From Cape to Congo

A project of the International Peace Academy

From Cape to Congo

Southern Africa's Evolving Security Challenges

edited by
Mwesiga Baregu
Christopher Landsberg

LYNNE RIENNER PUBLISHERS
BOULDER
LONDON

Published in the United States of America in 2003 by
Lynne Rienner Publishers, Inc.
1800 30th Street, Boulder, Colorado 80301
www.rienner.com

and in the United Kingdom by
Lynne Rienner Publishers, Inc.
3 Henrietta Street, Covent Garden, London WC2E 8LU

Library of Congress Cataloging-in-Publication Data
From Cape to Congo : Southern Africa's evolving security challenges / edited by
Mwesiga Baregu and Christopher Landsberg.
p. cm.
Includes bibliographical references and index.
ISBN 1-58826-102-6 (hc : alk. paper)
ISBN 1-58826-127-1 (pb : alk. paper)
1. Africa, Southern—Politics and government—1994- —Congresses. 2. Africa, Southern—Economic conditions—1994- —Congresses. 3. Africa, Southern—Social conditions—1994- —Congresses. 4. National security—Africa, Southern—Congresses. I. Baregu, Mwesiga Laurent. II. Landsberg, Christopher. III. International Peace Academy.
DT1182.F76 2002
968.06'4—dc21

2002075157

British Cataloguing in Publication Data
A Cataloguing in Publication record for this book
is available from the British Library.

Printed and bound in the United States of America

∞ The paper used in this publication meets the requirements
of the American National Standard for Permanence of
Paper for Printed Library Materials Z39.48-1984.

5 4 3 2 1

Contents

Foreword, *David M. Malone* vii
Acknowledgments ix

1 Introduction, *Christopher Landsberg and Mwesiga Baregu* 1

Part 1 Southern Africa's Security Challenges

2 Economic and Military Security, *Mwesiga Baregu* 19
3 Redefining Security, *Agostinho Zacarias* 31
4 The Quest for Good Governance, *Tandeka C. Nkiwane* 53
5 The Politics of Land Reform in Zimbabwe, *Sam Moyo and Prosper Matondi* 73
6 Land Reform: The South African Case, *Ruth Hall and Gavin Williams* 97
7 AIDS as a New Security Threat, *Jacqui Ala* 131

Part 2 National and Regional Actors

8 Civil Society in Southern Africa, *Patrick Molutsi* 159
9 South Africa and Nigeria as Regional Hegemons, *Adekeye Adebajo and Christopher Landsberg* 171
10 From the Organization of African Unity to the African Union, *Musifiky Mwanasali* 205

11 The Intergovernmental Authority on Development and the East African Community, *Monica Kathina Juma* 225

Part 3 Extraregional Actors

12 The United Nations, *Ibrahim A. Gambari* 255

13 The United States, *Jendayi E. Frazer* 275

14 The European Union, *Talitha Bertelsmann-Scott* 301

15 The Commonwealth, *Kaye Whiteman* 317

Part 4 Conclusion

16 Southern Africa's Security Architecture: Challenges and Prospects, *Mwesiga Baregu and Christopher Landsberg* 345

List of Acronyms and Abbreviations 355
Bibliography 359
The Contributors 383
Index 389
About the Book 403

Foreword

DAVID M. MALONE
PRESIDENT, INTERNATIONAL PEACE ACADEMY

It is with great pride and pleasure that the International Peace Academy (IPA) presents this volume, written primarily by African scholars of the highest order, joined by several leading non-African practitioners and academics.

The IPA's Africa Program—initiated by my predecessor, Olara Otunnu, and by Margaret Vogt, both eminent African activists and scholars—has for many years focused on means of enhancing African capacity to reduce the continent's tensions, resolve its conflicts, and prevent violence.

During the 1990s, the IPA worked with the Organization of African Unity (OAU) to encourage more frequent and convincing resort to the OAU's conflict-resolution organs and processes. Africa is a vast and diverse continent. For this reason, subregional security initiatives are more likely to prove substantive and substantial than are those at the mercy of continent-wide consensus. Subregional organizations are a source of considerable hope, if not yet always current satisfaction, in Africa. IPA scholars have studied intensively all of the deployments of ECOMOG, the military arm of the Economic Community of West African States (ECOWAS), and held a seminar with ECOWAS in Abuja, Nigeria, in September 2001 to determine how the need for such deployments can best be averted and, when inevitable, managed. We looked at eastern Africa and its security needs in 2002. In all of this activity, we have involved impressive African civil society actors. Indeed, a priority of the IPA Africa Program has been to highlight the important role civil society can play in conflict prevention and resolution continent-wide.

In 2000, we focused extensively on southern Africa's evolving security architecture, convening a meeting in Gaborone, Botswana, to discuss achievements in the subregion to date and improvements required. This volume reflects discussions at the Gaborone seminar. It makes clear how diverse, deep, and daunting are the challenges facing the Southern African

Development Community in moving beyond rhetoric to action on subregional security. But these are early days still, and many of the authors display considerable optimism. We hope their views will be widely read.

We are grateful to the funders of the IPA's Africa Program: the governments of Denmark, Germany, and the Netherlands, and the United Kingdom's Department for International Development. Without their financial and moral support, my colleagues within the program could tackle none of the fascinating challenges they have been exploring for some time and will be addressing in years to come.

This unique volume is intended for policymakers, activists, and scholars, both within and outside Africa. We hope that this exciting scholarly contribution will encourage meaningful steps toward subregionally designed and implemented security in southern Africa and beyond.

Acknowledgments

We would first like to thank David M. Malone and Adekeye Adebajo of the International Peace Academy (IPA) in New York for affording us an opportunity to produce this volume, which we hope will make a modest contribution to the discourse and debates about challenges faced by southern Africa. We would particularly like to thank Dr. Adebajo and his very able IPA Africa Program team, especially Aida Mengistu and Angela Muvumba, for their managerial and logistical efficiency and for keeping the flow of communication among New York, Dar es Salaam, Harare, and Johannesburg open. The leadership and intellectual guidance of friend and colleague Dr. Adebajo, and his weird and wonderful sense of humor, served as a constant source of inspiration.

We must also thank other colleagues who took the time to read through early drafts of various chapters and offered many insightful comments and suggestions that helped to sharpen the analysis. These individuals include John Hirsch, senior fellow at the IPA; Monica Juma, formerly with the IPA's Africa Program; John Stremlau, Francis Kornegay, and David Monyae of the Centre for Africa's International Relations at the University of the Witwatersrand; Shaun Mackay of the Centre for Policy Studies in Johannesburg; and Norman Mlambo, Jenifer Chiriga, and Viola Chidembe of the Southern African Regional Institute for Policy Studies (SARIPS) in Harare, Zimbabwe. We would also like to acknowledge the brilliant copyediting skills of Sara Lodge. IPA associate, Dorina Bekoe, ably assisted in the final stages of proofreading.

Karin Wermester, senior program officer at the IPA, served as a crucial interface among the editors, the IPA, and Lynne Rienner Publishers. She was ably assisted by Cyrus Samii, also at the IPA. Mpho Mashaba and Simon Marobe, two young students in the Department of International Relations at the University of the Witwatersrand, provided great assistance in compiling the bibliography for the book.

Finally, the idea for this volume grew out of the IPA's Africa Program, and in particular the December 2000 seminar, "Southern Africa's Regional Security Architecture: Problems and Prospects," held in Gaborone, Botswana. The seminar was hosted by the IPA, in partnership with the Department of International Relations at the University of the Witwatersrand, the African Renaissance Institute in Gaborone, and SARIPS. The editors and the IPA Africa Program therefore gratefully acknowledge the support of the governments of Denmark, Germany, and the Netherlands, as well as the United Kingdom's Department for International Development, for funding the seminar as well as the IPA's Africa Program.

—Mwesiga Baregu,
Christopher Landsberg

1

Introduction

Christopher Landsberg and Mwesiga Baregu

During the apartheid years in South Africa and the Cold War period, especially during the 1970s and 1980s, southern Africa was defined by a realist paradigm of war, destabilization, and mistrust. Toward the latter part of the 1980s, after the end of the Cold War, Namibia's independence in 1990, the defeat of Kenneth Kaunda by the Movement for Multiparty Democracy's Frederick Chiluba in Zambia in October 1991, Mozambique's transition from civil war to multiparty politics in 1992, Bakili Muluzi's defeat of Kamuzu Banda in Malawi's 1994 presidential election, and the erosion of apartheid rule in South Africa, the region appeared to be moving toward a cooperative architecture. Such an architecture held the promise of giving due regard to human security and broader social justice in the region.[1]

With the trends in regional democratization and the negotiated settlement in South Africa, southern Africa was widely acclaimed as an emerging political, economic, and security role model for Africa, a "pivotal" region that provided a good test case for applying such a paradigm shift.

But grand proclamations depicting southern Africa's "miraculous" experience or touting the region as a continental role model have yet to be tested. It is still unclear, for instance, whether the newly democratized South Africa will provide the model for democracy, stability, and promised prosperity for the rest of the continent, a model that the region and Africa as a whole can seek to emulate. Given that the Southern African Development Community (SADC) is highly dependent on external donor funding, should the SADC be externally funded at all, and what implications does that funding hold? Could it still be, as T. Ohlson, S. Stedman, and R. Davies asserted in 1994, that "the new is not yet born?"[2] In 1996, one of the most respected Africanists, Adebayo Adedeji, referring to South Africa's emergence from decades of apartheid rule and its anticipated role in the region, also asked, "Will due attention be given to restructuring hegemonic relations with South Africa's neighbors towards more equitable, fair and less tense ones?"[3] How has the region matched up to Adedeji's expectations? Have these premonitions been fulfilled?

The Elusive Security Architecture

There is no doubt that, at the beginning of a new millennium, a different picture prevails in southern Africa from that which characterized the Cold War and apartheid eras. But what are the real features of southern Africa's evolving security architecture?

In 1969, with the proclamation of the Lusaka Manifesto, the Frontline States was formed as a special organization to aid southern African liberation struggles in tandem with the Organization of African Unity's (OAU) liberation committee. In 1979, black-ruled states agreed to create their own subcontinental integration entity, and in 1980 in Lusaka, Zambia, they established the Southern African Development Coordination Conference (SADCC) to promote regional integration and lessen dependence on apartheid-ruled South Africa.[4] The founding members were Angola, Botswana, Lesotho, Malawi, Mozambique, Swaziland, Tanzania, Zambia, and Zimbabwe. Namibia joined in 1990, shortly after gaining its independence. In January 1992, more than a decade later, the regional states signed a declaration and treaty in Windhoek, Namibia, which turned the SADCC into the SADC. Whereas the SADCC was premised on the political solidarity of majority-ruled states in the region to promote economic welfare and counter white minority–ruled South Africa, the Windhoek treaty of 1992 promoted a level of regional integration that would address the region's deep-seated political, economic, and military challenges. More specifically, the treaty defined the objectives of the regional community, the Common Agenda, as:

- development and economic growth;
- the alleviation of poverty;
- enhancement of the standard and quality of life of the peoples of southern Africa and support for the socially disadvantaged through regional integration;
- the evolution of common political values, systems, and institutions;
- the promotion and defense of peace and security, the promotion of self-sustaining development on the basis of collective self-reliance, and the interdependence of member states;
- complementarity between national and regional strategies and programs and the promotion and maximum productive employment of the region's resources;

- sustainable use of the natural resources and effective protection of the environment; and
- the strengthening and consolidation of the long-standing historical, social, and cultural affinities and links among the people of the region.[5]

The SADC treaty appreciates the boundless link between peace and human security in southern Africa: the two streams constantly converge. The challenge to the SADC, therefore, is to articulate an integration strategy that is holistic and focuses simultaneously on the economic, political, and security dimensions.

By the time the SADC was established in 1992, some daunting challenges faced the region. Jan Isaksen and Elling N. Tjønneland, for example, asserted that, "by the mid-1990s it was becoming clear that the SADC was experiencing major difficulties and constraints. It was felt that the SADC secretariat lacked the power, authority and resources required to facilitate regional integration."[6]

A number of nonmilitary factors were already having an effect on the conflict dynamics of the region. Growth rates in almost every SADC state were not high enough to improve the living standards of the people. Even in states with high growth rates such as Botswana, which maintained an average growth rate of between 4 percent and 6 percent per annum, such a rate typically ensued from a low industrial and development base. According to Prega Ramsamy, executive secretary of the SADC, "In the last half of the 1990s real gross domestic product (GDP) growth averaged 3 percent annually. The highest GDP growth rate was attained in 1996 at 4.1 percent but was then followed by a declining trend in 1997 (2.2 percent) and 1998 (1.7 percent)."[7] Additionally, the economic growth rates of states in the region continue to be constrained by low rates of exports, low investment rates, generally high rates of unemployment, adverse terms of trade, and HIV/AIDS, among other factors.[8] In terms of HIV/AIDS alone, Ramsamy stressed that

> the pandemic continues to escalate in our Community. Available statistics indicate that the rates of infected people in the region could be as high as one in five in some member states. At least four member states have rates higher than 400 per 100,000 population, indicating the magnitude of the problem.[9]

On the macroeconomic side, fiscal uncertainty and instability characterize the region, which continues to experience high budget deficits, high rates of inflation, high balance-of-payments deficits, high levels of external public debt, and exchange rate volatility. Southern Africa additionally experiences what some scholars have labeled "hegemonic" economic relations, characterized by gross domestic product, trade, and investment imbalances in South Africa's favor.

In 1997, the SADC Parliamentary Forum was established outside the SADC's formal structures to be a consultative body without legislative powers.[10] The forum seeks to strengthen the SADC's implementation capacity by involving parliamentarians in SADC activities and facilitating the effective implementation of its policies and projects. Germane to this study on southern Africa's security architecture is the forum's promotion of peace, democracy, security, and stability on the basis of collective responsibility and its support for the development of permanent conflict-resolution mechanisms in the subregion.

Another consultative structure, the SADC Electoral Commissions Forum, was created in 1998—also without any executive powers—to affect electoral processes in the subregion. The idea behind the electoral forum was to strengthen cooperation among the bodies managing elections in member nations, with a view to enhancing democratic electoral processes and a democratic culture as well as developing standard electoral practices.

The link between democracy and security became more marked as democracy became an important means of conflict resolution. While the majority of the regions' states are today formal democracies, based on a minimal definition of democracy to mean conduct of free and fair elections at regular intervals, democracy continues to face many strains and stresses. Taking this most basic view of the term, only two states, the Democratic Republic of Congo (DRC) and Swaziland, would not qualify as democracies. Yet, increasing pressure for democratization and change are easily negated by continuing violent conflict in states other than these two. "Façade" or "virtual" democracies, where incumbent regimes manipulate the democratic process while pretending to be highly democratic, are the standard in southern Africa. In fact, many states are caught between democracy and authoritarianism.

Until the death of National Union for the Total Independence of Angola leader Jonas Savimbi in February 2002, government and opposition in Angola continued to interact not through parliament but through war, with hostile factions fighting for control of diamond and oil fields. In Lesotho, after a protracted period of political struggle, credible parliamentary elections finally took place in May 2002. Zambia has witnessed constitutional changes to limit the opposition's right to contest elections and failed attempts by the president to usher in a third term of presidential rule, followed by a highly contested election in December 2001. Meanwhile, in Zimbabwe, the relationship between the opposition Movement for Democratic Change and President Robert Mugabe's government spilled over into serious tensions and violence, even after the highly disputed elections of March 2002, in which Mugabe was accused of using legitimate questions over land for political gain. In Namibia, the decade-old democratic consensus was threatened when President Sam Nujoma contested and won for a third presidential term. In Tanzania, the ruling party's victory at the 2000 polls triggered major violence in Zanzibar and a conflict that threatened to engulf the island part of the union and the mainland in a drawn-out battle. An agreement to normalize the political situation has since been reached between the major political parties. In Mozambique, some of the opposition parties boycotted the 1998 local government elections, and the Mozambique National Resistance Movement questioned not only the outcome of that poll but threatened that, unless a rapprochement was found between themselves and the government, there could be a reversion to full-scale civil war. In Malawi, political party competition is weak, and this has given President Bakili Muluzi of Malawi the wrong idea that he, too, should stage a bid for a third term. A national referendum has since overwhelmingly rejected the idea. In South Africa, political and economic contestation continues to run along racial lines and could easily erode the prospects for a functioning democracy. Though Botswana's democracy is typically celebrated as an "exception," that state has yet to survive the test of a governing party defeat at the polls. Even Mauritius, often hailed as probably the only consolidated democracy in the region, faces its challenges.

On the defense and security front, important initiatives in the direction of collective peace and security have appeared to be under way. During the two decades that preceded the establishment of the SADC in 1992, states in the region undertook collective security arrangements through the FLS in 1970 and the SADCC in 1980. It was only with the proposed establishment of the SADC Organ on Politics, Defense, and Security (OPDS) in 1996 that the subregion seemed to be moving in the direction of constructing a concrete and stable regional security architecture. The concept of an OPDS was proposed at a meeting of the SADC Ministers of Foreign Affairs, Defense, and Security, held in Gaborone, Botswana, on 18 January 1996. The SADC heads of state and government then adopted and approved the concept on 28 June 1996.

The noble, if ambitious, functions and objectives of the SADC OPDS included:

- protecting the people and safeguarding the development of the region against instability arising from a breakdown of law and order and interstate conflict;
- promoting political cooperation among member states and evolving common political value systems and institutions;
- developing a common foreign policy in areas of mutual concern and interest and lobbying as a region on issues of common interest in international forums;

- cooperating fully on regional security and defense through conflict prevention, management, and resolution;
- mediating in inter- and intrastate disputes;
- using preventive diplomacy to preempt conflict in the region, both within and between states, through an early warning system;
- using diplomatic means to end conflicts;
- promoting and enhancing the development of democratic institutions and practices within member states and encouraging them to observe universal human rights codes;
- developing a collective security capacity, concluding a mutual defense pact for responding to external threats, and building up regional peacekeeping capacity within national armies that could be called on to act within the region or elsewhere;
- developing close cooperation between the police and security services of the region with a view to addressing cross-border crime as well as promoting a community-based approach on matters of security;
- encouraging the United Nations, the OAU, and other international conventions and treaties on arms control and disarmament, human rights, and peaceful relations between states; and
- addressing conflicts outside the region that affect peace and security in southern Africa.[11]

With the establishment of the OPDS, regional leaders hoped to put in place a consultative structure to "allow more flexibility and a timely response, at the highest level, to sensitive and potentially explosive situations." It seems fair to state that if it had been properly operationalized, the OPDS would have brought about a revolutionary shift in peace and security thinking and practice in the region. It would have laid the foundation for a fully coherent regional security architecture in southern Africa. However, the practice since 1992 has revealed major weaknesses and pitfalls, and the hopes that accompanied the establishment of the OPDS have yet to be fulfilled. Thus, although Article 4 of the SADC treaty embraces the principles of "solidarity, peace and security" and Article 5 commits member states to "defend and promote peace and security," the consolidation of a coherent and stable regional security architecture has been negatively affected by tensions and conflicts.

By 1998—two years after the OPDS was established and military interventions had occurred in Lesotho and Zaire—intraregional relations were under greater stress, and power struggles had become part of the regional character of southern Africa. South Africa and Botswana spearheaded the military intervention in Lesotho, ostensibly under the auspices of the SADC. Zaire became the DRC, obtained considerable military backing from Angola, Namibia, and Zimbabwe, and acquired SADC membership, thus making it possible for forces from the aforementioned states to intervene when the new government was threatened by external invasion and internal rebellion.

The 1998 intervention in the DRC by three of the SADC's most influential member states—Zimbabwe, Angola, and Namibia—brought into sharp relief the challenges facing the OPDS. That intervention, and South Africa's refusal to join in the military action, illuminated tensions around several issues:

- autonomy (the relationship between the OPDS and the SADC summit);
- the legal framework in which the OPDS should be operating; and
- the hegemonic power struggles in the postliberation, postapartheid era.[12]

Apart from the interventions in Lesotho and the DRC, the civil war in Angola had escalated and threatened to engulf the region; this, too, brought tensions within the OPDS to the fore. These bellicose situations showed that Makau wa Mutua's 1994 depiction of an alleged "war fatigue"[13] in southern Africa was at best premature. Peter Vale and Khabele Matlosa were more accurate when they wrote, "Southern Africa's search for a different future will be complicated by the legacy of long wars and the differentials between rich and poor."[14]

Tensions over the mechanics of the OPDS were exacerbated by political and economic strain, most notably between South Africa and Zimbabwe. The accusation by some member states that South Africa was pursuing selfish (and even hostile) economic policies and an inhospitable immigration regime added to the tensions. By 1999, the signs were evident that the southern African region might very well become polarized, and the acrimony would revolve around two poles, a South Africa–led grouping and a Zimbabwe-led bloc. The SADC showed signs of severe stress when South Africa and Zimbabwe were at loggerheads over how best to address southern Africa's security challenges.

A 1999 SADC summit in Swaziland recognized some of the problems and challenges besetting the OPDS and requested Swaziland to review the OPDS and make recommendations for reforming it. Swaziland, in close consultation with other SADC countries, started a process that would lead to a definitive overhaul of the OPDS.

Persistent Challenges

In 2000, SADC member states continued to be actively engaged in efforts to break the impasse over the format and function of the OPDS as an appropriate instrument to formalize and operationalize collective security in this divided region. But such efforts continued to be plagued by difficulties stemming from the lack of consensus among SADC member states regarding the OPDS statute in relationship to the SADC treaty.

However, SADC member states had been hard at work attempting to resolve conflicts in Angola, in the DRC, and in Lesotho, while tackling the issue of land reform in Zimbabwe. In all these situations, southern African states have given concrete meaning to the idea of seeking to find "African solutions for African problems."

In March 2001, significant progress was reported. During the extraordinary SADC summit that took place on 16 March in Windhoek, Namibia, leaders decided to integrate the OPDS into SADC structures. Whereas the OPDS, since its inception, had been administered by the Ministry of Foreign Affairs of Zimbabwe and headed by President Mugabe, SADC leaders decided that the OPDS would not be accountable to the chair country of the structure but to the heads of states and government.[15] The OPDS will be integrated in the SADC structures but coordinated at the summit level, and it will rotate on an annual and troika basis reporting to the chairperson of the summit. The structure, operations, and functions of the OPDS will be regulated by the new Protocol on Politics, Defense, and Security Cooperation. The decisions at this summit signaled progress toward not only collective security but also collective accountability.

When the SADC heads of state and government met for the summit in Blantyre, Malawi, on 13 and 14 August 2001, they agreed to ratify and implement the Windhoek recommendations. The summit brought the OPDS firmly under SADC control and called into life the new Organ on Politics, Defense, and Security Cooperation (OPDSC) by adopting the Protocol on Politics, Defense, and Security Cooperation.[16] It adopted an elaborate new structure, which confirmed that the SADC secretariat would also serve as the secretariat for the OPDSC. The OPDSC will henceforth have its set of regional structures and mechanisms for policy formulation and implementation. The OPDSC will operate on a troika basis, with the troika members to be selected by the summit. However, the chairperson of the summit cannot at the same time have the chair of the SADC summit. According to the protocol, a ministerial committee consisting of ministers responsible for foreign affairs, defense, public security, or state security shall be established under the aegis of the OPDSC. The Blantyre summit elected President Joaquim Chissano of Mozambique as the new chairperson of the OPDSC, with outgoing chair President Robert Mugabe of Zimbabwe and incoming chair President Benjamin Mkapa of Tanzania serving as the deputy chairs as per the troika arrangement.[17]

The protocol also provides for the Inter-State Politics and Diplomacy Committee (ISPDC), which comprises the ministers of foreign affairs of all

SADC states. The ISPDC is expected to perform functions that would be deemed necessary to achieve the political and diplomatic objectives of the OPDSC and may establish such structures as it deems necessary.

The protocol further articulates a clear role for the Inter-State Defense and Security Committee (ISDSC), which comprises the ministers responsible for defense, public security, and state security. It already boasts a fairly elaborate structure, including a Defense Subcommittee and other subcommittees dealing with functional areas. Under the public security ministers will function the Southern African Regional Police Chiefs Cooperation Organization (SARPCCO). SARPCCO already has a permanent secretariat hosted by the Interpol Subregional Bureau for Southern Africa stationed in Harare.

The protocol also provides a framework for SADC policies and activities to promote, defend, and consolidate democracy, peace, security, and stability. It lists twelve specific objectives in this regard:

- Protect the people and safeguard the development of the region against instability arising from the breakdown of law and order, intrastate conflict, interstate conflict, and aggression.
- Promote political cooperation among state parties and the evolution of common political values and institutions.
- Develop common foreign policy approaches on issues of mutual concern and advance such policies collectively in international forums.
- Promote regional coordination and cooperation on matters related to security and defense and establish mechanisms to this end.
- Prevent, contain, and resolve inter- and intrastate conflict by peaceful means.
- Consider enforcement action in accordance with international law and as a matter of last resort where peaceful means have failed.
- Promote the development of democratic institutions and practices within the territories of state parties and encourage the observance of universal human rights as provided for in the charters and conventions of the Organization of African Unity and United Nations, respectively.
- Consider the development of a collective security capacity and conclude a Mutual Defence Pact to respond to external military threats.
- Develop close cooperation between the police and state security services in order to address cross border crime and promote a community-based approach to domestic security.
- Observe, and encourage state parties to implement United Nations, African Union, and other international conventions and treaties on arms control, disarmament, and peaceful relations between states.

- Develop peacekeeping capacity of national defense forces and coordinate the participation of state parties in international and regional peacekeeping operations.
- Enhance regional capacity in respect of disaster management and coordination of international humanitarian assistance.

Even with these breakthroughs, a proper operationalization of the OPDSC is not guaranteed. Now that the Protocol on Politics, Defense, and Security Cooperation has been adopted, the gap between policy and practice needs to be closed. The SADC needs to ensure that the protocol is effectively institutionalized. Only after that process has been completed will the OPDSC be allowed to establish institutions and put in place the necessary human resource backup.

Contribution of This Book

Constructing a viable peace and security framework for the region is an ongoing process. In this book, we investigate the roles of governments, subregional organizations, civil society groups (notably nongovernmental organizations [NGOs]), and external powers in building southern Africa's security architecture. We also address the challenge of conceiving an effective and collective SADC role in promoting regional security, in light of its political deadlocks, continuing tensions, and weak institutions.

Part 1, addressing southern Africa's security challenges, includes a chapter by Mwesiga Baregu on "Economic and Military Security." This chapter explores the tensions over the modalities that the SADC's security architecture should take between centralization and decentralization.

A critical assessment of the evolution of the security debate within the subregion is provided by Agostinho Zacarias. His chapter, "Redefining Security," records the origins and challenges of regional security.

The issue of "integration," or decentralization, within a member state posed by Baregu has been one of the enduring points of contention in the security debate surrounding the OPDS and the OPDSC. For a long time this debate was fueled by tensions between Zimbabwe, a proponent of centralized autonomy, and South Africa, which has advocated a decentralized approach. These tensions contributed to the lack of clarity and consistency within the SADC that was occasioned by the controversial 1998 interventions in Lesotho (led by South Africa and Botswana) and the Congo (led by Zimbabwe, Angola, and Namibia).

The issue of aligning the SADC's evolving security architecture with "people-centered" rather than state-centric security thinking is also examined. The new security thinking focuses on a broader array of "human security" issues rather than narrowly defined "state security." Agostinho Zacarias tackles this complex terrain in his chapter and complements his analysis with a critique of the politics of the OPDS. Subsequent to Zacarias's and Baregu's chapters, a special SADC summit did, in fact, reach consensus on the structure of the SADC organ and its relationship with the SADC proper—a position that is a fine compromise between an integrationist, centralizing framework and an autonomous structure.

Apart from these structural concerns, the conceptual issues related to a broader definition of security and the role of civil society remain unresolved. At this stage, according to Zacarias, the SADC has not moved very far in absorbing these new sets of challenges, challenges that raise questions about good governance and democracy as addressed in Tandeka Nkiwane's chapter, "The Quest for Good Governance." This chapter challenges the notion that the liberal democratic corollary of economic liberalization can deliver peace and security to the subregion's peoples within the broader definition of human security. Her chapter also revisits some of the terrain covered in Baregu's regarding the evolution of the SADC's response to security issues. Moreover, it poses serious questions as to whether the ascendant free market focus of globalization can enhance the security of a "democratic peace." Whether or not a democratic peace is a viable prospect in the age of globalization is the core issue Nkiwane explores.

Part 1 further reflects on some of the controversies that will continue to resonate after this volume has been published. The chapter by Sam Moyo and Prosper Matondi provides an assessment of "The Politics of Land Reform in Zimbabwe," which is complemented by "Land Reform: The South African Case" by Ruth Hall and Gavin Williams.

Moyo and Matondi examine the efficacy of Zimbabwe's compulsory "fast-track" land-reform model within the context of a historical overview of the turmoil that has attended the issue of land redistribution in other parts of the world. They point out that an element of coercion is inherent in such initiatives.

With regard to South Africa, however, Hall and Williams argue that what is at stake are the policy choices open to government for pursuing a more commercial-oriented approach. Should the postsettlement government focus on building up a new black farming class, or should the state pursue a more rural developmental approach linked to poverty alleviation? Their critique takes us through the thicket of the recent history of South Africa's postcompromise agricultural and land redistribution controversies. Like Moyo and Matondi, Hall and Williams amplify the security challenges facing the democratic peace within the SADC. The way these challenges are addressed at a national level can have wider subregional security implications, such as the spillover effects of political instability generated by domestic conflicts over such issues as land. On the land question in South Africa, for example, UN Secretary-General Kofi Annan wrote in 1997 that "land reform is a crucial issue affecting both employment and income generation. A main goal in this area is to improve the distribution of good farmland."[18]

One of the issues that emphasizes the urgency of redefining the term "security" is the challenge posed by the HIV/AIDS pandemic. Jacqui Ala's chapter, entitled "AIDS as a New Security Threat," is a relevant contribution to the ongoing debate on the causes and strategies of handling the HIV/AIDS pandemic in southern Africa. Ala argues that "HIV/AIDS in southern Africa has been heralded as an unprecedented crisis that demands unprecedented action." She goes on to assert that "the disease endangers not only economic and human development, state and regional security, but also the goal of an African Renaissance on the continent."

Part 2 of the book is devoted to the theme national and regional actors. Patrick Molutsi examines the civil society dimension of inter-African politics of security in a chapter entitled "Civil Society in Southern Africa." Molutsi's survey of civil society's performance in addressing challenges in the subregion provides a useful inventory of how different NGO sectors relate to the security picture. This assessment is coupled with a look at southern Africa's conflictual history of struggles and civil wars.

The controversial role of Africa's big powers in the security equation is investigated in "South Africa and Nigeria as Regional Hegemons" by Adekeye Adebajo and Christopher Landsberg. In this chapter, the authors consider the challenges faced by South Africa and Nigeria in their efforts to play stabilizing roles in the southern and West African regions. Adebajo and Landsberg explore the possibilities of, and constraints on, Nigeria and South Africa playing hegemonic roles in their respective subregions. They candidly caution that there are many challenges emanating from "bargainers" or unwilling associates—those smaller states that may feel threatened by these two countries' giantism—that need to be overcome if South Africa and Nigeria are to become constructive hegemons. The chapter also compares the security initiatives undertaken by the SADC and the Economic Community of West African States (ECOWAS). The leadership role that the presidents of both countries have assumed is noted, as well as their strategic partnership as enshrined in the South Africa–Nigeria Bi-National Commission. The discourse in this chapter is an indication of what will be a continuing debate over the role of the "big and powerful" among Africa's states and smaller states, especially now that the OAU has made its transition into the African Union (AU).

The role played by regional institutions is considered by Musifiky Mwanasali, whose chapter explores lessons for the AU from the OAU's experience. Mwanasali's chapter is complemented by Monica Juma's focus on subregional organizational actors in east Africa. Her chapter focuses on what southern Africa can learn from The Intergovernmental Authority on Development and the East African Community.

Both of these chapters lift the security debate beyond the national level. They consider human security challenges posed by such explosive issues as land redistribution to the macro-level of inter-African and subregional security architectures. According to Mwanasali, when it comes to the broader human security focus, the OAU's role and status was problematic, given that the state remained central to the OAU's security agenda and all that it meant in terms of the principles of noninterference and sovereignty. This problem continues to be compounded by the enormously uneven quality of nation-state formation in Africa and the amorphous nature of Africa's regional economic communities (RECs). The OAU's interaction with RECs such as the SADC was problematic and uneven, especially in terms of defining coherent divisions of labor in relation to subregional security architectures. Nevertheless, Juma's chapter highlights the possibilities that exist for building cooperative REC relationships with the AU in such areas as "early warning" and engaging civil society in conflict situations such as those in the Sudan and Somalia.

To a great extent, the nature of OAU and REC interaction was conditioned by the major powers within a subregion, a factor that inevitably raises issues around the roles of perceived and aspiring hegemons.

Part 3 of the book focuses on extraregional actors. Central in this cast of actors is the United Nations, which is the subject of Ibrahim A. Gambari's chapter. Gambari's contribution is followed by a country focus on the lone superpower, the United States. In her chapter, "The United States," Jendayi Frazer scrutinizes the policies toward the SADC and southern Africa under the Bill Clinton administration. "The European Union" is examined by Talitha Bertelsmann-Scott, followed by "The Commonwealth" by Kaye Whiteman.

Gambari's focus on the UN–SADC relationship surveys the major challenges confronting the SADC. These include recognition of the transition in the security environment since the 1994 negotiated settlement in South Africa and the emergence of nonmilitary threats such as HIV/AIDS, transnational organized crime, the proliferation of small arms, and economic development. Nevertheless, curbing conflicts remains a major preoccupation, even after the recent breakthroughs in the DRC and Angola.

The UN itself also faces the challenges of conflict prevention, peacekeeping, and postconflict peacebuilding, as well as nonmilitary challenges such as promoting human rights and ensuring that globalization serves all in an equal manner. Based on these challenges, Gambari explores several factors that require consideration in forging a UN–SADC partnership. Such a partnership, according to Gambari, should be based on Article 52,

Chapter 8 of the UN Charter, which encourages the development of regional organizations for promoting peace and security.

Jendayi Frazer's chapter comes almost two years after the Clinton administration (1993–2000) left power and into the Bush administration, in which she currently serves as senior adviser on Africa on the National Security Council. Her contribution attempts a realistic evaluation of U.S.–southern African relations during the Clinton years. Frazer argues against the notion that the United States had a grand strategy toward Africa in general, or southern Africa and the SADC in particular. Rather, a complicated picture emerged of interbureaucratic influences combining with U.S. interests that need to be factored into any analysis of U.S.–Africa policy.

Talitha Bertelsmann-Scott follows up Frazer's treatment of U.S.–southern African relations by describing the relationship between the European Union and the SADC. As with other contributors to this volume, Bertelsmann-Scott takes the "new definition of security" as her entry point for examining European Union (EU) foreign policy and notes that "the largest external actor active in the southern African region is the European Union." Though security concerns in southern Africa were never included on any EU agenda, there are potential security implications for the SADC from its "overdependence on EU funding." This situation is compounded by the balkanizing trade implications of the Cotonou agreement (2000), the successor to the Lomé convention (1975).

Bertelsmann-Scott charts the history of the European Economic Community's involvement in supporting southern Africa's efforts to resist apartheid through its support for regional cooperation. She notes that the EU's Common Foreign and Security Policy has not, in the post-1994 period, translated into greater European involvement in conflict resolution in the subregion. The author further asserts that "nonactive means of contributing to peacekeeping" are preferred. A strong sense of disjunction between the ideals of the EU and its actual peace and security commitments in the subregion emerges from this analysis, which is coupled with the threat that the SADC's overdependence on the EU could pose.

Because of the British colonial legacy in southern Africa, the Commonwealth has a unique history as an extraregional actor that has been intimately involved in subregional politics. This involvement extends from the difficult period of Rhodesia's unilateral declaration of independence to the negotiated settlement in South Africa and the incorporation of a non–English-speaking Mozambique into the Commonwealth fold. Whiteman analyzes the Commonwealth's interest in international security and how it has played out in Africa during the Cold War and post–Cold War periods, through to its preoccupation with the promotion of democracy since the 1990s.

The book ends on a cautionary note, stressing that the future of peace and security in the region is conditional upon understanding the contradictions that define the contemporary environment in southern Africa. The critical contradiction is the counterposition between the forces and actors that seek to consolidate the gains of liberation—power, democracy, redistribution, and the possibilities of socioeconomic transformation. However, there are those forces and actors that seek to reverse the gains of the liberation struggle and democratization. This is evident in the conflicts over transformation and social justice. Indeed, even current debates over the need to redefine security fail to appreciate the centrality of social justice as crucial to any broadly defined security architecture.

Notes

1. Xavier Carim, "Strategic Perspective for Southern Africa in the 1990s: Theoretical and Practical Considerations," working paper, Southern Africa Perspectives, Centre for Southern African Studies, University of the Western Cape, August 1993, 1–4.

2. T. Ohlson, S. Stedman, and R. Davies, *The New Is Not Yet Born: Conflict Resolution in Southern Africa* (Washington, D.C.: Brookings Institution, 1994).

3. A. Adedeji, ed., *South Africa and Africa: Within or Apart?* African Centre for Development and Strategic Studies (Cape Town: SADRI Books; London: Zed Books, 1996), 3–4.

4. For two overviews of the origins of the SADCC, see I. Mandaza and A. Tostensen, *Southern Africa in Search of a Common Future: From the Conference to the Community* (Gaborone, Botswana: SADC, 1994); and Institute for Global Dialogue, *The IGD Guide to the Southern African Development Community* (Johannesburg: Institute for Global Dialogue, 2001).

5. SADC, "Treaty of the Southern African Development Community," Windhoek, Namibia, January 1992.

6. Jan Isaksen and Elling N. Tjønneland, "Assessing the Restructuring of the SADC—Positions, Policies and Progress," report commissioned by the Norwegian Agency for Development and Cooperation, Christian Michelsen Institute, Oslo, Norway, December 2001, vii.

7. Prega Ramsamy, "SADC: The Way Forward," in *Regional Integration in Southern Africa, Comparative Perspectives,* ed. Christopher Clapham, Gregg Mills, Anna Morner, and Elizabeth Sidiropolous (Johannesburg: South African Institute of International Affairs, 2001), 35.

8. SADC, *SADC Regional Human Development Report 2000: Challenges and Opportunities for Regional Integration* (Harare, Zimbabwe: SAPES Books, 2000), 23.

9. Ramsamy, "SADC: The Way Forward," 35.

10. For a perspective on the forum, see Masai Steppe, "The Windhoek Initiative: SADC Parliamentary Forum," consultative meeting report, Windhoek, Namibia, 20–22 October 1993.

11. M. Baregu, "Preventive Diplomacy and Peace-Building in Southern Africa," SARIPS Peace and Security Series 2, Harare, Zimbabwe, 1999, 73–75.

12. SADC, *Human Development Report 2000*, 131.

13. Makau wa Mutua, "New Challenges in Southern Africa: From Regional Conflict to Internal Reconstruction," *Brown Journal of World Affairs* (Winter 1994): 183.

14. Peter Vale and Khabele Matlosa, "Beyond and Below: The Future of the Nation-State in Southern Africa," working paper, Southern African Perspectives no. 53, Centre for Southern African Studies, University of the Western Cape, 1996, 3.

15. ACCORD, "Trends in Preventive Action," ACCORD online publications, 2001 [http://www.accord.org.za/publications/ct-2001/preventive.htm].

16. Over the past three years or so, the SADC has attempted to develop and institutionalize common approaches and policies through protocols, making use of legal instruments that commit member states to cooperate, coordinate, harmonize, and integrate policies and strategies in various sectors, including the security sector. See Isaksen and Tjønneland, "Assessing the Restructuring of the SADC," 2.

17. South African Department of Foreign Affairs, "Statement on the SADC Summit and Accompanying Meetings in Blantyre, Malawi," Pretoria, 14 August 2001.

18. Kofi Annan, "South Africa and the United Nations," address delivered to the South African Institute of International Affairs, Johannesburg, 21 March 1997, 10.

Part I

Southern Africa's Security Challenges

2

Economic and Military Security

MWESIGA BAREGU

As the Southern African Development Community (SADC) just celebrated the end of its first decade of existence, it is appropriate to reflect on where it is coming from and where it stands now, in order to project its possible future trajectory. Considering the SADC's progress is of importance particularly as it relates to assessment of the organization's problems, achievements, and prospects.

While opening the 2000 SADC Consultative Conference on "Peace, Progress and Prosperity in the new Millennium," King Mswati III of Swaziland noted

> that SADC was making steady progress towards full economic integration with all member states strongly committed to creating the right conditions for accelerated economic growth, creation of jobs and the reduction of poverty. He reiterated SADC's determination to bring sustainable peace to the whole region and said the prosperity of individual member states rests entirely on the fortunes of the region as a whole.[1]

It is against this background that this chapter will attempt to present a comprehensive picture of the state of the SADC, particularly in the areas of peace and security, integration, and trade and development. The argument of the chapter is that the picture presented by the Swazi king is too sanguine and rosy and that the existence of the political commitment he refers to cannot be taken for granted. At the very least such commitment needs to be cultivated and nurtured, for currently it is only aspired to. There are strong tendencies in the organization to indulge in formalities rather than substantive issues, despite the truth of the king's insight that "the prosperity of individual member states rests entirely on the fortunes of the region as a whole."

One reason why strong commitment cannot be taken for granted has to do with its source. The SADC region is defined and structured by a history of conflicts. *Apartheid, wars of liberation,* and *destabilization campaigns* are terms whose conceptual origins lie in the southern African conflict landscape, attesting to the structural conflict that afflicted the region until the early 1990s. Given this historical legacy, it is unlikely that political will and commitment will emerge spontaneously.

The SADC itself, founded in 1992, is a child of this history and continues to carry some of the legacy of these conflicts. On the one hand, the organization was founded to succeed the Southern African Development Coordination Conference (SADCC), which itself was built on the Frontline States (FLS) in the liberation struggles. The SADC thus embodies some elements of the liberation legacy. On the other hand, the SADCC was founded to curtail the involvement of the FLS in the liberation struggles in southern Africa and to serve as a defensive mechanism against apartheid South Africa. The organization has been deeply affected by this double heritage and has continuously vacillated between being defensive toward South Africa and seeking closer cooperation with it. The tensions that have emerged between South Africa and the SADC Allied Forces over the war in the Democratic Republic of Congo (DRC), for example, stem, at least in part, from these differences. The alliance between Zimbabwe, Angola, and Namibia recalls the alliance they forged during the liberation struggle, in which all the three countries, in one way or another, confronted apartheid South Africa as the regional enemy. This partly explains why South Africa initially reacted against the alliance, although it rationalized its action by claiming to embrace peaceful methods of resolving conflicts in the region. The truth is that, for South Africa, this alliance brought back memories of the liberation struggle and conjured up images of "total onslaught," to which the natural response in the 1980s was "total strategy."

Related to the tension between South Africa and the SADC is the whole question of hegemonic struggles in the region. These struggles emerge both from regional and from international political dynamics. At the regional level, South Africa, with a higher gross domestic product (GDP) than all the other SADC countries combined, perceives itself as the natural regional hegemon, although it lacks the legitimacy and capacity to exercise such a role. Its hegemonic legitimacy is brought into question by the legacy and enduring characteristics of apartheid. Its capacity is brought into question by its resource base, the absence of domestic coherence and political consensus, and the growing crime and violence that has come to characterize the South African social landscape.

South Africa's sense of identity is another source of tension in the region. South Africa is rather ambivalent (some would say schizophrenic) in its interregional relations. Whereas it is clear about being in Africa, it is not quite so clear whether it is also "of Africa." In 1998, for example, South Africa signed a bilateral trade and investment agreement with the European Union (EU) precisely at the time when the EU was involved in the negotiations for a post-Lomé successor agreement between the African-Caribbean-Pacific (ACP) countries and the EU. Furthermore, South Africa was at the same time involved in negotiations for a liberal trade regime among the SADC countries. That South Africa did not consult with the SADC allies on the EU relationship, even as it was extending its commercial interest in southern Africa, has caused considerable anxiety in the region. The other SADC members are deeply suspicious of South Africa. They wonder whether South Africa is an SADC team player or is driven purely by self-interest and is therefore in league with the EU and being used as a wedge for deepening and intensifying exploitation of southern Africa.

Regional Integration and Development

Apart from the problems emanating from South Africa's European connections, there are issues linked to South Africa's attitude toward regional integration. The SADC as a regional integration regime is held together by certain shared principles, norms, values, and practices. Although these have not fully evolved, minimum elements exist. There are at least four arguments that have been made to support the logic of regional integration in southern Africa. They may be referred to as the *affection*, *gain*, *threat,* and *power* models.

The affection model postulates that the southern African countries are natural allies not only because of their common history but also because of complex filial bonds that cut across the borders of the individual countries in the region. For proponents of this school of thought, regional integration should follow easily from the historical connections and filial bonds of southern Africans. This model, though not explicit, has partly dominated thinking among SADC members. Such thinking may be responsible for some of the weaknesses in the organization.[2]

The gain model emphasizes the potential for mutual, chiefly economic, benefits to be gained from integration. To this school of thought, integration is the rational choice if the countries in the region wish to benefit from economies of large-scale production and enlarged markets for interregional trade. Failure to integrate may be explained by lack of rationality on the part of the countries, as there exists plenty of scope for all to gain in a win-win arrangement. This argument has been at the center of the negotiations in the area of trade, but it was also responsible for the collapse of the East African Community due to unequal distribution of gains among members.

The threat model stresses *necessity* rather than *choice*. Under this argument it is postulated that countries will tend to come closer together if they develop a shared sense of external threat. In this context, globalization is perceived as threatening to the region as a whole. Whereas globalization has an integrating and centralizing tendency in the North, it tends toward disintegration and fragmentation in the South. Access to northern markets becomes harder for the South as export competition intensifies. The natural response to this challenge should be inward-looking regional integration with the aim of creating new regional divisions of labor and stimulating dormant markets by producing goods for the region. To some extent, this model applies to the EU, particularly to the founding of the European Coal and Steel Community.

The power model suggests that countries will tend to integrate under the aegis of a dominant state that is willing and able to impose hegemony and sustain the requisite costs. It is postulated that the natural hegemon in the region is South Africa. This model is associated with the North American Free Trade Agreement, in which the United States occupies the hegemonic position. As mentioned, however, South Africa has neither the capacity, legitimacy, nor willingness to impose a viable hegemony in the region.

Each of the above models embodies some features that may be applicable to the southern African situation, and they are by no means mutually exclusive. It is the contention of this chapter, however, that the threat argument is the most relevant to the conditions in southern Africa. It applies to all countries in the region, including South Africa, which may in the short term hitch its economic fortunes to Europe but will have to return to the region in the long term. It is illusory and shortsighted for any country in the region to imagine that its long-term economic prosperity is tied to Europe, except as a partner of a strong southern African economic bloc that must be created and nurtured in the short and medium terms. Unfortunately, the threat argument has not received sufficient attention.

Regional Security

The treaty that established the SADC in 1992 commits the member states to peace and security, human rights, democracy and the rule of law, and the peaceful settlement of disputes. Rather than empowering a committee of foreign ministers to manage the affairs of the SADC, the treaty envisages that the ministers of economic planning and finance will form the Council of Ministers; this structure of governance marginalized issues of politics, defense, and security. In an effort to rectify this situation, the 1996 Summit of Heads of State and Government of the SADC met in Gaborone and launched the SADC Organ on Politics, Defense, and Security under Article 22 of the SADC treaty, which provides for the conclusion of protocols "as may be necessary in each area of cooperation within the Community."[3]

With reference to the institutional framework, paragraph 4.3.1 of the communiqué of the 1996 summit states that

> the SADC Organ on Politics, Defense and Security shall operate at the Summit level and shall function independently of other SADC structures. The Organ shall also operate at Ministerial and technical levels. The Chairmanship of the Organ shall rotate on an annual and on a troika basis.[4]

Under subparagraph 4.3.3, the summit additionally agreed that the Inter-State Defence and Security Committee (ISDSC) should be one of the institutions of the organ, which was also empowered to "establish other structures as the need arises."[5] These two subparagraphs of the summit communiqué have been the major bone of contention between SADC members with respect to their interpretation of the operationalization of the organ. The 1997 summit in Blantyre, Malawi, failed to resolve outstanding differences. The 1998 deployment of what has come to be known as the SADC Allied Forces in the DRC (Angola, Namibia, the DRC, and Zimbabwe) has accentuated the debate. In brief, South Africa has taken the position that in accordance with Article 10 of the SADC treaty, which states that the summit is the "supreme policy making institution," the organ is answerable to the SADC summit. Zimbabwe and other countries, on the other hand, maintain that the Gaborone summit created a separate summit for the organ based on the principles of the FLS. Underlying these apparently legal and institutional differences are serious and enduring issues of regional political hegemonic struggles, begging for a clear framework for common security. The search for consensus has remained elusive.

A Framework for a Collective Security Community

Chapter VII of the UN Charter provides for action with respect to threats to peace, breaches of the peace, and acts of aggression. Article 51 states:

> Nothing in the present Charter shall impair the inherent right of individual or collective self-defence if an armed attack occurs against a member of the United Nations, until the Security Council has taken measures necessary to maintain international peace and security.

Chapter VIII of the UN Charter provides a general framework for regional arrangements in pursuit of world peace. Article 52, in part, states:

> Nothing in the present Charter precludes the existence of regional arrangements or agencies for dealing with such matters relating to the maintenance of international peace and security as are appropriate for regional action, provided that such arrangements or agencies and their activities are consistent with the Purposes and Principles of the United Nations.

Article 53(1) further states:

> The Security Council shall, where appropriate, utilize such regional arrangements or agencies for enforcement action under its authority. But no enforcement action shall be taken under regional arrangements or by regional agencies without the authorization of the Security Council.

Whereas the SADC allies in the DRC have been accused of acting without the authorization of the UN Security Council, the same accusation has not been directed at the North Atlantic Treaty Organization (NATO) intervention in the bombing of the Federal Republic of Yugoslavia or in the campaign against Iraq, neither of which had Security Council authorization. This is clearly the application of double standards. Both the NATO and SADC cases point to the erosion of the authority of the United Nations. This is particularly serious in the case of NATO, which includes three of the five permanent members of the Security Council.

The deployment and continued presence of the forces of Zimbabwe, Angola, and Namibia in the DRC has given rise to a heated debate that bears critical implications for long-term regional peacemaking, peacekeeping, and peacebuilding in the region. Apart from questions of the authority and legitimacy of the allied intervention, other questions have also been raised:

- What motivated the decision of the three countries to intervene in the DRC? Was it self-interest on the part of these countries, or was intervention undertaken in the interest of maintaining peace and security in the region?
- Even if they had the will and capacity, did these countries have the authority and legitimacy to intervene?
- Did these countries follow the UN rules and procedures, including obtaining the authorization of the Security Council, under Chapter VIII of the charter? If not, why not?
- Was there a regional consensus on armed intervention? Was it the decision of a few countries, and were there other peaceful options that were deliberately or imprudently ignored?
- What are the obligations of the allies, the SADC, and the UN given the facts on the ground?
- What should be the appropriate arrangements, rules of engagement, and procedure for authoritative and legitimate regional common security in southern Africa?

The intention here is not to answer these questions in any depth. Rather, it is to provide a framework in which the questions can be addressed. The debate surrounding the authority and legitimacy of SADC allied intervention in the DRC has more to do with the emerging competing doctrines of *hegemonic* as opposed to *collective* intervention than with the issue of whether the UN or SADC rules and procedures were followed. In the context of historical and contemporary hegemonic power struggles in the region, even if the SADC allied countries had followed the rules and procedures to the letter, they still would have been opposed by South Africa and the Western group of the permanent members of the Security Council. This is essentially because the SADC alliance runs counter to, and indeed challenges, the dominant emerging doctrine of hegemonic regional intervention.

Under the hegemonic doctrine, which has been seen in action in Kosovo, in East Timor, and, to some extent, in the Economic Community of West African States Cease-Fire Monitoring Group (ECOMOG) regional operations in Liberia and Sierra Leone, intervention should only be undertaken under a regional lead nation. This nation should emerge from a global hierarchy in which the United States is the lead nation in the Western regional security arrangement (NATO), which is globally the lead security arrangement. Other regional arrangements, which are subordinate to NATO, shall, under this doctrine, come under the leadership of lead nations appointed and anointed by the United States. This is the sense in which the United States was the lead nation in Kosovo, Australia the lead nation in East Timor, and Nigeria the lead nation in West Africa. According to this model, South Africa is supposed to be the lead nation in southern Africa.

Such an interpretation presents at least two challenges for conventional UN thinking about international peace that require critical attention. First, the lead nation model departs radically from the model centered on the UN Security Council acting, through the General Assembly, as the ultimate custodian of world peace. Second, it departs from the UN Charter, which embraces the multilateral collective international security model of Chapters VII and VIII. Instead, it leans on organized unilateralism.

This competition between hegemonic and collective security models arises, in the first instance, from the inherent tension between nation-states or regional authorities on the one hand and collective international rule on the other. S. Schlessinger traces this tension back to the founding of the UN in 1945. Although the permanent members of the Security Council (first the United States, Britain, and the Soviet Union, and later France and China) had veto power in the Security Council, the smaller powers, desirous of protecting their authority within regional groupings, insisted that the UN undertake in its charter to recognize the right of their regional pacts to serve as the forums of first resort for handling local crises before the UN assumed responsibility.[6]

At the regional level, however, the same problems are likely to recur.

Although there are no UN Security Council–type rules among the regional security arrangements, problems arising from the asymmetry of power manifest themselves in such situations. Such manifestations may be structural and embedded in the distribution of power in the region, or they may relate to particular situations as they arise. Under these conditions regional organizations may become instruments of regional hegemony if they are dominated by a single regional power.[7] In such situations, some argue, collaboration with the UN may temper domination by a hegemon. However, others argue that lead nations not only are likely to provide the necessary resources but can also galvanize political and organizational efforts, offering coherence to a mission and maintaining the resolve to meet agreed objectives.

Reforming or Reconfiguring the SADC Organ

Addressing the functioning of the organ in the wake of the intervention in the DRC, Horst Brammer of the SADC Political Affairs in the South African Department of Foreign Affairs, summed up the situation as follows:

> Due to the non-functioning of the Organ, attempts to find a solution were not and could not be conducted in an entirely unified way. Whereas the South African–initiated response was to engage all belligerents for a peaceful settlement, Zimbabwe and its "allies" (Namibia and Angola) preferred to engage the anti-Kabila forces in military confrontation. The difference in approach was identifiable along the same lines as the debate on the Organ.[8]

Needless to say, the above statement is an oversimplification of the reality. It does not attempt to explain the reason behind the difference in approach. Also, it wrongly associates particular responses with the positions taken on the organ. Brammer almost suggests that those advocating an independent organ are inclined toward a military solution, while those advocating centralization are likely to favor a peaceful solution.

Problems of organization and operationalization have continued to afflict the organ. At the August 1997 Blantyre summit, the question of the status of the organ vis-à-vis the summit was taken up with considerable tension between the SADC and the organ chairs. Decisions were deferred to a later summit in Angola, which did not take place. In March 1998, however, the summit held in Maputo tasked Mozambique, Malawi, and Namibia with studying the issue and making appropriate recommendations. Nothing was done until the August 1999 Maputo summit directed the Council of Ministers to review the operations of all SADC institutions, including the organ, and to report back within six months. At a subsequent meeting of the

ISDSC and SADC Ministers for Foreign Affairs in Swaziland in October 1999, the singular recommendation was made that the organ was part of the SADC and should report to the SADC summit. This recommendation was to be forwarded to the SADC Heads of State and Government for consideration. There are three possible structures of the SADC organ that have been proposed at various stages in its life (see Figures 2.1–2.3). Figure 2.2 is clearly the integrationist option. But does it necessarily guarantee a stable peace and security in the region? A competing, more autonomous structure is depicted in Figure 2.3.

Figure 2.1 Proposed Structure of the SADC Organ by Senior Officials (1997)

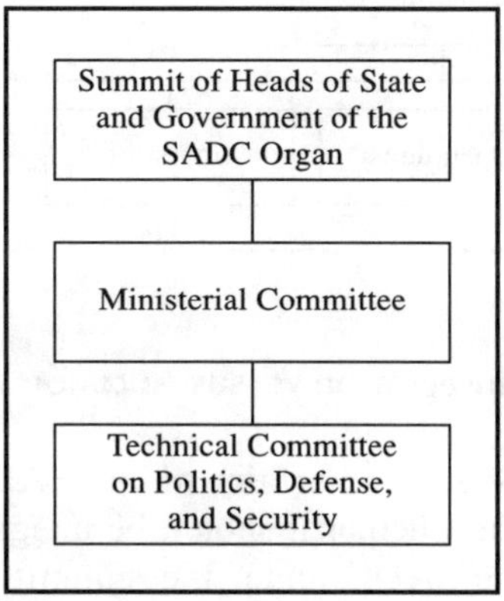

Figure 2.2 SADC Organ Organization Structure, Swaziland (1999)

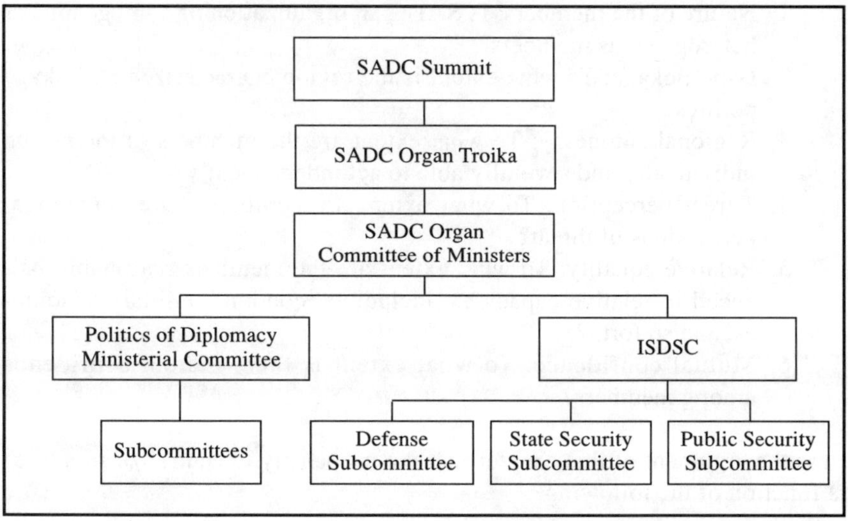

Figure 2.3 Autonomous SADC Organ Organization Structure

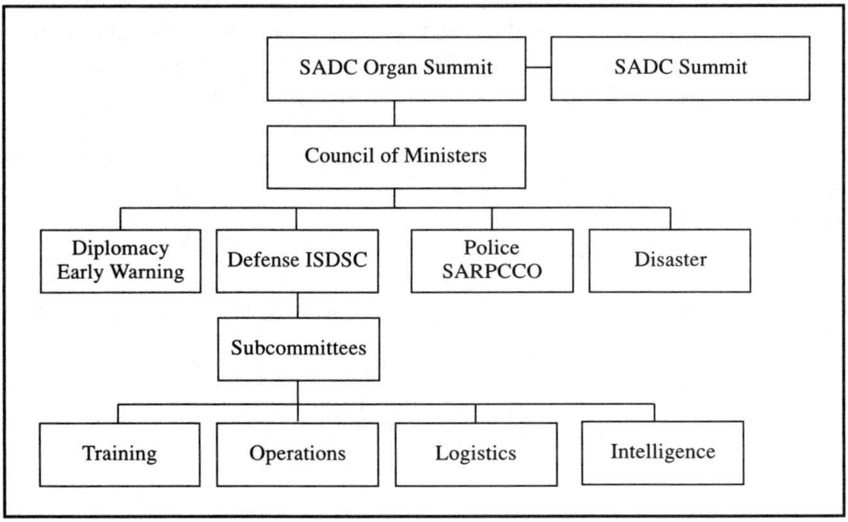

Integration Versus Autonomy

The issue that has dogged the affairs of the SADC Organ on Politics, Defense, and Security is whether it should be integrated within the overall unified structure of the SADC under the summit or have some relative autonomy and a capacity to act independently when such need arises.

The choice depends on at least six critical factors:

1. Nature of the members: Is SADC an organization of homogenous or heterogeneous members?
2. Issue linkage: To what extent is the region characterized by linkage politics?
3. Regional autonomy: To what extent are the members of the region individually and severally able to act independently?
4. Threat perception: To what extent do members share convergent perceptions of threat?
5. Relative equality: To what extent are the members reasonably balanced in relative capacities, including economic, military, resources, and so forth?
6. Mutual confidence: To what extent is there mutual confidence among members?

It is the argument of this chapter that the propensity to centralize should be a function of the following:

1. The group is more homogenous than heterogeneous.
2. Issue linkage politics is low.
3. Members are, individually and severally, autonomous actors.
4. Members share similar perceptions.
5. Members are relatively equal in capacities.
6. The level of mutual confidence is high.

A careful look at the southern Africa region suggests the following responses to the questions on the six critical factors outlined above:

1. The region is more heterogeneous than homogenous.
2. The tendency for issue linkage is high, as evidenced, for example, by the linkage between the domestic economic crisis in Zimbabwe, the land question, and the intervention in the DRC.
3. Members are not autonomous actors, as they are all overexposed to external international influences. South Africa's EU agreement is a case in point.
4. Members do not share threat perceptions. On the contrary, they have divergent perceptions of threat and conceptions of defense.
5. Inequality defines the structure of relationships in the region.
6. Mutual confidence, particularly between the could-be hegemony and the rest of the region, is very low.

Conclusion

The recommendations of the Swaziland meeting of the Committee of Foreign Ministers that the SADC Organ on Politics, Defence, and Security be brought under direct authority of the SADC summit were presented to the SADC Windhoek summit in August 2000 in the Council of Ministers' report on the review of the operations of SADC institutions.

Debate and discussion of the report were deferred. The 2000 SADC summit communiqué states that because there was a "need for member states to undertake further consultations, the Summit gave the Council of Ministers a three months extension to complete the exercise."[9] This suggests that there is a need to study the report carefully. Apart from the issues raised in that report, it will be extremely important to consider the following questions in the "further consultations" envisaged by the communiqué:

- The mutual defense treaty entered into between Angola, the DRC, Namibia, and Zimbabwe in 1999 in the course of their alliance in the war in the DRC. Whatever is decided must take this treaty into account to avoid conflicts surrounding sovereignty.
- Existing bilateral defense treaties and agreements among SADC

members and between them and other countries in the region and beyond.

- Threat perceptions and conceptions of defense and security both at the national and regional levels, as well as members' defense postures.
- The peace and security profiles of the SADC members, including defense expenditure patterns; nature, structure, and size of forces; and military capabilities.
- Mechanisms for ensuring multilateral action, particularly in the light of asymmetrical capabilities.

The creation of an independent organ would be best for the region. If, however, the integrationist view comes to prevail, it will at least be necessary to pursue a gradualist strategy, with the process phased in over time. This is in accordance with the conditions mentioned above. Any attempt to move more rapidly is likely to create strains that may have negative repercussions for the SADC as a whole.

Notes

1. SADC, communiqué from the SADC Annual Consultative Conference, Royal Swazi Sun Convention Centre, Mbabane, Swaziland, 20–22 February 2000.
2. See David Evans, Peter Holmes, and Ibbo Mandaza, *SADC: The Cost of Non-Integration* (Harare, Zimbabwe: SAPES Books, 1999).
3. SADC, "Treaty for the Southern African Development Community," Windhoek, Namibia, January 1992, Article 22.
4. SADC, "Protocol on Politics, Defense and Security in Southern Africa Development Community (SADC) Region," Maseru, Lesotho, 30 June 1996, 1.
5. Ibid.
6. S. Schlessinger, "Transcending or Defending the World of States? The United Nations and Its Members," *Politik und Gesellschaft: International Politics and Society* 4 (1999): 352.
7. SWP (Stiftung Wissenschaft Und Politik), Fourth International Workshop, Berlin, 24–26 June 1999.
8. Horst Brammer, "In Search of an Effective Regional Security Mechanism for Southern Africa," *Global Dialogue* 4, 2 (August 1999): 21–22.
9. SADC communiqué, Windhoek, Namibia, 7 August 2000.

3

Redefining Security

AGOSTINHO ZACARIAS

The argument has been made repeatedly that in the post–Cold War era, security in the southern Africa region should move away from the traditional state-centric approach to a people-centered approach guided by collective interest and based in regional settings.[1] Various political statements by leaders and the creation, in 1996, of the SADC Organ on Politics, Defense, and Security (OPDS) show that this view has gained currency in the region. Experience, however, has demonstrated that the vision is more easily articulated in words than performed in deeds. Since its creation, the OPDS has not achieved much in promoting collective security in the region, let alone in providing incentives or a clear justification for new security thinking through concrete policies. The OPDS has failed to prevent or arrest conflicts in the Democratic Republic of Congo (DRC), Lesotho, the Caprivi Strip in Namibia, and Zimbabwe. Its strategic vision on how to address the insecurity facing the region is still unclear.

This chapter argues that the main difficulty faced in translating the OPDS vision into concrete policies derives from the fact that security planners are still captive to old mindsets. Security in the region is still largely seen in traditional terms, as an exclusive preserve of the military, police, and securocrats who find it comfortable to do business as usual. The institutional framework needed to formulate policy in line with new security thinking in most SADC member states is weak to nonexistent. National bodies in charge of implementing the new security thinking are still dominated by the military and the police force.[2] There has not been a level of institutional reform capable of facilitating the implementation of the new security thinking or the involvement of academia in generating policy thinking. Because of these factors, the declared intent of moving from state-centric to people-centered security risks remaining an empty platitude. Admittedly, the challenges facing southern African states in translating this vision into reality are enormous. These include the need to transform the theoretical framework on which the concept of security rests, to transform institutions, and to coordinate between the military, social, economic, and political sectors. There is also a need for political will and for leaders to commit resources that will transform these institutions.

The first part of this chapter discusses the traditional concept of security and reviews its limitations. The second part examines some of the structural obstacles that have hampered progress in implementing the new thinking. The third part focuses on a new conceptual framework for security and its policy implications.

The Traditional Concept of Security and Its Limitations

The traditional concept of security borrows its core thinking from the realist school of international relations, which tends to see the international system as anarchical and determined by power. Military power, in particular, is seen to be central in relations between states. This view implies that states should be entirely self-reliant for their security. The traditional school of security thus views security as the absence of threats from other states. The insecurity of people living within a given state can only come from threats from other states, and as the major threat to the existence of states is the threat of war, military threats take precedence over any other threats.[3] W. Lippman's 1943 work set the stage for what was commonly accepted and practiced as security. He stated that "a nation is secure to the extent to which it is not in danger of having to sacrifice its core values, if it wishes to avoid war, and is able if challenged, to maintain them by victory in such a war."[4]

Although Lippman's view of security became dominant, especially in the West, for a long time the concept remained underdeveloped. It was the incidence of violent conflict in the third world in the 1970s that generated a renewed interest in finding an answer to the issues of conflict and insecurity. However, most of the literature at that time explained third world insecurity in terms of East-West competition. The first serious attempt to unravel the concept came from Barry Buzan, writing in 1983. His work nevertheless reaffirms the view of security in traditional terms. Buzan argues that, to be useful, the concept of security needs to be considered on three levels: the individual, the state (national), and the international. In the international system, security is primarily about sovereign territorial states, and the anarchical structure of the international system can lead to security if states are strong. Strong states are those with strong sociopolitical cohesion, the ideal type being nation-states such as Denmark or Japan, where ethnolinguistic boundaries coincide with geographical boundaries.[5] Buzan also asserts that in international relations, the security of the state, or the concept of national security, is of the greatest importance because it tends to organize the other two levels of security, the individual and the international.[6] For him, national security means the security of the whole sociopolitical entity: "It is about the country as well as states. It concerns the way of life of self-governing people including their social, cultural, political and economic modes of organisation and the right to develop themselves under their own rule."[7]

Buzan believes that in weak states—those with weak sociopolitical cohesion—and in anarchical states—those with no practical sociopolitical cohesion—the referent object of security is much harder to identify and, by implication, the concept of national security becomes difficult to apply. In weak states there is a lack of a cohesive locus of power that can turn its influence outward against extraneous threats. Elsewhere, Buzan concludes that the concept of national security is not applicable to third world countries.[8]

As the post–World War II period has shown, this view of security tended to emphasize state interest over people's interests and, as a consequence, militarism became paramount over people's welfare. In many countries, political stability, economic development, and environmental protection were relegated to second place, as arms buildups became synonymous with security. However, arms buildups and confrontation defeated the purpose of creating security, as tension, instability, and insecurity resulting from the threat of nuclear destruction grew in unparalleled fashion, and terrorism uncovered some of the vulnerabilities of Western security systems.[9] In Eastern bloc countries, and in most third world countries, the situation was worse, as militarization was attained at the expense of social welfare and economic development. Although statesmen claimed that their states were secure, insecurity was exacerbated.

John Herz, in his seminal work of 1957 "Rise and Demise of the Territorial State," demonstrates the flaws in the traditional concept of security. He argues that this approach led to the "security dilemma." That states pursue their own security—regardless of their intentions—increases the insecurity of other states, and ultimately their own insecurity.

Scholars such as Caroline Thomas, looking at security in the third world, have observed that the traditional concept fails to deal with other dimensions of state existence that are essential to security in the third world.[10] Edward Azar and Chung-In Moon have added that issues related to legitimacy and policy capacity are more important in the security of the third world than physical power.[11] Socioeconomists have argued that military power was an inadequate response to domestic crises of legitimacy, failed economic development, and poverty. As Stephen Walt puts it, "military power does not guarantee the well-being of the society and . . . nonmilitary phenomena can also threaten states and individuals."[12] For evidence of this, one has only to consider the devastating impact of the drought that affected southern African states in 1991–1992 and the recent floods in Mozambique, let alone the impact of the HIV/AIDS pandemic across the African continent.

Traditional Security and Southern Africa

While the traditional concept of security dominated thinking in Europe and across the Atlantic, southern Africa did not escape its influence. This is entirely understandable, as states in southern Africa resulted from the expansion of the European state system and the political ideas underpinning it.[13] Moreover, regional dynamics spawned by the frenzied economic interests of colonial powers, the need to protect white supremacy in the region, the cold war context, and the attempt by apartheid South Africa to establish a regional order founded on relations of domination and subordination all helped to develop the view that armed confrontation was the only way to attain security.[14]

In consequence, the region has witnessed increased militarization since the 1960s, on the one hand by forces that viewed colonial regimes as hampering their freedom, independence, and security and on the other hand by the colonial powers, who saw their acquired benefits and interests in peril.[15] Security was then seen in zero-sum terms: the security of one meant the insecurity of the other, a view that deepened even further as the conflict gained a regional character. At the heart of this model was the attempt by apartheid South Africa to structure a regional order founded on its hegemony through the Constellation of Southern African States project.[16] When the project was rejected by majority-ruled states, South Africa tried to co-opt and coerce most of the southern African states. Confrontation became inevitable as the Eastern bloc countries provided military support to many of the newly independent states, and South Africa defined this threat as a "total onslaught" to which the minority regime in Pretoria responded with a "total strategy" aimed at protecting its national interests, allegedly threatened by communists.[17]

Conceiving security from a militaristic point of view had an adverse impact on the region. Effects included the further weakening of states, the proliferation of land mines and light weapons, unstable political order, poor economic development, transnational crime, money laundering, and inadequate attention to food insecurity and epidemics such as HIV/AIDS.

The weakening of states was perceptible in terms of not only sociopolitical cohesion but also physical infrastructure and the whole idea of the state. In some countries, the state limits its existence to urban areas and is either virtually nonexistent or present at a level that makes it inefficient in handling problems that affect social groups in most remaining areas. The ability of such states to protect civilians, to mobilize resources, to collect taxes, to implement and oversee policies, and to face organized crime is limited. They are thus unable to cater to the security of the whole national entity.

Poor economic performance in the region has been associated with several factors, both economic and noneconomic. They include natural disasters, such as droughts, cyclones, and floods; mismanagement and poor macroeconomic policies; the debt overhang; lack of foreign direct investment; and an inability to sustain macroeconomic reforms. In addition, there are high levels of transnational crime, including drugs, car theft, money laundering, capital flight, and illegal arms sales. The proliferation of light weapons continues to be a major challenge that also impacts political instability.

Political instability was associated in the past with the apartheid regime's destabilization policies and, in the present, is associated with the difficulties of establishing all-inclusive democratic systems. Political instability makes most states of southern Africa less attractive for foreign direct investment, which in turn reinforces their poor development. This situation has resulted in migration from poor and less stable countries to richer ones: specifically the most dynamic economy of the region, South Africa. The majority of countries have relied upon migrant laborers to reduce their employment pressures. Migration to South Africa has become a source of tension in the region—not so much among authorities as among ordinary citizens of South Africa who feel that their employment opportunities are being usurped by foreigners. The need to resolve the problem of growing unemployment among the black population, and to introduce technological innovation to revamp the economy, has compelled South Africa to reduce the number of migrants in the country. Weak economies have caused massive unemployment, which in turn has caused crime rates to rise.

The problems faced by the southern African states cannot be resolved by a single state acting individually. They require a transnational approach founded on cooperation and a coordinated strategy that responds to military, economic, political, and social challenges. The traditional concept of security is nationally focused. This disjunction has led many scholars to call for a new security thinking in the region. The new dispensation that emerged as a result of the waning of the Cold War and the demise of apartheid provided the region with an opportunity to rethink security in much broader terms, encompassing military and nonmilitary phenomena.

The OPDS and Its Politics

The signing of the SADC treaty by the then Southern African Development Coordination Conference (SADCC) members in Windhoek, in 1992, constituted a major milestone toward the implementation of the new concept of security. The event led many commentators to hope that the SADC would adopt a concept of security that would permit it to tackle military and non-military problems. The declaration by heads of state that accompanied the SADC treaty states that "good and strengthened political relations among the countries of the region and peace and mutual security are critical components for regional cooperation and integration. The region needs therefore to establish a framework and mechanisms to strengthen regional solidarity and provide for mutual peace and security."[18]

Article 4 of the treaty stipulates that peace and security should guide the actions of the SADC member states; Article 5 specifies that one of the objectives of SADC members is to promote and defend peace and security, while Article 21 obliges SADC members to cooperate in these two areas. The treaty does not provide details about mechanisms by, and forms in which, security cooperation will be affected, save for mentioning that member states will conclude the necessary protocols in such areas of cooperation. However, experience has shown that concluding protocols that define mechanisms of cooperation in the area of security is not an easy exercise.

Soon after the signing of the SADC treaty, recurrent statements by regional leaders called for a new security agenda that would favor peaceful resolution of conflicts, prefer conflict prevention to conflict resolution, and be based on concrete problem-solving methods. This rhetoric was followed by a series of initiatives by the SADC secretariat aimed at fostering common understanding and identifying ways in which security cooperation could be effected. The secretariat commissioned a number of studies that invariably recommended the adoption of the new concept of security and cooperation among member states. Following these recommendations, the 1993 SADC program for action stressed the need for a strategy to advance regional security that included adopting the wider definition of security, establishing a forum for mediation and arbitration, and reducing the level of military expenditure.[19] In July 1994 in Windhoek, the secretariat convened a ministerial-level workshop on democracy, peace, and security. The workshop recommended the creation of a sector dedicated to conflict resolution and political cooperation, the coordination of which would be assigned to one member state, a common practice within the SADC.[20] The Council of Ministers meeting, held later that year in Gaborone, concluded that conflict prevention and mediation should be a wing of the sector of Politics, International Relations, Defense, and Security rather than a sector in itself.[21] But the ministers did not specify the means and mechanisms by which this wing was supposed to function, let alone the entire sector. There were still many questions to be answered on the nature of the structure and how wide-ranging issues such as defense, security, international relations, and politics could be dealt with in a meaningful and coherent manner and incorporated into one sector. From the outset, it was clear that the mandate for this sector would be cumbersome and difficult to manage.

In the debate that followed, some member states felt that bringing the issue of security within the SADC framework would divert the organization's attention from its main objective: economic development. Others felt that the new concept of security—which was strongly influenced by the debate within the Conference for Security and Co-operation in Europe—tended to view development as an integral part of building common security in the region.[22] The region's development was inseparable from the security problems it was facing, as much of its insecurity arose from the way resources were distributed and political space was shared. Development and security were intricately linked and required military and nonmilitary experts to work closely using a common framework, as the new concept of security called for cooperation in areas such as labor, the rule of law and human rights, the environment, science and technology, and military and economic issues.[23] According to this view, the issue of security was too important and sensitive to be subordinated to the debate on economic development and handled by bureaucrats at the SADC secretariat or the SADC summit meeting once a year, which largely deals with development problems.

This line of argument led some SADC members to advance a proposal to create the Association of Southern African States (ASAS), which would function independently of the SADC secretariat and would report directly to the heads of state summit. ASAS would have two main divisions, one dealing with the political aspects of security and the other dealing with the military aspects.

For some members, the ASAS proposal meant structuring a military alliance similar to the North Atlantic Treaty Organization, in a context in which the end of the Cold War meant that the dominant discourse was on reducing military expenditure. Furthermore, the proposal implied the establishment of a new secretariat to deal with security affairs in a situation where the SADC was extraregionally funded, as the economies of the region were still grappling with their rehabilitation and recovery. SADC members found it hard to justify the creation of a new secretariat dedicated solely to security affairs. Another reason the ASAS idea became unpopular was that its leadership was going to be allocated to one member, as had been the case with other sectors in the SADC. Many members disliked the idea of having one country alone handling sensitive issues such as politics, defense, and security. Still others saw it as a bid by Zimbabwe's president Robert Mugabe for a prominent role in regional politics, since the Frontline States (FLS), the organization he had chaired up to that point, had lost its relevance and consequently disbanded. These factors led the summit of heads of state and government meeting in August 1995 to reject the ASAS proposal. The communiqué issued at the end of the summit referred to the need for further consultations among the Ministers of Defence and Security on structures, terms of reference, and operational procedures before the summit approved ASAS.[24]

However, contrary to what had been promised, the Ministers of Defense and Security developed a new proposal—the Organ on Politics, Defense, and Security (OPDS)—in lieu of ASAS and recommended its creation in January 1996. The summit meeting in June 1996 formally endorsed this proposal. The new proposal made an effort to provide a response to many of the issues raised with respect to the ASAS proposal as well as the one proposing the creation of the Sector on Politics, Defence, and Security. The OPDS was charged with protecting people and safeguarding the development of the region against instability arising from the breakdown of law and order, interstate conflict, and external aggression. It would also promote political cooperation among members, enhance democratic institutions, use preventive diplomacy to preempt conflict between and within the states, and promote the political, economic, social, and environmental dimensions of security.[25]

The OPDS would function at the summit, ministerial, and technical levels, operating independently of SADC structures. Its chair would rotate on an annual basis among the troika presiding over the community.[26] The OPDS could also create new structures as it deemed necessary, including technical committees, while the Inter-State Defence and Security Committee (ISDSC), which had been established in 1994, would act as its secretariat.

It soon became clear that there was no consensus among members with regard to the ways in which this newly created OPDS should function. The existence of a chairperson for the SADC and a chairperson for the OPDS gave the impression that there were two separate organizations with no connection between them. That the chairman of the SADC was appointed for three years while that of the OPDS was supposed to rotate on an annual basis constituted another discrepancy. Furthermore, no institutional mechanism was established to harmonize or coordinate the work between the OPDS and the SADC. At the summit held in Malawi in August 1997, President Nelson Mandela of South Africa, acting as the chairman of the organization, expressed dissatisfaction that the OPDS functioned outside the SADC framework. He insisted that security should be dealt with as a substructure of the SADC, under the same chairmanship, and that the OPDS should report to the summit, as mandated by Article 10 of the SADC treaty,[27] rather than functioning with two independent chairs. Because of the differences between him and the newly elected chair of the organ,

President Mugabe, President Mandela threatened to resign from the SADC chairmanship if a solution aimed at bringing the OPDS under the framework of the SADC could not be found. Mandela's ultimatum led the summit to put the OPDS on hold temporarily and to appoint a committee composed of Malawi, Mozambique, and Namibia to identify a suitable solution.

From 1997 until early 2001, the SADC struggled to find solutions to these discordances. Proposals ranged from transforming the OPDS into committees and working on an ad hoc basis to integrating the OPDS into the SADC framework and having it chaired by one of the deputy chairpersons in the troika.[28] Others believe that the OPDS should operate on the basis of specific protocols, which have yet to be signed.[29] However, the Windhoek summit in August 2000 failed to endorse any of these proposals. The issue was resolved at the Maputo summit, in August 2001, which decided that the OPDS would function as an SADC substructure and report to the summit. The summit also agreed that the OPDS would be chaired by someone who is not at the same time chairman of the SADC. This troika would have a chairman and two deputies. The second deputy is the incoming chair, as the chairman will be rotated on an annual basis.[30] The newly introduced model offers the advantage of guaranteeing continuity, as the troika presiding over the SADC remains unchanged for three consecutive years. It also provides room for harmonizing security policies with economic and development policies, as all policymaking issues will be dealt with by the same body, the SADC summit.

However, the ISDSC—a structure comprising the ministers of defense, police commissioners, heads of intelligence, and their respective officials—continues to act as the secretariat of the OPDS. Their administration of the organ implies that, although there is talk about adopting a new concept of security, in practical terms, the SADC still views security in traditional militaristic terms. The debate between the old thinking—the one that tends to view security in strictly militaristic terms—and the new thinking—which understands security as an all-embracing concept—does not seem to have been resolved. The debate on security is not yet cross-sectoral or interdepartmental but remains the purview of the traditional institutions of security, which are primarily concerned with propping up the status quo rather than ensuring security for all or introducing new approaches to security. SADC security meetings organized under the auspices of the OPDS are still dominated by the military, officials of the ministries of defense, the police, and intelligence. The dialogue between these functionaries and their colleagues in civilian think tanks and academia has not been considered essential in policymaking or allowed the new security concept to permeate policymaking and implementation. The new security thinking is present in the minds of certain élites in the security establishment and academia, but so far it has failed to create a common vision that can transform the region. Traditional institutions of security are often insensitive to issues such as how politics, bad governance, the lack of environmental policy, the lack of social welfare, and bad economic management affect the security of individuals and society. They still conceptualize security in terms of threat perception and national disasters, and their policies are consequently reactive rather than proactive.

The lack of common vision in an environment of competing priorities has affected cooperation. Indeed, cooperation has been confined to the military, police, and intelligence. For example, high-level hotline satellite communications were established to allow communication on defense matters. There has been a commitment to establishing a standby force at the level of a brigade to intervene in regional conflicts, to which SADC member states would contribute with combat units and headquarters staff, but there has been little progress on this issue. There have been talks for regional joint training, especially in the areas of peacekeeping, and there have been a limited number of officials who have benefited from this training, but its impact and scope is very limited. There have also been some ad hoc cooperative police operations involving Mozambique and South Africa, and South Africa and Zambia; the intervention of South Africa in Lesotho to quell the rebellion that emerged after 1998 elections; and the military intervention by Angola, Zimbabwe, and Namibia in the DRC. None of these activities, however, can be said to have taken place within the framework defined by the SADC or the OPDS. Rather, they were a result of ad hoc agreements between departments, top officials of departments, or ministers responsible for those specific portfolios in the countries involved and heads of state acting outside the structures of the SADC. Indeed, a multidisciplinary approach to security is lacking, and the governance of the security sector is still following the traditional ways. In many countries, civil society and the public at large does not debate, contribute with ideas, or control the expenditure and activities of the security forces. Civilian control of security forces is still unclear. These are issues that should all have been addressed by the Protocol on Politics, Defense, and Security Cooperation.

Southern African states still do not share common values. Although many have embraced multiparty democracy, the democratic culture does not prevail in the subcontinent. The prolonged conflict in Angola has impeded the consolidation of democracy, and with the death of Jonas Savimbi hopefully politics in Angola will cease to be dominated by the rivalry between the Popular Movement for the Liberation of Angola and the National Union for the Total Independence of Angola (UNITA). The monarchies of Lesotho and Swaziland are still grappling with the ways in which democracy could be made viable in their countries. While Lesotho might move ahead with constitutional reforms aimed at establishing a balanced representation of political forces in the parliament after the May 2002 elections, pressure is mounting on the Swazi monarch to democratize the country. Not long ago, Namibia was forced to change its constitution to allow the president to run for a third term, while an attempt by former Zambian president Frederick Chiluba to run for the third time was received with bitter opposition. These conditions testify that the fundamental principles of democracy are not yet shared by all, making it difficult to democratize the governance of the security sector.

The differences that emerged between Zimbabwe, Angola, and Namibia on the one hand and South Africa on the other, when the first three countries decided to intervene in the DRC, show the lack of common principles on the basis of which security can be viewed in the region. Zimbabwe, Angola, and Namibia justified their intervention as occurring at the invitation of the legitimate government of an SADC member state under attack by proxy forces supported by Uganda and Rwanda. South Africa, having used the same justification to intervene in Lesotho on 22 September 1998, thought that intervention in the DRC was unjustified and preferred diplomacy as a means to solve the conflict.

Suspicion still reigns in the region and precludes the emergence of full-fledged relations of cooperation in the area of security. SADC member states have signed a protocol guaranteeing free circulation of SADC nationals in the region, but the ratification of this protocol and implementation by national governments is still pending. There are still fears that the nationals of one state may take advantage of the protocol either to compete for limited employment opportunities—causing brain drain, especially from weaker states to strong members—or to facilitate transnational crime. Relations of suspicion curtail the ability of SADC members to use the full potential available in the region to strengthen security relations. Suspicion had dominated the relations between Zimbabwe and South Africa, which continue to maintain an economic and military rivalry. Similar distrust governed the relations between Angola and South Africa and between Angola and Zambia, based on the Angolan government's suspicion that both those countries support UNITA. It also haunted the relations between South Africa and Namibia, which suspects that South Africa wishes to continue to dominate it.

These factors account for the difficulty in achieving a common vision and common policy planning that looks at security as an all-embracing concept, and in delegating power to a supranational structure to define new directions. Instead, SADC member states find it easier to cooperate minimally and half-heartedly in military and paramilitary spheres.

Where Do We Go from Here?

Reconceptualizing Security

There is a need to reflect on the theoretical basis on which the concept of security in the region rests. A theoretical shift would imply viewing security in terms of the philosophical underpinnings pertaining to the idea of "the good life," which implies looking at security as an all-embracing conceptual architecture of which peace, justice, order, and economics are the main pillars. The coexistence of these four pillars in a structural relationship forms the environment for security: the conditions in which the fulfillment of human aspirations is best served.

The term *peace* here is employed to mean different things. There is the classical definition of peace as the "absence of war"; there is peace as stability and tranquility; and peace as the absence of structural violence. The word is also employed to mean a political process of conflict management.[31] However, reduced to its practical meaning in all these cases, the concept of peace refers to a condition of minimal understanding between real and potential adversaries, in which cooperative efforts become possible. The predictability of peaceful behavior among members of society or between states is essential for security, as it is only in peaceful times that human beings can best fulfill their political, economic, and social aspirations and maximize their intellect and energy for the benefit of society.

The concept of *justice* is harder to define, due to difficulties in arriving at any conception of justice that is substantially founded, value-free, and neutral. The concept is shaped by several factors, material and nonmaterial; it is subject to many interpretations of a subjective nature; and it is strongly influenced by perceptions and culture. Nevertheless, justice is one of the most prevalent virtues at the core of any societal life. It is the basis of order and determines the stability of relations in a society. It provides the sense of fairness of the structures that mediate relations between members of a given society, and it ensures the protection of private and collective property. Justice is also seen as a set of principles assigning rights and duties in the basic institutions of society and the appropriate distribution of the benefits and burdens of social cooperation.[32]

The concept of justice is prominent and overriding in social life but is a hotly contested topic. This makes it difficult to present a concept of justice that is widely accepted yet regarded as neutral before rival claims. This situation by no means hinders the emergence of collective views of justice. Indeed, collective views of justice have been arrived at by indoctrination, education, imposition, and through free dialogue. However, given that the concept of justice is essentially contested, a collective view that can bring consensus can only be obtained by defining a framework and overarching rules within which people can conduct their inevitable disputes over the meaning of justice. Conceptions of security considerations that do not engender a sense of justice are not sustainable.

The term *order* refers to a predictable pattern of relations, which may or may not involve hierarchy. This pattern is achieved through the commitment of individuals to a certain level of minimal repression: submission to certain rules aimed solely at ensuring the existence of organized society. Order should thus be distinguished from surplus repression, which is aimed at assuring a particular sort of society.[33] Order assures the predictability of peaceful behavior among social members and states, which is attained when humans suppress their competitive instinct for the benefit of the community by submitting to commonly accepted principles. Only when individuals are in an environment governed by commonly accepted principles do they occupy a predictable and peaceful state in which they can share common expectations and plan and implement their aspirations without danger of physical damage or compromise of their values. Order also ensures the protection of property and the material assets of people and states, which are essential for the quality of life.

Economics is used here to mean resources, material assets, and a set of institutions and rules governing the production, management, and distribution of material benefits that human beings need in their lives. Material assets such as shelter and food are vital for human survival, whereas things such as clothing, means of transport, employment, wealth, and other social benefits define the quality of life that humans are likely to have. It is this idea of "quality of life," more specifically the idea of "the good life," that relates to security. An individual without stable sources of income (employment, private wealth, social security) is unlikely to have the same quality of life as someone with stable sources of income or wealth, and their type of housing, food, health care, and status in society will correlate strongly with their possession or lack of a stable income. If there is no sense of fair distribution of a society's assets, the management of these assets, as well as the rules governing their production, stability, justice, and order, cannot be guaranteed.

Security becomes possible if its four pillars—order, justice, peace, and economics—coexist in a condition of dynamic equilibrium. The equilibrium needs to be dynamic and not static because society changes and these changes need to be accommodated for security to be realized. People's concerns, priorities, and interests change over time, and the environment of security needs to respond to these changes. The changes reflect the evolutionary character of the society. In order to produce an environment for security, the change—in conception, interests, or concerns—should not disrupt the balance between pillars. This approach allows us to see security as a result of the interaction between individuals and the milieu, and security is obtained if the environment resulting from this process of interaction and change can still assure the same or better conditions for the fulfillment of human aspirations.

Historically, states that tended to emphasize one pillar at the expense of another did not provide a good security environment for their citizens. The Soviet Union, for example, which tended to emphasize order at the expense of justice, did not in the end provide effective security. Equally, states such South Africa during the apartheid era, insisted on a particular sense of justice at the expense of peace. This undermined the security of citizens. Furthermore, if peace is emphasized over order and justice—as it might be, for example, by a hippie who equated peace with tranquility—it does not lead to security. The prevailing social conditions that inspired Marxist revolutions in Russia, Eastern Europe, Asia, Africa, and Latin America embodied grievances founded on the insensitivity of capitalist economies and their failure to extend benefits to the majority of the population, while the counterrevolutions that followed—especially after the Cold War—were founded on the realization that Marxist economics did not work.

The balance between the pillars—the creation of an environment of security—is assured by the quality of the political process and the interaction among different social agents aimed at making decisions that affect society. The political process determines the principles guiding the functioning of the society and the values that are deemed important and need to be preserved and protected. That process also defines the allocation of resources, the determination of which development projects should be executed, the size of the army and police forces, and the national priorities that reflect the true inspirations of the people. The political process ultimately determines whether or not there will be peace, and whether the prevailing sense of justice is conducive to an orderly society. Therefore, building security in states such as those in southern Africa implies working toward the improvement of the quality of the political process.

Managing the Regional Security Variables

The reconceptualization of security along the lines defined above needs to be followed by an appropriate management of power,[34] fear, political fragmentation, and interdependence, which are the main variables that affect the southern Africa security system. Whether or not the security community to which the SADC aspires can be achieved will depend on how these variables are managed, that is, if changes in these variables can be oriented toward reinforcing cooperation, common vision, and consensus—the prerequisites for dealing effectively with various security concerns affecting the region.

South Africa remains the regional hegemon on account of its military strength, the size of its economy, its population, and its technology. However, until the end of apartheid in 1994, South Africa's power has not been used to effect positive change in the region. Moreover, the extent of its power has both been regarded with a suspicious eye by some neighboring states and attracted large numbers of immigrants. These immigrants have inspired xenophobia in South Africa and become a source of regional tension. South African nationals tend to see immigrants as the source of criminal activities in the country and as usurpers of the scarce employment opportunities available for nationals, while their increased deportation has not been much appreciated by their home countries. Regional states view this deportation as exhibiting a lack of appreciation for the role played by South Africa's neighbors and other African states in bringing apartheid to an end. This has fueled suspicions between South Africa and its neighbors, who question South Africa's commitment to helping African states overcome the economic difficulties they face.

Power is also a source of suspicion, as many southern African states hold the view that South Africa could dominate the region economically and militarily. This suspicion has led South Africa to be cautious in its relations with its neighbors and not to exert enough influence to bring the region together.

Power needs to be stabilized to reduce fears and inequalities. Excessive concentration of power in one member contributes to maintaining or inducing further dislocations, imbalances, and rivalries. That said, it is very difficult to find the right formula to balance power between states such as South Africa, Swaziland, and Lesotho, to mention only the extreme cases. The flip side of this argument is that unrestrained power will undoubtedly encourage relations of domination and subordination. A balance needs to be found between maintaining or increasing South Africa's power and enhancing the power of its neighbors to leverage their extraregional relations and consolidate their position in the international arena.

The variables of fear and fragmentation need also to be managed properly. Here, these words are used in the context of domestic and regional polarization, exclusion of communities in the decisionmaking process, alienation, intrastate and interstate conflict caused by military attacks, and any other forms of domination and discrimination.

In the past, the hegemonic ambitions of apartheid South Africa were spawned by the fears of a privileged white minority surrounded by black majorities constantly threatening to dispossess them of their privileges. To protect its supremacy, the white minority sought to consolidate its power through repression at home and expansion of its domination in the region. Fear also precipitated political fragmentation in South Africa, as the regime tried to appease domestic opposition and led the nation to encourage dissidence and subversion throughout the region. This enhanced the division of national communities into subnational structures, hampering the emergence of united national polities. Fear was also instrumental in the creation of the SADCC, as military and economic domination by South Africa was found to be a real possibility. This led South Africa's neighbors to constitute a front aimed at reducing dependence on South Africa in opposition to its domination while, at the national level, fear hindered the full participation of citizens in domestic political life. As Buzan justly observes, when fears are high, cooperation is low and, as a consequence, regional security cooperation suffers. Fears of economic domination by South Africa still persist and are likely to continue as the gap between South Africa's economy and the economies of the rest of the region remains large. Therefore, the variable of fear needs to be kept low by mounting confidence-building initiatives and mutually supporting strategies, and by promoting cooperation that strengthens the sense of community in the region.

Interdependence is another variable that needs careful management. It refers to mutual dependence between members of a system, or as Robert Keohane and Joseph Nye put it, "reciprocal effects among countries or among actors in different countries."[35] Interdependence is important because it reduces the potential for an interstate conflict, even if it does not always translate into symmetry. When fear is high, interdependence is low, and unless fear is low, it is unlikely that interdependence will be high.[36] Although there was a degree of interdependence between South Africa and its neighbors at the time when the latter decided to create the SADCC, this interdependence was not sufficient to prevent them from engaging in violent confrontation with South Africa. Indeed, the FLS members were weaker and extracted more benefits from South Africa than the latter did from them. Yet this did not stop them from providing sanctuary to the apartheid combatants and seeking ways to reduce dependence on South Africa. Moreover, interdependence among FLS members was low. Their levels of trade, capital flows, and circulation of goods and labor were modest, but they shared the commitment of fighting apartheid, which became the glue that bound them.

Therefore, the level of interdependence is not the most important factor, but the principles on which this interdependence rests (i.e., whether it binds states around common values and shared interests or is founded on relations of domination). The variable of interdependence needs to be managed in a manner that is mutually reinforcing, to make the settlement of disputes by force not only nonviable but also unthinkable.

Power, fear, fragmentation, and interdependence are not concepts applied to relations between states or variables for regional security but to national polities in intercommunity and interregional relations. Depending on how these variables are managed, cooperation or indifference in addressing the sources of insecurity at national and regional levels can be found.

Implications for the OPDSC

For the Organ on Politics, Defense, and Security Cooperation (OPDSC) to be effective in its challenge of building security in the region, it needs first to make a theoretical shift in the way it conceptualizes security. It needs to adopt a concept of security that takes into account military, political, economic, social, and environmental issues. Military and police matters are but one aspect of security; they do not constitute its totality. The OPDSC needs to be structured in such a way that it can respond to political, economic, and social challenges to security. One of the SADC's weaknesses is its lack of integrated systems, processes, and methods to deal with sources of insecurity, from poor governance to lack of respect for human rights; from poverty and unemployment to the abundance of light weapons; from deprivation and exclusion to violent behavior and transnational crime.

Building security in southern Africa also implies promoting and protecting common values. Freedom, democracy, human rights, nonviolent means of resolving disputes, peace, justice, and cooperation in lieu of confrontation are essential values that affect the security of a society. The SADC countries do not share these values to a sufficient degree. Because they constitute the foundation of a stable society, and of the idea of the good life, these values need to be promoted and protected and their compatibility in the region needs to be ensured. However, as the OPDSC is currently structured, it cannot respond to these challenges. Common values are important because they ensure common vision and act as the glue that binds a society or community. If common values are not ensured in the region, the OPDSC will find it difficult to assume a principled position and cannot, therefore, be effective in its task of promoting regional security.

The assurance of common values requires new institutions or transformations of old institutions. One institution that needs transforming is the state. The state continues to be an important player in promoting and protecting the idea of the good life, and hence security; it is an important instrument for the creation of an orderly environment, reducing injustices and inequalities in society and building peace. States are important mediating instruments for various social agents such as classes, interest groups, corporations, and individuals. These social agents find it important to operate in an orderly environment, a legal framework created and legitimized by the state, despite disputes as to whether or not it can perform certain functions.

The question facing southern Africa is, what type of states are necessary to promote regional security in the present era? Past experience has demonstrated that authoritarian states are not the best arrangement for security. They are often insensitive to diversity and competing needs in society and out of touch with the reality they are supposed to serve. They end up not harnessing the full potential that societies can offer and are thus ineffective in the promotion of security for all. We need states that can operate on a different basis: those that can adopt interactive and inclusive approaches and democratic values, those that can place the people they are serving at the center. Ministries of defense and security need to interact more with other social agents and increase the participation of nonmilitary sectors in making national security plans. It is also important to have states that can factor mainstream economic, political, and social concerns into the regional security equation. The OPDSC should spearhead the transformation of states by adopting a structure that can ensure the promotion of democratic order, good governance, and economic, social, and operational issues. There must be a linkage between activity at the national level and regional policies. The OPDSC is well positioned to draw expertise and ideas from other sources, such as research institutions, think tanks, civil society organizations, and private security organizations. It is also well suited to developing thinking that can influence policy and action in the region and contribute to strengthening capacity—especially in the civilian sectors dealing with security, such as the parliaments, civilian ministries of defense, ministries of justice, and the offices of heads of government.

Interaction between military, intelligence, and police institutions and other nonmilitary social agents will allow the latter's preoccupations to be taken into account when planning national security. Underlying this wide participation of social agents in the business of security is the idea that the state and its institutions should not maintain security as its exclusive preserve, as the state does not constitute the totality of life. There are other agents, such as civic organizations, pressure groups, and community-based organizations, that converge under the umbrella of civil society. For example, the evidence shows that the position of women, and of large numbers of others in society, has improved in the last decades thanks to work conducted by women's organizations and human rights activists with little or no connection with the state. Equally undeniable is the influence of peace movements on issues such as nuclear disarmament and the reduction of conventional forces in Europe. Social movements have also played an important role in raising awareness as to how the misuse of the environment places global security in peril.

In southern Africa, large numbers of people depend on nonstate entities for their emergency relief, food, education, heath care, sanitation, and personal security. Civil society also plays an important role in crime prevention and the protection of the environment. It makes no sense to conceptualize a people-centric approach to security without involving civil society organizations.

The OPDSC also needs to pay attention to operational issues. The establishment of early warning systems throughout the region is paramount to allow timely action. There is already cooperation in the area of intelligence, but not all intelligence institutions in the region have the same capacity, nor do the same principles and vision necessarily guide them. Some institutions still act within the framework of secret police rather than intelligence gatherers as processors and important components of preventive action. Common vision among intelligence institutions is crucial for the type of security articulated in the SADC treaty. The OPDSC should also be charged with establishing the principles and the framework on which intelligence institutions should cooperate. It should also plan the operationalization of the new concept of security and provide national institutions with ideas and policy proposals as to how this concept could be practiced and strengthened.

Putting the new security concept into practice implies the establishment or improvement of legal frameworks that can facilitate action by appropriate actors. The signing of collective and nonaggression pacts, human rights protection acts, moratoriums to limit arms smuggling, and pacts for environmental protection and the protection of the rights of children and vulnerable groups in conflict could be the first step. Next, the region will need to embark on institutional development, at both the national and the regional level, to implement and monitor the various accords established. Finally, it will be necessary to establish priorities and a program of action and to draw up a calendar to be ratified by national institutions. There is a need to examine critically the role of the defense industry in the region, and whether or not it can play a role in meeting the region's defense needs, especially in supplying equipment and servicing training, research, and development. There is also a need to examine how the conversion of military installations and technological capabilities can enhance regional security. However, none of these tasks is likely to be performed if some of the sovereignty of member states is not surrendered to the OPDSC.

Notes

1. See, for example, Peter Vale, "The Case for a Conference for Security and Cooperation in Southern Africa," in *Southern Africa at the Cross Roads,* ed. Anthoni Van Nieuwkerk and A. G. Van Staden (Cape Town: South African Institute of International Affairs, 1991); Andre du Pisani, "Security and Peace in Post

Apartheid Southern Africa," *International Affairs Bulletin* 13, 3 (1992); and Peter Vale and Ken Booth, "Security and Co-operation in Southern Africa: Post-Apartheid and Beyond Realism," *International Affairs* 71, 2 (1995).

2. By the "new security thinking," I mean that defined by SADC intellectuals and the SADC itself. See, for example, final communiqué of SADC summit, Gaborone, 28 June 1996. This communiqué articulates a broad range of security thinking, including using preventive diplomacy to preempt conflict; promoting the political, economic, and social dimensions of security; developing a collective security capacity; and concluding a mutual defense pact for responding to external threats and promoting regional peacekeeping.

3. See W. Lippman, *U.S. Foreign Policy: Shield of the Republic* (Boston: Little, Brown, 1943).

4. Ibid., 51.

5. See Barry Buzan, *People, States, and Fear: An Agenda for International Security Studies in the Post–Cold War Era,* 2d. ed. (Boulder, Colo.: Lynne Rienner Publishers, 1991).

6. Ibid., 1.

7. Ibid., 16–17.

8. See Barry Buzan, "People, States, and Fear: The National Security Problem in the Third World," in *National Security in the Third World,* ed. Edward E. Azar and Chung-In Moon (Aldershot, UK: Edward Elgar, 1988), 40–41.

9. The conflict in Northern Ireland and the bombing of the Pan-Am flight over Lockerbie, Scotland, in 1988 typify some of the threats difficult to defend against using conventional security systems.

10. See Caroline Thomas, *In Search for Security: The Third World and International Relations* (London: Harvester Wheatsheaf, 1987).

11. See Edward Azar and Chung-In Moon, eds., *National Security in the Third World* (Aldershot, UK: Edward Elgar, 1988).

12. See Stephen M. Walt, "The Renaissance of Security Studies," *International Studies Quarterly* 3 (1991): 211–239.

13. See, for example, Hedely Bull and Adam Watson, *The Expansion of International Society* (Oxford: Oxford University Press, 1985).

14. See, for example, Kenneth Grundy, *The Militarization of Southern African Politics* (London: I. B. Tauris, 1986); Christopher Coker, "South Africa: A Military Role in Southern Africa, 1969–92," in *Southern Africa Regional Security: Problems and Prospects,* ed. Robert Jaster (London: Gower, 1985); and Deon Geldenhuys and Denis Venter, "Regional Cooperation in Southern Africa: A Constellation of States?" *International Affairs Bulletin,* December 1979.

15. See Agostinho Zacarias, *Security and the State in Southern Africa* (London: I. B. Tauris, 1999), 46–51.

16. See Geldenhuys and Venter, "Constellation of Southern African States," 149.

17. South African Department of Defense, white paper on defence, Pretoria, 1977.

18. SADC, "Towards a Southern African Development Community," declaration by heads of state and government, Windhoek, Namibia, 17 August 1992.

19. See SADC, *Southern Africa: A Framework and Strategy for Building the Community* (SADC Secretariat, Gaborone, 1993), 24–25.

20. For details, see, for example, Mark Malan, *SADC and Sub-Regional Security,* ISS Monograph Series no. 19, February (Pretoria: Institute of Security Studies, 1998).

21. See "Military and Economic Pressure from South Africa Forces King's Yield South," *Scan*, 16 September 1994, 270.

22. See, for example, Vincent Maphai and Peter Vale, "From Swords to Plough-shares," in *Rethinking Strategies for Mozambique and Southern Africa,* ed. A. Zacarias (Maputo, Mozambique: ISRI, 1991). See also Peter Vale, *The Case for Baskets: The Watershed Years* (Cape Town: Leadership Publication, 1991), and "Case for a Conference on Security and Cooperation"; and Laurie Nathan, "Towards a Conference on Security, Stability, Development and Cooperation in Africa," paper prepared for Asian Peace Research Conference, Aukland, New Zealand, 1992.

23. Ibid.; see also Peter Vale and Ken Booth, "Security in Southern Africa After Apartheid: Beyond Realism," *International Affairs* 71, 2 (1995).

24. See SADC summit communiqué, Johannesburg, 28 August 1995.

25. See SADC summit communiqué, Gaborone, 28 June1996.

26. After the 1996 summit, the SADC introduced a system in which the community would be presided over by a troika composed of one chair and two vice-chairs: the outgoing and incoming chair (SADC summit, communiqué, Gaborone, 28 June 1996).

27. Article 10 of the SADC treaty defines the summit as the supreme policy-making institution of the SADC and makes it responsible for the overall policy direction and control of the functions of the SADC.

28. See Mark Malan and Jakkie Cilliers, "SADC Organ on Politics, Defence, and Security: Future Development," ISS Occasional Paper Series no. 19, Johannesburg, March 1997.

29. The proposal was formulated in the meeting of Ministers of Defence and Security in 2000.

30. See SADC, communiqué, Windhoek, Namibia, 16 March 2001.

31. See Michael Banks, "Four Conceptions of Peace," in *Conflict Management and Problem Solving: Inter-Personal to International Applications,* ed. Dennis Sandole and Ingrid Sandole-Staroste (London: Pinter, 1987).

32. See J. Rawls, *A Theory of Justice* (Oxford: Oxford University Press, 1971), 4.

33. Herbert Marcuse, *Heroes and Civilisation* (London: Sphere, 1969), 203.

34. *Power* is defined here in Waltz's terms. It means an aggregate of capabilities in the social, political, military, and economic sectors to conduct state and community interests internationally. Hence, according to Buzan, to be powerful is to possess a broadly based, relatively large and reasonable economy; to control advanced technology and support a sufficient military establishment to sustain a plausible self-defense against other powers; and to have sufficient sociopolitical cohesion that these assets can be maintained and controlled so that their influence can be turned outward.

35. See Robert Keohane and Joseph Nye, *Power and Interdependence: World Politics in Transition* (Boston: Little, Brown, 1971), 8.

36. See Barry Buzan, Morton Keltrup, Pierre Lemaitre, Elizabieta Tromer, and Ole Waever, *The European Security Order Recast* (London: Pinter, 1990), 166.

4

The Quest for Good Governance

Tandeka C. Nkiwane

The relationship between democratization and security in a southern African context is extremely complex, with much of the current discourse on the nexus between the two deriving from the liberal democratic model, as it is understood in international relations. Democratic politics, claim the proponents of this model, foster a climate particularly conducive to security; in the southern African context this claim is generally understood to revolve around the end of apartheid in South Africa as the central "security" question for the region. Scholars of the liberal view have looked to shifting patterns of domestic politics, the fortunes of democratization within states, the expansion of institutions in helping states maximize common interests, and the impact of a region's insertion in the global economy in order to link regional security to political democracy.

Good governance is often viewed as the outcome of the democratization process. The concept of good governance remains extremely fluid and is often associated with the World Bank's discourse on governance as applied in the context of political conditionality. As such, its central aspects have been described by the World Bank as "(i) the form of political regime; (ii) the process by which authority is exercised in the management of a country's economic and social resources for development; and (iii) the capacity of governments to design, formulate, and implement policies and discharge functions."[1] The legitimacy of government, according to this view, is linked to the degree of democratization in its broadest sense, with human rights and participatory development equally important to the overall definition.

Of the claims that may be derived from the liberal democratic position, two have special significance to the issue of security in southern Africa. The first broad claim is that democracies do not fight each other and that, almost self-evidently, democratization should automatically lead to regional security. This is sometimes referred to as the democratic presumption.

The second claim is that economic liberalization and regional integration feed naturally into the creation of a positive regional security order. The formation of the Southern African Development Community (SADC) in 1992, and the creation of an SADC Organ on Politics, Defense, and Security (OPDS) in 1996, if the logic holds, should illustrate the deepening of a regional security order in the postcolonial and postapartheid era.

This chapter examines these broad assertions. First, it analyzes the democratic peace model, noting the difficulties of applying this to the region of southern Africa, especially in light of the region's history of conflict and cooperation. Second, the chapter examines the link between economic liberalization and peace in the region. It recognizes, in particular, that the relationship between economic integration and peace is complex, with regional examples offering some insight into this mixed picture. Third, the chapter outlines the various transitions in the regional political and economic institutions, most notably the SADC and the OPDS, with a view to deepening understanding of notions of security in southern Africa.

Debating the Democratic Peace

Liberalism claims to explain the systemic outcomes of interstate actions. Much of the literature on the "democratic peace" assumes that systemic predictions can follow from domestic theories of preferences. According to the logic of the new world order, under the theory of a democratic peace, there is a tendency for liberal regimes not to fight each other, as well as a tendency for liberal regimes to fight nonliberal regimes. This construct has come to define the liberal promise of international peace and cooperation through the promotion of democracy and democratic institutions.

Southern African examples are rarely mentioned in the debate over whether democracies fight each other because it is asserted that there are no true democracies in Africa. Not only is this untrue, but the entire notion of democracy in this case is also open to disputation. Although the theory of a democratic peace has been criticized on the grounds that, both historically and in the present day, the debate is very selective in the examples its proponents use to argue their case, this criticism is not exclusive to the region or to the continent.

The spread of liberal democracy and consumer capitalism has not resolved many of the contradictions in southern Africa. Rather, in many cases it has exacerbated internal sociopolitical struggles, which have been externalized in a variety of forms. The logic of the new world order disenfranchises the poorest regions, and this has led to an increasing income distribution gap. In most southern African countries, the gini coefficient (measuring income distribution) has demonstrated an increasing income distribution gap, widening in tandem with liberalization. The South African Human Development Report of 2000 notes that "virtually every social indicator betrays the extreme inequalities that define South African society. Measured by the gini coefficient, inequality in South Africa is among the highest in the world. South Africa is ranked as the third most unequal society, surpassed only by Brazil and Guatemala."[2] The statistical inequality quoted in the report with respect to both poverty and inequality has deepened since the introduction in 1996 of South Africa's macroeconomic liberalization program Growth, Employment, and Redistribution (GEAR), which replaced the Reconstruction and Development Program. This pattern is not unique to South Africa and indeed holds in many southern African nations, particularly those that have undergone structural adjustment programs (SAPs).

In southern Africa, the prospects for peace arguably have less to do with democracy in its liberal sense than with questions of socioeconomic distribution or a broader understanding of the democratic question. The land question in Zimbabwe, unemployment and trade union unrest in South Africa, and poverty in Angola all exemplify the complexity of the democratic question. The promise of peace has proven elusive in many southern African countries that have undertaken liberal institutional reform. The litmus test for a democratic peace theory is its ability to define its variables in a comprehensive format, rather than dismissing African countries as anomalies. The relationships between political and economic reform, as well as issues of distribution, must be taken into account.

A proper understanding of the historical nature of the state in Africa is key in this regard. Liberal scholars have made a concession in acknowledging that liberalism can have imperial consequences or can lead to imperial pursuits. As Robert O. Keohane puts it, normatively, liberalism is "distressingly plastic," and it accommodates too easily to dominant interests seeking to use its institutional skills to improve the situation rather than fundamentally restructure it.[3] This normative orientation of liberalism is significant in the sense that the democratic ethos is a conservative project and has had contentious consequences, from "civilizing missions" to the promotion of "good governance."

The nations and peoples of southern Africa have pursued violent conflict over a variety of fundamental principles—most notably the anticolonial struggle—where the territorial state is not the sole strategic representative body. Whereas Michael Doyle makes the argument that democracies have forms of institutional constraints, he avoids a crucial question in southern Africa, where a variety of economic weaknesses have tended to feed other weaknesses in the sociopolitical sphere.[4] Democracy, then, is not necessarily the primary factor that prevents war in African international relations; indeed, it can actively promote war.

Liberalization, Democratization, and Security

An important debate related to the discussion on the democratic peace has been best exemplified by the questions of structural adjustment programs (SAPs), as advocated by the International Monetary Fund and the World Bank, and whether southern Africa has reached a "postadjustment" period. One of the most problematic aspects of the democratic peace model regards the marriage of the propagation of democracy to foreign economic and political penetration. The debate about structural adjustment in Africa has most clearly outlined this concern.

The advocates of liberal market reform throughout Africa have faced a sustained challenge on the implications of allowing an unfettered market mechanism to operate in highly dependent and vulnerable economies.[5] The sphere of economics throughout the 1980s and 1990s was characterized by both enforced constraint and market failure, which led to the movement toward a postadjustment discourse in Africa and in the international financial institutions.

The current transnational, neoliberal economic offensive to open up African markets to foreign penetration seeks to claim, in the face of strong internal opposition, that Africa is being prepared for democracy. This argument is made especially loudly in southern Africa. Are countries, then, being designated as "'choiceless' democracies"?[6] In other words, who are the agents of market reform, and to whom are they responsible? The hostility with which international financial institutions have approached the question of state intervention in Africa has been the subject of much discussion, particularly with respect to the economic, social, and political effects of structural adjustment on the continent. In southern Africa, this hostility has been exemplified in the South African debate over GEAR and the various debates over SAPs, particularly in Zimbabwe, Zambia, Mozambique, Tanzania, and Malawi.

The economic argument that neoliberal programs foster general prosperity, and hence democracy, has been challenged from a pragmatic perspective, after over two decades of liberal market reform throughout much of Africa. As Claude Ake notes, since the 1970s there have been some parts of Africa that have declined so decisively due to market reforms that they have established once and for all the notion of the reversibility of development.[7] The belief in the ability of the mythical market to alleviate the African economic condition, therefore, is open to empirical contestation. There exists no firm consensus on the effects of liberal market reforms in Africa; instead, a powerful and growing African perspective argues that these reforms have not only failed to improve the African condition but have actually worsened it. The importance of this perspective as a criticism of the liberal paradigm cannot be overstated because, if true, the liberal assumption that open markets offer opportunities for mutual gain will, of necessity, become increasingly questionable. In southern Africa, neoliberalism's limits are particularly poignant, as economic liberalization has led to deepening inequity both within and between the region's states.

Regionalization in Southern Africa

The politics reshaping the African continent need to be understood from a historical perspective that is integrated with a sensitivity to the contemporary realities tugging at the African social fabric. Regional politics are clearly a manifestation of both the old and the new, and regional blocs in southern Africa are often pursued as an attempt to create a political framework for a variety of forms of economic activity.

Regionalism has both an external and an internal logic. A region, in international relations, can be a phenomenon imposed from the outside. Regions were formed, for example, in a cold war context, through military and economic alliances. In Africa, the external imposition and composition of regions is a phenomenon shaped by the colonial experience but reinforced during the postcolonial period. Regions, in addition, generally have an internal logic and coherence, which binds nations with threads of commonality. The notion of a region usually implies some form of territorial contiguity, although regions in Africa have also been delineated along historic, political, or linguistic lines. This arbitrary definition of regions generally has Africa divided into five: east, west, north, south, and central. With reference to the SADC, James Sidaway and Richard Gibb note, "Its members are linked through a certain functional unity, derived from the (colonial) network of labor migration, trade and communications that was centered on the industrial, minerals-energy economy of South Africa."[8]

The political and foreign policy landscape in southern Africa has changed dramatically in the last eight years. A geostrategic focus on military security and destabilization pitted apartheid South Africa against the Frontline States (FLS) of southern Africa, in a politico-military confrontation that enveloped the foreign policy debates from the mid-1970s until the mid-1990s. Freed from the main obstacle to building cooperative regional mechanisms, namely apartheid South Africa, new and expansive agendas have dominated the debates in the region. This has brought to the fore a complex set of competing interests and actors, not necessarily confined to the politico-military sphere. Following the demise of white minority rule and the holding of democratic elections in April 1994, South Africa is being integrated into the African whole, drastically changing the range of possibilities now present in the foreign policy realm.

Two contending perspectives have emerged with respect to South

Africa's foreign policy in southern Africa regarding the security realm. One line of reasoning has argued that the removal of the security threat posed by apartheid South Africa would bring about a new level of regional cooperation. This perspective, which has dominated the discourse in recent southern African scholarship, advocates the creation of new avenues of political cooperation to replace the FLS.[9] This position is reflected in the 1992 Treaty on the Establishment of a Southern African Development Community. The counterperspective, often associated with those of a realist persuasion, has taken the line that while a black majority government may reign in South Africa, the South African state remains a regional hegemon and will persist in its external relations as a regional hegemon.[10] In this scenario, there would be no impetus for South Africa suddenly to change its foreign policy dictates, given its geostrategic constraints. These include regional economic and military dominance, as well as political positioning.

On 17 August 1992, the SADC treaty was signed, heralding a new phase in regional cooperation and security in southern Africa. A resurgence, experienced by many countries in the discourse on integration and security beginning in the early 1990s, is often considered a by-product of the end of the Cold War. In southern Africa, it was the end of apartheid in South Africa in 1994 that marked a watershed in regional politics. With South Africa as the alleged "engine of growth," many observers anticipated that southern Africa as a region would, through SADC structures, promote and maintain regional security, stability, and growth.

For almost half a century the South African apartheid state was the main source of insecurity and instability in southern Africa, and on the African continent. Regional arrangements, namely the FLS and the Southern African Development Coordination Conference (SADCC), were formed to exclude the Republic of South Africa, as well as to extend and promote cooperative relations in the political and economic spheres. Negotiations leading to democratic elections in South Africa began in 1990; the SADCC was converted into the SADC in 1992, in recognition of the positive developments in the region, not to mention the removal of a main source of insecurity. As Roger Southall expressed it,

> An era of regeneration and interstate cooperation throughout the Southern African region seems possible with the fall of *apartheid*, the democratization process that has taken place throughout the region, and the winding down of the externally fuelled civil conflicts in Angola and Mozambique. . . . Central to this new optimism that now defines the region has been the conviction that relations between South Africa and its neighbors will now be based on mutual trust in a shared project of regional peace and development.[11]

Nearly a decade after the signing of the SADC treaty, the institutionalization of regional structures and protocols remains unfulfilled. According to Patrick Bond, the SADC in the year 2000 "remained feeble as an institution."[12] The four-year-old SADC trade protocol remains "stalled," troops from SADC member states have been involved in regional conflicts in the Democratic Republic of Congo (DRC) and Lesotho, and there is ongoing political strife in a variety of SADC member states including Angola, Zimbabwe, Swaziland, and Zambia. The much-anticipated "fortress southern Africa" has crumbled since the end of apartheid, and the SADC as a regional arrangement remains deeply divided on a number of crucial matters. The question, therefore, is why?

Outside the realm of security, a number of intriguing foreign policy concerns have emerged. Questions related to economic integration and trade, shared water resources, constitutionalism and democracy, border disputes, and the recognition and involvement of nonstate actors in the foreign policy decisionmaking process have surfaced, representing new challenges to the nation-states of southern Africa. Increasingly, nonmilitary threats have come to represent major foreign policy concerns, widening the parameters of cooperation and conflict. The foreign policies of a variety of states are still taking shape, reflecting a change in political leadership and the goals of political elites. President Ketumile Masire of Botswana's voluntary decision to step down on 31 March 1998, as well as President Nelson Mandela's like decision in South Africa in 1999, represents the withdrawal of powerful regional figures associated with the foreign policies of their respective countries. In the multiparty "wave" of the early 1990s, new presidents were installed in Zambia, Lesotho, Tanzania, and Malawi, with the leadership of Swaziland currently under constitutional debate. Of the postliberation generation of leaders, Presidents Robert Mugabe of Zimbabwe, Joaquim Chissano of Mozambique, Jose Eduardo Dos Santos of Angola, and Sam Nujoma of Namibia remain. A number of these leaders have shuffled their foreign ministers in recent years, another reflection of the political changes now under way.

Throughout the 1970s, South Africa systematically used the threat or use of force, as well as economic sanctions, as policy instruments in the southern African region. South African prime minister Johannes Vorster, who proposed in 1975 the establishment of a Constellation of Southern African States, first elaborated this model of aggression, encompassing both military and economic measures. P. W. Botha, who took over from Vorster in 1977, expanded on the security problem in the subregion by proposing the policy of "total strategy."

The concept of total strategy was based on South Africa's claim of a right to intervene in any African state south of the equator, and South

Africa's perception that it was surrounded by a "total onslaught" of liberation forces. This, of course, was part of apartheid South Africa's flagrant violation and refusal to comply with accepted norms of international law. Between 1975 and 1985, South Africa's allocations for defense rose dramatically from 692 million to 4.27 billion rand, with military incursions and destabilization of neighboring states, including Lesotho, Mozambique, Angola, Botswana, and Zimbabwe.

As a political response to both apartheid South Africa and colonial rule in southern Africa, the FLS was born in 1974, spearheaded by Tanzania and Zambia, but also consisting of Congo-Brazzaville, Zaire (Democratic Republic of Congo), and Botswana. The fall, in 1975, of the Portuguese colonial regime drastically altered the regional balance of forces, leading to the withdrawal of Zaire and Congo-Brazzaville from the FLS and an increased effort by South Africa to block the attempts of states in the subregion to escape its political and economic dominance. Nigeria also played an important role in countering apartheid's dominance in Africa.

One of South Africa's first foreign policy acts in 1994, after Nelson Mandela's democratically elected government came to power, was to join the FLS. Until its conversion in 1995, the organization comprised eight members—Angola, Botswana, Mozambique, Namibia, South Africa, Tanzania, Zambia, and Zimbabwe (historically omitting Lesotho, Swaziland, and Malawi).[13]

The FLS has also faced severe nonmilitary threats. After the demise of apartheid in South Africa, economic and political threats are often as severe as military threats. In such circumstances, self-seeking behavior on the part of any one state can profoundly destabilize the system, as well as the position of actors within it, and unilateral measures taken without regard to the interests of neighbor states may weaken an already unstable economic, political, or military order. In order to combat multiple threats and prevent further destabilization, states are often willing to give up some freedom of action to a consultation process that helps to gradually formalize and institutionalize an alliance. This would appear to be the only realistic means of combating nonmilitary threats, since any exit strategies potentially pursued as solutions are counterproductive.

The distinctive aspect of many of the nonmilitary threats in southern Africa is that they transcend borders. Economic instability, environmental problems, and social movements respect no boundaries and, as such, often demand a regional or subregional response. Many of the political crises in recent years in southern Africa have had potentially serious repercussions for the entire region and have also demanded a regional response. This chapter will now explore some of these recent peace and security questions in southern Africa.

The SADC Organ on Politics, Defense, and Security

The Southern African Development Coordination Conference was in essence the economic outgrowth of the FLS and was formally constituted in April 1980, following the Lusaka declaration entitled "Southern Africa: Towards Economic Liberation." Key objectives of the SADCC were to harmonize development among the countries of southern Africa (excluding South Africa and South West Africa/Namibia) and to reduce economic dependence on South Africa, while simultaneously supporting the liberation struggles through the FLS. The declaration and treaty establishing the SADC was signed in Windhoek, Namibia, in August 1992 with the expanded mandate of more comprehensive regional integration, as well as political integration of the subregion. The mandate also called for the development of a common foreign policy in the region. The SADC at its formation comprised Angola, Botswana, Lesotho, Malawi, Mozambique, Namibia, Swaziland, Tanzania, Zambia, and Zimbabwe. In 1994, the SADC admitted South Africa, following democratic multiracial elections. In 1995, Mauritius was admitted, following a year of controversy about its candidacy; and, in 1997, Seychelles and the Democratic Republic of Congo (DRC) were admitted.

When the SADC was formed, it was committed to the formation of "a framework and mechanisms to strengthen regional solidarity and provide for mutual peace and security."[14] This commitment signified an expansion of the former SADCC's directive, in light of positive changes in international and subregional politics. The focus on political issues in addition to economic cooperation culminated in a workshop in Windhoek in July 1994, which recommended SADC cooperation in political, human rights, and security spheres—a recommendation that formed the basis for the decision at the SADC Gaborone summit in August 1994 to establish a formal SADC sector on Political Cooperation, Democracy, Peace, and Security. These proposals were endorsed by southern African nongovernmental organizations (NGOs) in Windhoek, in particular supporting the formation of a human rights commission within the SADC. It was further agreed that the FLS would disband, and all operations would be integrated into this SADC sector. As with all SADC sectors, there would be one country responsible for coordinating its operations.

Whereas the international community, or even the African community, may be wary of becoming involved in a particular crisis, neighbors cannot ignore the potential repercussions of a conflict in their territorial proximity and therefore have an impetus to involve themselves. The potential for national conflicts to transform into regional conflicts is an ever-present threat, and nations are always keen to prevent this eventuality. The SADC region has experienced the mass flow of refugees across borders, the fomenting of armed insurgencies, and many other security threats that make regional cooperation in the sphere of politics and security not only desirable but indeed necessary.

The logic behind the establishment of a formal sector on Political Cooperation, Democracy, Peace, and Security stemmed from both a short-term commitment to cooperate and a long-term focus toward the development of a common defense policy. This commitment centered on both exogenous integration, or the process of military cooperation developed in the face of an explicit external or internal threat, and endogenous integration, or the process of eventually developing a political and economic union. The formation of a sector has many inherent advantages, which states took into account. First, the SADC is an intergovernmental organization and operates on this basis; therefore, an institutional approach toward cooperation is probably the most functional. Second, and more important, the SADC was established in order to form an economic and political community; therefore, cooperation in this area will logically lead to progress in the security sphere. The theory of regional integration supports this argument, as integration itself can contribute toward security, stability, and peace.

The other potential approach was the establishment of an Association of Southern African States (ASAS) as a successor organization to the FLS. A meeting was held in Harare, Zimbabwe, on 3 March 1995, in order to harmonize the ASAS and SADC proposals, as the suggested characteristics of this new organization were sometimes contradictory. It was eventually proposed that the ASAS be established as the political arm of the SADC, with conflict prevention, management, and resolution as its major area of focus.

The ASAS represented a new look for the FLS, with informality and flexibility paramount to governing its operations. It was further proposed that the ASAS be supported by two committees, one on political matters and the other on defense and security matters; and, as had been the case with its predecessor, the FLS, the foreign ministry of the chair nation would service the ASAS. Most important, the chairmanship of ASAS was to rotate every two years. The ASAS proposal was taken to the 1995 SADC summit in Johannesburg and eventually the matter was deferred, the stated reason being that the ministers of foreign affairs needed more time to consult with their ministers of defense and security.[15] South Africa and Zimbabwe were to play a dominant role in this process.

Postapartheid South Africa is in many senses the newest political player in the subregion, and it is in the process of redefining its postapartheid foreign policy. South Africa has joined the SADC, the Organization of

African Unity, the Commonwealth, and the UN and has been keen to assert itself as a center of democracy and reconciliation. In October 1995, during the UN's fiftieth anniversary celebrations, South Africa intimated that it would lobby for a permanent seat on the Security Council should the UN reform process allocate one to Africa. Undoubtedly, South Africa is the most powerful country in the subregion. Its gross domestic product (GDP) is three times greater than that of the other SADC countries combined, and its military is the most sophisticated in Africa, comprising 137,900 regular troops, a part-time reserve force of 475,000, commandos totaling 76,000, and an active citizen reserve force of 275,000. South Africa has an army, navy, air force, paramilitary force, and a latent nuclear arsenal.[16]

Zimbabwe's foreign policy has been described as activist, with much of its effort being concentrated on regional affairs. Similar to the foreign policies of small states, the vision encompassed in Zimbabwe's foreign policy is strongly associated with its leader, Robert Mugabe. When the FLS was formed it was decided that the chairmanship would rotate according to seniority; hence, it began with Julius Nyerere of Tanzania and moved to Kenneth Kaunda of Zambia. The next in line in the FLS in terms of seniority was Jose Eduardo dos Santos of Angola, who, because of the civil war in his country, decided to pass the mantle on to Mugabe. Mugabe therefore considers himself to be the senior statesperson in southern Africa, as customarily defined.

On 18 January 1996, SADC ministers responsible for foreign affairs, defense, and SADC affairs met in Gaborone to make a final decision on the best option for the SADC with respect to peace and security. There were considerable differences revolving around integration with or autonomy from the SADC. The compromise position that emerged was what was termed the SADC Organ on Politics, Defence, and Security. The SADC organ, as proposed, would be an institutional structure of the SADC but operating only at the summit (heads-of-state and government) level, on a troika (three-member) basis and independent of other SADC structures. It was proposed that the chairmanship of this organ rotate annually and that the powerful Inter-State Defence and Security Committee (ISDSC) be one of the institutions of the OPDS.

On 28 June 1996, at an extraordinary summit in Gaborone, the SADC heads of state formally established the OPDS with the objective of evolving common political value systems and institutions among the twelve SADC member states, as well as evolving a common foreign policy in areas of mutual interest. The SADC has developed a protocol on peace, security, and conflict resolution and also to develop a collective security capacity and a mutual defense pact for responding to external threats. In addition, it was stated that the development of a regional peacekeeping capacity within national armies would be of relevance both within the subregion and, more broadly, for Africa. President Mugabe was elected the first chairman of the OPDS.

This SADC compromise position contained both strong and weak elements. Perhaps its greatest strengths are the inclusion of the ISDSC as a sub-body of the organ and its institutionalization. It is also instructive that SADC member states employed the troika system in their deliberations. The rotation of the OPDS, though, is still a cause for concern. The extent of the involvement of nongovernmental actors in the SADC and their impact on this intergovernmental body are also still unclear. NGOs, in particular Amnesty International, have criticized the formation of the SADC organ on the grounds that while paying lip service to the necessity for democracy and the promotion of human rights, no formal institutional structures were considered, let alone put into place, contrary to both the letter and spirit of the 1994 Windhoek declaration.

Things nearly fell apart at the September 1997 SADC summit in Blantyre, Malawi, in a conflict between President Mandela as chairman of the SADC, and President Mugabe as chairman of the OPDS. In a startling revelation, it was acknowledged that "although the organ was established in May, 1996, its functions, structure, operating procedure, and relationship with the other SADC institutions have not been discussed."[17]

President Mandela, in a surprise announcement, threatened to quit as SADC chairman unless the institutionalization of the OPDS was accomplished. President Mugabe maintained the position that the various components necessary for the maintenance of peace and security in the subregion must not be overbureaucratized. The question of the OPDS remained unresolved. It is only with the Windhoek summit in 2000 that we witnessed progress in talks and the decision to form a ministerial working group on the OPDS. The 2001 Blantyre summit agreed on a compromise and decided that the OPDS would have its own leadership outside the SADC chairperson.

Broadening Regional Disputes

An issue that has gained prominence in the realm of foreign policy in southern Africa has been the escalating dispute between Botswana and Namibia over the Sidudu/Kasikili Island. This is a broader dispute over the territorial border along the Linyati/Chobe River. It is also one of the few foreign policy disputes in which regional mediation failed, and both countries subsequently submitted the case to the International Court of Justice (ICJ) for binding arbitration. What makes the bilateral dispute intriguing is that the three-square-kilometer island in dispute is not a strategic asset to either country and does not possess any known resources. Namibian farmers have been using the island only for small-scale agricultural production on territory that Botswana claims; Botswana has deployed military personnel to evict the farmers. This has prompted the feeling that the aggressive acquisition by Botswana of military hardware and the construction of a U.S.-built air force base could signify an increasingly militaristic foreign policy stance by Botswana.

The Anglo-German Treaty of 1890 demarcated the territorial possessions for both colonial powers; it states that the center line of the river defines the boundary between Namibia and Botswana. The matter in dispute, on which the ICJ had to decide, was the definition of the main channel of the river. Following a failed effort at resolution by a bilateral commission and a failed attempt at mediation by President Mugabe in Harare between presidents Nujoma and Masire in 1995, both countries informed the ICJ of the submission of their dispute on 29 May 1996. The issue was eventually decided in favor of Botswana.

A second important and emergent foreign policy issue is that of water resources in southern Africa. Water naturally knows no national boundaries and in a drought-prone region such as southern Africa, the struggle for the control of water resources has intensified in recent years and has become a major foreign policy question. SADC heads of states and government in 1995 signed a protocol on shared watercourse systems, and, in 1997, a formal SADC sector responsible for water was established under the auspices of Lesotho. In southern Africa there are eleven shared watercourse systems; the Zambezi River is the largest and is shared by eight countries.[18] The Zambezi River basin has two large hydroelectric dams, one at Kariba on the border between Zimbabwe and Zambia, which is a current source of dispute, and the other at Cahora Bassa in Mozambique.

Munyaradzi Chenje and Phyllis Johnson note that, "the mean annual renewable water resources for Southern Africa are about 1,870 cubic kilometers per year, of which 80 percent is available in the Congo basin, most of which is outside the SADC region."[19] When the DRC was admitted as a member of the SADC in 1997, the debate on shared water resources was a central foreign policy concern, and despite arguments coming from outside of the southern African region concerning the geographic location of Congo as traditionally defined, the country was admitted as a member.

The issue of trade in southern Africa has emerged as a major foreign-policy concern and will remain on the agenda of the SADC members for the foreseeable future. The SADC has adopted a trade protocol in order "to further liberalize intra-regional trade in goods and services on the basis of fair, mutually equitable and beneficial trade arrangements."[20] The idea behind the trade protocol is at the heart of the SADC's raison d'être, specifically the establishment of a "fortress southern Africa" with a common external tariff among SADC member states. In May 1995, South Africa was assigned the finance and investment portfolio of the SADC and tasked with promoting both intraregional and external trade on behalf of the organization.

A major foreign policy debate has emerged over access to the South African market by its neighbors, with Zimbabwe, Zambia, and Mauritius complaining about South Africa's positive trade balance with the rest of the region and alleging unfair trade practices by South African businesses in cooperation with the government. Trade disputes are not limited to South Africa. In March 1997, the "cement war" occurred between Zambia and Zimbabwe, after Zimbabwe unilaterally increased the import duty on cement from Zambia.

The level at which trade becomes a major foreign policy issue was best exemplified in 1996, following the circulation of the SADC finance and investment report for the annual consultative conference. The Zimbabwean government through its foreign minister, Stan Mudenge, referred to the report as a "conspiracy" meant to undermine both Zimbabwe and the SADC.[21] The report alleged that Zimbabwe's GDP in 1995 had declined by 10 percent—an allegation that was untrue. The representatives of Angola, Botswana, Zambia, Swaziland, Lesotho, and Namibia all demanded an explanation, and a formal apology was delivered to the Zimbabwean government the next day by South African foreign minister Alfred Nzo, South African finance minister Chris Liebenberg, and SADC executive secretary Kaire Mbuende. A formal inquiry was instituted into the report and a further apology was demanded and received.

The issue of trade will remain a central foreign policy concern, and the states of southern Africa will need to harmonize their positions with respect to the protocol on trade. A related issue is that of overlap between organizations formed in southern Africa to deal with trade. These include the Southern African Customs Union (SACU), comprising South Africa, Namibia, Botswana, Lesotho, and Swaziland, and the Common Market of Eastern and Southern Africa (COMESA).

The SADC/COMESA overlap is of particular concern to many analysts. COMESA, formerly the Preferential Trade Area, was established in 1981 to promote integration among eastern and southern African states and envisaged the establishment of a common market by the year 2000. COMESA comprises twenty member states and has its secretariat in Lusaka. Nine of the SADC states (the exceptions being South Africa, Botswana, and Tanzania, which withdrew recently) belong to COMESA.

Similarly, the SADC envisaged the creation of a common market by the year 2012. With SADC member states accounting for 81 percent of Africa's gross national product, 81 percent of total imports, and 80 percent of total exports, it is very plausible to see it as the most promising subregional organization, with South Africa as its economic anchor. It is no accident that upon being appointed a SADC member, South Africa was assigned the finance and investment portfolio. A joint SADC/COMESA ministerial committee was appointed in 1996 to examine a possible merger of the two organizations to rationalize responsibilities because so many of the economic and political initiatives overlap. This proposal, while initially endorsed by a majority of the joint ministerial committee, was rejected in August of 1996, though there was advocacy for "modalities of cooperation in specific areas between the two bodies."[22] At the COMESA summit of April 1997, both Lesotho and Mozambique gave notice that they would leave COMESA in 1998; Namibia also threatened to pull out of the organization due to its overlap with the SADC, setting the stage for a strengthened and more cohesive SADC.

The DRC and Lesotho

Realpolitik, couched in the discourse of constitutionalism and democracy, is part of the evolving foreign policy agendas of southern African states. This was first exemplified by the intervention of Botswana, Zimbabwe, and South Africa in the 1994 Lesotho crisis but is part of a larger discourse at both the governmental and nongovernmental level. Following a political and military crisis in Lesotho throughout 1993 and 1994, King Letsie III suspended the constitution and fired Prime Minister Ntsu Mokhehle in a "royal coup" that sent shockwaves through southern Africa. Determined not to allow a military coup in southern Africa, the troika stated that they borrowed their political intervention from the Harare declaration of 1991, which calls for the "protection and promotion of the fundamental political values of the Commonwealth; democracy, democratic processes, and institutions which reflect national circumstances, the rule of law, and the independence of the judiciary, just and honest government."[23] Whether the issue of democracy and constitutionalism will be the basis of future political interventions in similar situations is open to question, but the Lesotho intervention certainly placed questions of democratic rule at the forefront of the foreign policy of southern Africa, a position from which it will be difficult to retreat.[24]

A similar debate emerged in 1998, couched in the discourse of "sovereignty" and the protection of legitimate government, with respect to the ongoing regional conflicts in the DRC and Lesotho. The decision taken in Harare on 18 August 1998 by SADC defense ministers under the auspices of the ISDSC to intervene militarily in the DRC exposed a political rift in the SADC that cannot easily be healed.

In May 1997, when the Allied Forces for the Liberation of Congo/Zaire under the leadership of Laurent Kabila ousted Mobutu Sese Seko from power, it was not only with the overt military assistance of Rwanda and Uganda but also of Angola and Zimbabwe in southern Africa.[25] The failed attempt by South Africa to mediate a negotiated exit from power by Mobutu additionally led to the reversal of a number of economically strategic pacts in Zaire, particularly by prominent South African multinational corporations involved in the mining industry. South African losses were Zimbabwean gains, with private- and public-sector companies moving in quickly to establish bilateral relationships. These gains were under threat when Kabila's former allies, Rwanda and Uganda, instigated a rebel uprising in eastern DRC in August of 1998, which almost succeeded in capturing the capital, Kinshasa. The DRC, now a member of SADC, appealed for help.

Announcing the decision to intervene militarily, Mugabe stated, "We have considered it our duty to respond to the call of appeal by *one of us* for assistance to be given so that peace and stability can be restored in the Congo and in our region. . . . The people of the DRC are as much our people who constitute our individual population."[26] The contribution of military personnel by Zimbabwe, Angola, and Namibia in support of President Laurent Kabila, which effectively reversed the rebel advance on the capital, Kinshasa, prompted the South African government to take a public stance against the military intervention. This stance was subsequently publicly reversed at the Nonaligned Movement summit in Durban, South Africa, in early September 1998.[27] The prolonged political dispute between South Africa and Zimbabwe on the resolution of the conflict in the DRC has expanded to include numerous state and nonstate actors and highlighted the larger and complex issue of regional leadership and vision. The dispute has also driven home the fact that the inconclusive status of the OPDS has left it open to manipulation and intensified jockeying for its control.

In September 1998, after a seven-week political dispute over general elections that were deemed flawed by the SADC-appointed Langa commission,[28] Lesotho prime minister Pakalitha Mosisili requested preemptive intervention by South Africa, Zimbabwe, Mozambique, and Botswana. The South African military intervention, aided forty-eight hours later by Botswana, has prompted further controversy within the SADC, exposing the varying political agendas within the development community.

As already mentioned, there has been a change in leadership with respect to foreign policy decisionmaking in southern Africa. The older "liberation struggle generation" of political elites is slowly retreating from the center stage; the process of political transformation is attended by new problems and prospects. There is an increasing trend toward the institutionalization of a variety of key decisionmaking processes in the foreign policy realm and the broadening involvement of a vast array of sectors and actors in these processes. The expansion of nonmilitary security and foreign policy concerns necessitates consultation on a wide array of subjects including home affairs, finance, development, social welfare, industry, and commerce. This consultation includes research organizations, the university community, populations in border areas and drought-prone areas, private-sector and informal traders, and populations that are subject to relocation for the benefit of the "greater" southern African good.

The populations of southern Africa are increasingly vocal with respect to foreign policy matters, and they are demanding a place in the formulation, and at times the implementation, of key foreign policy measures. The 1994 Windhoek SADC workshop was one of the first occasions on which nonstate actors and groups were asked to contribute to the foreign policy debates of southern Africa on a large scale, and regional institutions are increasingly demanding a place in the foreign policy decisionmaking process. The DRC and Lesotho interventions have made communities more aware of the necessity to engage in foreign policy and to demand accountability from governments. The expression "you get the government that you deserve" has touched many individuals and groups in southern Africa, and people are increasingly demanding transparency and participation in foreign policy making.

Conclusion

This chapter has highlighted several points. First, the theory of a democratic peace encounters many difficulties when applied to the southern African region. It provides a very partial and often misleading guide to understanding the history of interstate conflict in southern Africa, particularly with regard to the development of the FLS and the SADC. Since the end of apartheid, scholars of the liberal tradition have defined regional order and security in terms of the collective defense of democracy in its broadest sense, but this definition offers little explanation of what a strong regional community means and what it takes to create a set of functioning regional political structures within which both traditional and nontraditional security threats can be handled.

Second, the chapter has recognized that economic liberalization and regionalization can simultaneously bring potential problems for regional order and be a source of nontraditional security problems. This is especially true with respect to internal conflict.

The regional alliance in southern Africa has persisted well beyond the historical and political circumstances that initially gave rise to it. The ascendance of nonmilitary security concerns in defining foreign policy objectives poses some interesting questions that speak to issues whose scope extends far beyond southern Africa. A major litmus test of the OPDS will be its ability to respond to this expansive array of foreign policy concerns in a comprehensive manner. The issues and actors have evolved since the formation of the FLS, but the necessity for cooperation in the sphere of security remains, particularly in a structurally integrated region.

In the future, nonmilitary threats, particularly those emanating from political or economic instability, will be the most prominent security threats in southern Africa. The effects of millions of cross-border immigrants have introduced growing tensions both within South Africa and between South Africa and its neighboring states. Trade wars and economic tensions now characterize disputes within southern Africa, as does internal strife—exemplified by recent labor strikes and riots in Zimbabwe; police and military tensions in Zambia, Swaziland, and Lesotho; and political tension in South Africa associated with both the transformation of governmental decision-making bodies and the upcoming elections. The export of civil war from Angola to neighboring states is a most disturbing development, as are increasing political tensions in Namibia.

The biggest challenge facing the SADC will be management of the conflict in the DRC and the political fallout subsequent to the restoration of stability. The line dividing southern and central Africa is increasingly blurred by economic and political realities that are threatening to engulf the entire region. The political alliances in formation and under contestation will not only determine the future of the OPDS but will also redefine the very meaning of security in the region.

The change of political leadership throughout southern Africa has affected foreign policy decisionmaking in a significant manner, as a new generation of elites will be forced to find innovative ways of understanding one another and projecting a common foreign policy vision. Part of the challenge will be to achieve a critical and nuanced understanding of the relationship between democratization and security.

Notes

1. World Bank, *Governance: The World Bank's Experience* (Washington, D.C.: World Bank, 1996), xiv.

2. UNDP (United Nations Development Program), *South Africa: Transformation for Human Development 2000* (Pretoria: UNDP, 2000), 63–64.

3. Robert O. Keohane, "International Liberalism Reconsidered," in *The Economic Limits of Modern Politics,* ed. John Dunn (Cambridge: Cambridge University Press, 1990), 192.

4. See Michael Doyle, "Liberalism and the End of the Cold War," in *International Relations Theory and the End of the Cold War,* ed. Richard Ned Lebow and Thomas Risse-Kappen (New York: Columbia University Press, 1995).

5. See Adebajo Olukoshi, "The State, Conflict, and Democracy in Africa," in

State, Conflict, and Democracy in Africa, ed. Richard Joseph (Boulder, Colo.: Lynne Rienner Publishers, 1999).

6. Thandika Mkandawire, "Crisis Management in the Making of 'Choiceless' Democracies," in Joseph, *State, Conflict, and Democracy.*

7. See Claude Ake, "The New World Order: A View from Africa," in *Whose World Order? Uneven Globalization and the End of the Cold War,* eds. H. Holm and G. Sorenson (Boulder, Colo.: Westview Press, 1995), 19–42.

8. James Sidaway and Richard Gibb, "SADC, COMESA, SACU: Contradictory Formats for Regional Integration in Southern Africa?" in *South Africa in Southern Africa: Reconfiguring the Region,* ed. David Simon (Oxford: James Currey; Athens: Ohio University Press, 1998), 171.

9. Ibid.

10. See David Myers, ed., *Regional Hegemons: Threat, Perception, and Strategic Response* (Boulder, Colo.: Westview Press, 1991), and Ibbo Mandaza, ed., *Peace and Security in Southern Africa* (Harare, Zimbabwe: SAPES Trust, 1996).

11. Roger Southall, cited in Larry Swatuk and Abillah H. Omari, *Regional Security: Southern Africa's Mobile "Front Line."* Southern African Perspectives no. 61 (Cape Town: Centre for Southern African Studies, 1997), 2.

12. Patrick Bond, *Elite Transitions: From Apartheid to Neoliberalism in South Africa* (London: Pluto Press, 2000), 232.

13. For a more comprehensive discussion on the FLS, see Ronald T. Libby, *The Politics of Economic Power in Southern Africa* (Princeton, N.J.: Princeton University Press, 1987).

14. See SADC, "Towards a Southern African Development Community," declaration by heads of state and government, Windhoek, Namibia, 17 August 1992.

15. See SADC, communiqué, Johannesburg, 28 August 1995, 3.

16. The economic statistic was compiled prior to Mauritius joining the SADC. The military statistics are from IISS, *The Military Balance 1996–1997* (Oxford: Oxford University Press, 1996), 264–265.

17. See South African Department of Foreign Affairs, "South Africa as Chair of SADC and Review of the SADC Programme of Action," Pretoria, 20 November 1996, 2.

18. Munyaradzi Chenje and Phyllis Johnson, eds., *Water in Southern Africa* (Maseru and Harare, Zimbabwe: SADC/IUCN/SARDC, 1996), 166.

19. Ibid., 189.

20. See SADC, "Protocol on Trade," Gaborone, Botswana, 25 January 2000.

21. See the SADC Annual Consultative Conference, Gallager Estate, Midrand, South Africa, Report 4, 1.

22. See COMESA secretariat, statement, 6 August 1996.

23. Commonwealth, Harare Commonwealth Declaration, heads of government meeting, Harare, Zimbabwe, 16–22 October 1991.

24. For a wider discussion of the 1994 Lesotho intervention, see Tandeka C. Nkiwane, "My Brother's Keeper: The Lesotho Crisis in Perspective," African Association of Political Science Occasional Paper Series no. 1, Harare, Zimbabwe, 1997.

25. The assistance of Eritrea was also involved.

26. *The Harare Herald,* 18 August 1998, 1.

27. The rebel advance was propelled by Uganda and Rwanda; their contribution to the war, whether as an "act of aggression" or in support of a legitimate

internal political rebellion, is at the heart of the dispute between Zimbabwe and South Africa.

28. The extent of electoral fraud was (and still is) a matter of dispute. It has been argued quite authoritatively that the Langa commission report was watered down at the SADC summit in September 1998.

5

The Politics of Land Reform in Zimbabwe

Sam Moyo and Prosper Matondi

The struggles over land reform and redistribution in Zimbabwe have drawn the international community's attention to the land issue in southern Africa and beyond. Attempts at reforming the structural ownership and access to land raise a number of critical questions for Zimbabwe, with lessons for other countries in the southern African region. Whereas independence ended the violent conflict of the liberation struggle over land in the name of peacemaking, the structural forms of conflict remained.

This chapter provides a historical analysis and broad-based treatment of the various forms of conflict and struggle over land, including the complex and competing social and political tendencies that underline and define many of the social actors engaged in land reform.[1] This includes a focus on how different actors compete for various resources, including land, and the historical basis for such contestations. The major social and interest groups (or stakeholders) involved in policymaking and implementation processes and the actual social practices are discussed. Instead of assuming that certain groups will have predetermined interests or outlooks, the chapter examines the social dynamics involved in how groups articulate certain positions in particular circumstances and how they also change as those circumstances change. Social groups are not immune to the wider political and economic contests.

Given that land reform and resettlement are by nature material processes, and given the crucial role sustainable environmental management plays in the economic well-being of the southern African region,[2] attention will also be directed toward the agrarian dynamics of the land-reform process. The chapter also elaborates on the attempts to resolve land conflicts in the postindependence period. The variety of land conflicts of different intensities and magnitudes at both the local and national level are discussed within the context of six main thematic areas: land acquisition, beneficiary selection, agrarian issues, land rights and land tenure, institutional processes, and international capital and donors.

The Land Question in Zimbabwe

In postcolonial Zimbabwe, the land question is the most wrenching unresolved issue from the liberation struggle. Previous research has documented various phases and intensifications in Zimbabwe's land conflicts.[3] Sam Moyo provides the most comprehensive treatment of the land question in Zimbabwe, employing a methodological approach derived from political economy.[4] Yet various writers have contributed immensely to the subject from historical, class, gender, and race perspectives.[5]

Land conflicts in Zimbabwe have a long history, spanning over a century. Many of the less informed or less honest discussions today lean toward presenting the current land conflicts as a new phenomenon, despite persistent intense conflicts over land, sometimes involving physical violence, both before and after independence. Land occupancy and other local, national, and international pressures have led to a variety of attempts by postcolonial governments to mediate the conflict over land, including through responding to the demands for land itself.

Table 5.1 provides a periodization of the main phases of conflict over land since 1980. During this period, conflict has centered on how land should be acquired, the mode of resettlement (model types and tenure arrangements), the criteria for beneficiary selection, and, more recently, how to respond to the needs of farmworkers and women.[6] Despite changes in specific issues and types of conflict over time, these basic sources of conflict have remained consistent, highlighting the importance of approaching the current conflicts in historical perspective.

In the period 1980 to 1985, conflicts revolved around the transition from the liberation struggle to the actual implementation of those longstanding objectives for which the war was fought.[7] During this period, a large number of spontaneous land occupations took place across the country.[8] By 1986/1987, the government moved to put a stop to what were deemed to be illegal occupations of commercial farms, communal lands, national parks, urban areas, and state land, often through violent means.

The brutality with which these evictions were carried out, both by police and farmers, was reminiscent of earlier evictions carried out in the decades prior to independence.[9] Land occupations, and the overall pace of land reform, slowed down substantially after 1986.[10] Beginning in 1997, however, the incidence of land invasions began to grow, and from February 2000 the number of land occupations increased exponentially.

Nonetheless, for the last twenty years discussion of the land question

Table 5.1 A Synopsis of Conflicts over Land in Zimbabwe Since 1980

Period	Issue	Type of Conflict
1980–1985	Rehabilitation, transition. Farmers fleeing the country. Accelerated resettlement schemes. Selection of the beneficiary of land reform. Prime minister's directive creating VIDCOs and WARDCOs.	Squatting on abandoned farms. Some people not taking government reconciliation policies seriously. People unwilling to accept resettlement (*minda mirefu*—long fields) because of fear of working for government benefit. Conflicts between new institutional structures and traditional leaders.
1986–1989	Black bidding for equal opportunities, affirmative action, and empowerment. Growing demand for land expressed through stream bank cultivation and natural resources poaching. Subsidies on agriculture. Ill treatment of farmworkers, poor social services (housing, education, and health).	Intolerance toward squatters. Violence against farmworkers. Government prosecution of stream bank cultivators. Slow progress in meeting land reform targets. Subsidies seen as a drain, yet government felt it had a social responsibility to its citizenry.
1990–1996	Land use (what is the most suitable land use in the prime lands). Land pressure as more workers are retrenched. Farm leases. Evictions for development of infrastructure. Compensation for contributing to the liberation struggle. Land acquisition. Beneficiary selection.	Negative state view of wildlife in prime lands. Farmers diversifying into wildlife. Growing squatting in communal areas. More natural resources poaching. Farmers punishing villagers, ill treating them for trespassing. Corruption in the issuing of government leases. Politically driven evictions. Farm leases and the wider society's negative view of them. Conflicts between farmers and government as farmers contested. Farmworkers, women, disabled, and youths who are excluded and engage in confrontation.
1997–2000	Stakeholder participation in the land reform. Donor conference. ICFSS origin, beneficiaries, transparency. Progressive increases in land occupations. Land and the constitution. Rejection of the constitution. Amendment to the constitution.	Reactionary civil society movement. Donor conference promised too much but delivered too little. Disagreement as to who pays for land and capital improvements. Elites getting larger benefits from land reform. Disagreements on criteria and proceedures on land acquisition prevent peaceful resolution. Farmers against war veterans. Government support of the war veterans. Compulsory acquisition and change of constitution. Rule of law in 2000 versus rule of law before independence. Party contestation and tensions over land reform.

Notes: Village Development Committee (VIDCO); Ward Development Committee (WARDCO); Indigenous Commercial Farm Settlement Scheme (ICFSS).

has been marked by entrenched positions at local, national, and international levels bolstered by contrasting understandings of land use, race, and history itself. These positions have led to rhetorical and physical conflicts between a changing constellation of interest groups, including the central government, local governments, commercial farmers, communal land communities, traditional leaders, commercial farmworkers, veterans of the liberation struggle, international donors, political parties, and farmers on existing resettlement schemes. Such conflict has emerged even more explicitly within the ruling party itself. More militant tendencies grew stronger within the Zimbabwe African National Union (Patriotic Front) [ZANU(PF)] concerning issues of land reform, indigenization, and market reforms. This conflict also needs to be placed within the context of economic collapse in the country starting in 1996, which has seen a steady erosion of living standards for the majority of the population, exacerbating divisions within the ruling party and the larger polity itself.

Six Analytical Dimensions of the Land Question

Conflict over land started when Europeans expropriated land, forcibly expelling Africans and resettling them in predominantly poor agricultural areas. Native reserves were created to make way for European farms, towns, and mines during the colonial period; and ever since, conflict and struggles over land have continued to erupt over the landscape of the region. The conflicts not only surround land acquisition itself and its pace but also include the type of land tenure to be implemented on resettlement schemes, the models of land use, the selection of beneficiaries, the institutional setup of the schemes, and the role of donors in the land reform.

Land Acquisition

The key conflict of the land question is the structural inequality in land ownership and access. This conflict has been fanned by both competing methods of land acquisition and dissatisfaction with the different methods by various actors. Since the late 1990s, there have been five means of acquiring land either proposed or implemented. The first approach entails depending on the market to purchase land on a *willing seller–willing buyer basis*. This was the dominant method used in the 1980s, and donors and commercial farmers still strongly promote it while it is resisted by the government and other stakeholders. The second approach is *compulsory acquisition,* whereby the government gazettes land for acquisition and only pays for improvements to the land and not for the land itself, with the obligation to pay for the land being placed on the United Kingdom to compensate for its role in colonial expropriation. This approach is favored by the government and by some segments of civil society but opposed by the commercial farmers and donors. The third approach involves *negotiated sales,* whereby individual farmers and government negotiate a sale of the land or a swap of one of the farms owned by the individual farmer. Some commercial farmers support this approach. The fourth approach relies on individual nongovernmental organizations (NGOs) to devise their own way of land acquisition and resettlement in consultation with government. The final approach is *land occupations,* whereby individuals and groups occupy private or state land and allocate themselves stands or plots.

Recently, war veterans have spearheaded land occupations, while combinations of different levels of government, politicians, and traditional leaders either support their actions or their eviction. Landholders, donors, and many other groups in Zimbabwe who want stability are against occupations.[11] Differing forms of land acquisition are also colored by political competition. Before the June 2000 parliamentary elections, ZANU(PF) leaders were calling for a speedy reclamation of land from the "whites" and supporting the land occupations, while leaders of the Movement for Democratic Change (MDC) called for a more orderly process of land resettlement. Aside from the issue of compensation for landowners, there is also the recurring question of compensation for farmworkers who are retrenched by such acquisition.[12]

The policy debates over the forms of land acquisition at the macrolevel are thus informed by actual practices of land acquisition; groups and individuals that invade land are motivated by many, sometimes competing motives, ranging from restitution of lost lands to the need for residential stands, from the need for agricultural land to fulfillment of the liberation struggle promises, from local leaders' attempts to bolster their authority drawing on colonial-era frameworks of traditional leadership[13] to politicians carrying out terror tactics on farmers to fulfill personal ambitions. Such diversity of possible forms of "local-level legitimacy" can lead to clashes of different groups of people on occupied land. The inherent conflicts in different modes of land acquisition are thus exacerbated by localized power struggles as well as by party politics. Bad relations between individual commercial farmers and farmworkers, or neighboring resettlement farmers or communal land farmers, can also exacerbate conflicts.

Some of the factors that aggravate conflict over land acquisition include lack of agreement on the means and the scale of acquiring land; the type and source of payment for the land acquired; confrontational approaches by all sides involved, intensified by biased media reports; rigid donor policies; macroeconomic forces like budgetary allocation for land resettlement, donor support or lack thereof for land acquisition, and the general investment climate that affects the land market itself; the level of violence of the land occupations; the pace of actual land acquisition and resettlement; the type of support or pressure from regional governments, particularly South Africa's; and overt political party positions and perceptions of the various moves by the key stakeholders.

Beneficiaries Selection

There is conflict over who decides who will be selected for land resettlement and by what criteria decisions are made. There are also debates and conflicts over the number of farmers needing to be resettled, the proper racial mix of large-scale farmers, and the classifications of access between smallholder and large farmers. Contentious issues can include settlers' prerequisites such as financial capital, farming history, location of settlers' home area compared to the area of resettlement scheme, and political party connections or lack thereof. The characteristics of settlers are also divisive: the mix of war veterans, peasant farmers, town dwellers, and farmworkers; the weight of settler "capability" versus "need" and how these terms are defined and operationalized; the gender and age of the settler; whether the settler needs to be a full-time farmer or not; whether the settler should be from district or neighboring chiefdom or not. Selection committees can also give rise to wrangling (due to the differing roles and powers of traditional leaders, district administrators, councillors, war veteran organizations, and others), as can the question of whether settlers will have to meet certain requirements (productivity levels, amount of construction, investment) and, if so, what the penalties for failure should be. There is also the debate over what infrastructure is provided and by whom (beneficiaries, donors, NGOs, the state, or some combination thereof). Beneficiaries selection is ideologically charged by intense competition for access to land and resources.[14]

Land redistribution in the early 1980s aimed at rehabilitating society and included refugees, displaced persons, the landless, war veterans, and displaced farmworkers.[15] Some of these were placed on very productive resettlement farms,[16] but others got the most marginal land and farms that had been run down during the war. The resettlement program was not adequate in terms of its goals, coverage, quality, and equality. Even today there are no proper records or a systematic way of quantifying the types of war veterans who benefited from the land reform program in relation to their various groups (the disabled, women, unemployed, civil servants, politicians, widowed, etc.). The majority of the ex-combatants did not benefit from all the other programs of rehabilitation. There are different classes of criteria that can be used to say who did not qualify or benefit; major examples are rural women, the destitute, and the disabled.

In the 1990s, the new criteria for beneficiaries of land redistribution were broadened even more toward indigenization through farm leases, and some people started looking at beneficiaries based on their history and political status. Some civil servants, businesspersons, academics, military officers, ex-combatants, and politicians who were also ex-combatants benefited much to the chagrin of those who felt that they too "sacrificed to the liberation struggle to become marginalized" after independence.

The Agrarian Context of Land Reform

One of the more intractable policy debates is that of the balance between land and agrarian reform. The main argument from critics is that agrarian reform involves changes in the property relations, and therefore ownership, as well as access to land to promote equitability in resource benefits.[17] The success of agrarian reform depends to a larger extent on access to productive land, yet the availability of land using the market principles has been in vain. Less than 30 percent of the land in the Mashonaland provinces has been accessed for resettlement purposes.[18] The agrarian transformations that have taken place include policy reforms, tax incentives, financial reorganization, institutional reforms, and water sectoral reforms that have benefited the current landowners and land users in the large-scale commercial farms.[19]

Moyo discovered that in the 1990s the pressure to evolve "efficient" large-scale commercial farms (LSCF) land markets by relaxing the subdivision and land-use conversion regulations and provision of export incentives stimulated production, diversification, and agricultural growth.[20] Visible gains were made from new land uses such as horticulture and tourism, which yield higher profits on smaller land units than were the norm in the LSCF. This, however, did not lead to more land redistribution as was expected. The Economic and Social Adjustment Program (ESAP) adopted by the government in the 1990s offered no concrete resources to black smallholder export-led growth in commodity production (as had happened in Kenya), due to the restrictive land, water, and infrastructural conditions of communal areas. Large-scale farmers, with their long disproportionate access to such resources, responded to ESAP incentives, which influenced changes in Zimbabwe's land use and land tenure tendencies and consolidated the move toward an increasingly market-oriented conception of Zimbabwe's land question. The effect of ESAP policy influences was to sharpen the class- and racially based inequalities over access to land and resources and to give ammunition to elements within the ruling party arguing for a more radical, equitable, and rapid land-reform process.

While these conflicts shape the scope, pace, and support of the Land Redistribution and Resettlement Program (LRRP), the conflicts on the ground are often characterized by attempts by authorities to mandate particular land uses against the wishes of the farmers themselves. All of these debates are fueled by ESAP's emphasis on nontraditional exports and tourism in agriculture. This changing macro-environment also led to revaluation of formerly underutilized land among all landholders and to new struggles and alliances over that land. An example of this is the new (white and black, state and private) capital investment in communal lands through the Communal Areas Management Programme for Indigenous Resources and other forms of tourism and outcropping that lead to the displacement of some farmers from land for the benefit of the tourist industry.[21]

Differences between smallholders and large-scale commercial farms in terms of productivity, efficiency, and environmental impact have been noted by donors, government officials, researchers, the Commercial Farmers' Union (CFU), and NGOs. But the various actors' assumptions based on ideology, race, and modernity have varied.[22] Indeed evaluations of the first LRRP are marked by similar debates.[23] These assumptions also influence discussion of policy instruments such as the land tax. Although there have been significant academic contributions to these debates, there needs to be more research on the actual land uses of resettlement farmers, including environmental impacts,[24] rather than resting claims on ideological assumptions about the size of the farm and the race of the farmer.

Land Rights and Tenure

At the heart of the land question is the debate about the needs and forms of security of tenure desired by various classes and groups including the landless, the land short, (white) large-scale commercial farmers, women, farmworkers, and other claimants to Zimbabwe's LSCF lands. Even once land is acquired, many questions remain concerning the land rights and tenure regime of the settlers. In policymaking documents there is agreement that the permit system should be discontinued and that leaseholds or freehold rights should eventually be given to settlers (and, by extension, to farmers in the communal lands). There seems to be a growing consensus on this approach among government officials, donors, and farmers' groups. Yet it goes against existing forms of land rights and tenure, such as security through ruling lineages; permission given by local leaders, councillors, and, more recently, war veterans; a growing informal "land market" in communal areas; and resettlement schemes.

The divergences of these practices from existing policy have led to many confrontations between different levels of the state and smallholders.[25] There is also the debate over the possibility of resettling farmworkers or providing them with residential stands.[26] This too has been a source of conflict during the current occupations, as farmworkers either join the occupiers or team up with their employees to fight them back because of the insecurity of tenure. Here, the scale of farmworker families in need of land, or who would be displaced as a result of land redistribution, tends to be exaggerated. Farmworkers have reasons besides insecurity of tenure for siding with the war veterans. Violence committed by some commercial farmers against farmworkers has a long and historic legacy in Zimbabwe. To this day, there is much brutality committed against farmworkers. Their pay is very low; their living conditions are substandard; they are often exploited; and severe punishments are meted out for even the most minor infractions. Finally, there is the pressing question of the security of tenure for women raised by many NGOs but often resisted by policymakers and traditional leaders.[27] All of these questions and conflicts regarding land rights are amplified in particular locales by growing land demands, which then exacerbate divisions between various groups.

Institutional Processes and Actors

There is a wide and complex array of actors involved in the policy formulation and implementation stages of the government's national land policy. At the formal institutional level, responsibility for formulating and implementing policy is "shared" between the various central government ministries, including the Ministry of Lands, Agriculture, and Rural Resettlement; the Ministry of Rural Resources and Water Development; and the Ministry of Environment, Mines, and Tourism. The lines of responsibility then shift downward, to the provincial governments, the rural district councils, and the village committees and traditional leaders. Conflict-inducing problems have characterized all levels of the formal institutional policy process, stemming from lack of coordination between various ministries and departments, lack of capacity, the preservation of turf, and the intrusion of personal interest in the land acquisition and resettlement process. Furthermore, problems have arisen out of the imperfect decentralization process, generating additional conflict on the roles of local government structure and traditional leaders.

Enmeshed within this formal institutional structure is a web of other nonstate actors, with varying degrees of direct and indirect involvement in the policy process. These include the donor agencies; a wide range of NGOs (whose activities involve policy advocacy, the provision of technical support, academic consulting, and local-level policy implementation); and the various farmers' unions, farmworkers' organizations, and local-level community-based organizations. Attempts to formalize the role of these various actors in the policymaking and implementation process are reflected in their inclusion in the Inter-Ministerial Committee on Resettlement and Rural Development and the National Economic Consultative Forum's Land Reform Task Force, under the Inception Phase Framework Plan (1999–2000).

Interaction among these various actors, and between them and the government, has been highly conflictual, from 1980 to the present. The sources of conflict stem, in part, from the vastly divergent power positions of these actors, where some enjoy superior organizational capacity and considerable financial resources (e.g., donor agencies and the CFU), while others are significantly weaker (e.g., the Women's Land Lobby Group, the Zimbabwe Farmers' Union, and the General Agricultural and Plantation Workers' Union of Zimbabwe [GAPWUZ]). Serious conflict has also risen over the highly divergent policy preferences and priorities of these organizations, as well as their differing abilities to promote their interests and the difficulty of building consensus among them.[28] The policy process has been further complicated by the "intrusion" of actors not formally invited to play a role, most notably the war veterans, the landless, and the land-stressed in the communal areas.

The role of the ruling party creates an additional layer of complexity. While a clear conceptual distinction must be made between the government and the ruling ZANU(PF), in practice that distinction is often less clear. The political interests and priorities of the ruling party have impinged on the land policy process at every level of government, and at the intersection between the government and the various nonstate actors. There are serious internal divisions within the ruling party over key issues such as the land tenure question, as well as over succession politics. The rift within ZANU(PF) has exacerbated conflict through the insertion of political considerations in the land policy process, the espousing of contradictory policies, and the willingness to use extreme measures, such as intimidation and fear.

Conflicts within and between the various governmental, party, and nonstate actors (both domestic and external) are usually played out in a nonviolent manner but, more recently, have been associated with violence. In the most recent phase of the land struggle, the police have been both unwilling and unable to maintain "law and order" (a value-laden term), and the Zimbabwe National Army has come to play a more visible role. This has both potentially positive and negative implications for the alleviation of conflict.

International Capital and Donors

Mutual suspicion and distrust have often characterized Zimbabwe's relationship with international donors, including bilateral donor agencies and multilateral donors such as the World Bank and International Monetary Fund. Although an understanding was reached in the late 1980s with the World Bank over market-based reforms, culminating in the introduction of ESAP in 1991, relations have since soured for a variety of reasons (not all directly related to the land question).[29] ESAP, which failed to integrate the need for land reform in its design, introduced new sources of conflict (and aggravated old ones) with direct implications for the land question. The program reinforced an extremely inequitable land ownership structure, and it soon became apparent that the mostly white commercial farmers were the main beneficiaries of reforms promoting production for export markets. Furthermore, ESAP had the effect of altering land use practices discussed earlier, which created new demands for land and new sources of conflict between white and black elite with easy access to capital.[30] Depending on the issue, the small black commercial elite have formed alliances with white commercial farmers; however, the push to indigenize the commercial farming sector is clearly contradictory to the interests of white farmers.

Another effect of ESAP has been to internationalize interests in the land question through the introduction of stock-owning and shareholder arrangements, introducing yet another source of conflict in the land equation and creating new allies for commercial farmers.[31] The intrusion of foreign interests in the land question has added yet another layer of complexity in terms of national politics. The role of international capital in funding NGOs, in particular those lending their support to opposition, adds complication to the political process. Up to now, up-to-date foreign ownership of huge tracts of underutilized agricultural land, mining concession areas, and productive eco-tourism projects have been a key source of the internal and external dimension of land conflicts. Thus, British, South African, and German multinationals, including highly influential groups such as the Anglo-American Corporation, are major actors in the tensions between Zimbabwe and the rest of the world. At the regional level, there is a surprising amount of public support among SADC countries for Zimbabwe's land-reform program, but this support may wane if more donor pressure is exerted on these countries.

The World Bank and the United Nations Development Programme (UNDP) are the major multilateral donors taking initiative on the land question. There appears to be considerable policy coordination between them and the major bilateral donor agencies, most notably the UK Department for International Development and the U.S. Agency for International Development (USAID). This has resulted in a united policy front over such issues as transparency in the land acquisition and resettlement processes, the preference for respect for private property rights, and a minimal role for the state in the land-reform process. The preferences of the government with respect to its national land policy are often diametrically opposed to those of the multilateral and bilateral donors, generating conflict and stalemate in resolving the struggles over the land. The result is that international donors have missed important opportunities for moving forward on land reform.[32] The policy effect of missed opportunities for resolving conflict has been the strengthening of those elements within ZANU(PF), in alliance with the powerful war veterans, who prefer a radical solution to the land issue. There has been a shift in government thinking on whether land reform is dependent on donor support. The reality is that farms are being acquired—both by force and voluntarily—without the provision of compensation, with the government's position being that Britain should compensate farmers for the value of the land.

Impasse with Land Reform in Zimbabwe

Stalled Negotiations, 1997–1999

In 1997, the government of Zimbabwe (GoZ) announced measures to redress the land question once and for all through the acquisition of 5 million hectares of land in the "Year of Our Lord 1997."[33] The context of that attempt has to be analyzed in the failed negotiations of the 1996 GoZ mission to the UK and the new Labour government there. The GoZ, faced with the slow pace of land reform due to lack of resources, renewed its attempts to negotiate with the British. Verbal promises were made with the Tories, but no funds were forthcoming and this was worsened with the election of the Labour government. The Labour government naively pointed out that they were not responsible for the actions of their colonial peers and were therefore not going to pay for a land reform based on "colonial reparations" but would focus on poverty reduction through land reform.

At least 1,471 farms were identified throughout the country as part of reaching the 5 million hectares targeted in the 1990 National Land Policy.[34] This led to an international outcry on the economic implications of this move, contributing to positive pressure brought to bear on all stakeholders to dialogue and map the way forward with the land reform. A donor's conference in 1998, coupled with a resurgence in land occupations, kept the land reform on the agenda until the state made contingency plans for land redistribution by developing a comprehensive national land policy,[35] an implementation plan of the Second Phase of Land Reform and Resettlement, and an inception phase to try out various innovative approaches to land reform and resettlement. With the 1,471 commercial farms targeted for compulsory acquisition and an unbudgeted payout to the war veterans promised in August of 1997, donors and the international financial institutions began raising concerns about the government's macroeconomic stability and its plans for land resettlement.

Broader Land Policymaking Processes

The government of Zimbabwe, with the strong participation of international donors and national civil society groups, prepared several frameworks and policies for a second phase of the Land Redistribution and Resettlement Program to build on the first phase of the program that occurred in the 1980s. The key focus of these consultations was the Donor Conference held in September 1998, when government and donor representatives agreed that land redistribution remains one of the most critical issues to be resolved in Zimbabwe. They further agreed that the approaches to land acquisition and resettlement needed to be widened to facilitate participation by other stakeholders, as well as beneficiaries, and that the program would begin immediately with an inception phase starting with the farms currently on offer to the government.

Out of these consultations came the national land policy document and the Inception Phase Framework Plan (IPFP). The policy document outlines the broad framework of land reform and resettlement and was presented to the government for consideration and adoption in November 1998. The IPFP, introduced in early 1999, was a detailed implementation plan and budget that set out specific principles and objectives for proceeding with a limited land redistribution exercise over twenty-four months involving 1 million hectares. But many of the people who have been involved in preparing these frameworks or who are said to be the beneficiaries have reacted to various components of the framework with suspicion, distrust, or bad faith, given the deep-seated conflict over the land question. It is fair to say that all the major parties to the agreement did not meet the expectations.

In 1997, spurred on by pressure from the powerful war veterans, the government employed the relevant sections of the Land Acquisition Act to designate 1,471 large-scale commercial farms for compulsory acquisition. The top-down approach of the government, and its failure to consult widely with interested stakeholders, compromised the success of this initiative. The government then launched a broad-based consultation process with a wide variety of nonstate actors in order to develop a national land policy and the LRRP Phase 2 that embraced the principles of transparency, accountability, and democratic participation. In 1998, the government launched its national land policy and the LRRP Phase 2. The changing land policy interest reflected by the main operational policy documents of the government of Zimbabwe, including the IPFP, reflects a gradual acceptance of a variety of civil society organizations participating in the land reform process.

The IPFP reflected the eventual compromise that would be used to implement the government resettlement models and to test out a variety of approaches to land redistribution, with the key objective of "learning by doing." During this phase, the government aimed to finalize a new land policy, which would introduce an agricultural land tax, streamline subdivision regulations, and improve land tenure arrangements. The IPFP was founded on a "twin-track" approach, which anticipated harmonious collaboration between government and nonstate actors' efforts to enhance land reform. The plan that was supposed to be implemented through the Inter-Ministerial Committee on Resettlement and Rural Development, supported by a technical support unit, coordinated the work of various line ministries and departments, rural district councils, stakeholder organizations, and private or NGO agencies to be engaged in the LRRP. The inception phase was to be financed by the government and donors, while it promoted the direct disbursement of funds to implementing agencies in and outside of government. The framework plan promised to improve the existing government land acquisition and resettlement approaches and for nonstate actors to try out new approaches of land acquisition, including selecting settlers, procuring finance, and planning infrastructure for the resettlement program.

The IPFP was severely challenged by the widespread and at times violent land occupations that began after the defeat of the draft constitution in a national referendum in February 2000. The latent conflicts over the pace and type of land redistribution, when coupled with intense political contests between ZANU(PF) and the Movement for Democratic Change (MDC), emerged in the form of mass land occupations led by veterans of the liberation war. The violence directed toward white farmers and black farmworkers as part of a political campaign on behalf of the ruling party for the June parliamentary elections led to the freezing of donor support to the IPFP, which donors had already only half-heartedly financially supported. This led the government to adopt a fast-track land resettlement program (June 2000), based on the compulsory acquisition of farms, with compensation to be paid only for the value of improvements on the land. In response to this move, there have been simultaneous negotiations between government officials, leaders of the war veterans and the CFU, and with some of the major donors, but these do not seem to have been able to keep pace with the developments on the ground.

Context of the Land Occupations

Periodization of Land Occupations

The land occupancies have remained on the political agenda in the last twenty years with scant attention being provided by the state, civil society, opposition political parties, and the private sector. The first phase saw low-profile, high-intensity occupations throughout the country from 1980 to

1985, while a parallel process of land resettlement funded mainly by the British was moving in tandem with the occupancies.[36] The period between 1985 and 1990 witnessed normal, low-intensity occupations, which began in the context of dwindling resources for continued land resettlement and economic liberalization due to retrenchments as most people lost their jobs in urban areas and the mines.

The severe drought in the 1991–1992 farming season led to extensive commercial farm retrenchments, adding to the pressure on communal area land resources.[37] Yet during this time the state had the ability to solve the land question with the enactment of the Land Acquisition Act in 1992. The grounds for severe conflicts were created during this time and acutely captured through research on new land uses in the Mashonaland provinces by Sam Moyo.[38] From the middle of the 1980s, the state began to evict, often in violent fashion, those deemed to be occupying land illegally on commercial farms, communal lands, national parks, urban areas, and state property.[39] This occurred simultaneously with increasing violence taken by property owners, particularly white farmers, on illegal occupants, often with implicit or explicit state approval. Land occupancies then slowed slightly in the late 1980s but then expanded more and more, culminating in an intense period of high-profile land occupancies involving war veterans and rural peasants from 1997 onward.

In August/September 1997, land occupations started to occur in isolated areas of the country; those taking part had the explicit aim of redistributing land from white farmers to landless villagers and war veterans. The occupations came in waves, starting with just a few in 1997 and reaching well over a thousand by 2000. The constitutional reform process created a form of discord that ultimately became linked to the land question. Before the draft constitution was put to a referendum in February 2000, the government introduced a number of changes to the final draft. Included in these changes were an additional clause that reinforced the right to compulsory acquisition, and qualified the existing market criteria for compensation of the land, and a statement that obliged the British to pay for land compulsorily acquired by the state. The National Constitutional Assembly (NCA), formed to push for constitutional reform, and the MDC, a political party launched in September 1999, both campaigned against the draft constitution, contributing to its defeat in the referendum. Shortly thereafter, twelve war veterans occupied farms in Masvingo, complaining that the white farmers had connived to defeat the constitution in the referendum. The former governor of Mashonaland Central and the Zimbabwe National Liberation War Veterans Association (ZNLWVA) came in full support of the actions of the veterans. When leaders of the ZNLWVA and the ruling party realized by the end of March that white farmers were actively campaigning for the MDC, and encouraging farmworkers to do the same, farm occupations grew violent, becoming intertwined with the political campaign for the June 2000 parliamentary elections.

The interest of the international community and the international media has been focused, rather narrowly, on the current land occupations and the murder of white farmers and MDC supporters. Approximately 1,000 commercial farms, owned and operated mainly by white farmers, have reportedly been occupied by war veterans and their supporters in the peasant areas and the cities.[40] Available information bulletins suggest that about one-third of the occupations have been marked by violence, and serious human rights abuses, including rape and torture, have characterized the period both before and after the June elections. Yet various other data sources, including fieldwork, suggest that the scale of the invasions and violence at their peak could have affected 60 percent of the above figures, given the uneven range and iterative nature of the land occupations.

However, the period since mid-February 2000 represents an intense propagation of the land question in Zimbabwe, as it has been for the second time brought to the attention of the world.[41] The interest of the international community and the international media has been focused on the current land occupations and the growing rift over procedures with land reform. It is estimated that from 800 (survey data) to over 1,500 (CFU reports) commercial farms owned and operated mainly by white farmers (but also including farms owned by black farmers, multinational corporations, and the state) have been occupied by veterans of the liberation struggle and their supporters in the peasant areas and the cities. The occupation has been marked by sporadic violence, with many people injured and the levels of tension remaining high on many of the farms.

The 2000 Election and Political Competition over Land

The parliamentary election campaign of 2000 was the most bruising in the history of elections in Zimbabwe. The campaign focused on land and the economy as major issues. The ruling ZANU(PF) Party campaigned on the basis of land through its campaign slogan of "Land is the Economy, the Economy is land," whereas the opposition MDC emphasized the economy, not land. A host of other smaller parties became submerged, and it was difficult for them to sell their agenda to the electorate. The campaign became a two-party affair, with accusations and counter accusations between the two. For instance, ZANU(PF) accused the MDC of trying to reverse land reform, of wanting to sell the country to the former colonial masters (as the party was alleged to be receiving financial assistance from the white farmers, white business, and a host of civil society organizations linked to the UK such as the NCA). The MDC accused ZANU(PF) of giving land to the cronies,[42] and of monopolizing the land issue—an argument that the party had continued to use as a campaign strategy in every election since 1980 and had failed to resolve in twenty years.

The land issue will always be a campaign issue, in spite of the oppositional politics that argue that it is a national issue and not for party politics. There is a critical need for opposition parties to come up with strategies or positions on land reform to keep it on the national agenda. However, the last election proved that indeed most of the smaller parties do not have a firm land-reform agenda. Internationally, all parties that yearn to govern tend to identify major development issues around which they campaign for political office. It is within this scope that ZANU(PF) has used the land issue as a campaign strategy. There are indications that it has kept its election campaign momentum on the land issue to prove that it was campaigning beyond the elections. However, the party's critics interpreted this as ZANU(PF)'s official campaign strategy for the 2002 presidential elections. At the same time, since the election the MDC has rhetorically opposed the government land-reform program but has failed to develop its own position on land issues.

Within the MDC, there seems to be no agreement as to what the party position on land reform should be. In its election manifesto, the MDC advocated a land commission to lead the land-reform processes. While a land commission will be the most appropriate framework to deal with all aspects of land,[43] there is a need to craft a framework to deal with the current occupations so as not to evoke violent reactions from the stakeholders, particularly the war veterans occupying farms. Furthermore, the land commission, which will come into being as a result of cumbersome procedures that involve statutory reform, must not be seen as a diversionary tactic or a process of delaying land reform.

In early June the government gazetted a list of 804 farms for compulsory acquisition. The election later that month saw ZANU(PF) win 62 and the MDC 57 of the 120 contested parliamentary seats. The war veterans began to reemphasize the demand for land on the occupied farms as the government, the CFU, and donors negotiated the way forward. The latest policy framework on land reform has been emerging out of the negotiations and actions taken to respond to the land occupations in 2000. The government in June adopted a "fast-track" LRRP to speedily resettle war veterans and villagers on at least twenty farms per province to kick-start their aim to acquire 5 million hectares. In response to court cases brought against President Mugabe in July by the CFU and others, the government announced it was going to resettle people on over 3,000 farms by the start of the rains in October. Debates and negotiations continue around questions such as when and how land occupations will end and farms will be acquired and resettled, especially given the context of conflicting expectations for the land acquired. The uncertainty and conflict on farms remains an important national issue.

The Regional Dimension of Land Questions in Southern Africa

There is an important regional dimension to the land question in Zimbabwe, given the impact of settler history on current land use, labor migration patterns, and markets, as well as on the growing regional political, economic, and communications ties. The debates surrounding land reform in southern Africa have had an influence on those in Zimbabwe. Furthermore, land-reform developments in Zimbabwe are having a significant impact on the region as a whole.

Although the exact contours of the struggles over land are shaped by the national histories of individual countries, conflict remains universal to the land question throughout the region. While governments, donors, and national lobby groups debate about the need for and models of land reform, the structural imbalance of land ownership and use inherited from colonial times continues to fuel antagonism. Conflicts over the land tend to focus on the following areas: land use and demands, land administration, approaches to land reform, the impact of liberalization, and the notion of community-driven land reform. In terms of land use and demands, compelling and unresolved dilemmas persist that are centered around the impact of land on social distribution, utilization efficiency, and the contribution it makes to improving the welfare of the majority of people in the region. The dynamics of land reform raise difficult questions about the goals being accomplished and issues surrounding kinship, land use, and gender bias in favor of males.

In land administration, conflicts have polarized around competing claims over jurisdiction on matters that impinge on the realization of land rights. The legitimate rights and roles of various authorities, ranging from the central government to provincial governments, local authorities, and traditional authorities in allocating land and adjudicating land disputes need to be clarified.

Variations in approaches to land reform relate to whether priority is attached to the redressing of past grievances, and the promotion of justice and equity, or to the narrower concerns of economic efficiency. Underlying these different land-reform approaches is the distinction that is emerging regarding the relative merits of land-rights-based approaches to land transfers, as opposed to land redistribution approaches. The latter are based on the identification of generalized demands for land for survival, agricultural growth, and rural development. The legally sanctioned approaches to the restoration of land rights have been termed the "land restitution" approach. The relative merits of these approaches are controversial, warranting further investigation.

The pressure on southern African countries to liberalize their economies through structural adjustment programs (SAPs) has altered strategies for land reform. The preference for market-assisted approaches by donors and interested national stakeholders influenced a shift from radical to more liberal land-reform strategies that privilege guarantees for uninterrupted land productivity for globalized markets.[44] The neoliberal preference for a minimal role for the state, and for decentralization, have further driven the encouragement of community-driven or "negotiated" land reform. A key—and questionable—assumption of this approach is that impoverished and marginal rural populations can initiate land reform themselves, without falling prey to the hegemony of traditional chieftancy and dominant-party political systems.[45]

Conflicts over land in the 1980s centered around two tensions: between the government's push for land reform and redistribution based on a social justice criteria of redressing colonial wrongs and those who resisted that demand, and between administrators who called for an orderly, well-planned, and heavily controlled land resettlement exercise and popular demands for land and for following other forms of governance and land-use practices.[46] In the 1990s, the conflicts over land were between, on the one hand, donors, the government (at times), commercial farmers, and a few other groups promoting more of an economic efficiency criteria for land resettlement and, on the other hand, those communities and their supporters among traditional leaders, politicians, war veterans, and at times the government itself, who were upset with the slow pace and the selection process of beneficiaries.

Conclusion

In Zimbabwe, conflict mediation has been complicated by the overly rigid positions of some NGOs and donor agencies over the land issue, the contradictions within the ruling party, and the way in which those contradictions get played out in the policy process. The media (both national and international) have played an unhelpful role by distorting the policy positions on all sides to the dispute, as well as negatively shaping people's perceptions of what is actually happening on the ground. During the recent violence, the intense emotional atmosphere and state of uncertainty have complicated the task of mediation efforts. The most crucial mediation effort is to keep the channels of communication open and encourage dialogue.

Further research needs to explore the extent to which the state has an independent view on the land question, in the face of a multitude of societal actors, with different interests and ideologies based on class, gender, race, and ethnicity. A better understanding is needed of the alliances formed both between domestic actors and between domestic and external actors (e.g., NGOs and donor agencies), and of their comparative ability to position themselves in the various forums for debate (e.g., the National Economic Consultative Forum). The relationships among different organizations and those they claim to represent, the overlapping membership between various organizations, and the impact of those acting outside formal organizational structures (e.g., peasant protest) need further exploration.

An obvious means to ameliorate the conflict would be for both donors and the government to be more flexible in their policy stances. This appeared to have been accomplished with the cooperation between donors, the government, and a variety of other stakeholders in the preparation of the IPFP, which grew out of the second phase of the Land Reform and Resettlement Program. The IPFP basically entailed a compromise between the government's preferred approaches to implementing the LRRP Phase 2 and other "complementary approaches" (all favoring a market approach) preferred by the international donors. However, it is not clear to what extent either the donors or the government were truly committed to the compromise reflected in the IPFP, and events have (temporarily at least) minimized its relevance. The degree of the apparent policy coordination between the various donors needs to be validated empirically, in order to determine the extent to which some potential donors might be persuaded to relax their policy positions.

The chapter has also taken as a starting point the understanding (or assumption) that it may not always be possible to avoid violent conflict in the realization of important and legitimate national goals, such as land redistribution and resettlement. International donors tend to privilege the preservation of (law and) order, but in doing so, this may entail the maintenance of unjust and inequitable social structures. If the avoidance of all violence comes at the expense of meaningful change through legitimate processes, then the value attached to the preservation of order may be questioned. However, the outbreak of violence can unleash forces that ultimately undermine legitimate social goals, which points to the critical importance of minimizing violent conflict.

Notes

1. Sam Moyo, *Land and Democracy in Zimbabwe* (Harare, Zimbabwe: SAPES Books, 1999).

2. Sam Moyo and Dan Tevera, "Regional Environmental Security in Southern Africa," in *Environmental Security in Southern Africa,* ed. Dan Tevera and

Sam Moyo (Harare, Zimbabwe: SAPES Books, 2000), 3–24; Lawrence Tshuma, *A Matter of (In)Justice: Law, State and the Agrarian Question in Zimbabwe* (Harare, Zimbabwe: SAPES Books, 1997).

3. Sam Moyo, *The Land Question in Zimbabwe* (Harare, Zimbabwe: SAPES Books, 1995); Sam Moyo, "The Political Economy of Land Acquisition and Redistribution in Zimbabwe, 1990–1999," *Journal of Southern African Studies* 26, 1 (2000); Sam Moyo, *Land Reform Under Structural Adjustment in Zimbabwe* (Uppsala, Sweden: Afrika Nordiska Institute, 2000); Paris Yeros, "Peasant Struggles for Land and Security in Zimbabwe: A Global Moral Economy at the Close of the Twentieth Century," working chapter (Harare, Zimbabwe: SAPES Books, 2000); Terence Ranger, "The Communal Areas of Zimbabwe," In *Land in African Agrarian Systems,* ed. T. J. Bassett and D. G. Crummey (Madison: University of Wisconsin Press, 1993), 354–385.

4. Moyo, *Land Question in Zimbabwe*; Susie Jacobs, "Women and Land Resettlement in Zimbabwe," *Review of African Political Economy* 27 (1984): 33–50.

5. H. V. Moyana, *The Political Economy of Land in Zimbabwe* (Gweru, Zimbabwe: Mambo Press, 1984); Mandivamba Rukuni, *Report of the Commission of Inquiry into Appropriate Land Tenure Systems,* Harare, Zimbabwe, 1994; L. Tshuma, *A Matter of (In)justice: Law, State, and the Agrarian Question in Zimbabwe* (Harare: SAPES Books, 1997).

6. Angela Cheater, "The Role and Position of Women in Pre-Colonial and Colonial Zimbabwe," *Zambezia* 13 (1983): 65–79; Rudo Gaidzanwa, "Women's Land Rights in Zimbabwe: An Overview," Department of Rural and Urban Planning Occasional Chapter no. 13, University of Zimbabwe, Harare, 1998; Jacobs, "Women and Land Resettlement in Zimbabwe."

7. Moyo, *Land Question in Zimbabwe;* Sam Moyo, "The Land Question," in *Zimbabwe: The Political Economy of Transition, 1980–1986,* ed. I. Mandaza (Dakar, Senegal: CODESRIA, 1986).

8. Jeffrey Herbst, *State Politics in Zimbabwe* (Harare: University of Zimbabwe Press, 1990); Tor Skalnes, *Politics of Economic Reform in Zimbabwe: Continuity and Change in Development* (New York: St. Martin's, 1995).

9. Moyo and Tevera, "Regional Environmental Security."

10. Sam Moyo, "Peasant Organisations and Rural Civil Society in Africa: An Introduction," in *Peasant Organisations and the Democratisation Process in Africa,* ed. S. Moyo and B. Romdhane (Dakar, Senegal: CODESRIA, 2000); Ben Cousins, Dan Weiner, and Nick Amin, "Social Differentiation in the Communal Lands of Zimbabwe," *Review of African Political Economy* 53 (1992): 5–24.

11. Moyo and Tevera, "Regional Environmental Security."

12. GAPWUZ, report on the Workshop on Living Conditions of Farm Workers in Zimbabwe, Darwendale, Zimbabwe, 23–25 February 1997.

13. David Hughes, "To Spread Opportunity Across Space: Smallholder-led Resettlement in Eastern Zimbabwe," report to the Southern Alliance for Indigenous Resource (SAFIRE), 2000.

14. Moyo, *Land and Democracy in Zimbabwe;* Moyo, "Political Economy of Land Acquisition"; Prosper Matondi, "Access to Land and Water Resources in Zimbabwe's Rural Environment," in *Environmental Security in Southern Africa,* ed. D. Tevera and S. Moyo (Harare, Zimbabwe: SAPES Books, 2000), 101–116.

15. The beneficiary selection changed in 1985 to include master farmers and other high producers; Bill H. Kinsey, "Emerging Issues in Zimbabwe's Land Resettlement Program," *Development Policy Review* 1 (1983): 163–196.

16. Moyo, *Land Question in Zimbabwe.*

17. Moyo, *Land and Democracy in Zimbabwe.*

18. Moyo, *Land Reform Under Structural Adjustment.*

19. Ibid.

20. Moyo, "Political Economy of Land Acquisition"; Sam Moyo, "The Land Question and Land Reform in Southern Africa," in *Environmental Security in Southern Africa,* ed. D. Tevera and S. Moyo (Harare, Zimbabwe: SAPES Books, 2000), 53–74; Moyo, *Land Reform Under Structural Adjustment.*

21. Steve Robins, "Contesting the Social Geometry of State Power: A Case Study of Land-Use Planning in Matabeleland, Zimbabwe," *Social Dynamics* 20, 2 (1994); Alison Goebel, "Process, Perception and Power: Notes from 'Participatory' Research in a Zimbabwean Resettlement Area," *Development and Change* 29, 2 (1998): 277–306.

22. Moyo, "Political Economy of Land Acquisition"; Moyo and Tevera, "Regional Environmental Security."

23. Moyo, *Land Question in Zimbabwe;* Bill H. Kinsey, "Determinants of Rural Household Incomes and Their Impact on Poverty and Food Security in Zimbabwe," report for the Department of Urban Planning, University of Zimbabwe, and the Economic and Social Institute, Free University of Amsterdam, 1999.

24. Ian Scoones, "Range Management Science and Policy: Politics, Polemics, and Pasture in Southern Africa," in *The Lie of the Land: Challenging Received Wisdom on the African Environment,* ed. M. Leach and R. Mearns (London: Heinemann, 1996); Ian Scoones, "Landscapes, Fields, and Soils: Understanding the History of Soil Fertility Management in Southern Zimbabwe," *Journal of Southern African Studies* 23, 4 (1997): 615–634.

25. Cousins, Weiner, and Amin, "Social Differentiation"; Donald Moore, "Contesting Terrain in Zimbabwe's Eastern Highlands: Political Ecology, Ethnography, and Peasant Resource Struggles," *Economic Geography* 69, 4 (1993); Jocelyn Alexander, "The Unsettled Land: The Politics of Land Redistribution in Matabeleland, 1980–1990," *Journal of Southern African Studies* 17, 4 (1991); Moyo, *Land Question in Zimbabwe;* Land Tenure Commission, *Report of the Commission of Inquiry into Appropriate Land Tenure Systems* (Harare, Zimbabwe: Government Printer, 1994); Blair Rutherford, "Another Side to Rural Zimbabwe: Social Constructs and the Administration of Farm Workers in Urungwe District, 1940s," *Journal of Southern African Studies* 23, 1 (1997): 107–126; Blair Rutherford, *Working on the Margins: Black Workers, White Farmers in Postcolonial Zimbabwe* (London: Zed Books; Harare, Zimbabwe: Weaver Press, 2001); Goebel, "Process, Perception and Power"; David M. Hughes, "Refugees and Squatters: Immigration and the Politics of Territory on the Zimbabwe-Mozambique Border," *Journal of Southern African Studies* 25, 4 (1998): 533–552; Matondi, "Access to Land and Water Resources."

26. Lloyd Sachikonye and Oliver Zishiri, "Tenure Security for Farm-Workers in Zimbabwe," Working Chapter no. 27 (Harare, Zimbabwe: Friedrich Ebert Stiftung, 1999); Sam Moyo, Blair Rutherford, and Dede Amanor-Wilks, "Land Reform and Changing Social Relations for Farm Workers in Zimbabwe," *Review of African Political Economy* 84 (2000): 181–202.

27. Cheater, "Women and Their Participation"; Mahmood Mamdani, *Citizen and Subject: Contemporary Africa and the Legacy of Late Colonialism* (Princeton, N.J.: Princeton University Press, 1996).

28. Hevina Dashwood, *Zimbabwe: The Political Economy of Transformation* (Toronto: University of Toronto Press, 2000); Dashwood, Hevina, "Social Welfarism, Poverty Alleviation, and Political Stability in Zimbabwe," *Canadian*

Journal of Development Studies 3 (1999): 566–592; Herbst, *State Politics in Zimbabwe;* Moyo, *Land and Democracy in Zimbabwe;* Moyo, *Land Reform Under Structural Adjustment;* Matondi, "Access to Land and Water Resources."

29. Dashwood, *Zimbabwe;* Dashwood, "Social Welfarism."

30. Moyo, *Land Question in Zimbabwe;* Moyo, *Land Reform Under Structural Adjustment.*

31. Ibid.

32. Dashwood, *Zimbabwe.*

33. Moyo, *Land Reform Under Structural Adjustment.*

34. Moyo, *Land Question in Zimbabwe;* Tshuma, *Matter of (In)Justice.*

35. Issa Shivji, Sam Moyo, Welshman Ncube, and D. Gunby, "Draft National Land Policy for the Government of Zimbabwe," discussion paper, Food and Agricultural Organisation and Ministry of Lands and Agriculture, Harare, Zimbabwe, 1998.

36. Moyo, "Peasant Organisations and Rural Civil Society."

37. Moyo, *Land Reform Under Structural Adjustment*; Moyo, "Peasant Organisations and Rural Civil Society."

38. Moyo, *Land Reform Under Structural Adjustment.*

39. Herbst, *State Politics in Zimbabwe.*

40. CFU, Land reform proposal, Commercial Farmers' Union, Harare, Zimbabwe, 1998.

41. Moyo, "The Land Question," pointed out that the land question drew foreign interest through the funding of technical reports by USAID, the World Bank, Overseas Development Institute, Food and Agricultural Organisation, European Economic Union, and the Whitsun Foundation. Many local organizations and departments of the University of Zimbabwe are funded and staffed with American expatriates.

42. This is an issue that had also been overemphasized by the UK ministers in foreign affairs (Robin Cook and Peter Hain).

43. Shivji, Moyo, Ncube, and Gunby, "Draft National Land Policy."

44. World Bank, Zimbabwe: Agricultural Sector Memorandum, vols. 1 and 2, no. 9429-Zim (Washington, D.C.: World Bank, 1991); World Bank, *Zimbabwe Achieving Shared Growth,* Country Economic Memorandum, vol. 2 (Washington, D.C.: World Bank, 1995); CFU, Land Reform Proposal.

45. Moyo, *Land Question in Zimbabwe.*

46. Ibid.; Moore, "Contesting Terrain," 380–401.

6

Land Reform: The South African Case

RUTH HALL AND GAVIN WILLIAMS

The "land question" in South Africa is a source of conflict between and within communities and a key challenge to the state's aims to advance the objectives of reconstruction, redistribution, and development. The South African government and its citizens have closely followed the widespread occupations of private farms in Zimbabwe from 1998 to 2002—out of concern for a close neighbor and also with fears, hopes, and questions about what these events signify for South Africa. Land reform has proven to be far more complex and difficult to implement in South Africa than policymakers and their international advisers expected. The government has neither given it priority nor found coherent solutions to the problems of acquiring and transferring land.

The tardy pace of land restitution and redistribution, the patchy enforcement of tenure rights, and contending claims to land and to rights in land have resulted in evictions of farm dwellers and attacks on farmworkers. Farmers and their families have been murdered. Commercial farming land and vacant urban land have been illegally occupied. People resort to direct action because of the inadequacy of the supply of land for redistribution and also to stake preemptive claims on land that is, or may be, available for reallocation.

Impatience with official land reform and its failure to provide relief to those who are landless or homeless, or who have insecure tenure over the land on which they live, has increased. It has been given voice in the name of the landless by the Landless People's Movement, the National Land Committee (NLC), and the Pan Africanist Congress, most notably during a campaign surrounding the 2001 UN World Conference Against Racism in Durban, under the slogan "Landlessness = Racism."

Substantial land reform may well be necessary to avoid wider conflicts. Ironically, the process of land redistribution itself and the claims to which it gives rise may also create or intensify local conflicts.

Reforming Land and Agriculture

Land reform is one of the ways in which past racial exclusions and inequalities are being addressed in the "new South Africa." The South African Department of Land Affairs (DLA) is responsible for restoring land to those unjustly deprived of land rights since 1913, redistributing land to those denied equitable access to it under segregation and apartheid, and securing the tenure rights of those excluded in the past from acquiring title to land.[1]

At the outset, the DLA was a "new South African" department, with its own minister, Derek Hanekom. It recruited key staff from nongovernmental organizations (NGOs) active in land-oriented struggles and focused its activities on changing the unequal distribution of land. It took over the responsibilities of the Department of Regional and Land Affairs, itself the heir to the bankrupt Department of Development Aid.[2] The National Department of Agriculture (NDA) inherited from the apartheid past ways of thinking and institutional structures; links to "organised [i.e., white] agriculture";[3] initially, key staff; and even, from 1994–1996, its minister. In 1996, Hanekom replaced Kraai van Niekerk of the National Party, and combined his responsibilities for the Departments of Agriculture and Land Affairs within one ministry. Thoko Didiza replaced Hanekom as minister of agriculture and land affairs after the 1999 elections.

Since 1994, the NDA has carried through radical policies of liberalizing external and internal agricultural markets. It has ended the twenty-two statutory marketing schemes and the statutory control of the markets for sugar and vine products that lay at the heart of the cozy relations between organized agriculture and the old regime.[4] However, it has failed dismally to reorient itself toward serving a new client group, beneficiaries of the land reform program, whose needs differ from those of white commercial farmers.

In 1993, the World Bank put forward a model for a radical redistribution of 30 percent of medium- and high-quality land from large-scale white commercial farmers to 600,000 small-scale, part-time black farm households.[5] The World Bank's "model" was converted into a "target" in the 1993 Reconstruction and Development Program (RDP) of the African National Congress (ANC). Hanekom abandoned the target as fiscally and administratively unrealistic. The land redistribution program enabled approved beneficiaries to claim settlement/land allocation grants (SLAGs) of 15,000 rand (that is approximately U.S.$2,000) per household.

In its first five years, the DLA fell far short of the objectives it had set itself, let alone the ambitious targets implied in the World Bank's models.[6] The department failed to spend the modest budget that had been allocated to it, and most of that went to pay salaries rather than to purchase land.[7] An official review of the department's work described it as "a highly centralized and fragmented bureaucracy," riven by "poor race relations" and a "high black staff turnover."[8]

In 2000, under a new minister, Thoko Didiza, the ministry produced a new redistribution policy: an Integrated Programme of Land Redistribution for Agricultural Development in South Africa (IPLRAD). Its language and proposals shifted the emphasis away from the previous focus of DLA policy statements on alleviating the plight of the rural poor to the NDA's new concern to promote agricultural production and commercial farming by establishing a class of black commercial farmers. The change of direction in the DLA's policies was accompanied by a displacement of senior white staff recruited from NGOs and an exodus of senior officials of all colors, followed by bitter exchanges between Gilingwe Mayende, the new director-general of the DLA, and critics of the new policies.[9]

The new program to redistribute land to historically disadvantaged people turns the focus from poverty to race. It gives weight to the arguments for the relative economic merits of medium- and large-scale farming over smallholder farming. It brings out tensions between those who wish to promote a class of smallholder farmers and those who see this as a way of limiting the opportunities for Africans to engage in commercial farming. The thinking that underlies the new policies shows unintended continuities with the strategies of colonial government in Africa and the apartheid government in South Africa to allocate land to Africans for agricultural production. The new policies, like the previous ones, are unable to address the pressing, and diverse, demands of people in urban and rural areas for land for a variety of purposes. They do not identify or provide ways to manage the conflicts, as to guiding who is to allocate land to whom and on what terms—conflicts that may take, or threaten to take, very violent forms.

The Integration of Land Reform and Agricultural Development

IPLRAD went through a series of drafts in 2000. It finally dropped its claim to integration and became the Land Redistribution for Agricultural Development (LRAD): A Sub-Programme of the Land Redistribution Progamme.[10] The drafts were inflected in ways that reflect black aspirations to commercial success and, at the same time, the thinking of colonial and apartheid-era agricultural departments. The initial drafts of IPLRAD insisted on the department's commitment to providing farming opportunities, rather than "unsustainable handouts" for the rural poor; the program focuses explicitly on "emergent farmers," an elastic category that covers those wishing to produce for subsistence and to farm commercially on a small, medium, or large scale.[11] LRAD adds the objective of "de-congesting over-crowded former homeland areas."[12]

The initial aims of the new policy were to redistribute over twenty years 30 percent of farmland to black people, to establish black commercial farmers, and to provide appropriate mechanisms to deliver and support the new policies.[13] The focus on commercial farmers was muted to "assisting black people who want to establish small- and medium-sized farms." Subsequent drafts brought the timescale down to fifteen years and specified the transfer of 30 percent of "medium to high quality land," changed in the final version to the more explicit "commercial agricultural land [i.e., formerly 'white commercial farmland']."[14] The final drafts make it clear that *black* means "Africans, Coloreds, and Indians" and commits the department to overcome the legacy of past gender discrimination as well as racial discrimination. It also intends to facilitate "better productive use of land" by people in communal areas and promote "environmental sustainability of land and other social resources."[15]

Two main programs were distinguished in the first draft of IPLRAD.[16] The Food Safety-Net Programme was to take over where the SLAGs left off and to be raised to 20,000 rand per household. The key innovation in the first draft of IPLRAD was the Commercial Farmer Programme. This initiative was aimed at those with five or ten years' experience in agriculture and agricultural diplomas. In subsequent drafts, the two separate programs were unified through the provision for a sliding scale into a single, overarching program. Within this framework, explicit provision for these two quite different sets of beneficiaries remains.[17]

These proposals revive the World Bank's original targets—though over a longer timescale—and its suggestions for a basic grant, supplemented by a matching grant and loan.[18] The mechanism to achieve the aims of the program is a new sliding scale of state grants, which must be matched by a proportionate "own contribution" from participants—in the forms of cash and/or assets and/or labor.[19]

The grants range from 20,000 to 100,000 rand per applicant. The "own contribution" ranges from 5,000 rand at the bottom of the scale to 400,000 rand at the top (see Figure 6.1). Own contribution may consist partly or (seemingly) entirely of bank loans.[20] These may be supplemented by loans from the State Land Bank and Land Reform Credit Facility.[21] At the top end, the grants will therefore be directed toward the creditworthy, among whom earners of high salaries in urban employment are likely to be prominent. The share of own contributions to be met from the participants' own labor is restricted to a value of 5,000 rand for one year of full-time labor. In practice, the new policy will create incentives for participants to apply for lower levels of grant, where the entirety of their own contribution can be paid in labor. The DLA has acknowledged that the contribution of labor can neither be monitored nor enforced.[22]

Figure 6.1 Sliding Scale of Grants and Own Contribution

The minimum grant is 20,000 rand, requiring an own contribution of 5,000 rand. The maximum grant is 100,000 rand, requiring an own contribution of at least 400,000 rand. Between the minimum and maximum amount, a continuum of grants is available, depending on the participant's own contribution, as highlighted in the graph.

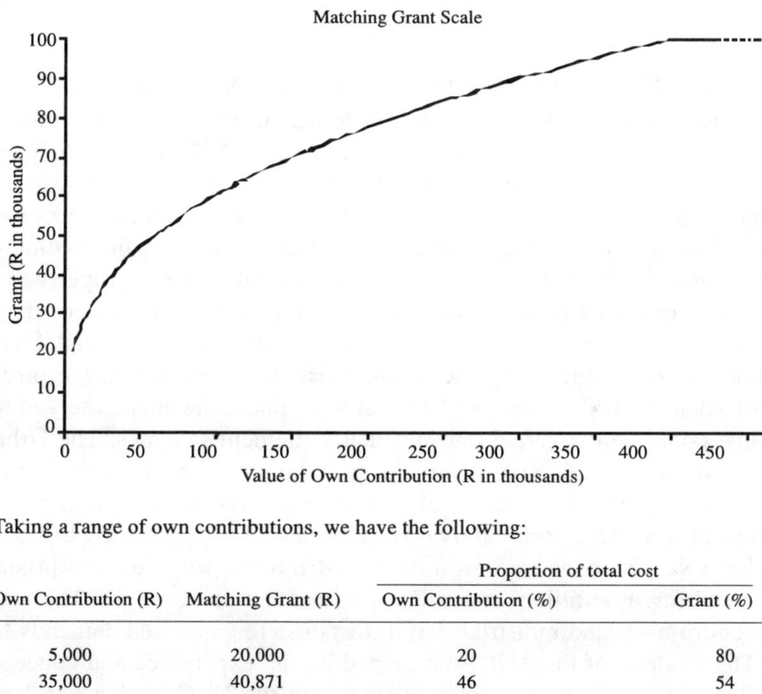

Taking a range of own contributions, we have the following:

		Proportion of total cost	
Own Contribution (R)	Matching Grant (R)	Own Contribution (%)	Grant (%)
5,000	20,000	20	80
35,000	40,871	46	54
45,000	68,888	68	32
400,000	100,000	80	20

Source: South African MALA, "An Integrated Programme for Land Redistribution and Agricultural Development in South Africa," 23 October 2000, 4.

Race alone, not means, is now the criterion of eligibility for grants. The only criteria for applicants are that they be black South Africans and that they intend to use the land for agricultural purposes and to live on it or nearby. To facilitate "graduation," recipients may acquire several grants, up to the cumulative ceiling of 100,000 rand. Assets acquired from the program, or from land restitution or the acquisition of land tenure rights, cannot subsequently be used to provide own contributions for a further claim. There is no provision for rights to land being counted as contributions.[23]

If we wish to understand the new policy, we need to identify its origins and analyze the process through which it has come into existence. We can then return to examine in more detail the proposal and its implications.

Defining Policy Agenda

Once they had released Nelson Mandela in 1990, the National Party government recognized that it could no longer sustain the segregation of land and its unequal distribution under the land acts of 1913 and 1936.[24] The 1991 land acts,[25] the associated white paper, and the 1993 Provision of Certain Land for Resettlement Act sought to find ways to broaden access to land previously reserved for whites, without "any form of redistribution of agricultural land."[26] They gave priority to individual freehold property over other forms of rights in land, while maintaining state regulation over the use and division of land in the name of conservation and commercial development.[27] Land acquired by the South African Development [formerly Native] Trust (SADT), under the 1936 act to augment the areas reserved for Africans, could be converted into planned settlement schemes. The Urban Foundation advocated "state acquisition of land for special agricultural areas for new farmers . . . on land near to cities and towns, or irrigation schemes, or near large corporately owned estates."[28]

The ANC, in response, outlined a land reform program, comprising three elements: restitution, redistribution, and tenure reform.[29] The state would coordinate land redistribution in response to expressed demands for land. The strategy of the ANC was shaped by the experience and concerns of NGOs, many of whom were affiliated with the NLC, which had been active in resisting removals and supporting communities who wished to reclaim their land.[30] The NGOs' priority was to restore or redistribute land to poor rural people. This was resisted not only by white farming and business interests and agricultural officials but also by the National African Farmers Union (NAFU), which saw the promotion of small-scale farming as "another ploy . . . to restrict blacks from the more profitable and competitive large scale farming."[31] Chiefs sought to reassert their patriarchal authority over land against the NLC's commitment to egalitarian forms, which would explicitly grant independent land rights to rural women.[32]

Enter the World Bank

In 1992, the World Bank initiated a report on the agricultural sector in South Africa.[33] Later that year, an array of "international experts," brought together by the World Bank at a conference at the Royal Swazi Sun Hotel in Mbabane, Swaziland, presented analyses of international experience for applied land reform and agricultural policy in South Africa. Hans Binswanger and Klaus Deininger of the World Bank argued that small farms were more efficient than large ones and urged the removal of the system of protection and subsidies that had sustained inefficient white farmers.[34] However, if small farmers, lacking initial capital of their own, were to pay the full interest charges on the value of land, they would be unable to sustain viable farms and an improved standard of living. Consequently, "a free land market alone will not be able to transfer land to smaller and poorer farmers, unless these are provided with grant financing in addition to or instead of mortgage financing."[35]

Binswanger and Deininger recognized that successful transfers of large-scale, mechanized commercial farms are difficult, "since there are not enough families with farming skills and implements available on these capital-intensive farms to result in the establishment of efficient small farms able to rely on low-cost family labor."[36] They require "a change in the pattern of production, subdivision of the farm and construction of complementary infrastructure."[37] Political considerations in South Africa necessitated a "major restructuring of the rural economy centered on significant land transfers and small scale production units." It was not enough "to tinker at the margin with land reform and resettlement," as "in Zimbabwe after independence."[38]

The World Bank put forward Kenya, or rather their construction of it, as the positive model for South Africa to follow.[39] Their proposals recall the proposals of the 1954 Swynnerton Report in Kenya.[40] The Kenyan land reforms of the 1950s and the plan to transfer land at independence in 1962 from white farmers to a hierarchy of African large-scale yeomen and peasant farms turned out rather differently from official intentions, and from the interpretations of World Bank economists.[41] The World Bank's proposal for South Africa, developed by Binswanger and Deininger, argued that

> Settlers should be selected based on their prior farming skills and their ability to pay for part of the land cost. They should be allowed to purchase (with credit) relatively small plots of land, to which the successful ones could add via rental or additional purchases. Unsuccessful settlers should be allowed to rent out or sell their land and take on off-farm employment. A settlement agency should only be responsible for very basic infrastructure. Extension and marketing must be organized for the settlement areas. . . .
>
> The above argument implies that settlement schemes will not directly benefit the poorest, who lack the skills and capital resources to be successful. Since infrastructure suited to small farm-cultivation would have to be established and the ensuing path of agricultural development would

> be more labor-intensive, they would, however, be able to derive considerable indirect benefits as tenants or workers.[42]

The South Africans to whom these lessons were directed were offended by the patronizing attitude of the international experts who lectured them. The exclusion of the poorest people from the direct benefits of land reform was contrary to the mood of the time. ANC supporters and civil society organizations involved in rural people's struggles for land expected that the transition to democracy would establish an ANC-led government, which would prioritize the redistribution of both resources and opportunities to the poorest South Africans. However, the ANC did not have well-developed proposals for land reform, nor did they have experience in agricultural policy. Advice and expertise were needed.

In 1993, the Land and Agricultural Policy Centre (LAPC) was set up with donor funds. The LAPC and the World Bank drew South Africans of various persuasions into the process of drafting policy documents for which the Bank and the LAPC set the terms of reference. In 1993, Binswanger and Deininger modified their earlier proposals to allow communities, not only individuals, to acquire land, and they suggested the introduction of vouchers to buy land, which would be "targeted to the poor . . . to avoid having the scheme benefit the middle class, bureaucrats and tribal chiefs."[43]

Options for Land Reform

Hans Binswanger and Robert Christiansen presented the World Bank's "Options for Land Reform and Rural Restructuring in South Africa" to the LAPC "Land Redistribution Options" conference in September 1993.[44] The document explicitly declared "its guiding principle" to be "political and economic liberalization."[45] The World Bank economists linked agricultural policies to land reforms. There was a clear institutional and ideological separation between the South Africans preparing papers on agricultural policies and those working on land issues. These differences in perspective would be repeated in the divisions between the DLA and the NDA after 1994.

The World Bank's "Options" recognized the central tension "between the *desire to address welfare objectives* through the redistribution of land and the *need to promote the productive use of agricultural land*."[46] In setting the terms of reference for the conference, the World Bank made provision for groups willing to "commit some of their own resources to part- or full-time farming" to "gain access to land . . . using a combination of own resources [*sic*], loans and a matching grant."[47] As the program "was neither intended to nor able to meet the legitimate welfare needs of the entire population," an assessment would have to be made of "Rural Social 'Safety Net Requirements.'"[48] "Options" therefore suggested "a basic grant scheme" "at a level sufficient to pay for a major share of a rural housing site" to meet welfare aims—5,000 rand was suggested. For those who would "use land in a productive manner," an additional grant could be provided, to match the beneficiaries' own contribution, and augmented by a loan.[49] A rural public-works program would create economic infrastructure and provide rural employment. "Options" discussed a variety of criteria for selecting beneficiaries. It did not ask whether workers currently resident on farms might have some prior claim to the farm over settlers.[50]

The World Bank's "Options" paper argued specifically that the constitution should allow the state to acquire land for redistribution. It suggested that district land committees, separate from elected district councils, should compile land records, document land claims, and administer applications for land redistribution. If insufficient land became available for redistribution, these committees would also be able to recommend expropriation.[51] As with the ANC's 1992 proposals, the process would be "demand-led." Demand would be determined by the market, enhanced by state grants to beneficiaries and reserve powers of expropriation.

"Options" outlined a model in which 30 percent of white-owned medium- to high-quality land would be transferred to 600,000 black households within five years. Its cost would be "surprisingly small,"[52] 3.5 billion rand per annum, of which less than 10 percent would be spent on administration. The World Bank's model, converted into a target in the ANC's RDP in 1993, was abandoned by Derek Hanekom in 1995 as fiscally and administratively unrealistic.

Squaring Circles

The apparent convergence of views, notably at the Land Redistribution Options conference, masked fundamental differences as to which objectives should be prioritized and which policy instruments employed.[53] These differences were exacerbated by the need to coordinate the work of institutions with different outlooks and priorities, and to reconcile the divergent objectives that land reform policies were intended to realize. The divergences centered on the priority to be given to promoting the commercially productive use of land, relative to meeting the needs of the rural poor, including rural women, and to changing the racial composition of land ownership.[54]

The DLA land reform program followed the lines initially drawn by the ANC: *restitution* of land of which people had been deprived since 1913 because of racially discriminatory laws and practices; *redistribution* of land to "poor and disadvantaged people"; and land *tenure reform*.[55] The NGOs now looked to the DLA and the LAPC for contracts to implement and to evaluate land reform projects. They were weakened by the loss of staff to the DLA and the LAPC, and into consultancies working for both, but this meant that their agendas tended to permeate these structures.[56]

Land Restitution

The complex architecture of land claims courts, supported by the Commission on the Restitution of Land Rights and provincial land claims commissioners, was created to adjudicate claims for land restitution. These included claims made by second-generation labor tenants under the Land Reform (Labour Tenants) Act. This act suffers from lack of a clear definition of "labor tenants" and amalgamates under a single heading the rather different claims of people with different farming and livestock strategies and relations to land and to wage employment.[57]

The narrative of dispossession drove much of the anti-apartheid activism on land issues and the demand that people be returned to their land.[58] Attempting such returns was not always practical or desirable.[59] It might offer rural people the prospects of yet another move to an isolated area without access to facilities and employment. Urban land, in particular, had often been transformed in ways that precluded any return to the status quo ante.

Between 1994 and 1998, land was restored to a small number of dispossessed communities. The majority of claims, urban and rural, were yet to be dealt with. The process and the achievement of reclaiming land expose divisions between rival claimants to the same land, between former owners and their tenants, and between different claims to the authority to allocate land. Some, particularly older men, may be determined to return to lost lands. Others, especially women and younger people, may prefer to stay in places where they have lived their lives and to seek financial compensation and make a living elsewhere.[60]

The department speeded up the settlement of claims, especially in urban areas, by moving from the legal process of restoring land to the administrative process of making offers of financial compensation.[61] "Standard settlement offers" of 40,000 rand per urban claim were mooted, but in practice the level of financial compensation has been made in a more flexible way, in both urban and rural settings, taking into account how the claimants were dispossessed from their land, the value of the land at the time (adjusted for market inflation), and other relevant factors. The potential costs of adjudicating and meeting these claims could easily exhaust future land reform budgets. After the first three years of restitution, fewer than ten of the 63,455 claims lodged had been settled. By mid-2000, almost 4,000 claims had been resolved.[62]

The "Review of the Land Reform Pilot Programme" suggests that, whether claims are to be met by restoration, alternative land, or compensation, they should be subject to district planning requirements.[63] In practice, land transfers are settled separately from district plans by different offices, each of which lacks adequate means to realize its own objectives.[64]

Land Rights

Land tenure reforms were intended to end racially defined forms of rights to land and at the same time to allow for different forms of tenure within which de facto rights would be protected. Problems of administering land rights, whether through traditional authorities or by recognizing individual property rights, have led the government to revert to reissuing permissions to occupy in the former homelands.[65]

Communal property associations (CPAs) and community trusts were created to allow beneficiaries of land reforms to acquire, hold, and manage property in terms of a written constitution. They are more likely to provide a fictive legal framework behind which political entrepreneurs, civic organizations, or traditional authorities control the allocation of resources rather than an effective mechanism for holding decisionmakers accountable to their communities.[66] Scholars have observed a process of "privatization" of land allocation by land administrators in the Tribal Authorities in KwaZulu-Natal, subsequently extended to land redistributed under the land reform program.[67] The process of compiling lists of members of "communities" making claims conferred claims on those included, hence the concern of their spokesmen to keep the lists under their own control rather than make them available to state officials.[68]

A new Land Rights Bill was drafted in 1999. It was framed in terms of the constitutional requirement that the state enact legislation of general application to protect and secure tenure rights.[69] This aimed to vest rights in the people—women and men—who occupy, use, or have access to the land, not in institutions such as traditional authorities or municipalities. The bill would protect those who had established occupation, use, or access rights and would be implemented by land rights officers employed by the DLA and advised by local land-rights boards.[70] Key issues remained. How to secure, or to compensate for, the overlapping rights of landowners and of tenants, who may have been allowed to use land for specific purposes? How to adjudicate competing claims to the same rights, especially in areas opened for occupation by land reforms? How to facilitate and allocate the benefits arising from external investment in a community's land? How to adapt tenure rules to changing circumstances? Above all, who would manage rights to and allocate land held in common and decide who can succeed to rights to use land?[71]

The Extension of Security of Tenure Act of 1997 (ESTA) was designed to protect workers and other occupiers against arbitrary eviction. It aims to give occupiers rights to their own land, either on the farm or off it, through the government housing subsidy program or through grants under the land reform policy. It also gives occupancy rights to former or current farmworkers resident on land acquired by the SADT or available for acquisition for land reform purposes.[72] The prospect of the act, like the Land Reform (Labour Tenants) Act of 1996, prompted evictions it was designed to prevent. ESTA discourages farmers from building, providing, or improving housing on their farms for employees. Police and magistrates have not treated illegal evictions with the severity required in a criminal matter.[73] Local governments have largely failed to provide the "suitable alternative accommodation" required by the act for occupiers evicted in accordance with ESTA procedures, resulting in the growth of poor informal settlements on the edges of commercial farming areas and around rural towns.[74]

Donna Hornby shows how inadequate government staff resources are to perform the complex tasks of dealing with the many ill-defined claims of labor tenants to land rights and protection from eviction.[75] The DLA is currently in breach of the Land Reform (Labour Tenants) Act for failing to process immediately the claims of those who have registered as labor tenants and may face eviction under other legislation, without due recognition of their rights in terms of this act.[76]

Land Redistribution

The policy of land redistribution is formally a market-based process, relying on sales between willing buyers and willing sellers funded by state grants. "Communities" articulate their claims in a language very different from the discourse of market exchange.[77] They pursue these claims through the state-managed process of making grants to "beneficiary" households in accordance with "business plans" designed to demonstrate the commercial viability of the project. The plans are often far removed from the diverse aims of the members of the communities, who differ from one another in their age, gender, sources of income, and in their possession of cattle and other assets.

The DLA provided that households earning less than 1,500 rand per month were eligible to apply for a settlement/land allocation grant of 15,000 rand. The grant was pegged to the state housing grant, and applicants were allowed to apply for only one of the two grants. The SLAGs were subsequently raised to 16,500 rand, 1,000 less than the increase in housing grants. In this way, the DLA sought, with a single grant, to realize the twin aims of providing rural housing and opportunities to farm. SLAG applications were to include a business plan. Settlement planning grants could pay for the services of a planner. The cost of land relative to the size of the grants encouraged the hasty constitution of communities, often of over 100 households, to purchase farms. Beneficiaries were generally unable or unwilling to commit their own resources to the project. This has been named the "rent-a-crowd" syndrome. Little money is left to buy farm implements or build houses, and the land is either occupied by only a few of the families listed on the grant application or becomes another crowded settlement similar to those established by the apartheid regime.[78]

In February 1994, the NLC convened the Community Land Conference (CLC), which brought together more than 700 representatives of 357 black rural communities. The CLC adopted a land charter, which demanded that the state expropriate land and deliver it to dispossessed communities. It called for women to have equal rights in land with men and to be represented equally in community decisionmaking bodies.[79]

The DLA called the National Conference on Land Policy in 1995 to bring representatives of black rural communities and white farming interests into accord with its thinking, as reflected in the department's "Draft Land Policy Principles."[80] As at the CLC, community representatives opposed the exclusion of claims for dispossession before 1913, called for the constitutional clause protecting property rights to be scrapped, and pointed out that the SLAG was too low.[81]

The RDP allocated 35 rand each to land reform pilot projects (LRPPs), one in each province. Whereas agriculture is primarily a provincial responsibility, land reform was a national competency, directed centrally by the DLA through its own officials in the nine provinces and the districts in which the projects were situated. Private planning agencies took on a large share of the projects' implementation because of the lack of planning capacity at the district level.[82] LRPPs could involve officials from the DLA, from provincial (and national) departments of agriculture, land claims commissioners, white farmers, agricultural unions, planning consultants, the NGOs, community-based organizations (CBOs), traditional authorities, and claimants to land. They each have their own interests, jurisdictions, forms of authority, and accountability. It has proved difficult to coordinate their activities and complete the transfer of land.[83]

Pilot projects were chosen to include districts "faced with land-related issues of the greatest complexity and urgency."[84] By mid-1997, pilot projects had been completed and land transfers registered only in KwaZulu-Natal, Eastern Cape, and Mpumalamga; Free State had also completed several nonpilot projects.[85] A pilot project in the Northern Province was confronted by local opposition from the rural poor.[86] LRPPs adopted diverse strategies to meet the varied conditions in their districts. The Northern Cape and the Free State gave poor rural people access to municipal commonage to graze stock.[87] In KwaZulu-Natal, the Association for Rural Advancement, the provincial agricultural union, and the DLA set up a tripartite arrangement to deal with conflicts regarding security of tenure and labor tenancy rights.[88]

In KwaZulu-Natal, the provincial office of the DLA found itself confronting conflicts between and within communities as to whose claims to land available for redistribution would be recognized and who would exercise authority over the land once it had been transferred.[89] Scott Drimie shows how and why land at Impendle, Natal, which the SADT had acquired before 1994, was not transferred to any of the rival beneficiaries. Chiefs and their followers in neighboring areas, former labor tenants, people evicted from "black spots," aspirant commercial farmers, and conservation officials all either lived on or laid claim to one or more farms. The moral and legal claims invoked arose from different laws and policy objectives (restitution and redistribution, reform of labor tenancy and protection of security of tenure, nature conservation). Without any resolution to the issue of who had what sort of right to land tenure, no redistribution of land could take place. Drimie argues that the DLA's ability to hold the ring among contending claimants without transferring land may be counted a success in the volatile political context of the Natal Midlands.[90]

In the Eastern Cape in the 1990s, various groups occupied land, including state land and white farms adjacent to the Ciskei, thereby constructing their own patronage networks and aligning, often uneasily, with local, provincial, and national political organizations and state institutions. Residents' and civic associations found themselves exercising state functions without the means to secure order or impose their authority. Even the ANC could not resolve competing claims, as it sought to ensure its support from groups with conflicting objectives and different principles.[91]

In the Western Cape in particular, farmers and agribusiness companies have used grants to fund the acquisition of shares in farm enterprises by workers' trusts. These schemes circumvent the problems of delayed returns on the high costs of land and of establishing vineyards and orchards. They can enable workers to share in the returns from marketing fruit and making wine and not only from growing grapes and other fruit. They depend on the use of the farmers' or the company's capital, equipment, skills, and access to markets and must therefore fit in with the farmers' objectives. They may enable employers to acquire additional land and water resources, as well as capital for the enterprise, and to raise productivity by restructuring incentives. Ownership of shares in the enterprise has not contributed sufficiently to changed power relations between employers and employees. Nor has it necessarily produced tangible financial benefits: in the deciduous fruit industry, falling international prices have deprived workers of dividends and caused the values of their shares, which are locked into their employment, to collapse.[92] SLAGs can also be used to meet housing costs. In this way, SLAGs replace the subsidies that the previous government gave farmers to build farm housing. Since the passage of ESTA in 1997, it suits farmers if workers are housed on their own land rather than, as in the past, tied to farm housing.

Most "equity-share" schemes were initiated by farmers or by firms, who retain direction of financial management. Some looked to funds from land reform grants to find ways out of their financial difficulties.[93] As there are no independent smallholders, such as there would be in contract farming schemes, these equity-share schemes "do not look like land reforms" but the "vision of independent small-scale production" may be "inappropriate in high-value horticulture."[94]

Outgrower schemes, alongside established estates, might offer a way of integrating small-scale producers into international markets. This strategy has been successful in other industries, such as Kenyan tea production or small-scale cane growing in Natal,[95] where smallholder producers sell the high-value products to a monopsony processor and can earn a better return from their labor than local alternatives. These schemes do not, however, overcome the problem of high establishment costs for orchards and vineyards; nor do they enable producers to share in the generally more profitable returns from processing and marketing.[96]

The Contradictions of Land Reform

There is an obvious tension between the aims of providing resources to the rural poor and encouraging commercial production, whether by the emerging farmers favored by the NDA or by the smallholders envisaged in the World Bank's model. The first priority for most people wanting land is to acquire residential sites and gardens (from which they may produce for sale) before grazing for stock and arable land.[97] Poor, and not so poor, people who acquire land will use it for several purposes and combine it with other sources of income and security. These multifaceted and adaptive strategies have fitted badly with the business plans required for grants.[98]

The SLAG offered the majority of potential beneficiaries little scope for expanding agricultural production on their own and encouraged purchases by communities who have lacked the resources or capacity to farm effectively the land they have acquired. Viewed in this way, land reform appears to be a form of welfare provision and is seen as a cost to be minimized rather than an investment in future production. Unsurprisingly, government allocated few funds to it—and the DLA found it difficult to spend them on acquiring and transferring land.[99] Most of its budget was spent on salaries rather than on grants for purchasing land.

The DLA gave explicit priority to the marginalized and, in particular, to the needs of women. In practice, the demand-led nature of land reform has meant that benefits are more likely to be claimed by those with "literacy, money, transport, political contacts and the ability to submit and continue pressing their claims."[100] Local "dynamics of social differentiation, resources access and political contestation"[101] are more likely to decide who gets what, when, and how, than the rules set out by the DLA. Beneficiaries of land, as in the former bantustans, have been drawn disproportionately from those groups able to pay for land, farming activities, and finance from salaries or commercial activities.[102]

The structures for allocating land formed an extended hierarchy of patron-client relations from the DLA and provincial officials via NGOs to CBOs to rural people seeking grants to acquire land. An alternative route goes through farmers and facilitators to farmworkers, to enable them to pay for housing, buy land, and acquire equity in the farm business. Claims for restitution and redistribution of land validate the authority of those who speak and act on behalf of their communities—largely men. They act as brokers between rural people and outside institutions and can charge fees to outsiders seeking land. Communal property arrangements may meet the formal requirements for transferring land but are out of line with the informal, hierarchical, and gendered networks through which common property will be managed or allocated.

Demand for land is most intense along the borders of the former bantustans, where farmers increasingly find it difficult to protect their fences, their stock, and their own and their families' lives, and to resist the encroachment of people and cattle on their land.[103] Over the seven years up to November 2000, more than 930 white farmers have been murdered.[104] Many farmers look to the government to buy them out, as the previous regime did when it consolidated the territories of the bantustans. Claims are shaped by the availability of land for sale rather than by the purpose to which claimants might put the land they acquire.[105] Because these areas are in high demand from land reform applicants, the price of land acquired for redistribution is inflated.[106] As in several other respects, a policy designed to reverse the patterns of the past continues to extend features of previous practices.

The three pillars of land restitution, land rights, and land redistribution are, in practice, not separate from one another. Nor are they necessarily compatible with one another, or with other legislation to secure rights for rural people, such as ESTA or the Land Reform (Labour Tenants) Act.

Going Back to the Beginning

The evident shortcomings of the DLA's plans to reform land redistribution and the appointment of a new minister of agriculture and land affairs in 1999 made the Review of the Land Reform Programme, produced in draft for the DLA and external donors on 27 September 1999, particularly timely. It built on the work, and went beyond the recommendations, of the 1997 midterm review and provided a basis for bringing current arrangements and policies into question and opening the way for new initiatives.

Reviewing Reforms

The first two chapters of the 1999 review identified key flaws in the land reform program. A longer third chapter focused on the structure and procedures of the DLA itself. This chapter identified racial tensions common to other government departments and institutions and lack of information on the DLA's expenditure, activities, and outcomes. Its financial management system "was designed for use in centralized government departments"[107] and was unsuitable for facilitating activities carried out at provincial and district levels. The implementation of policies depended on the institutions that carried them out. Requiring the DLA to bring its practices into line with managerial discourses may not be sufficient to ensure its effectiveness in carrying out its policies.

The 1999 review identified the key problems of the land-restitution policy in its "largely-legal and rights-driven process."[108] Similarly, the redistribution process suffers from

> its application basis, which required applicants to apply for particular pieces of land, often without reference to need, available infrastructure or provincial or municipal planning. Second is the "grant-based approach" and the size of the grant. This is insufficient to generate a livelihood. . . . It has also encouraged large groups to apply for land to make up the price. This is the fundamental problem from which most other problems (after-care, reproduction of poverty, etc.) stem.[109]

The review further questioned the capacity of Community Trusts and Communal Property Associations "to hold and manage land."[110] This undermines the three pillars of the land reform policy fairly conclusively.

The difficulties of getting support from other organs of government, at the national, provincial, and district level led the provincial offices of the DLA to accumulate functions, despite its attempts to form cooperative relations with the provincial departments of agriculture and district councils.[111]

The review therefore advocated a reversal of policy from a demand-led to a supply-side approach. The state could make land available to eligible beneficiaries. This would be implemented as part of a coherent, interdepartmental rural development policy, within which the DLA would concentrate on its core activities rather than try to solve all the related problems itself. Claims for restitution, and whether they are to be met by restoration, alternative land, or compensation, should be subject to district planning requirements.[112] The large, centralized bureaucracy in Pretoria should be reduced in favor of a district planning approach, in which "in theory at least" local development activity is coordinated through "developmental local government."[113] Theory may be a poor guide to the limited capacity of rural district councils to plan and implement complex land reform projects.

The review insisted that government should decide how much it is willing to spend to meet restitution claims and insulate other land reform programs from spending on restitution. It emphasized the urgent need to establish an effective and flexible policy to define and recognize individual and group rights to land.[114]

The review recommended, without extensive discussion, that the DLA should clearly differentiate between different "products" for different beneficiaries. These products are, first, the promotion of medium- and large-scale black commercial farmers, as advocated in provincial and national departments of agriculture. This is a key element for the growth of commercial agricultural. Second, there is the promotion of small-scale farming enterprises, which combine commercial production with other sources of livelihood, as in the outgrower schemes for sugar and timber. Third, there is the acquisition of land for commercial or semicommercial purposes other than agriculture, specifically ecotourism; mining; and small, medium, and micro enterprises. Fourth, there is accommodation of the needs for settlement of the very poor, who are at the center of DLA discourse but have gained little from its practice.[115] The problems identified by the review are clearly inherited from the apartheid era. There are also continuities in the policies that the review recommends to deal with this heritage.

Land Reform in Historical and Comparative Perspectives

The 1913 Natives Land Act reserved 7 percent of South Africa's land for "native reserves" and prohibited Africans from buying land elsewhere. The issue of the augmentation of the reserves was unresolved until the 1936 Native Trust and Land Act made provision for the acquisition of additional land by the Native Trust (later the South African Development Trust). This would raise the area of the reserves to 13.6 percent, a process that had not been completed by 1991. In the border region of the Eastern Cape, purchases of white-owned land for transfer to Africans to consolidate the boundaries of the Ciskei bantustan increased the land area set aside for African occupation.[116] The SADT continued to transfer land to homeland governments, even after the 1991 land acts.

The government evicted African communities from areas designated for white ownership. In this, it was only partially successful in the face of resistance by local communities and the strength of the historic land rights of Africans to freehold or quitrent titles.[117] Farmworkers and farm tenants were forcibly removed, mainly to "closer settlements" in the bantustans.[118] Labor tenancy survived its legal abolition in parts of KwaZulu-Natal because it allowed African producers a place to live and to keep stock, albeit on steadily worsening terms.[119] African farmers in the reserves were directed to separate residential, arable, grazing, and woodland areas in accordance with the requirements of "betterment" schemes, which—as in colonial east and central Africa—reduced their capacity to grow crops or keep stock and provoked rural resistance.[120] The Tomlinson Commission was set up to report on the socioeconomic development of the "Bantu areas." It proposed to grant freehold title in the South African reserves to a class of full-time farmers on "economic farm units" (*vollebestaans-boerderyeenhede*), with a target income of £60 per annum.[121] This would displace half the rural population. The government rejected this plan to make half the population of the reserves landless. Betterment continued—as part of a policy of settling even more people into the reserves.

Some of the land acquired under the 1936 act was made available to displaced communities or to tenants of land held by Africans, or to meet the expanding claims of the next generation. Local political authority is closely linked to the capacity to allocate land to outsiders for funds and following. Luvuyo Wotshela's study of the politics of land in the border region reveals the interaction of the politics of chieftaincy, church, class, and land within communities. He shows how regional NGOs and national political organizations were drawn into the local politics of land and patronage in conflict with the government of the Ciskeian bantustan.[122]

In the bantustans, politically connected traders and civil servants acquired some large farms. Resident farmworkers lost their livelihoods without the benefit of the compensation paid to landowners. The SADT leased much of the land it acquired to white farmers for grazing.

After 1987, the Development Bank of Southern Africa (DBSA) directed agricultural development in the bantustans away from large-scale farms and settlement to farmer support programs (FSPs). The DBSA distinguished between three categories of farmers: "commercial farmers," "emergent farmers" and "(sub-)subsistence" farmers, echoing the tripartite categories of colonial planners in Kenya. It focused on the supply of inputs, including machinery, extension, credit, and marketing services. Most FSPs were successors to failed settlement projects. Their clients were former farmworkers, labor tenants, and residents of reserves, who brought with them different experiences, skills, resources, and objectives. Farmers participated in FSPs to get access to credit and inputs but found themselves without the money to repay their debts. Project recommendations and technologies were often inappropriate. Two projects were successful in that they enabled farmers, mainly women in one instance, to increase maize production for their own consumption. In several cases, FSP farmers were more likely than others to use inputs and to achieve higher yields and incomes, but these were the groups for whom the program had been designed in the first place. In two cases, farmers who did not participate in the FSP were more successful than those who did. Hardly any commercial farmers emerged from the process.[123]

After 1994, the Department of Agriculture initiated the Broadening Access to Agriculture Thrust to extend services to "previously disadvantaged farmers."[124] This built on the assumptions of the FSP, to which they added a graduation farmer support scheme, replicating colonial strategy in Southern Rhodesia (Zimbabwe). The department failed to get the program off the ground and abandoned it in 1998.[125] Ironically, its approach and objectives are central to the focus of the new strategy of providing support for "emergent" farmers.

In 1998, the DLA acquired three farms in the Northern Province for redistribution to the Monyamane Farmers Association, a CPA of 201 members. The business plans expected them to manage it as a purely commercial, as opposed to subsistence, enterprise, raising pedigree livestock, and employing only wage labor, ignoring the members' own cattle and labor and the issues of how to manage the farm collectively.[126]

In KwaZulu-Natal, outgrower schemes allowed men and women to enter into cane production on land held in small parcels in customary tenure under the direction of milling companies. Credit and extension services facilitated expansion of cane growing, but the recovery of credit from the sale price created tensions between growers and millers, and extension services were often neither timely nor appropriate. Income from cane supplemented remittances from migrants and pensions and was spent predominantly on education, housing, and consumer durables. In KaNgwane, dispossession of people to make way for state plantations made it possible for cane farmers to be established on "economically-viable units," each employing on average three laborers, at the expense of excluding their neighbors from access to land. Tomlinson's recommendations had at last come into their own.[127] Outgrower schemes made a significant impact on production and incomes in cane-growing areas and allowed millers to increase their cane supply. Agricultural development programs proved to be most successful when they involved a commitment from agro-industry and fitted in with the industry's needs.

The Ironies of the New

The DLA's new strategy initially envisaged a hierarchy of black farmers who were characterized as "subsistence," "semi-commercial," "pre-commercial," and "commercial." "Broadly aimed interventions" should "assist large numbers of people" at the subsistence level. "More focused interventions" would "seek to move particularly promising and desiring candidates from one level to the next" (i.e., from subsistence to commercial production). "Commercial farmers tend to be—but are not necessarily—larger, and are more likely to consider farming to be their *full-time* occupation. Subsistence farmers . . . tend to be small, and treat agriculture as a subsidiary activity to support the household."[128] The chain of progress is thus one of increasing scale, commercialization of inputs and outputs, and commitment to full-time farming.

According to the initial drafts, Food Safety-Net projects "aim to provide households with individual resource bases, especially where arable land is concerned."[129] Farms would usually be acquired by a group, or "tribe," or by state purchases of blocks of land for communities and subdivided among or allocated to its members under individual, sectional, group, or "tribal" title. The later drafts simply refer, under this heading, to beneficiaries acquiring land for food-crop or livestock production to improve household food security, either on an individual or a group basis. The DLA would allow groups to acquire land and subdivide it but, after the experience of rent-a-crowd projects, would discourage group production.[130] Initially, grants for equity schemes, in which employees can become co-owners of the farms on which they work, were also to be limited to 20,000 rand, but, under the new proposal to integrate all grants within a sliding scale, these limits disappeared.[131]

At a workshop on 25 February, 2000, the minister stressed that municipal commonage should allow the emergent farmers easy access to the commercial grants for black commercial farmers.[132] A draft document proposed that "the Commonage Product" be bifurcated to allow municipal commonage to be leased on a communal basis for subsistence purposes and individually to emergent farmers.[133] The final drafts left municipal and tribal commonage projects—one low-cost and effective manner in which the previous land reform program was able to contribute to poverty alleviation—outside LRAD. Similarly, projects oriented toward housing and settlement and supporting a range of productive and income-generating activities rather than agricultural production alone would be separate from LRAD; grants for the acquisition of land could not be used to acquire "housing top-structure."[134]

Transferring Land

The first priority of the DLA would be to dispose of state land "to unlock the economic potential of rural communities whilst simultaneously addressing current inequalities in access to commercial agriculture by black farmers."[135] However, land would still have to be paid for. The state would advertise land for disposal to enable beneficiaries to bid for the land and secure grants to finance their purchases.[136] Hitherto, the Departments of Defence and Public Works, as well as the Department of Agriculture and agricultural parastatals have been very reluctant to release land for redistribution.[137]

The disposal of state land was originally envisaged as part of a proactive strategy, encompassing public and private land. The DLA would contract with a firm to create a database of available land. Planning grants of up to 15 percent of total project costs might be paid to "design agents" on approval of the project.[138] Farmers and developers might subdivide large plots for sale under the program. Approval would be devolved to the provincial land officials. Local officials would identify land, confirm the seller's title and provide technical advice on the proposed farm plan and use of land and its impact on the environment. Professional valuers would confirm that the price was comparable to recent sales in the area, and estate agents would handle the transfer. Department of Agriculture officials would be trained to advise beneficiaries before and after the land was transferred.[139] The outsourcing of these administrative tasks is designed to hasten decisions and save money. It may not prove profitable within the limited budgets available.

Although the new policy makes reference to a wide range of beneficiaries, these procedures define the profile of its preferred applicants:

> They select the chosen amount of the grant, engage a design agent if required, identify available land, enter into a contingent contract with the seller, apply for a normal bank loan through standard banking procedures, if necessary, engage a transfer agent, prepare a farm plan, submit all documentation to the local agricultural officer for an opinion, assemble the completed proposal package, and submit it to the provincial grants committee.[140]

The transfer of state land, as well as private land, to black commercial farmers may dispossess workers or tenants currently occupying that land. This would conflict with rights created by the Extension of Security of

Tenure Act and the Interim Protection of Informal Land Rights Acts.[141] The final version of the new policy recognizes, at last, that

> frequently, farm workers or former farm workers may be residing on the land being contemplated for purchase. The interests of these existing residents must be borne in mind. A number of different solutions are possible, including accommodating them within the group of applicants, and assisting them to apply for separate tenure security grants.[142]

They clearly have no prior claim to the land on which they live and work.

The program does not, despite its name, make provision for agricultural development or specify how it can be oriented to the needs of small-scale producers and beneficiaries of land reform. State and private-sector extension services are presumably expected to provide for black commercial farmers as they have always provided for whites.[143]

Traditional leaders have vehemently opposed any measures that would undermine their authority to allocate land.[144] The new minister, Thoko Didiza, withdrew the Land Rights Bill in 1999 for further revision. She originally intended to transfer state land held in trust (i.e., land held under communal tenure and, presumably, acquired by the former SADT) to ownership by "tribes," later glossed as "traditional authorities" or "African traditional communities."[145] These provisions are absent from the final drafts.[146] The minister planned to replace permissions to occupy by introducing new regulations for the administration of land in the former bantustans and SADT areas, after consultation with traditional leaders.[147] IPLRAD's initial drafts provided, rather implausibly, for people to buy sectional title to land they already held under communal tenure.[148] The final drafts refer to existing laws designed to protect tenure security and to the opportunities that LRAD offers to those who have regained tenure rights or lack secure tenure rights, but they make no mention of any replacement for the Land Rights Bill.[149] A draft Communal Land Rights Bill was released in November 2001 and is unlikely to be promulgated before 2003. The state has yet to fulfill its constitutional obligation.

The Interim Protection of Informal Land Rights Act of 1996 was intended to provide immediate protection to occupiers of land, pending legislation to define and secure land rights. It was due to lapse on 31 December 2000 but, in the absence of a Land Rights Act, was renewed for another year to avert a situation in which the DLA would be in violation of its constitutional obligation to provide security of tenure.

The final drafts do secure gender equality in one way, by allowing "adult individuals" "to apply for grants in their own right, rather than as members of households."[150] This will facilitate grants for women-only projects. It may also enable households to maximize benefits by aggregating the grants to individuals and to expand the claims made on the budget for redistribution.[151] Further, at least "one third of the transferred land must accrue to women."[152] How this is to be achieved and what this means in practice, and across generations, is not clear.

Policies, Plans, and Outcomes

The conceptions underlying the new strategies recall the Kenyan land reform, on which the World Bank modeled its proposals for South Africa. This distinguished between "commercial," "yeomen," and "peasant" farmers, all above "subsistence" level. The proposal is unrealistic in assuming that there is a definite relation between scale, commercialization, and full-time farming. For example, producers with access to small areas of irrigated land and markets for their produce may well grow vegetables intensively and buy their staple food. The most successful commercial farmers often draw on past or present earnings from salaries or business activities. The strategy wrongly assumes that there is a smooth progression up the scale rather than a multiplicity of optimal combinations of skills, money, and material resources. These are appropriate to different crops under different conditions, for people with different endowments of assets and capabilities and with no direct path connecting one with another. One reason for the failure of policies to promote yeomen farmers in Kenya was that they operated on a scale too large to manage family-labor-based smallholdings and too small to enjoy the economies of scale of large owner-managed capitalist farms.[153]

The minister presented the final draft of the new strategy to an Indaba (meeting) on 6–7 November 2000,[154] eighteen months after a moratorium on new land redistribution projects and in the face of outcries in the press about the abandonment of the poor. She was pleased that the plan had been debated so widely; the task at hand was to implement it. Land reform would address the needs both of the landless and of potential entrepreneurs, who would contribute to economic growth. The Indaba and, by implication, the policy was concerned with the latter. Invited participants from black and white commercial agriculture, financial institutions, agribusiness, NGOs and trade unions, and uninvited rural communities were divided about policies and priorities. NAFU looked to the state to make state and private land available to African farmers, and called for expropriation of private land, to the alarm of Agriculture SA, which represented commercial farmers. The NLC wanted government to acquire and allocate land in a proactive approach, but it did not regard expropriation as its first option. They all complained about the department's lack of genuine consultation on the new policies they were being asked to implement.

The ministry may well be fatally underestimating the political imperative and economic viability of providing land for subsistence and nonagricultural purposes. Land invasions continue, and violent attacks on white farmers are becoming more and more frequent. Community lobbies are mobilizing for non-market-based land reforms in several provinces. These developments may indicate a realization that state policy does not offer a route to acquiring land for the majority of rural South Africans.

The department has made changes to each subsequent draft of the policy. These have been largely cosmetic, addressing the barrage of criticism while retaining intact the priority to commit resources to altering the racial profile of the commercial agricultural sector, which is itself in crisis. The aims and mechanisms of the policy have stayed the same. As in 1994, the new policy combines a change in discourse with institutional continuities and a return to strategies that have been tried and tested and have often failed elsewhere or in the past.

No definite conclusions can be drawn from experiences elsewhere; all other things are not equal. The failures of land reform thus far in South Africa give reason for adopting a different approach from those tried by the old regime or put forward by colonial planners in Kenya. Those examples suggest that it may prove difficult and expensive to foster and sustain a successful class of semicommercial and commercial black farmers, let alone enable the former to turn themselves into the latter.[155] The new policy blueprints may fail to realize their goals, as previous plans did in colonial and postcolonial Kenya and in the old and the new South Africa. Even if they were to succeed, in their own terms, the policies may not quell the demand for land and the social conflict associated with it.

Notes

This chapter draws on Gavin Williams, "Policies and Prospects: Land Reform in South Africa," presented at the workshop on "The Politics of Land Reform in the New South Africa," Development Studies Institute, London School of Economics, June 2000 (hereafter referred to as the DESTIN workshop); and Ruth Hall, "Contested Terrain: The Politics of Land Reform Policy in Post-Apartheid South Africa," Ph.D. thesis, University of Oxford, 1998. We are grateful to the Leverhulme Trust for a research grant provided to Gavin Williams. We are indebted to contributors to the DESTIN workshop and to Richard Johnson and Colin Murray, for comments, advice, and ideas. Gavin Williams is a Fellow of St. Peter's College, Oxford. Ruth Hall is a researcher at the Program for Land and Agrarian Studies (PLAAS) in the School of Government, University of the Western Cape; at the time of writing, she was a researcher at the Centre for Rural Legal Studies (CRLS), Stellenbosch. CRLS and PLAAS are not responsible for the views put forward in this chapter.

1. Constitution of the Republic of South Africa, Sections 25.5–25.7.
2. The Department of Development Aid was finally abolished in 1992 in the wake of revelations of extensive corruption. It was the direct successor to the

renamed Department of Native Affairs/Bantu Administration/Plural Relations/Co-operation and Development.

3. Merle Lipton, "The Politics of Rural Reform in South Africa," in *Land, Labour, and Livelihoods in Rural South Africa: Volume One: Western Cape,* ed. Michael Lipton, Mike de Klerk, and Merle Lipton (Durban, South Africa: Indicator Press, 1996), 407–409; H. Bernstein, "The Political Economy of the Maize Filière," *Journal of Peasant Studies* 23, 2 (1996).

4. G. Williams, J. Ewert, J. Hamman, and N. Vink, "Liberalising Markets and Reforming Land in South Africa," *Journal of Contemporary African Studies* 16, 1 (1998): 65–69; B. Bayley, *A Revolution in the Market: The Deregulation of South African Agriculture* (Oxford: Oxford Policy Management, 2000). For a critical view, see C. Mather, "South African Agriculture and Rural Livelihoods in the Era of Liberalisation," in *At the Crossroads: Land and Agrarian Reform in South Africa into the 21st Century*, ed. Ben Cousins (Bellville, South Africa: PLAAS; Johannesburg: NLC, 2000).

5. World Bank, "Options for Land Reform and Rural Restructuring in South Africa," Land and Agricultural Policy Centre Conference, Johannesburg, October 1993, summarized in Land Redistribution Options Conference, Johannesburg, 1994. R. van den Brink, M. de Klerk, and H. Binswanger, "Rural Livelihoods, Fiscal Costs, and Financing Options: A First Attempt at Quantifying the Implications of Redistributive Land Reform," in *Agricultural Land Reform in South Africa: Policies, Markets and Mechanisms,* ed. J. van Zyl, J. Kirsten, and H. Binswanger (Cape Town: Oxford University Press, 1996), 424.

6. South African Department of Land Affairs (DLA) figures for approvals and transfers of land from 1994 to April 2000 are cited in S. Turner and H. Ibsen, "Land and Agrarian Reform in South Africa: A Status Report," PLAAS Research Report no. 6, University of the Western Cape, Bellville, South Africa, November 2000, 17–19.

7. B. Streek, "Land Reform Underspends Budget by R1.4 Billion," *Johannesburg Mail and Guardian,* 26 May 2000. Between 1994 and 1998, the Department of Welfare and Population Development surrendered 197.7 million rand of its budget unspent.

8. McIntosh Xaba and Associates, "Review of the Land Reform Pilot Programme," draft report for the DLA, European Union, the Department for International Development, and DANIDA, 1999, 6, 38.

9. Turner and Ibsen, "Land and Agrarian Reform," 40, 46; G. Mayende, "Myth and Reality in Land Reform," *East London Daily Dispatch,* 8 August 2000, and "Didiza's Doing What She Should," *Johannesburg Mail and Guardian,* 25 August 2000; L. Cook, "Land Affairs Is Now 'a Sick Department,'" *Johannesburg Business Day,* 15 August 2000; Ben Cousins, "Didiza's Recipe for Disaster," *Johannesburg Mail and Guardian,* 18 August 2000, and "Who Will Benefit from Land Reform," *Johannesburg Mail and Guardian,* 15 September 2000.

10. Thoko Didiza, minister of land affairs, parliamentary media briefing, 11 February 2000. South African Ministry of Agriculture and Land Affairs, "An Integrated Programme of Land Redistribution and Agricultural Development in South Africa" (hereafter referred to as IPLRAD), draft framework policy document, draft 4.1, 8 May 2000; IPLRAD, proposed second draft, 15 May 2000; IPLRAD, final draft document, 8 June 2000; IPLRAD, final draft document, version 2, 23 October 2000. South African MALA, "Land Redistribution for Agricultural Development: A Sub-Programme of the Land Redistribution Progamme" (hereafter referred to as LRAD), final version 3, 6 November 2000. The "properties" of the

computer files suggest that all drafts and the final version of LRAD were written by J. F. Kirsten for a company called "World Bank."

11. Media briefing document put out by the DLA Media Conference, Durban, South Africa, 22 June 2000. The language differs but the strategy is the same in IPLRAD, 8 June 2000, 5, and 23 October 2000, 2.

12. LRAD, 1.

13. IPLRAD, 8 May 2000, 6. The minister's initial statement aimed at "redistributing at least 15% of farmland in five years to emergent black farmers" (Didiza, briefing, 2).

14. IPLRAD, 23 October 2000, 1; LRAD, 3.

15. LRAD, 3.

16. IPLRAD, 8 May 2000, 6–9.

17. LRAD, 2, 9, 10.

18. World Bank, "Options for Land Reform," 2, 35.

19. IPLRAD, 8 May 2000, 20–23; South African MALA, "The Commercial Farmer Programme: A Component of an Integrated Land Redistribution Programme of the Ministry of Agriculture and Land Affairs," draft 2.7, 10 May 2000.

20. LRAD, 4.

21. Turner and Ibsen, "Land and Agrarian Reform," 24–25.

22. LRAD, 1, 2, 4, 9; IPLRAD, 23 October 2000, 3.

23. LRAD, 4–9.

24. These were the Natives Land Act of 1913 and Natives Trust and Land Act of 1936, as amended, and renamed ("Native" was replaced, first by "Bantu" and then by "Development").

25. These are the Abolition of Racially Based Land Measures Act, the Upgrading of Land Tenure Rights Act, and the Less Formal Township Establishment Act.

26. Republic of South Africa, "White Paper on Land Reform," Pretoria, 1991, 13.

27. E. Francis and G. Williams, "The Land Question (in Kenya and South Africa)," *Canadian Journal of African Studies* 29, 3 (1993).

28. Urban Foundation, "Land Reform: An Analysis and a Challenge" and "Rural Development: Towards a New Future," *Policies for a New Urban Future* 4, Urban Foundation, Johannesburg, undated [1990], 3.

29. African National Congress, "Land Manifesto for ANC Policy Conference," endorsed final draft, Johannesburg, 1992.

30. Lipton, "Politics of Rural Reform," 420–421.

31. Ibid., 420.

32. Ibid., 426–427.

33. M. Roth, H. Dolny, and K. Wiebe, "Employment, Efficiency, and Land Markets in South Africa's Agricultural Sector: Opportunities for Land Reform," draft report for the Land Tenure Center, Madison, Wis., and the World Bank, 1992.

34. H. Binswanger and K. Deininger, "South African Land Policy: The Legacy of History and Current Options, *World Development* 21, 9 (1993). See also H. Binswanger, K. Deininger, and G. Feder, "Power, Distortions, Revolt, and Reform in Agricultural Land Relations," World Bank Working Paper Series no. 1164 (1993), in *Handbook of Development Economics*, ed. J. Behrman and T. N. Srinivasan, vol. 3 (Washington, D.C.: World Bank, 1995). For a critique of their use of evidence and analysis, see Gavin Williams, "Setting the Agenda: A Critique of the World Bank's 'Options for Land Reform and Rural Restructuring,'" *Journal of Southern African Studies* 23, 1 (1996): 146–157.

35. Binswanger and Deininger, "South African Land Policy."

36. Binswanger, Deininger, and Feder, "Power, Distortions, Revolt, and Reform," 27.

37. H. Binswanger and K. Deininger, "The Evolution of the World Bank's Land Policy," *World Bank Research Observer* 14, 2 (August 1999), 257.

38. World Bank, "South African Rural Restructuring Program," 15 June 1993, 3.

39. Binswanger and Deininger, "South African Land Policy." For a critique of their account of land reform in Kenya, see Williams, "Setting the Agenda."

40. Colony and Protectorate of Kenya, *A Plan to Intensify the Development of African Agriculture in Kenya*. The classic account of the Swynnerton Plan and its outcomes is M. J. K. Sorrenson, *Land Reform in the Kikuyu Country* (Nairobi: Oxford University Press, 1967).

41. E. Francis, *Making a Living: Changing Livelihoods in Rural Africa* (London: Routledge, 2000), 1–17; C. Leo, *Land and Class in Kenya*, (Toronto: University of Toronto Press, 1984); Francis and Williams, "Land Question"; Williams, "Setting the Agenda."

42. H. Binswanger and K. Deininger, "Are Large Farms More Efficient Than Small Ones? Government Intervention, Large-Scale Agriculture and Resettlement in Kenya and Zimbabwe," World Bank conference, Mbabane, Swaziland, November 1992. "South African Land Policy," is a modified version of this paper.

43. Binswanger and Deininger, "South African Land Policy," 1467.

44. The conference papers are summarized in LAPC, *Proceedings: Land Redistribution Options Conference* (Johannesburg: LAPC, 1994), and some are published in Johan van Zyl, Johann Kirsten, and Hans P. Binswanger, eds., *Agricultural Land Reform in South Africa: Policies, Markets, and Mechanisms* (Cape Town: Oxford University Press, 1996). The first version of Williams, "Setting the Agenda," was an invited (licensed?) critique produced for the conference.

45. World Bank, "Options for Land Reform," 1, 11.

46. Ibid., 2, 34. Emphasis in original.

47. World Bank, "South African Rural Restructuring Program," 3.

48. Ibid., 10.

49. World Bank, "Options for Land Reform," 2, 34.

50. Rosalie Kingwill, James Putzel, participant details/briefings, "The Politics of Land Reform," DESTIN workshop, 7 June 2000.

51. World Bank, "Options for Land Reform," 49 and in Annex 4: Costings; World Bank, "Rural Restructuring Program," 11.

52. World Bank, "Options for Land Reform," 3, 63. The assumptions and arithmetic on which the model is based are criticized as unrealistic in Williams, "Setting the Agenda," 161–163.

53. Hall, "Contested Terrain," 24.

54. South African DLA "Mid-Term Review of the Pilot Land Programme," report in association with the DANIDA, the European Commission and DFID, 24 September 1997, p. 10.

55. South African DLA, "White Paper on South African Land Policy," Pretoria, 1997.

56. Hall, "Contested Terrain," 29.

57. Donna Hornby, "All We Need Is a Piece of Land," report for the National Land Committee Investigation into Labour Tenancy, March 1998; Gavin Williams, "Transforming Labour Tenants," in *Land, Labour, and Livelihoods in Rural South*

Africa, Volume Two: KwaZulu-Natal and Northern Province, ed. Michael Lipton, Frank Ellis, and Merle Lipton (Durban, South Africa: Indicator Press, 1996).

58. C. Walker "Relocating Restitution," *Transformation* 44 (2000).

59. Richard Levin, "Towards a National Implementation Strategy for Land Redistribution," and Andries du Toit, "The End of Restitution: Getting Real About Land Claims," in Cousins, *At the Crossroads*.

60. McIntosh Xaba, "Review," 12–13; Catherine Cross et al., "Making a Living Under Land Reform," and Richard Levin, "Politics and Land Reform in the Northern Province: A Case Study of the Mojapelo Land Claim," in Lipton et al., *Land, Labour, and Livelihoods, Volume Two;* Andries du Toit, "Piloting Land Redistribution in the Western Cape," report, PLAAS, University of the Western Cape, Bellville, South Africa, 1996; Chris de Wet, "Land Reform in South Africa: A Vehicle for Justice and Reconciliation, or a Source of Further Inequality and Conflict?" *New Routes* 2, 2 (1997); D. James, "Hill of Thorns: Custom, Knowledge and the Reclaiming of a Lost Land in the New South Africa," *Development and Change* 31, 3 (2000), and "After 'Years in the Wilderness': Development and the Discourse of Land Claims in the New South Africa," *Journal of Peasant Studies* 27, 3 (2000); Walker, "Relocating Restitution"; Scott Drimie, "Unravelling the Redistribution of Impendle State Land: Prospects and Process of Land Reform in Kwazulu-Natal, South Africa," Ph.D. thesis, Cambridge University, 2000.

61. South African DLA, media briefing, 3.

62. Statistics come from the South African DLA Web site (www.dla.pwv.gov.za) and from the chief land claim commissioner's overview in the *Annual Report* of the Commission on the Restitution of Land Rights, Pretoria, June 2000.

63. McIntosh Xaba, "Review," 81.

64. E. Lahiff, "The Impact of Land Reform Policy on the Northern Province," and A. McIntosh and A. Vaughan, "Experiences of Agricultural Reform in South Africa: The Limits of Intervention," 101–102, in Cousins, *At the Crossroads*.

65. McIntosh Xaba, "Review," 17.

66. Cross et al., "Making a Living Under Land Reform"; McIntosh Xaba, "Review," 12; McIntosh and Vaughan, "Experiences of Agricultural Reform," 227–228; M. Adams, *Breaking Ground: Development Aid for Land Reform* (London: Overseas Development Institute, 2000), 77–78.

67. Cross et al., "Making a Living Under Land Reform," 152–153.

68. C. MacDonald, "The Construction of State and Development Subject in Rural Kwazulu-Natal: Implications of Dominant Discourses in the Kwazulu-Natal Land Reform Pilot Programme," *Transformation* 37 (1998).

69. Bill of Rights, Chap. 2, in the Constitution of the Republic of South Africa, cited in Adams, *Breaking Ground*, 47.

70. "Update on the Land Rights Bill 1999," *Tenure Newsletter* 3, 1 (1999); S. Sibanda, "Proposals for the Management of Land Rights in Rural South Africa," in Cousins, *At the Crossroads*.

71. M. Adams, B. Cousins, and S. Manona, "Land Tenure and Economic Development in Rural South Africa: Constraints and Opportunities"; A. Claassens, "Land Rights and Local Decision Making Processes: Proposals for Tenure Reform"; S. Mankopi, "How to Provide Security of Tenure and Comparable Redress"; Sibanda, "Proposals for the Management of Land Rights"; D. Hornby, "Tenure Rights and Practices on a State-Owned Farm: the Community of Ekuthuleni," all in Cousins, *At the Crossroads*.

72. South African DLA, "What the Extension of Security of Tenure Act

(ESTA) Means for Owners and Occupiers: Know Your Land Rights," information leaflet, December 1997.

73. R. Hall, K. Kleinbooi, and N. Mvambo, "What Land Reform Has Meant and Could Mean to Farm Workers in South Africa," Centre for Rural Legal Studies, paper presented at the Human Sciences Research Council Conference, "Land Reform and Poverty Alleviation in Southern Africa," Pretoria, 4–5 June 2001, 3–4; Lahiff, "Impact of Land Reform," 97–98, 105.

74. South African DLA, media briefing, 4; Hornby, "All We Need," 19, 22, 84–90.

75. Hornby, "All We Need," 61–82.

76. Donna Hornby, personal communication to Ruth Hall, 6 September 2001.

77. MacDonald, "Construction of State," 53.

78. G. McIntosh, "Don't Use Bantustan Solutions," *Johannesburg Mail and Guardian*, 31 March 1995; Cross et al., "Making a Living Under Land Reform"; South African DLA, "Mid-Term Review," x, 11, 24; C. de Wet, "Managing Togetherness: Establishing a Collective-Ownership Farm in the Eastern Cape," presentation to the Department of Anthropology, Rhodes University, January 1998; Lahiff, "Impact of Land Reform," 95–97.

79. Sue Wixley, "Report from the Community Land Conference, 12–13 February 1994," NLC, Johannesburg, 1994; NLC, "Land Reform Policy Proposals," Johannesburg, 1995.

80. South African DLA, "Draft Land Policy Principles," from the National Conference on Land Policy, Kempton Park, South Africa, 31 August–1 September 1995.

81. South African DLA, *Proceedings of the National Conference on Land Policy, Kempton Park,* Pretoria, 1995.

82. Levin, "Towards a National Implementation Strategy," 69–71.

83. Du Toit, "Piloting Land Redistribution"; South African DLA, "Mid-Term Review," 11, 22–24.

84. Ibid., 8–10.

85. Ibid., 29; South African DLA, "Directorate: Redistribution Policy and Systems," *The Commonage Product*, 18 April 2000, 5–6.

86. South African DLA, "Mid-Term Review," 19–20.

87. Ibid., 29; South African DLA, "Directorate," 5–6.

88. McIntosh Xaba, "Review," 13.

89. Richard Clacey, interview by Gavin Williams, DLA Office, Pietermaritzburg, South Africa, September 1997; MacDonald "Construction of State."

90. Drimie, "Unravelling."

91. Luvuyo Wotshela, "Homeland Consolidation, Resettlement and Local Politics in the Border and the Ciskei Region of the Eastern Cape, South Africa, 1960–1996," Ph.D. thesis, Oxford University, 2001, Chap. 6.

92. J. Eckert, J. Hamman and J. Lombard, "Perceiving a New Future: Empowering Farmworkers Through Equity Sharing," *Development South Africa* 13, 5 (1996); J. Hamman and J. Ewert, "A Historical Irony in the Making? State, Private Sector and Land Reform in the South African Wine Industry," *Development South Africa* 16, 3 (1999); H. Fast, "An Examination of the Impact of Share Equity Schemes on Beneficiaries in the Western Cape and Mpumalanga," report for the Surplus People's Project, Cape Town, and the Land and Agricultural Policy Center, Johannesburg, 1999; N. Humphries, "Land Reform in the Western Cape, South Africa: Policy and Practice," B.A. thesis, St. Peter's College, Oxford, 2000.

93. Fast, "Examination"; South African DLA, "Mid-Term Review," 28.

94. Humphries, "Land Reform in the Western Cape," 49.

95. On Kenya, see M. Cowen, "Commodity Production in Kenya's Central Province," in *Rural Development in Tropical Africa*, ed. J. Heyer, P. Roberts, and G. Williams (London: Macmillan, 1981); Francis, *Making a Living*, 17–19, 80–87.

96. Charles Back, interview by Gavin Williams, Fairview, Paarl, South Africa, 22 August 2000; South Africa DLA, "Mid-Term Review," 27.

97. T. Marcus, K. Eales, and A. Wildschut, *Land Demand in the New South Africa* (Johannesburg: LAPC, 1996); South African DLA, "Mid-Term Review," 10. On the significance of wild resources, livestock, and agriculture for rural households, and the tendency to underestimate it in surveys and official sources, see S. Shackleton, C. Shackleton, and B. Cousins, "The Economic Value of Land and Natural Resources to Rural Livelihoods: Case Studies from South Africa"; Lahiff, "Impact of Land Reform"; and Adams, Cousins, and Manona, "Land Tenure and Economic Development," all in Cousins, *At the Crossroads*.

98. Lahiff, "Impact of Land Reform," 95–97; Deborah Potts and Deborah James, LSE workshop participant details/briefings, DESTIN.

99. McIntosh Xaba, "Review," 10.

100. de Wet, "Land Reform in South Africa," 15.

101. Gavin Capps, participant details/ briefings, "The Politics of Land Reform," DESTIN workshop, 7 June 2002.

102. C. Murray, "Land Reform in the Eastern Free State: Policy Dilemmas and Political Conflicts," *Journal of Peasant Studies* 23, 2/3 (1996), and "South African Land Reform: Case Studies in 'Demand' and 'Participation' in the Free State," *African Affairs* 96 (1997).

103. W. Beinart and R. Kingwill, "Eastern Cape Land Reform Project: Preplanning Report," Working Paper no. 25, LAPC, Johannesburg, 1996; Murray, "Land Reform in the Eastern Free State."

104. Agriculture SA, personal communication to Ruth Hall, November 2000. See also R. W. Johnson and L. Schlemmer, "Farmers and Farmworkers in Kwazulu-Natal: Employment Conditions, Labour Tenancy, Land Reform, Attitudes and Relationships," Helen Suzman Foundation for the Kwazulu-Natal Agricultural Union, Johannesburg, 1998, 7, Fig. 1.

105. Lahiff, "Impact of Land Reform," 103–104.

106. South African DLA, "Mid-Term Review," 21.

107. McIntosh Xaba, "Review," 46; South African DLA, "Mid-Term Review."

108. McIntosh Xaba, "Review," v.

109. Ibid.

110. Ibid., vi; South African DLA, "Mid-Term Review," 18.

111. McIntosh Xaba, "Review," vi.

112. Ibid., 81.

113. Ibid., 7; see also vi–vii, 79–81.

114. Ibid., vii, 78.

115. Ibid., vi, 78.

116. Wotshela, "Homeland Consolidation," Chaps. 1, 4, 5.

117. Ibid., Chaps. 2–3. For the previous period, see A. Mager, *Gender and the Making of a South African Bantustan: A Social History of the Ciskei, 1945–1959* (Oxford: James Currey, 1999).

118. C. Desmond, *The Discarded People: An Account of Forced Resettlement in South Africa* (Harmondsworth, UK: Penguin, 1971); Surplus People's Project, *Forced Removals in South Africa*, 5 vols. (Cape Town: SPP, 1983); L. Platzky and

C. Walker, *The Surplus People: Forced Removals in South Africa* (Johannesburg: Ravan Press, 1985).

119. T. McClendon, *Genders and Generations Apart: Labour Tenants, Customary Law and Segregation in Natal* (New York: Heinemann, 2000); Williams, "Transforming Labour Tenants." For other provinces, see Timothy Keegan, *Rural Transformations in Industrializing South Africa: The Southern Highveld to 1914* (Basingstoke, UK: Macmillan, 1987); S. Schirmer, "Land, Legislation and Tenants: Resistance in Lydenburg, 1938," and C. Mather, "Wage Workers and Labour Tenants in Barberton, 1920–1950," in *White Farms, Black Labor: The State and Agrarian Change in Southern Africa, 1910–1950*, ed. A. H. Jeeves and J. Crush (Oxford: James Currey, 1997).

120. W. Beinart, ed., special issue: "The Politics of Colonial Conservation," *Journal of Southern African Studies* 15, 2 (1989); C. de Wet, "Resettlement and Land Reform in South Africa," *Review of African Political Economy* 61 (1994); Mager, *Gender and the Making of the Ciskei.* For Kenya, see D. W. Throup, *The Economic and Social Origins of Mau Mau, 1945–1953*, (London: J. Currey, 1988).

121. *Summary of the Report of the Commission for the Socio-economic Development of the Bantu Areas Within the Union of South Africa,* Pretoria, 1955, 118.

122. Wotshela, "Homeland Consolidation," Chap. 3.

123. For sources, see Williams, "Setting the Agenda," 145 n.32. See also R. Singini and J. van Rooyen, "Serving Small Farmers: An Evaluation of the DBSA's Farmer Support Programmes," report for the Development Bank of South Africa, Midrand, South Africa, 1985.

124. South African Department of Agriculture, "White Paper on Agriculture," Pretoria, 1995 (available at: www.nda.agric.za). See Abie Dithlake, citing Richard Levin, participant details/briefings, "The Politics of Land Reform," DESTIN workshop, 7 June 2000.

125. Drimie, "Unravelling."

126. Lahiff, "Impact of Land Reform," 96–97.

127. A. McIntosh and A. Vaughan, "Enhancing Rural Livelihoods in South Africa," in Lipton et al., *Land, Labour, and Livelihoods, Volume Two,* and "State and Capital in the Regeneration of a South African Peasantry," *Canadian Journal of African Studies*, 29, 3, 1993.

128. IPLRAD, 8 May 2000, 7.

129. Ibid., 13; South African DLA, "The Food Safety-Net Programme: A Component of the Land Redistribution Programme," draft discussion document, version 2.5, Pretoria, 8 May 2000, 5.

130. LRAD, 4; IPLRAD, 23 October 2000, 3, 7; IPLRAD, 8 May 2000, 14–15; South African DLA, "Food Safety-Net," 7–9; IPLRAD, 8 June 2000, 9.

131. IPLRAD, 8 May 2000, 18–20; IPLRAD, 8 June 2000, 9–10; IPLRAD, 23 October 2000, 7; LRAD, 2, 9. Also South African DLA, "Farm Equity Scheme: Implementation Guide," Pretoria, 2000.

132. South African DLA, "Report to the Minister on the Proceedings of the Commonage Workshop, 25 February 2000," repeated in *The Commonage Product*, 18 April, 2000, 7; IPLRAD 8 May 2000, 7; IPLRAD 8 June 2000, 9.

133. South African DLA, "Report to the Minister; IPLRAD 8 May 2000.

134. LRAD 3, 5; Didiza, briefing, 4.

135. This statement was first made in the February 2000 Didiza media briefing (Didiza, briefing, 2); it was repeated later (South African DLA, media briefing, 2).

136. LRAD, 12–13.
137. Lahiff, "Impact of Land Reform," 104.
138. LRAD, 8–11.
139. Ibid., 11.
140. Ibid.
141. See *The Integrated Programme of Land Redistribution and Agricultural Development: A Response from Land NGOs,* prepared by the Centre for Rural Legal Studies (CRLS), Land Development Unit (LDU), Legal Resources Centre (LRC), Programme for Land and Agrarian Studies (PLAAS), Surplus People's Project (SPP), and Trust for Community Outreach and Education (TCOE) for the South African MALA Indaba on the IPLRAD, Johannesburg, 6–7 November 2000, 15. The report, however, was not presented at the Indaba.
142. LRAD, 11.
143. Ibid., 13–14.
144. L. Ntsebeza, "Traditional Authorities, Local Government and Land Rights," in Cousins, *At the Crossroads.*
145. Didiza, briefing, 2000, and IPLRAD, 8 May 2000, 14, refer to "tribes"; IPLRAD 8 June 2000 to "traditional authorities"; and South African MALA, media briefing, 3, to "African traditional communities." The political correction of colonial terminology has South African precedents.
146. LRAD; IPLRAD, 23 October 2000.
147. South African MALA, media briefing, 3. See criticisms by Ben Cousins, "Land Reform at the Crossroads," *Reconstruct*, 20 February 2000.
148. IPLRAD, 23 October 2000, 2; IPLRAD, 8 June 2000, 6–14, 20–21; IPLRAD, 15 May 2000.
149 *Integrated Programme*, 6.
150. LRAD, 3.
151. *Integrated Programme*, 8.
152. LRAD, 3.
153. For South African evidence, see P. Moll, "The Structure of Commercial Agriculture in South Africa: A Quantitative Approach to Economies of Scale, Farm Size Change and Technical Change," Ph.D. thesis, Oxford University, 1988.
154. Ruth Hall attended the Indaba. This account draws on her experiences and the observations of others who attended the meeting.
155. S. N. Hinga and J. Heyer, "The Development of Large Farms," in *Agricultural Development in Kenya,* ed. J. Heyer, J. Maitha, and W. Senga (Nairobi: Oxford University Press, 1976); J. Heyer, "Agricultural Development Policy in Kenya from the Colonial Period to 1975," in Heyer et al., *Rural Development;* Leo, *Land and Class in Kenya;* Francis, *Making a Living*, 15–16.

7

AIDS as a New Security Threat

Jacqui Ala

One of the many changes brought about by the end of the Cold War has been the way in which we define the term *security*. During the Cold War period, security was confined to a narrow realist interpretation that focused primarily on conventional military threats such as the proliferation of weapons of mass destruction and arms races. Although these conventional threats still exist, there has been a realization that there are many nonconventional threats that pose an equally serious risk to national and international peace and stability. These include issues such as ethnic violence, intrastate conflict, disease, and environmental degradation. This realization has resulted in an expanded agenda of international security concerns. A more holistic understanding of security has emerged that incorporates matters affecting the security of individuals and communities, not merely of states and the international system. Acknowledgment that ensuring the safety of these nonstate actors is as important as guaranteeing that of the state has led to the development of the concept of *human security* as part of this new security agenda. Human security recognizes that an individual's personal protection and preservation derives not only from the safeguarding of the state as a political entity but also from access to individual welfare and quality of life. However, human security does not merely encompass matters of individual benefit but also denotes protection from the structural violence that frequently accompanies many aspects of nonterritorial security (for example, violence due to food shortages in a country). Thus, the scope of human security concerns includes individuals in their personal surroundings, their community, and their environment.[1]

The United Nations Development Programme (UNDP) *Human Development Report* of 1994 was the first to use the specific phrase *human security* in an attempt to direct the post–Cold War security agenda toward more development-based concerns.[2] According to the UNDP, human security encompasses two main aspects: "safety from such chronic threats as hunger, disease, and repression [and] protection from sudden and hurtful disruptions in the pattern of daily life, whether in homes, in jobs, or in communities." The report proceeded to enumerate security threats as follows: economic insecurity; food insecurity; health insecurity; personal insecurity; environmental insecurity; community and cultural insecurity; and political insecurity.[3]

Based on the Joint UN Programme on HIV/AIDS' (UNAIDS') criteria, HIV/AIDS constitutes an immense human security threat, especially to those states with high infection rates. The pandemic not only causes health insecurity but also has repercussions for the other six categories. The UN set a precedent for considering HIV/AIDS as a human security concern in 2000 when Richard Holbrook, U.S. ambassador to the UN, placed the issue before the Security Council, citing it as a threat to international security and stability. This was the first time that a health issue was afforded this type of attention. The Security Council unanimously adopted a resolution calling for increased international cooperation and for concrete action by member countries to counteract the impact of HIV/AIDS on the health of international peacekeepers.

Given that southern Africa is at present generally believed to be the epicenter of this pandemic, HIV/AIDS has come to represent an unprecedented threat to the human security of the region's states in particular. Governments on the whole have failed to deal with their epidemics in a timely manner, resulting in enormous infection rates that are set to stabilize at exceptionally high levels. The political, social, and economic ramifications of the epidemic for this region are severe. Moreover, HIV/AIDS will also impact southern Africa's security architecture.

The region is classified by epidemiologists as having a generalized epidemic. Statistics for seven countries in this region indicate that one out of five adults is HIV positive. In Swaziland, HIV prevalence among pregnant women attending antenatal clinics in 2000 ranged from 32.2 percent in urban areas to 34.5 percent in the rural areas; in Botswana, the corresponding figures were 43.9 percent and 35.5 percent. In South Africa's KwaZulu-Natal Province, prevalence rates stood at 36.2 percent in 2000. Botswana currently has the world's highest infection rates, approximately 38 percent of the adult population is HIV positive. South Africa has the highest number of people living with HIV globally. It is estimated that one in nine South Africans is HIV positive, approximately 4.7 million total.[4]

Southern Africans' Vulnerability to HIV/AIDS Infections

The socioeconomic and political composition of many sub-Saharan African countries gives rise to numerous problems that increase a population's risk of becoming HIV positive. Individual behavior does not occur in a vacuum. The social, economic, and political conditions of a country all play a part in determining an individual's behavior. For prevention programs to be effective they need to address a myriad of issues. This understanding partially negates the view held by many scholars that prevention programs are the simplest, most cost-effective way of curbing HIV infections. Taken at face value, issues may look easy to solve, but many of the prevention programs strike at age-old cultural beliefs and ideas that are extremely resistant to change.

Although biological considerations, such as the length of infection and the presence of sexually transmitted diseases, play a major role in determining the extent of the epidemic, it is these factors in tandem with other socioeconomic circumstances that predispose sub-Saharan African communities to high rates of HIV infection. Most of these factors and circumstances are interrelated, and it is extremely difficult in many instances to separate them or to discuss any one of them in isolation. It is also impossible to single out one issue as being the major or sole contributor to high infection rates. For example, alleviating poverty without empowering women will still place them at risk of contracting the virus, as the social traditions that make them vulnerable will still exist.

Poverty and Malnutrition

The economic well-being of a society has a definite bearing on the population's physical health. The governments of developing states have less money to spend on health care. Although many endeavors to provide low-cost or free basic health care are under way, the standard of the services provided by governments is generally low. Medical facilities are often badly equipped and understaffed due to the lack of government resources. As many people in these countries fall into lower income brackets, the demand placed on the public health sector is enormous. The situation is further exacerbated by the limited number of medical facilities to service this growing demand, especially in the rural areas. Given their small resource base, many developing countries do not have the means to extend the public healthcare sector by building more clinics and hospitals or employing more people. Consequently, patients have to travel long distances and wait long periods of time to gain access to treatment in the public health care system. Due to resource shortages, these patients also have limited treatment choices. Newer, more effective medication, diagnostic procedures, and treatment regimes are often prohibitively expensive and simply not viable for the public health care sector.

In many countries, the diagnosis of HIV can only be performed in certain urban areas, as there exists no, or limited, diagnostic facilities in rural areas where the majority of the population resides. Without access to HIV/AIDS testing, people uninformed of their status may continue to expose themselves and others to infection. In addition, the lack of these facilities means that infected individuals are unable to access treatment for AIDS-related diseases. Many people who are HIV positive in sub-Saharan Africa have limited treatment options, as the public health sector cannot afford to purchase the drugs they require to treat opportunistic diseases. In South Africa, patients in the public health sector have not until recently been able to access the drug diflucan, which is effective in treating thrush, as the Department of Health could not afford to purchase the drug. Without access to drugs that treat opportunistic infections, the life expectancy of an HIV-positive person is substantially reduced. The high rates of HIV infections prevalent in sub-Saharan Africa put further demands on the public health sector, as those who are infected require long-term treatment. However, with the presence of other equally life-threatening diseases in Africa, such as tuberculosis and malaria, no government can afford to deploy all its health resources exclusively to treat HIV/AIDS.

The pressures of globalization have also contributed to poverty within sub-Saharan Africa. With governments being pushed to be more efficient and economies under pressure to grow more in line with those of the developed world, subsidies have been cut in important areas such as health care, education, and agriculture. Government-controlled industries have been privatized, leading in many instances to large-scale retrenchments. The result is that food, health care, and education now cost people in sub-Saharan Africa significantly more. However, there has not been a concomitant increase in the price of agricultural commodities or employment opportunities for populations to meet these increased costs.

Malnutrition is rife on the African continent, especially as economic situations in general continue to deteriorate. Malnutrition and parasitosis that appear to be endemic to poor countries have long been recognized as depressing the immune function. This has two important repercussions with regards to the HIV/AIDS pandemic in Africa. First, it is argued that malnutrition and the synergistic effects of infectious and parasitic disease increase the risk of contracting HIV with each sexual contact, regardless of the number of contacts. Recent work has shown the ways in which each of the elements of the immune system is undermined by both protein-energy malnutrition and micronutrient deficiency. Examining the immune system at the cellular level highlights the role of malnutrition and parasitosis in vulnerability to specific diseases, in particular to sexually transmitted diseases (STDs). Vitamin A, for example, is essential for epithelial integrity and plays an important role in protection from STDs, particularly of the ulcerative type that facilitate HIV transmission.[5]

Second, nutrition plays a significant role in allowing HIV-positive people to lead long, productive lives. Malnutrition and its negative effects on the human immune system leave these people vulnerable to opportunistic infections, which further weaken their immune response. This deterioration of the immune system ultimately results in death.

Education

UNAIDS studies reveal interesting correlations between education and the tendency to engage in high-risk behavior. On the whole, the well-educated lead healthier, more productive lives, as they have access to more information and can therefore make well-informed decisions regarding their health. Education also secures better-paying jobs, which in turn result in greater disposable income. This income can be used to procure a healthy lifestyle. However, it can also be used to purchase alcohol, drugs, and sex. UNAIDS surveys among fifteen to nineteen year olds in seventeen African and four Latin American countries revealed that as education increases, certain kinds of high-risk behavior increase, while others decrease. Better-educated girls start having sex later but the reverse is true of boys in many countries. Better-educated people are more likely to have casual sexual partners. Nevertheless, they are also more likely to use condoms during these encounters.[6] Although no study has found conclusively that a lack of education is a fundamental factor that makes people vulnerable to infection, those studies conducted by UNAIDS seem to indicate that, in countries hardest hit by HIV/AIDS, better-educated people are endeavoring to modify their behavior to decrease the risk of contracting the virus.

Stigmatization and Stereotyping

Despite the establishment of HIV/AIDS awareness programs in many sub-Saharan countries, there still exists fear and stigmatization of the disease. In sub-Saharan Africa, HIV/AIDS usually results in death and is mostly acquired through heterosexual contact, which makes it the perfect breeding ground for prejudice. Consequently, people are reluctant to learn their HIV status, as they fear rejection by family and the community. Too frequently this fear is not groundless, as a high degree of stigmatization exists toward the HIV positive. In South Africa, as in other southern African states, many HIV-positive people have been rejected by family members and thrown out of their households; they are often threatened with death by the community.[7] In addition, despite there frequently being legislation to the contrary, people also fear learning their HIV status, as they may be dismissed from their employment if they test positive.

Stigmatization is often linked to a lack of knowledge about HIV/AIDS among communities. Education, to a large extent, can counteract the prejudices associated with the disease. It is also vital that governments, as well as prominent civil society members, encourage a culture of openness about HIV/AIDS by addressing the issue publicly. In Uganda, government officials and prominent members of civil society strengthened the country's HIV/AIDS initiative by publicly announcing their HIV-positive status. This not only made people more aware of HIV/AIDS but also gave many people the courage to be tested. The government, especially President Yoweri Museveni, have facilitated the creation of an informed environment where people can disclose their HIV status without fear. People have come to be so open about HIV/AIDS that virtually no stigmatization exists in Uganda surrounding the disease.

Social Norms

To a large extent, society shapes individuals' perception of sex. It often dictates what type of behavior is acceptable or unacceptable in this regard. Social norms surrounding sexual activity can be both positive and negative. If they, for example, encourage abstinence among the unmarried or fidelity among those who are married, then they will contribute to decreasing high-risk behavior and subsequently HIV infection rates. However, in reality, social norms regarding sex often discriminate on the grounds of gender. In many societies, men are permitted to be promiscuous but women are expected to be chaste. In a study conducted in Rio de Janeiro 61 percent of interviewed men between the ages of fifteen and nineteen admitted to having had sex at least once in the past year but only 1 percent of women admitted to doing the same.[8] Societies that encourage this type of gender stereotyping tend to exhibit explosive HIV epidemics. Men in these societies usually make use of prostitutes and have a high rate of partner change. This factor puts them in a high-risk category. In addition, because this type of behavior does not encourage fidelity within marriage, their female partners are placed at risk of contracting HIV. This conduct allows the virus to spread from those people involved in high-risk activities into the general population. Over time, if this trend goes unchecked it will result in infection patterns moving from being concentrated to being generalized. This type of gender stereotyping results in both men and women being vulnerable to HIV infection.

In many African societies, women are forbidden from obtaining information about sex and reproductive health, thereby denying them the very information that will empower them to avoid HIV infection. Women who try to obtain such information are branded as promiscuous. Men are also reluctant to seek help on issues regarding sex, as they fear appearing less masculine. Sexually transmitted diseases in men thus often go untreated because the infected are usually ignorant of the dangers of STDs. This is extremely problematic, as STD infection substantially increases a person's chances of contracting HIV through sexual intercourse.

Another cultural practice exclusive to southern and central Africa, which puts women at risk, is widow cleansing. This practice requires a relative of the deceased, usually a brother, to have sexual intercourse with his widow. Participants are placed at risk of infection, as they are ignorant of each other's sexual history or HIV status. Women are particularly vulnerable. Due to their lack of social and economic status within traditional African society they have no power to resist such a cultural practice.

Within traditional African society, older men are encouraged to marry younger women as a display of their continued virility. Older men are attracted to adolescent women in particular, believing they are still virgins and therefore HIV negative. Problematically, many of these older men are themselves already HIV positive. They are thus not only infecting these younger women but, in so doing, are also spreading the epidemic to another generation. In addition, researchers in South Africa have attributed increased rape statistics among girls and young women to the fact that they are perceived to be low risk in terms of being HIV positive. It is thought that this increase has also been fueled by the myth that having sex with a virgin will cure one of HIV.

Despite many high-risk practices being associated with traditional values, the increase in HIV infection within a country is often attributed to the breakdown of these same values. As previously stated, many traditional values are not pernicious per se in an HIV/AIDS context. For example, polygamy poses a low risk for HIV infection, for as long as husband and wives remain faithful to each other. The advent of urbanization, coupled with the phenomenon of migrant labor, has definitely had an adverse effect on family units within many African countries. Men working away from their wives frequently make use of the services of prostitutes, exposing themselves and their wives to possible HIV infection. The southern Africa region has a large number of migrant workers, the majority of whom provide labor for South African mining and industry. The phenomenon of migrant labor has not only assisted the spread of HIV/AIDS from urban to rural areas but has also contributed to increased infection rates throughout the region.

Urbanization has also seen the increase of female-headed households, as men leave the family in search of employment in the cities. Frequently, husbands fail to remit some of the earnings back to their families. Thus, female-headed households are usually the most economically vulnerable. Women head 60 percent of households in the communal farming areas of Zimbabwe.[9] In situations in which the absent male partner does not regularly remit income back to the family and the woman head is unable to generate enough income to meet the needs of the family, these households tend to rank as the poorest of the poor. Gender-biased development policies on the part of governments, nongovernmental organizations (NGOs), and international organizations often exclude women from accessing the services they require to cultivate their land in the absence of their husbands. For example, agricultural extension services are often directed exclusively at male farmers. Loans are de facto only granted to men. NGOs target men to develop small businesses, but women are confined to low-key income-generating projects. Women who are economically vulnerable often exchange sex for money or other requirements such as food, clothing, and seed. Increased promiscuity, drug addiction, and crime within society, especially among youth, have also been attributed to the breakdown of traditional values, particularly the family unit.

One cannot generalize about the benefits of traditional values. Viewing traditional values from an idyllic vantage point can be extremely dangerous. Feminists especially allude to the fact that many traditional African values are rooted in patriarchy. As such, they discriminate, especially against women and the young. With the advent of HIV/AIDS on the continent, it is often these very values that have placed society at risk.

Status of Women

Despite large-scale efforts by community groups, national governments, and the international community, the political, economic, and social status of the majority of women in sub-Saharan Africa has still not improved substantially, if at all. Until recently, the predominant rationale for correcting this problem was to improve women's economic development and security. However, in the age of HIV/AIDS, women's status also makes them extremely vulnerable to infection. Many of the reasons for this low status can be attributed to patriarchal norms and values and, as such, much of this discussion is interconnected with that of the preceding section. However, this topic warrants a section of its own because sub-Saharan Africa is the only part of the world where HIV infection rates for women exceed those of men. In this region, 55 percent of HIV-positive adults are women.[10]

Within the gender and development discourse, much has been written about women's economic dependence on men. This economic dependence arises from the fact that women, due to numerous circumstances, are precluded from gaining access to activities that would allow them to generate enough income to enable them and their dependents to be economically self-sufficient. For example, the majority of rural African women are excluded from owning land, as land inheritance is usually patrilineal. In many countries, legislation has endeavored to give women greater access to economic resources, but patriarchy often overrides these as it continues to enforce the status quo. In Kenya, a survey showed that out of 135 households affected by land adjudication, only eight registered the land in the name of women. The official reason the government gave for this was that it was customary: men own land and women do not. In Zimbabwe, it is still culturally unacceptable for women to own property in rural areas, even though no legislation prevents them from doing so. The absence of land title limits women's access to resources such as credit, extension services, training, technology, and membership in cooperatives.[11]

The marginal economic position of women in sub-Saharan Africa can partly be ascribed to their limited access to education. In South Africa in 1995, 23 percent of African women above the age of twenty-five had no formal education at all, compared to 16 percent of African men. Over a quarter of African women had not passed grade five, compared to one-fifth of African men.[12] The introduction of structural adjustment programs (SAPs) in many African states has seen the elimination of government subsidies for education. Consequently, parents unable to afford the cost of education for their entire family frequently choose to educate boys over girls. The rationale is that boys will benefit more from an education, as this will facilitate greater employment opportunities. Girls, who are traditionally employed within the household, do not need education to fulfill this customary role. A study conducted in Côte d'Ivoire found that fewer women completed their secondary schooling after the introduction of SAPs in 1980.[13]

Economic dependence makes it almost impossible for a woman to leave an unfaithful spouse. Thus, economic dependency places women at increased risk of infection. Given their inferior status within society, and within the family, many women find it impossible to negotiate sexual relations. According to a study conducted by Gupta, Weiss, and Mane, it is usually men who initiate, dominate, and control sexual interactions and decisions, while the responsibility of contraceptive use is often borne by the women.[14] Women, although they lack the power to control sexual transactions, have been charged with the responsibility for safe sex. As the condom is a form of contraception that a woman does not have direct control over, her safety is dependent on her ability to negotiate its usage with an often reluctant partner.[15] Women risk physical abuse and ostracism from their male partners for requesting the use of a condom. Conversely, cases have been cited of male partners being reluctant to initiate condom usage, as this is often perceived to be a sign of infidelity on their part by the woman.[16] These factors contribute to low condom use in many communities, despite public awareness campaigns.

Poverty, accompanied by lack of education and subsequently limited employment opportunities, is often responsible for women turning to prostitution to generate income for themselves and their households. Studies have also indicated that many prostitutes shun condom use, as they can earn more from unprotected sex. In Gambia, sex workers earn three times more than women employed in the informal sector, and as much as a senior civil servant.[17]

Social and economic vulnerability also predisposes young women to be coerced into sex or enticed by older, richer men who offer money for education or gifts in return for sex. Approximately 17 percent of unmarried teenagers in rural Tanzania reported having had sex with a man at least ten years older than themselves.[18] A factor that places women and young children at further risk of contracting HIV/AIDS is the high level of sexual abuse in many African communities. Rape has also become a common feature of war. A random sample of twenty Ethiopians from a Somali refugee camp indicated that seventeen knew of someone from their village and thirteen knew of someone from their own family who had been raped by the Ethiopian militia.[19] In countries with high infections rates, women are placed under great risk of contracting HIV/AIDS when raped. Sexual abuse among children is also on the increase, particularly because children are perceived to be low HIV risks to perpetrators.

To decrease the high infection rates among women in Africa, policymakers need to grasp the nettle and address those factors that contribute to their inferior social, economic, and legal status. Unfortunately, this means challenging cultural norms and values that are very resistant to change. Nevertheless, many gender and development programs, especially those run by African communities themselves, have been successful and a concerted effort should be made to continue these processes.

Lack of Information Regarding HIV/AIDS

At present, there still exists much misinformation and a lack of knowledge on the subject of HIV/AIDS, especially among women. For example, as reported in the 2000 South African Health Review, although 97 percent of women had heard of AIDS, their knowledge of ways to avoid it was limited. Ten percent of female respondents stated that having one partner and using a condom during sexual intercourse would not protect them from AIDS. Twenty-one percent still believed that transmission could take place by sharing public toilets, while 38 percent felt that mosquitoes could spread HIV. Despite the presence of prevention programs, misinformation and ignorance still occur.[20]

In Carletonville, South Africa, where many HIV education programs have been initiated due to high prevalence rates, a survey indicated that only 40 percent of men and women respondents were aware that an individual could live with the virus for several years without any outward sign of infection. Approximately one-third of respondents were mistakenly convinced that all HIV-positive people would show symptoms of their infection, while one-quarter had no idea what to expect.[21] Another poll of 339 military recruits between the ages of eighteen and twenty-four in Bloemfontein, South Africa, showed that attitudes toward HIV/AIDS had not changed substantially, despite media information campaigns. One in ten interviewees stated that HIV-positive people should be kept in isolation. Twenty-three percent believed that AIDS was a punishment from God for sexual immorality. Twelve percent believed that AIDS could be cured, and nine percent said that healthy people could not contract the virus. Many felt that women could not infect men and that certain contraceptive pills would prevent transmission.[22]

Providing a population with information on how to prevent infection is one of the most important and effective weapons that exist to halt the spread of the virus. However, programs need to be extensive, endeavoring to reach the entire population of a country. They also need to be ongoing, as it takes time before people internalize the message and modify their behavior.

The Consequences of High Infection Rates

Population Growth

The HIV/AIDS pandemic is set to alter radically the demographic profile of many African states. On the whole, better standards of health and nutrition have brought with them decreases in child mortality rates and increases in life expectancy for many Africans. However, HIV/AIDS is reversing these gains. For example, in Botswana, whose HIV prevalence rate for those aged fifteen to forty-nine is 38.5 percent, the average life expectancy has fallen from almost seventy years to forty-four in less than a decade. By 2021, it is estimated that the population will have shrunk by 30 percent due to HIV/AIDS.[23] In South Africa, unless significant behavioral change takes place, 45 percent of the adult population will die of AIDS. Thus, by 2010, the probability of a fifteen year old not surviving to the age of sixty will have increased from approximately 30 percent in the mid-1990s to 75 percent.[24] Zimbabwe may already face a zero population growth in 2002 due to its rising AIDS death rate. Official statistics put the weekly AIDS death toll at 2,000.[25] The trend for other sub-Saharan countries with high prevalence rates is similar. According to the UN Population Division, life expectancy will decrease by at least seventeen years in Lesotho, Namibia, Swaziland, South Africa, Zambia, and

Zimbabwe.[26] In addition, infant mortality is on the rise as a result of mother to child transmission of the virus. Countries such as Zambia and Zimbabwe, which both have high adult prevalence rates, report a steep increase in child mortality.

Also of concern is the way in which HIV/AIDS is altering the demographics in these states. Prevalence rates are the highest in the age group fifteen to forty-nine. In the past, population pyramids depicted very low death rates for this group. However, population pyramids that account for HIV/AIDS in their projections look more like population chimneys. Death rates among children will increase due to AIDS-related deaths. There will also be a decrease in figures in the middle of the pyramid, as adults begin to die in their thirties and forties. For countries with high infection and prevalence rates like South Africa and Botswana, there will be more people in their sixties and seventies than in their forties and fifties. In South Africa, the total number of AIDS-related deaths over the next ten years is estimated at 5–6 million.[27] This has enormous social implications, as the missing people in the forty to fifty age groups are usually those who care for children and the elderly. With the advent of the HIV/AIDS pandemic, often it is now the young and the elderly who care for their dying parents or children. Unfortunately, as HIV/AIDS takes its toll in African society, there will be very few adults to take care of children and the elderly who have lost their immediate family to the epidemic. In other words, generalized depopulation threatens the continent.

Economic Impact

A government report states that Botswana's epidemic will cost almost one-third of the country's economic potential over the next ten years. Government revenue is also expected to drop over the same period, while expenditure is set to rise, creating a budget deficit of 21 percent.[28] These predictions are very serious, as the country is one of the wealthiest in Africa. The report labels HIV/AIDS as the single greatest threat to human welfare and development in Botswana. UNAIDS believes that the South African economy will be 17 percent smaller in 2010 than it would have been without HIV/AIDS. By that time the disease will have cost the country in excess of $22 billion.[29]

HIV/AIDS is expected to continue to dominate the business environment over the next five to fifteen years. Metropolitan Life forecasts that 20 percent of the workforce could be HIV positive by 2005 and 22.5 percent by 2010, if no interventions are taken.[30] The ramifications of HIV for business will depend on the type of business and whether it relies mainly on skilled or unskilled labor. Industries that rely on unskilled labor may not feel the effects of HIV/AIDS as harshly, as unskilled labor is fairly easy to replace. Those employing a greater number of skilled workers may find this workforce more difficult and costly to replace. Although the direct cost of HIV/AIDS to business in the form of healthcare and other employee benefits will be quite substantial, it is the indirect costs that will be the most significant.[31] These costs include high absenteeism due to illness, care for the sick, or funeral attendance; lost skills; training; recruitment costs; and reduced performance and lower productivity. HIV infection is likely to cost companies between one and six times the employee's annual salary, depending on the company's benefit structure (see Table 7.1).[32]

The loss of skilled labor will make South Africa and other African states less competitive internationally. Local turnover will also decline. The absentee rate of employees infected by the virus will probably increase. Business revenue will suffer. Consequently, the government's tax base will shrink.[33] This could spell an increase in taxation rates, especially corporate tax, to cope with the shortfall, which would make the country even less attractive to foreign investment. In addition, demand for health services and welfare support will rise and consume a substantial portion of the national budget. Given the demands placed on the national budget, it is possible that spending in other areas such as education will be cut. It is estimated that HIV/AIDS could reduce gross domestic product (GDP) growth rates in South Africa by 0.3 to 0.4 percent per annum over the next fifteen years. The impact on social and human development will be profound. Increased illness and death and lower life expectancy will undermine development objectives. People affected by the disease, especially orphans, have a lower chance of fulfilling their human potential, being less able to meet their physical and emotional needs. HIV/AIDS will inevitably lead to increased socioeconomic disparities.[34]

Table 7.1 Projected Costs of Risk Benefits as a Percentage of Salary in South Africa

Year	Lump Sum Death or Disability Benefit	Spouse's Pension	Disability Pension
1997	1.5	4.0	1.5
2002	2.9	5.9	2.1
2007	4.5	7.5	2.6

Source: LoveLife and ABT, Inc., "Impending Catastrophe Revisited: An Update on the HIV/AIDS Epidemic in South Africa," Kaiser Foundation, Parklands, South Africa, 2001.

Implications for the Health Care Sector

Although private health care does exist in many African states, it is the public sector that is used by the majority of the population. Thus, the cost of caring for the HIV positive will be borne largely by the government. Nevertheless, both public and private sectors will be seriously affected by the pandemic. However, the effects on the private sector are likely to be delayed. The cost of treating a patient infected with HIV varies according to the different stages of the disease, with treatment earlier on in the HIV stage costing less than when the person develops AIDS. Therefore, the more people a country has in the later stages of the disease, the more money it will be spending on their health care requirements. This factor should be considered in both private and public health care planning for the pandemic.

HIV/AIDS is already pushing the public health care sector to the limit, and in some cases it is reaching a breaking point. A report published in the *South African Medical Journal* states that the death rate among chronically ill patients in KwaZulu-Natal who were not HIV positive is increasing because hospitals are being flooded with AIDS-related illnesses that require hospitalization. Most state-run hospitals in the province report overcrowding, with many patients sharing beds and some even sleeping on the floor. Consequently, many seriously ill people are being turned away from hospitals. In addition, treating AIDS-related illnesses is being made a priority at the expense of other equally serious ailments such as malaria and tuberculosis. HIV/AIDS is expected to increase expenditure in both the inpatient and ambulatory components of health care in South Africa. To maintain 1995 levels of care in public-sector hospitals, expenditure would need to increase 2.3 times.[35]

None of the above figures include the use of antiretroviral treatment. The impact on ambulatory care is likely to be less severe. Projected expenditure will probably not be sustainable given financial constraints in both the public and private sector, resulting in the need to ration resources. The current increase in the numbers of HIV patients could give way to a situation in which hospitals refuse to admit people who are HIV positive. There is already anecdotal evidence that this is occurring in the public health sector in South Africa. At Baragwanth Hospital, figures indicate that there was already a decrease in hospitalization per AIDS-sick child between 1991 and 1996.[36] There is a clear need for both the public and private sectors to employ alternative measures to hospitalization as the main method of treating acute HIV/AIDS patients. Alternatives would include supporting hospice or community-based care. In countries with forward-thinking HIV/AIDS programs, like Uganda, community-based care has already been effectively employed to provide health care services to people with HIV/AIDS.

Unfortunately, HIV/AIDS is not the only health crisis faced by many of these states. There are other pressing issues such as malaria and tuberculosis, which also require government resources. On the whole, the HIV/AIDS pandemic is set to consume the meager health budgets of African states. A recent study estimates that in 1997, public health spending for AIDS alone already exceeded 2 percent of the GDP in seven out of the sixteen African countries sampled. This amount is staggering when one considers that these are countries where total health care expenditure usually accounts for 3 to 5 percent of the GDP.[37]

Education

The education sector is a vital component in the development equation for southern African states. Escalating HIV/AIDS rates have implications for both teachers and students. Globally, the teaching profession accounts for more HIV/AIDS infections and deaths than other professional groups. In the first ten months of 1998, HIV/AIDS cost Zambia 1,300 teachers. This number is the equivalent of two-thirds of all new teachers trained annually. HIV/AIDS-related absenteeism among teachers and students is also rife. Ironically, according to studies, it is teachers' higher income and community status that predisposes them to engage in high-risk activities.[38] HIV/AIDS also threatens to widen the disparity between rural and urban education, as it is the rural areas in most African countries that are presently the worst affected by the virus.

Although the impact of HIV/AIDS on the education sector in terms of absenteeism and death may not be any more severe than on other areas of the workforce, the ramifications of the pandemic, not only for the education sector but for society as a whole, are extremely serious. The death or absence of a single educator affects the education of twenty to fifty students. The current shortage of educators in critical fields such as science, mathematics, and technical skills will become more acute. The average age and experience of teachers is set to decrease. Depending on how the disease affects key people in leadership positions, continuity and quality in education policy could be compromised; thus, the overall standard of education is threatened by HIV/AIDS.

The high attrition rate of teachers will probably result in an increased demand for educators. However, the education sector in many countries like South Africa has been earmarked for rationalization. Consequently, many countries in Africa will need to reconsider their training requirements for teachers. Already shorter training periods for educators have been suggested in countries hard hit by HIV/AIDS in order to replace teachers at a fast enough rate. This could also contribute to the further lowering of educational standards.

With regards to learners, it is not illness and death that are the primary causes for concern but the growing number of AIDS orphans among this cohort. Although more research needs to be conducted in this area, initial studies conclude that there is a high percentage of school dropouts among orphans. A study conducted among commercial farmworkers in Zimbabwe that had high numbers of AIDS-related deaths among their workers indicated that 48 percent of primary school age orphans had dropped out of school either during their parents' illness or at the time of their death. Furthermore, no orphan of secondary school age was still in school.[39]

Financial constraints and the psychosocial implications of losing one or both parents to a disease that is still highly stigmatized in many parts of Africa contribute to orphans leaving their schooling prematurely. Peers and educators may enforce this psychological trauma by stigmatizing infected or affected children. Even though the extended family has mitigated to some extent the impact of the growing number of AIDS orphans on the African state, the increased financial commitment this poses means that they are unable in many cases to provide for the educational needs of all the children in the household. Thus, immediate family and boys are frequently given preference in such situations.

It is erroneous to assume that the disruption of a child's education occurs only when a parent dies. Many children leave school for short periods, either to care for a sick parent or sibling or to work to sustain the household. Thus, by the time the parent dies many learners are likely to be over the age of their class, which has also been cited as a reason for orphans leaving school. Students who are able to remain at school are less likely to afford to pay for books or uniforms. The pursuant economic and psychosocial vulnerability of AIDS orphans makes them more susceptible to abuse or engaging in prostitution, which in turn predisposes them to contracting HIV.

The increased number of students failing to complete their schooling will result in fewer people being able to enter skilled employment. This could negatively affect the economy of a country, depending on the amount of demand for skilled labor. The shrinkage in the pool of skilled workers will be further exacerbated by high HIV-incidence rates among those completing tertiary education and among the newly employed. In South Africa, it is estimated that AIDS deaths will peak in the age group thirty to forty years, the most productive age group for skilled labor.[40] Increased demand will be placed on the education system to train additional skilled workers to compensate for this decrease.

For the education sector to meet the challenge presented by HIV/AIDS, it will be necessary to extend its role beyond the academic and to place great emphasis on providing its learners with life-management skills and crisis support in order to prevent them from becoming victims of the virus and to enable them to cope with the various stresses that the epidemic will place on their lives. With regard to future strategic planning, policymakers need to take into account that numbers of people requiring education may decline as a result of decreased birthrates and higher infant mortality due to HIV/AIDS.

Agriculture

Many African economies are still basically agrarian. Approximately 80 percent of the continent's population rely on agriculture for their livelihoods. HIV/AIDS has had detrimental effects on the productivity of both commercial and subsistence farming. However, those who farm for subsistence purposes are hardest hit, as they do not have the financial resources and the labor supply possessed by the commercial sector to mitigate the impact of the disease. The overall ramifications of decreased productivity in this sector for the economic and social welfare of African states is dependent on the degree to which a specific country or community is reliant on agriculture to generate income. Nevertheless, HIV/AIDS threatens to reverse the development efforts of local governments and the international donor community in general, which have to a large extent focused their attention on this sector as an efficient means of uplifting the entire population.

AIDS-related illnesses decrease the amount of time the infected person can spend farming. Caregivers, usually women, also forfeit the opportunity to generate income or provide food for their households through farming. As subsistence farming is usually a labor-intensive activity, especially during planting and harvesting, prolonged periods of illness result in the loss of income because of unmarketed or unfarmed cash crops. Moreover, instead of growing food for household consumption, food must now be bought for this purpose. Frequently, farm equipment, together with other household goods such as radios and bicycles, must be sold to pay for healthcare expenses. The selling of farming implements, which were often provided as part of development initiatives, makes farming less efficient, more labor intensive, and less productive.

The death of a male head of household jeopardizes the food security of the remaining members of the household. Gender bias regarding inheritance rights sometimes results in livestock being surrendered to the husband's male relative, further undermining the economic security of the household. In addition, gender bias excludes women from securing loans or agricultural extension services that they require in order to continue or expand agricultural activities. Although many studies have focused on the problems surrounding female-headed households, very little has been done to address the phenomenon of child-headed households. Children are at a greater disadvantage than women; because of their age, they are excluded from accessing the services required to farm and many lack the necessary agricultural expertise to farm.

Impact on Households

The impact of HIV/AIDS on the household depends on how many members are infected, whether or not they are employed, and whether they are in the AIDS stage of the disease. The general trend is that HIV results in a decline in household income and savings. In South Africa, it is estimated that the financial impact of AIDS on households is 30 percent more than from deaths due to other causes.[41] As an employed infected person develops AIDS, he or she is often unable to work, resulting in a decrease in household income. Simultaneously, that person's medical expenses increase, creating a double burden on the household. That burden might be manageable if only one household member had AIDS. Unfortunately, many household members develop AIDS concurrently, stretching household finances to the limit. In African states with high employment or a large informal economic sector, the impact of HIV cannot be mitigated by the presence of a provident fund, private medical aid, or unemployment insurance. If HIV/AIDS is highly stigmatized in a particular community, it may also preclude unemployed infected people from accessing the few social support mechanisms for which they may be eligible.

The medical expenses of the HIV-positive person consume a considerable amount of the household's income. The amount expended on medical treatment becomes more severe the closer the sick person comes to death. In Rwanda, households with an HIV/AIDS patient spend on average twenty times more on healthcare annually than those without such a family member. Only one-third of those households can manage to meet these extra costs.[42] Although public health care is free in many African countries, HIV-positive people frequently pay to use private facilities and traditional healers in attempt to find a more effective method of treatment or, ultimately, a cure.

The decline in household income due to AIDS has ramifications for HIV-negative family members. The elderly are faced with having to care for grandchildren, and their meager resources become the sole source of income for the household. This is a reversal of societal norms, whereby the elderly are usually taken care of by their children. Frequently, household members have to forfeit formal or informal employment to care for sick family members. Either children are taken out of school when the household can no longer afford school fees, or they are regularly absent because they need to care for the sick. A study conducted in urban areas in Côte d'Ivoire reveals the extent of the damage inflicted by HIV/AIDS on the household. In AIDS-affected households, outlay on education was halved, food consumption dropped by 41 percent, and expenditure on health care quadrupled.[43]

The impact of HIV/AIDS on many household economies is so disastrous that they do not recover even after the AIDS sufferers die. Migration and urbanization have also undermined and often dissolved southern African societal structures. The care of infected or affected people is thereby handed over to state social services that are already overutilized due to poor economic conditions.

Orphans

An estimated 13.2 million children had lost either a mother or both parents to AIDS by the end of 1999. Ninety-five percent of these children live in sub-Saharan Africa. Minister of Health Manto Tshabalala-Msimang states that South Africa alone will have approximately 1 million AIDS orphans by 2005, and this number is expected to rise to 2.5 million by 2010.[44] In the past, despite conflicts and humanitarian disasters, Africa had relatively few orphans. However, since 1997, when AIDS-related deaths increased dramatically in most African states, there has been a phenomenal increase in the number of orphans. In certain states, these increases have been as high as 7 and 11 percent.

In Africa, it is primarily the community that has assumed the responsibility of caring for orphaned children—in line with the norms and values of African societies. Orphaned children are usually absorbed into their extended family. However, with the epidemic resulting in an explosion of orphans, this traditional coping mechanism is being pushed to capacity, with extended family units having to care for more and more children. It is not uncommon for a relative to be caring for ten additional children.

The increasing number of orphans is taking its toll on the extended families' ability to care for these children. Moreover, AIDS orphans are more vulnerable and neglected than other types of orphans. According to a joint United Nations Childrens' Fund and UNAIDS study, AIDS orphans are at a greater risk of malnutrition, illness, abuse, and sexual exploitation. They often face stigmatization and discrimination that, in turn, deprive them of basic social services and education. A World Bank report concurs with these findings, stating that AIDS orphans are frequently malnourished and less educated when compared to other children in the household.[45] The psychosocial effects of losing one or both parents to AIDS are enormous, and measures need to be put in place by the state or organizations that focus on these children to alleviate these issues. Additional complications arise when orphans themselves turn out to be HIV positive.

With the capacity of the extended household to absorb orphans failing, the phenomenon of child-headed households is increasing, as are the number of street children. These children are at an even greater disadvantage, as they must fend for themselves and often for their siblings. Many development institutions, both government and private, have not equipped themselves to deal with child-headed households. As a result, these children cannot access various social welfare or development facilities. Growing numbers of street children are also problematic, and many turn to crime or prostitution for survival. In general, AIDS orphans growing up under poor socioeconomic conditions are at higher risk of developing antisocial behavior and of becoming less-productive members of society. This will ultimately have profound implications for their societies.[46]

Political Stability

The state's ability to govern effectively will be compromised as valuable civil servants are lost to the disease. Already, essential services in many southern African states are being depleted. Government credibility may be called into question when it becomes more difficult to meet the basic needs of the population due to the inroads made by HIV/AIDS on the economy. This has the potential to lead to unrest within the state that could ultimately spill over into the region. Large-scale migration may occur to states where more favorable economic conditions exist or where better medical treatment is available. This could also lead to intrastate conflict, as local populations clash with migrants who are perceived to be encroaching on employment and social services and thereby limiting their availability. This tension already exists in South Africa within an economic context. Such conflict could have a negative impact on relations between members of the Southern Africa Development Community (SADC).

In the context of southern Africa, HIV/AIDS poses a human security threat to every one of the seven categories listed in the UNDP's *Human Development Report*. It is imperative that southern African states act quickly and decisively or the impact of HIV/AIDS on their societies will become even more severe. However, many of these states still insist on relegating the disease to a mere health care concern. This approach is exceptionally problematic, as the causes and impacts of HIV/AIDS on society will never be understood if viewed from this narrow vantage point. Only a multisectoral approach will allow states to deal fully with the complex, interconnected dynamics of the disease. Regarding HIV/AIDS as a human security threat provides a suitably broad focus for the adoption of such an approach. Evidence already indicates that states, such as Botswana and Uganda, that have adopted multisectoral approaches are pushing back the epidemic.

Elevating HIV/AIDS to a security issue also ensures that it receives the high-level response that it requires. Expanding its view of HIV/AIDS beyond a health care problem has allowed the UN to intensify its efforts in assisting states in confronting their epidemics. All UN organs are required to deal with HIV/AIDS as it pertains to their particular mandate. For instance, the UNDP will focus on various aspects of HIV/AIDS and development. Furthermore, UN Secretary-General Kofi Annan has secured the financial commitment of the international community to fighting HIV/AIDS by establishing the Global AIDS Fund. The fund intends to raise $7–10 billion annually from industrialized countries, including $2 million a year from the United States. Fifty percent of the funds will be used to purchase HIV/AIDS medicine for more than 10 percent of the estimated 25.3 million infected Africans. The remaining 50 percent would be used to strengthen and accelerate existing prevention programs. Although the fund's focus is almost exclusively on HIV/AIDS, the project also aims to improve treatment for other killer diseases in developing-world countries such as malaria and tuberculosis. Whether these funds can be raised remains doubtful.

Confronting the Challenges of HIV/AIDS

HIV/AIDS threatens to eclipse both the development and security agenda of the SADC. For example, one of the priority sectoral areas of cooperation from the inception of the SADC and its precursor, the Southern African Development Coordination Conference, has been food security. However, HIV/AIDS will make the attainment of this goal more difficult as both the commercial and subsistence agricultural sectors dwindle due to the incapacitation of large numbers of the region's farmers. Unfortunately, this will also affect other areas of regional concern such as rural development; the socioeconomic fabric of rural communities extending into urban areas; the heavily gendered dimension of the economic and personal security of women and girls, and their role as workers and caregivers; and the bedrock institutions of society contained in family and kinship relationships and how these link to the wider society.[47]

The HIV/AIDS pandemic is emblematic of the extent to which southern Africa's evolving security architecture will have to broaden its scope and capacity to deal with threats to regional stability beyond conventional political-military threats to state security. In the words of the SADC's executive secretary, there is a pressing need to adopt "a multisectoral approach to deal with the issue of HIV/AIDS as no longer solely a health problem, but an emergency development problem."[48] Unfortunately, many SADC initiatives still regard HIV/AIDS as a healthcare issue.

At present, southern African states are tackling HIV/AIDS primarily at a national level. This is necessary, in so far as the dynamics of the disease differ from state to state. Thus, a "one size fits all" HIV/AIDS policy would not be very effective. However, regional cooperation in the area of HIV/AIDS could augment and strengthen national efforts. It could also attempt to mitigate the impact of HIV/AIDS on society by strengthening development efforts and economic cooperation. The organization could also facilitate the exchange of information on the types of HIV/AIDS policies particular states have found to be effective. This could be especially helpful, given the fact that Botswana in particular has an exceptionally successful HIV/AIDS program involving public-private initiatives with both local and international actors. To some extent, this exchange of information is taking place. The ministers of health from SADC states have had meetings to discuss issues such as mother to child transmission, vaccine initiatives, the safety of blood, and access to antiretroviral drugs. Nevertheless, the need exists to hold these types of meetings more frequently and to expand their scope beyond issues of healthcare.

The SADC could endeavor to purchase anti-AIDS drugs in bulk for its members and negotiate discounted prices with the pharmaceutical companies for such bulk transactions. Drug manufacturers have in the past offered to reduce the price of AIDS drugs to the SADC and to assist these countries in establishing a health infrastructure. However, SADC health ministers believe that this is not a sustainable solution. They accuse drug manufacturers of not putting forward a clear offer. Instead they argue that manufacturers do not want to negotiate with the SADC but prefer to price their products according to what they believe each individual country can afford. It may be prudent to review this stance.

The region could also work together in order to achieve the objectives of the 2001 UN General Assembly on HIV/AIDS. At the General Assembly, governments pledged to pursue a series of benchmark targets relating to prevention, care, support, treatment, impact alleviation, and HIV/AIDS orphans. The SADC could devise regional responses to issues that spur the spread of the disease, such as migrant labor, refugees, and domestic violence, as a way of motivating states to improve their own domestic responses to HIV/AIDS. Unfortunately, regional organizations like the SADC cannot enforce the adoption of such initiatives by member states. At present, the organization has developed a code of conduct relating to HIV/AIDS and the workplace. This sets standards for addressing HIV/AIDS in the work environment in an ethical, nondiscriminatory, positive way. In addition, the SADC may consider using the Global AIDS Fund to finance regional HIV/AIDS initiatives.

HIV/AIDS and the Southern African Security Architecture

Although this chapter has discussed HIV/AIDS as a human security issue, the disease has ramifications for traditional security concerns. The pandemic is compromising the ability of the state to ensure law and order, as it disrupts institutions such as the courts, the police, and the army.

The military has come to represent a high-risk group for contracting HIV/AIDS. A 1995 study revealed that HIV infection rates among the Zimbabwean military were three to four times higher than the levels in the civilian population. This phenomenon is not unique to southern African armies but represents a global trend. A 2002 South African Defense Force report puts its infection rate at 23 percent.[49]

Military and peacekeeping service often includes lengthy periods spent away from home with the result that personnel look for ways to relieve stress, loneliness, and sexual tension. Also, the military's professional ethos tends to excuse or even encourage risk-taking. Most personnel are in the HIV/AIDS high-risk fifteen to twenty-four age group. Peacekeepers frequently use their disposable income to procure the services of sex workers. Military personnel and camps, including peacekeeping forces, attract sex workers and illicit drug dealers.[50]

The high HIV/AIDS infection and prevalence rates among many southern African states' armies have numerous consequences for their ability to ensure their own security, as well as that of the region. The operational readiness of these forces can be compromised if a large number of soldiers are too sick to be deployed. Military expenditure will increase if the state has to recruit and train more personnel to replace those who are dead or too sick to work. Costs will escalate more rapidly if large numbers of highly skilled personnel are lost. Ensuring the cohesion required by military units may be difficult if members of the team have to be replaced frequently, which in turn affects operational readiness. Furthermore, given the mobility of military personnel, armies with high prevalence rates risk spreading the disease rapidly throughout the country or region. This is an important consideration, especially when the SADC deploys peacekeeping forces. Already there has been an attempt, through large-scale condom distribution, to ensure that the peacekeeping force deployed in the Democratic Republic of Congo does not contribute to the spread of the disease in that country. If peacekeeping forces are perceived by the local population to be spreading HIV/AIDS, it undermines the credibility of the entire peacekeeping operation.

The military expenditure of southern African states could be curtailed by HIV/AIDS, as they are forced to allocate more funds to alleviating the effects of the disease on their populations. States could also refuse to contribute to peacekeeping operations for the same reasons. The upgrade of the South African military has been severely criticized by AIDS activists as unnecessary activity. They believe that the money would be better spent providing antiretroviral treatment to the growing number of HIV-positive people. Diverting funds away from the military impedes its ability to operate effectively and will ultimately limit the number of SADC peacekeeping activities. Prevention and treatment programs for soldiers could also increase military spending. However, this may prove cost-effective in the long term if it results in reducing infection rates as well as allowing HIV-positive personnel to continue in active service. Already Botswana and Zambia have instituted successful prevention programs among their armed forces.[51] The SADC should make prevention and treatment programs a fundamental part of its peacekeeping activities.

Conclusion

> Peace to have meaning for those who have known only suffering in both peace and war must be translated into bread or rice, shelter, health and education as well as freedom and human dignity.
>
> —Ralph Johnson Bunche,
> UN Undersecretary-General for Special Political Affairs,
> 1904–1971

HIV/AIDS in southern Africa has been heralded as an unprecedented crisis that demands unprecedented action. The disease endangers not only economic and human development and state and regional security but also the larger goal of an African renaissance on the continent. The concept of human security provides a useful framework for confronting HIV/AIDS in southern Africa, as it allows for the multidimensional focus that the pandemic requires. However, few southern African states have implemented the responses necessary to reverse infection rates.

The challenge facing southern African states is considerable, as they must institute both prevention and treatment campaigns because they have generalized epidemics. Combating HIV/AIDS in this region involves substantially expanding development programs at a time when such initiatives are under threat, ironically, from the disease itself as well as from other factors such as structural adjustment programs and the depressed global economy. Although the onus is primarily on individual states to address their epidemic, as the pandemic affects issues of common concern for states in the region such as trade, development, and migrant labor, it is essential that a multisectoral regional response be implemented. Furthermore, as most of these states lack the resources to launch comprehensive HIV/AIDS programs on their own, an accelerated response, especially at a financial level, from the developed world is vital. However, whether the political will exists to muster the required response at individual, community, state, regional, and international levels to this extraordinary threat to the human security of southern Africa remains to be seen.

Notes

1. G. Maclean, "The Changing Perception of Human Security: Coordinating National and Multilateral Responses," United Nations Association Canada, 1999 [available at: http://www.unac.org/en/link_learn/canada/security/perception.asp], 2.

2. L. Axworthy, *Human Security: Safety for People in a Changing World,* Department of Foreign Affairs and International Trade, Ottawa, Canada, 29 April 1999, 2.

3. UNDP, *Human Development Report 1999* (New York and Oxford: Oxford University Press, 1999), 36.

4. UNAIDS, "Report on the Global HIV/AIDS Epidemic," Geneva, December 2001, 14.

5. Eileen Stillwagon, "HIV Transmission in Latin America: A Comparison with Africa and Policy Implications," *South Africa Journal of Economics* 68, 5 (December 2000): 992.

6. UNAIDS, "Report on the Global HIV/AIDS Epidemic," Geneva, June 2000, 4.

7. J. McGeary, "Death Stalks a Continent," *Time,* 7 February 2001.

8. World Bank, *Confronting AIDS: Public Priorities in a Global Epidemic* (Oxford: Oxford University Press, 1997), 124.

9. The reasons for the absence of the male head of the household include divorce, migrant labor, abandonment, urbanization, and families split up due to war or internal displacement. Zimbabwean Women's Resource Centre and Network, "The Gender Dimensions of Access and Land Use Rights in Zimbabwe: Evidence to the Land Use Rights Commission," Harare, January 1994, 2.

10. Adults, as defined here, are those between fifteen and forty-nine years old. UNAIDS, December 2000, 3.

11. Jacqui Ala, "Gender Biases: Stumbling Blocks to Effective Development Policies," *Discussion Papers in International Relations* 1, 4 (September 1997): 12.

12. Passing grade five is often used as a measure of literacy. Liz Walker and Leah Gilbert, "Women at Risk: HIV/AIDS—A South African Case Study," paper presented at the AIDS in Context Conference, University of the Witwatersrand, Johannesburg, 4–7 April 2001, 18.

13. P. Sparr, *Mortgaging Women's Lives: A Feminist Critique of Structural Adjustment* (New Jersey: Zed Books, 1994), 27.

14. S. Hoosen and A. Collins, "Women, Culture and AIDS: How Discourses of Gender and Sexuality Affect Safe Sex Behaviour," paper presented at the AIDS in Context Conference, 12.

15. Ibid.

16. C. Kaboresa (Dept. of Women Studies, Mackere University) interview by Jacqui Ala, Kamparla, Uganda, 15 January 2001.

17. World Bank, *Confronting AIDS: Public Priorities in a Global Epidemic* (New York: Oxford University Press, 1997), 126.

18. UNAIDS, June 2000, 48.

19. Ibid., 50.

20. Walker and Gilbert, "Women at Risk," 21.

21. UNAIDS, June 2000, 40.

22. "Youth Still Ignorant on AIDS, Study Shows," *Johannesburg Star*, 18 July 2001, 6.

23. Claire Bisseker, "Botswana and Uganda Lead the Way in the Battle," *Financial Mail,* 15 June 2001, 34.

24. Claire Bisseker, "It's Worse Than You Thought—Unless Behaviour Changes," *Financial Mail*, 15 June 2001, 34.

25. UN Foundation, "Disease May Cause Zero Population Growth in Zimbabwe," *UN Wire*, 5 June 2001 [available at: http://unfoundation.org/unwire/2001/06/05/index.asp], 2.

26. Ibid., 1.

27. Bisseker, "It's Worse Than You Thought," 34.

28. UN Foundation, "Botswana to Lose One-Third of Economic Potential," *UN Wire,* 17 May 2000 [available at: http://www.unfoundation.org.unwire/archives/UNWIRE000517.cfm], 1.

29. A. Shevel, "AIDS Will Shrink Economy 17% by 2010," *Business Report,* 29 November 2000, 1.

30. Ibid.

31. However, direct costs will be mitigated depending on the number of unskilled laborers employed, as these usually receive fewer benefits.

32. LoveLife and ABT, Inc., "Impending Catastrophe Revisited: An Update on the HIV/AIDS Epidemic in South Africa," Kaiser Foundation, Parklands, South Africa, 2001, 13.

33. Mary Crewe, "A Grim Prognosis as Paralysis Grips Education Chiefs: Effects of Pandemic Underestimated or Ignored," *Financial Mail,* 28 January 2000, 6.

34. LoveLife and ABT, "Impending Catastrophe," 15.

35. Ibid., 21.

36. Ibid.

37. UNAIDS, June 2000, 31.

38. Ibid., 27, 29, 42.

39. Ibid., 30.

40. LoveLife and ABT, "Impending Catastrophe," 32.

41. UNAIDS, December 2001, 6.

42. UNAIDS, June 2000, 27.

43. Ibid.

44. Ibid., 8.

45. Ibid., 28.

46. LoveLife and ABT, "Impending Catastrophe," 11.

47. Francis Kornegay and Christopher Landsberg, "The HIV/AIDS Challenge to Southern Africa's Evolving Security Architecture," unpublished paper, Johannesburg, December 2001, 2.

48. Prega Ramsamy, "SADC: The Way Forward," in *Regional Integration in Southern Africa, Comparative Perspectives,* ed. Christopher Clapham, Gregg Mills, Anna Morner, and Elizabeth Sidiropolous (Johannesburg: South African Institute of International Affairs, 2001), 38.

49. UNAIDS, "AIDS and the Military," Best Practices Collection [available at http://www.unaids.org].

50. UNAIDS, "AIDS and the Military," Geneva, May 1998, 3.

51. Ibid., 6.

Part 2

National and Regional Actors

8

Civil Society in Southern Africa

PATRICK MOLUTSI

Currently, conflict is endemic on the African political landscape. As Richard Sandbrook notes, although deadly conflicts have afflicted most continents since 1980, no part of the world has been more negatively affected than Africa.[1] Even the conflicts in Bosnia, Kosovo, and Tajikistan in Europe; Sri Lanka, Cambodia, and Afghanistan in Asia; and Peru, Colombia, Haiti, and El Salvador in South and Central America have not approached the protracted violence of conflicts in Africa. African conflicts are both persistent and widespread; they have taken an enormous toll on human life, social and physical infrastructure, and other resources. In 1997, Richard Joseph observed that during the last two decades of the twentieth century, over forty of the fifty-one African countries were afflicted by either intrastate or interstate conflict.[2] Conflict not only is a direct military threat to the physical security of African countries but also undermines national and regional efforts toward their peace and development; it is thus a threat to human security in its broadest sense. Therefore, it is important that evolving security processes and strategies are made integral to broader processes of democratization and development planning and that they involve a wide spectrum of society. Civil society has much to contribute to peacebuilding, peacekeeping, humanitarian efforts, and democratization in southern Africa.

Human Security

Southern Africa remains one of the continent's conflict-ridden regions. Despite the early optimism and triumphalism that followed the collapse of apartheid, peaceful transition to majority rule in South Africa, and the end to conflict in Mozambique, the region has been beset by disputes of new and complex dimensions.[3] The return to civil war in Angola following the refusal of the National Union for the Total Independence of Angola (UNITA) to accept the results of the 1992 elections; the postelection turmoil and destruction of property in Lesotho in 1994; and the war in the Democratic Republic of Congo (DRC) have surrounded southern Africa with fresh and tortuous conflicts. Political tensions and economic breakdown in Zimbabwe during 2000–2001 have also shown that the roots of past conflict are still strong in the region. Present conflict situations are perhaps even more difficult and demanding in character than colonial ones.

Three distinct features separate the present regional conflicts from earlier manifestations. First, in the current conflicts there is no single enemy; typically many enemies are involved. In the past, it was easy to blame conflict on colonial forces, Cold War politics, and secessionist surrogates and their superpower supporters. Today the enemy is the internal section of the population that demands the same unmet rights and opportunities contested in the anticolonial struggles. Second, present conflicts cannot be dismissed on ideological grounds of communism or religious fundamentalism. On the contrary, they are predicated on a broad liberal democratic and development agenda. The actors in these conflicts often have a strong moral ground for inclusiveness, representation, and participation in national and community affairs to which their group is historically attached. Third, the worst aspect of the current conflicts is that by dividing states that were previously fighting fraternal wars, they are also destroying the social and institutional capital developed over the past decades.

In the past five years of conflict in the DRC and, more recently, Zimbabwe, both the Southern African Development Community (SADC) and its Organ on Politics, Defense, and Security have become ineffective and have often themselves become battlegrounds for contending forces in regional conflicts. The activities of UNITA have created tensions between Angola and Zambia, while those of the Capri secessionist groups have embroiled Botswana and Namibia in a new refugee problem.

The above examples demonstrate the multifaceted nature of the present forms of conflict in the SADC. The nature and form of these conflicts have direct implications for the type of security architecture that the region seeks to establish. This means that our definition of security must be broadly based, to cover not only the security of states but also human security, with a strong developmental orientation. Even though the SADC has begun to identify human security as a priority, it has not yet put sufficient emphasis on operationalizing it so that individuals, communities, states, and regional entities can all feel that their political, environmental, economic, health, physical, and military security are being protected. Michael Renners concisely presented this need in 1997:

> Unlike traditional military security, human security is much less about procuring arms and deploying troops than it is about strengthening the social and environmental fabric of societies and improving their governance. To avoid the instability and breakdown now witnessed in countless areas around the globe, a human security policy must take into account a complex web of social, economic, environmental and other factors.[4]

Civil society has played a vital role in determining a human security framework in the past, and it will need to remain a key actor in the new security processes and strategy in southern Africa.

Understanding Civil Society

The concept of civil society has been—and remains—a subject of intense academic debate. Although the concept is an old one in political science vocabulary, like the concept of governance it has gained considerable currency only in the past few decades. In the 1980s, the Solidarity revolts—the trade union uprisings in Poland and subsequently in the rest of the former Soviet Union bloc—were popularized in the West as the efforts of civil society to distance itself from authoritarian regimes. Since then, the reformist and transformative roles played by trade unions, women's groups, churches and church organizations, and human rights and environmental protection groups against authoritarian regimes in Africa, Asia, and Latin America have attracted the sympathy and support of many donor organizations. As articulated by several Western analysts, having started in the 1980s as a critical complement to the market and democracy as a mean for development, civil society now stands as a main cure for social ills.

Outside the Gramscian conception that separates civil society from political society, civil society is increasingly accepted as an independent entity, voluntarily formed by citizens, that ensures the state guards or promotes society's values. Augustine Ikelegbe has emphasized that civil society is a layer of voluntary, popular, public, and social actions of nonstate actors that utilizes social, cultural, political, and ethnic networks and nonstate activities in pursuance of objectives, which are usually of a public nature.[5]

Civil society in southern Africa is made up of organizations of professions; academic and research institutes; and labor, youth, women's, peasants', communal, social, cultural, urban neighborhood, development, environmental, civil, and human rights groups that build identities and platforms in respect of collective claims and civic actions.[6] Civil society in this context is not merely an urban phenomenon. As in other parts of

Africa, civil society includes traditional ethnic, religious, and cultural groups. Some of these were critical in the decolonization process.[7] Many have also survived the hostile environment of the one-party state and military regimes of the past forty years that have followed independence. Thus, rather than being a modern phenomenon, civil society in one form or another is historically embedded in the political, social, cultural, and economic aspects of African societies in much the same way as in Western and other societies elsewhere.

This raises the fundamental question of why African civil society seems to have emerged only recently, with the fall of authoritarian regimes. Also relevant is the question of why African civil society apparently has not made much impact on the continent's development.

The answers to these questions are crucial to understanding the role of civil society in conflict management and democracy promotion in Africa today. First, for many years civil society in Africa was suppressed, manipulated, divided, and incorporated by the authoritarian state. This weakened and derailed it from its independent work. Second, in the past, the majority of bilateral donors considered it interference to fund civil society directly without going through the state. This gave the state control over what the donors gave to civil society and on what civil society groups could receive funding. In the end, this gave the state greater clout and a financial muscle to control the agenda of the civil society.[8] Current work with civil society should not only consider past mistakes but, more important, seek to create a new environment of inclusiveness for all agents of development—the state, civil society, the private sector, and external development agencies.

Civil society is not without its limitations and problems. Whereas, in general, literature has tended to be populist and unrealistic about the potential and role of civil society, there is growing evidence that shows that civil society, like the market, will not serve as a panacea for all developmental, political, and human security challenges in southern Africa. On the contrary, some civil society groups, including trade unions, the church, women's groups, and ethnic communities that advocate peace and democracy, have themselves experienced conflict, intolerance, and democratic deficit. Some have leadership that were last elected to power through questionable electoral processes more than two decades or so ago. Thus, J. A. Odera was right to note as early as 1997 that "the impact of civil society in conflict management can be either positive or negative."[9]

As she further observed, the strength of civil society will ideally depend on its commitment to pursue, without fear or favor, respect for human rights and thus to promote the building of a just society.[10] Like

Odera, we do not wish to underestimate the importance and critical role that civil society has played in the liberation wars and struggles for democratic change in southern Africa; we nonetheless caution against a populist portrayal of civil society as a panacea for social ills. Also, the proliferation of civil society organizations may fragment, and this weakens communities.

Main Characteristics of Civil Society in Southern Africa

The role and contribution of civil society in Africa has differed from one subregion to another, and within the same subregion from one country to another, depending on the character of colonialism and the nature of the postcolonial state. Civil society in southern Africa is diverse and complex but still largely building its capacity. Its strength differs from one country to another. The stronger, more experienced, and better-resourced civil society entities are found most prevalently in countries with a history of liberation struggle, followed by those countries where the one-party state and dictatorship were strong. Zimbabwe, Namibia, and South Africa, for instance, were involved in long liberation struggles, which galvanized their civil societies into unusually strong entities, able to organize widespread political and civil disobedience. The least organized and politically weak civil societies are found in countries with low levels of economic difficulty and limited tensions over land, and where liberal democratic openings have existed for a longer period, for example, in Botswana and Mauritius.

There are, of course, exceptions to this general classification. For instance, although it had a long experience of one-party state rule and major economic difficulties, Tanzanian civil society has always been low-key and is considered to be less radical within the same cluster as Botswana's civil society. In countries such as Lesotho, Angola, and Mozambique civil society has been at different times coopted, politicized, and used by contending political elites.

In short, southern African civil society exhibits the following features:

- Unequal levels of social and political sophistication.
- High concentration in urban areas.
- Considerable preoccupation with the welfare aspects of members.
- Predominance of ethnic and cultural groups that tend to have more of a local than a national or regional focus.
- Low levels of management, negotiation, and lobbying skills.
- Low command of resources and high dependence on state and other external support.

A survey of the literature shows the main sectors of the civil society in southern Africa to be trade unions, church and church organizations, human rights and legal aid centers, women's organizations, environmental groups, youth organizations, the academic and research community, and ethnic and cultural groups.

Trade Unions

Trade unions have played a historic role in the decolonization process in southern Africa. Their role in different countries has been widely recognized and documented. From the early twentieth century, the embryonic trade unions in the commercial sector took the lead in mobilizing opinion against discriminatory legislation and oppressive political systems, not only in South Africa but also in Zimbabwe, Zambia, Tanzania, and Mozambique, to name but a few. In the later part of the twentieth century, trade unions across the subregion became the nucleus of the liberation movement. Trade unions are currently actively involved in political and economic reforms in many SADC countries. Examples include, in South Africa, the Confederation of South African Trade Unions (COSATU) and the National Union of Mineworkers; the Organizacao dos Trabalhadores des Mozambique; the Zimbabwe Congress of Trade Unions (ZCTU); the Zambian Congress of Trade Unions; and the Malawi Congress of Trade Unions. Trade unions in other SADC countries continue to be at the center of economic policy discussion, such as the debate on privatization.

Over the past decade, however, the trade unions have found themselves playing three contradictory roles:

- They have been, and continue to be, effective agents of political liberation and democratization. The COSATU, for instance, is giving a lot of moral and material support to the ZCTU in Zimbabwe and the Swaziland Federation of Trade Unions, given the debates over democratization in those two countries.
- Trade unions have also been strongly protective and have fought for restricted immigration policies.
- By transforming themselves into political parties, trade unions have weakened their role as civic organizations able to mobilize workers across party political lines.[11]

These roles might make it difficult for trade unions to defend democratic governance and help to build peace in their respective countries. However, in southern Africa trade unions have been and will remain central to popular struggles and resistance movements. The reformist agenda of unions makes them critical partners and players in human security, in that they fight for freedom, justice, equity, fairness, and good governance in individual countries but have also, more than any other institution in the region, adopted a pan-regional agenda and solidarity action.

The Church and Church Organizations

The church, too, boasts a rich history of resistance against injustice and war. It has also been a major force in educational and health developments in the region. It was an early founder of schools and health facilities in many countries in the region. As individual denominations, and increasingly as multidenominational groups, churches have played a pivotal role in ending wars in South Africa, Namibia, and Mozambique and oppressive rule in Malawi and Zambia. In Malawi, it is widely believed that the pastoral letter by the Catholic bishops of Malawi in 1993 calling for democratic change was decisive in mobilizing public opinion against the Banda regime.[12] Similar calls are currently being heard in Angola, Zimbabwe, and Swaziland. Following the end of apartheid, the church has continued to play a role in peaceful resolution of conflict at the national level, for example, in supporting the National Truth and Reconciliation Commission and also in conflict-ridden situations such as those in KwaZulu-Natal and in Western Cape in South Africa. Through umbrella organizations the church is very actively involved with postconflict communities in Mozambique, Namibia, South Africa, and in places such as Botswana, where it is supporting development among indigenous groups and the poor.

In Angola, the Catholic Justice and Peace Organ is reported to be exerting pressure on both the Movimento Popular de Libertação de Angola government and UNITA to end the twenty-five-year-long war in that country.[13]

Human Rights and Legal Aid Centers

A number of human rights and legal centers have been established across southern Africa in the past three decades. A number of the universities are also providing free legal services to students and the neediest sections of the population. Human rights commissions and groups have brought cases of injustice by the police and the army to public attention. However, human rights commissions, in particular, remain weak and largely dormant in a number of countries, including Botswana, Swaziland, and Tanzania, where they are almost dysfunctional or exist only on paper. Yet demands for legal defense by, among others, deserted women, disadvantaged prisoners, and minority ethnic groups have increased. The work of legal centers is spreading very fast into the large villages and towns in the subregion.

Women's Organizations

The reasons for the growth in women's groups have substantially reflected the positive international climate relating to declarations and conference resolutions on the issue of gender equality and women's rights. Across the subregion, governments have come under pressure to provide women a place in newly established development machinery, to revise laws that discriminated against women, and to formulate policies on women in development. On the whole, positive developments have occurred in this area in the past five years. These include the appointment of women into senior positions in the judiciary, management, and politics. The SADC Gender Division shows that, relative to the rest of sub-Saharan Africa, southern Africa has the highest number of women in decisionmaking positions. Although much more needs to be done, some SADC member states have made some progress leading to record proportions of over 30 percent women in parliament. Governments have also committed themselves to achieving higher levels of female participation at all levels but, more important, at least to a target of 30 percent in political and decisionmaking structures by 2005.[14]

Like the trade unions and church and human rights groups, women's organizations have been active in peacebuilding and democratization. Women's groups are widely involved with land-rights struggles, refugee problems, and support to communities emerging from conflict, particularly in Angola, Mozambique, and Zimbabwe.

Environmental Advocacy Groups

Environmental groups have also emerged as strong advocates of efficient and equitable use of land, water resources, wildlife, and mining operations. In the past few years, such groups have been central in managing conflict between government policy on wildlife and the rights of communities neighboring wildlife reserves, including indigenous peoples.[15] Both environmental and human rights groups are also actively involved in land-conflict and resettlement issues in Namibia and South Africa.[16] Environmental lobby groups seem to be more effective at managing conflict at the community level, as well as moderating policy in favor of local communities.

Youth Organizations

In the past five years, many countries have seen the reemergence of the youth or student movement that had been suppressed by oppressive and authoritarian regimes. Youth organizations are now reestablishing themselves and lobbying for policies and programs that favor young people. As a result, they are increasingly recognized as an emerging lobby group. Through protests and joint political activities with other civil society groups, the student lobby can become a useful anchor for debates and activities on conflict management and local development in the region. The youth movement is, however, weakened by both high levels of unemployment and a lack of lobbying skills.

The Academic and Research Community

The academic community in southern Africa is a critical and growing source of information on democratic development and conflict management. Research networks exist throughout the subregion and are producing extensive and useful comparative information on sources of conflict and required policy action. Universities in the region are collaborating with others from the North not only on conflict research but also in mounting training programs on this subject.[17] For example, the Southern African Regional Institute for Policy Studies has a standing annual training program with the Austrian Conflict Research Program and a regional research program on conflict prevention sponsored by the Danish government. There is a growing need to coordinate the activities of the research community with policymaking processes so that the policymakers are informed by detailed studies being done in the subregion by citizens themselves.

Ethnic and Cultural Groups

Ethnic groups of different kinds have played a role in the attainment of democratic reforms in their countries. Most of these groups have been politically, culturally, and economically excluded, exploited, and marginalized. Minority groups of Khoisan background are still involved in democratic struggles for accommodation, land rights, and social justice. This branch of civil society must also be recognized and involved in policy and strategy for human security in the region.

Bringing Civil Society into the Human Security Process

Both the Organization of African Unity and International Peace Academy promulgated a multilayered approach to peacebuilding and conflict management. This approach calls for the use of local and regional partners as important agents of conflict management. However, so far emphasis has been laid on national governments and subregional organizations such as the SADC and the Economic Community of West African States. Clearly, with more resources and better coordination, different civil society organizations can play an increased and effective role, complementing but not substituting for other players in conflict management. In a limited way, civil society has already been involved in conflict management. More important, it has become the anchor for development and democratic governance, both of which are the basis for lasting peace and grounded human security.

Which civil society groups may be best placed to play a role in conflict management? Table 8.1 seeks to illustrate the relative strengths of certain civil society groupings within each country in the SADC region. The table takes five types of civil society organizations and makes a comparative assessment based on their experience, strength, legitimacy, and potential. The characterization is limited and subjective—it excludes some groups and may inadequately represent others within an evolving reality. It is intended to be illustrative and indicative rather than exhaustive and definitive.

The strongest organs of civil society in the region are the media and women's groups. Religious and human rights groups come second, and labor groups come third in terms of strength of activity. However, in terms of relative legitimacy to engage in dialogue and undertake a mediating role, religious, women's, and labor groups seem more likely to be acceptable than, say, media or human rights groups. The latter groups are known for their critical roles and are therefore perceived as partisan. Groups omitted include traditional leaders and academic and professional groups. These two groups are well suited to community-based conflict resolution and arbitration in technical areas. Table 8.2 sketches some possible roles that different civil society groups can play in conflict management.

Table 8.1 Roles of Civil Society Groups in Conflict Management

Country	Labor	Religious	Women's	Human Rights	Media
South Africa	++	+++	+++	++	+++
Zimbabwe	+++	++	+++	++	++
Angola	–	++	++	++	+
Mozambique	+	+	++	++	+
Namibia	–	+	++	++	++
Lesotho	+	+++	+++	++	+++
Swaziland	++	–	+	+	+
Malawi	++	++	++	+	++
Mauritius	++	+	+	–	+
Botswana	–	–	+	+	+

Notes: +++ active, organized, and articulate; ++ active, well functioning, and visibly articulate on key issues; + young, evolving, and promising; – weak and dormant or inactive.

Table 8.2 Areas of Possible Civil Society Involvement

Organization	Possible Roles
Labor/trade unions	Mediation, protest, policy advocacy, and material support to those in conflict.
Religious groups	Mediation, reconciliation, advocacy, and welfare for the needy.
Women's and youth groups	Peacebuilding, democracy promotion, policy reform, and support to communities in conflict.
Human rights groups/the media	Monitoring conflict and postconflict situations, advocacy, and raising issues related to acquisition of military hardware and so forth.
Academic/professional groups	Monitoring, generating information, and providing platforms for debates.

Conclusion

Civil society has a potentially important role to play in peacebuilding and the human security architecture in southern Africa. Over the past century, different civil society groups, including trade unions, the church, the media, and human rights groups, have played a pivotal role in advocating democratic governance. Their role in this area continues to be relevant and essential for sustainable democracy. However, because of their past political role and close association with the struggle for democratic change in several countries, a number of key civil society groups find themselves limited or divided between supporting the government of the day and playing an advocacy role. This is particularly true of the trade unions in the region. Nonetheless, different sectors of civil society continue to play some role in peacebuilding, reconciliation, and humanitarian efforts. This role can be strengthened through the following measures:

- Better coordination of efforts.
- Closer collaboration with governments and regional organizations.
- Creation of information databases accessible to all involved.
- Creation of a network at the country level of conflict-management chapters bringing together human rights groups, academics, the media, and the church.

The conflict environment in southern Africa has become more complex. In current conflict situations it is easy neither to identify the enemy nor to justify the extent to which they should be confronted with military force. Although space here does not allow for an elaboration of this issue, democratic approaches such as inclusive electoral systems, comprehensive constitutions, and other democratic measures to ensure justice for all are critical prerequisites for human security in southern Africa and elsewhere on the continent.

Notes

The views expressed are those of the author and do not represent the views of the institutions with which he is associated.

1. Richard Sandbrook, *Closing the Circle: Democratisation and Development in Africa Between the Lines* (London: Zed Books, 2000).

2. Richard Joseph, "The International Community and Armed Conflict in Africa—Post Cold War Dilemmas," in *Out of Conflict: From War to Peace,* ed. Gunner M. Sørbø and Peter Vale (Uppsala, Sweden: Africa Nordiska Institute, 1997), 9–22.

3. Peter Vale, "Peace-Making in Southern Africa: Time for Questions," in Sørbø and Vale, *Out of Conflict*, 39–53.

4. Quoted in R. Williams, "Managing Regional Security," in *The IGD Guide to the Southern African Development Community,* ed. Riaan de Villers and Kato Lambreechts (Johannesburg: Institute for Global Dialogue, 2001), 118.

5. Ikelegbe, "Civil Society, Oil and Conflict."

6. Ibid.

7. In West African countries, for instance, social welfare, education, and political representation are often mediated through well-entrenched organizations such as the Ogoni People's Congress, Association of Ibo People, and so forth.

8. The subject of funding civil society remains a contentious one within the framework of the ACP–EU Cotonou agreement (2000).

9. J. A. Odera, "Civil Society and Conflict Management in Africa: A Re-emerging Role," in Sørbø and Vale, *Out of Conflict,* 150.

10. Ibid.

11. In Botswana, for instance, the Botswana Federation of Trade Unions was highly divided by partisan politics in the early years of its formation. Similar divisions seem to exist in the two ZCTUs of Zambia and Zimbabwe.

12. Martin Ott, Kings M. Phiri, and Nandini Patel, eds., *Malawi's Second Democratic Elections* (Blantyre, Malawi: Kachere Series, 2000).

13. BBC CUK–Africa reports have carried stories on the positive efforts by the church to end the war in Angola since the collapse of the peace agreement in 1992.

14. SADC, "Report of the Gender Division, 1999," paper presented at International IDEA's Conference Towards Sustainable Democratic Institutions, Gaborone, Botswana, May 2000.

15. In Botswana, for instance, the Kalahari Conservation Society and other small lobbying groups in the Okavango region joined Greenpeace and others to stop a government project to dam the swamps in 1991–1992.

16. See, for instance, the recent case in which the indigenous people are demanding their land rights in the Northern Province of South Africa.

17. See, for instance, Swedish Committee on Development and Security in Africa, "Report on Development Assistance to Africa," Department of Foreign Affairs, Stockholm, 21 February 1996, 65–80.

9

South Africa and Nigeria as Regional Hegemons

Adekeye Adebajo and Christopher Landsberg

"No Prophet is honored in his own country." The biblical saying sums up the quandary faced by Africa's two political prophets, South Africa's Thabo Mbeki[1] and Nigeria's General Olusegun Obasanjo.[2] Both leaders are respected internationally but face enormous economic and political difficulties at home that have eroded their popularity. Mbeki has inevitably struggled to fill the shoes of his saintly predecessor, Nelson Mandela. Obasanjo, rejected by his own Yoruba people in Nigeria's 1999 presidential elections, has not totally shaken off his military background. Both have faced severe criticism at home for embarking on frequent foreign trips and for not spending more time addressing pressing problems of poverty, unemployment, and crime. Mbeki has been criticized for his domestic AIDS policies; Obasanjo has been castigated for not preventing recurring massacres of civilians by his army. Both prophets have, however, indefatigably traversed the globe spreading the idea of an African renaissance (focusing largely on democracy, development, and security) and seeking foreign investment to revive their ailing economies.[3] Mbeki and Obasanjo have called for greater international burden-sharing in peacekeeping missions in Africa, campaigned for the annulment of Africa's external debt, championed better access for African goods entering Western markets, and called for Africa's integration into the global economy.

In the post–Cold War era, the reluctance of Western countries to intervene militarily in African countries after the U.S. debacle in Somalia in 1993[4] and France's embarrassing policy failures in Zaire and Rwanda in the 1990s[5] led many observers to question whether potential African hegemons like South Africa and Nigeria could fill the security vacuum.[6] It is important, however, to note from the outset some of the constraints upon both states acting as regional hegemons. South Africa and Nigeria can, at best, be described as aspiring or potential hegemons—largely due to military, political, and economic constraints faced by both countries in their efforts to influence the actions of their neighbors. Rather than "regional hegemons" it would be more accurate to describe South Africa and Nigeria as "pivotal states"[7] that, in their respective subregions, possess disproportionate military and economic power and influence relative to other states.

Though South Africa, accounting for about a third of Africa's gross domestic product (GDP), is economically more powerful than Nigeria, it faces even more powerful military challengers and political rivals in its own subregion. The apartheid-era army's destabilization of its neighbors has left a profound distrust of South African military interventionism, which remains strong today. During the 1990s, Nigeria was willing but unable to carry out swift and decisive military interventions in West Africa. South Africa was more able but largely unwilling to undertake such military actions in southern Africa. South Africa has military and economic capacity but lacks the legitimacy to play a hegemonic role. Nigeria arguably has more legitimacy in its own subregion but lacks the military and economic capacity to act as an effective hegemon.

Although South Africa and Nigeria are militarily and politically powerful relative to other subregional states, and may have the will, they lack the capacity and legitimacy to dominate their subregions effectively and often fail to convince other states to follow their lead on vital political, security, and economic issues. Pax Pretoriana has to contend with "bargainers" like Zimbabwe, Namibia, and Angola, while Pax Nigeriana faces "bargainers" like Côte d'Ivoire, Senegal, Liberia, and Burkina Faso. These states have the capability to increase significantly the costs of the aspiring hegemons' attempts to impose their will on their respective subregions.

Do South Africa and Nigeria have the internal cohesion and means to become genuine and constructive hegemons in Africa? Do both states have the ability to win over the confidence of a majority of African states and to convince these states to entrust them with a leadership role in Africa? Are Pretoria and Abuja so resented and envied by many African states that such states would undermine their attempts to act as regional hegemons? Are South Africa and Nigeria prepared to accept and bear the full burdens of hegemony?

As these questions imply, the idea of South Africa and Nigeria as regional hegemons is not one that will go unchallenged. Instead of serving as beacons of democracy and development in Africa, both countries' roles and positions could easily deepen divisions on the African continent. Instead of enhancing solidarity and partnerships in Africa, the role of South Africa and Nigeria could trigger antihegemonic alliances and deepen regional rivalries. While Obasanjo and Mbeki are trying to sell a Pax Africana, their roles could easily be construed as efforts at imposing Pax Pretoriana and Pax Nigeriana on the rest of the continent.[8]

Defining Hegemony

Hegemony is a concept that has often been interpreted in different ways by different analysts. In popular usage, the term conjures up negative images of a bullying, domineering power imposing its will on weaker states. But the technical definition of the term is one that is less value-laden and does not necessarily have such negative connotations. Daniel Bach reminds us of the origins of hegemony during the era of the ancient Greek city-states: "Respect for the autonomy of coalition partners distinguished *hegemonia* from imperial domination based on the use of coercive methods and, ultimately, territorial control. . . . *Hegemonia* represents a system of leadership where power is based on domination as much as cooptation."[9]

According to Graham Evans and Jeffrey Newnham, hegemony means "primacy or leadership. In an international system this leadership would be exercised by a 'hegemon,' a state possessing sufficient capability to fulfill this role."[10] David Myers defines regional hegemons as "states which possess power sufficient to dominate subordinate state systems."[11] Edward Mansfield defines hegemony as "the holding by one state of a preponderance of power in the international system or a regional subsystem, so that it can single-handedly dominate the rules and arrangements by which international and regional political and economic relations are conducted."[12] In a similar vein, Stewart Patrick defines hegemony as "legitimate single-power domination and coordination of the foreign security, political, and economic relations of sovereign states in international society."[13] Patrick argues that hegemony rests on a combination of preponderant power, a participatory ideology, and, very importantly, willing associates. In short, the ability to wield power in noncoercive ways with the consent of other states and the ability to pay military and economic costs are critical factors in exercising hegemony.[14]

The concept of hegemony has, over the decades, conjured up images of domination, bullying behavior, and arrogance on the part of great powers. Past and present hegemons, such as Britain during the late nineteenth century and the United States during the twentieth century, sometimes used their powers and primacy aggressively through colonialism and other forms of domination in Africa, Asia, Latin America, and the Caribbean. But hegemony need not be a negative phenomenon. The pound and dollar stabilized the international monetary system under Pax Britannica[15] and Pax Americana,[16] while after World War II, the United States helped Western Europe and Japan's economic recovery, provided its allies with a nuclear umbrella, and led the creation of the international trade system. During the Gulf War of 1991 and the North Atlantic Treaty Organization (NATO) interventions in Bosnia and Kosovo of the 1990s, the United States was able to rally its allies in support of military action under its leadership. It was willing to bear the principal costs, while convincing others to support these efforts. One can in fact talk of "constructive" hegemony in which hegemons are able not only to articulate the rules and norms for respective regions but also to convince other states to follow such rules and adhere to established norms. Hegemony is therefore principally about leverage and influence, not just bullying dominance.

Great power status is, however, insufficient to promote hegemony successfully. More often than not, the hegemon needs to have effective tools at its disposal, such as the ability to dispense foreign assistance, forge alliances, and use various sticks and carrots to achieve its policy objectives. In other words, the hegemon must make it clear to the hegemonized that it has the capacity to reward and punish. The constructive hegemon is able to promote solidarity and stitch together alliances. Like a sheriff, it must demonstrate the capacity and political will to gather a posse in defense of mutual regional security interests. A major challenge facing aspiring or potential hegemons, therefore, is that they must come to terms with their powerful status while allaying the fears of smaller states in their subregions. In short, the challenge of hegemony is leadership without bullying dominance, and the willing acceptance of such leadership by others.

One cannot do justice to a discussion about hegemony without considering the concept of hegemonic stability. This concept holds that hegemony provides some order in the international (or regional) system, reducing anarchy and performing some functions similar to a central government—deterring aggression, promoting free trade, and backing a hard currency that can be used as a world (or regional) standard.[17] Hegemons can help to resolve, or at least keep in check, conflicts among middle powers or small states.[18] However, from the perspective of less powerful states, such hegemony may seem like an infringement on their sovereignty, and the order the hegemon seeks to create may seem unjust or illegitimate.[19]

The idea of South Africa and Nigeria as potential hegemons in Africa often raises resentment among other African actors who challenge the notion that two countries can arrogate to themselves a divine right to lead Africa. Both South Africa and Nigeria have faced opposition from their neighbors to their foreign policies in Lesotho, the Democratic Republic of Congo (DRC), Liberia, and Sierra Leone. In some public and scholarly circles, South Africa and Nigeria are often associated with "giantism": they are perceived to be political, military, and economic giants who have the potential to use these resources in malignant and even destructive ways to threaten other states.

In stark contrast, other commentators have suggested that the future of the entire continent rests on the fate of South Africa and Nigeria. South African analyst Garth le Pere noted that a partnership between Nigeria and

South Africa is important because "the two countries represent the economic colossuses of Africa, accounting for more than half of the GDP of sub-Saharan Africa. In their respective geo-strategic locations—Nigeria in the West of Africa and South Africa in the South—they serve as Africa's global power perch."[20] Nigerian diplomat Olu Adeniji stated that "Nigeria and South Africa have always been considered as the two countries that should propel Africa, south of the Sahara, into the contemporary economic level."[21] U.S. foreign policy guru Henry Kissinger opined that "No state except Nigeria or South Africa is in a position to play a major role outside its immediate region. . . . African security issues . . . should be left largely to African nations, with South Africa and Nigeria playing the principal roles."[22]

Influential opinion-shapers in South Africa and Nigeria have, in recent times, openly promoted an alliance between their two states to work for Africa's political and economic renaissance. This may be overambitious, but it does suggest that Pretoria and Abuja possess some hegemonic attributes that could allow them to play a leadership role on African security issues.

The Prophet and the Pariah

The annus mirabilis of African independence, 1960, saw the birth of Nigeria amid great hopes for a political and economic giant that was to take its preordained place in the African sun. In the same year, South Africa was about to be expelled from the Commonwealth for another bloody round of killings of unarmed blacks in Sharpeville during another ugly display of its atavistic policy of legally sanctioned racism, and many felt that the apartheid state was heading toward civil war. In the three decades that followed, both African giants failed to achieve their leadership aspirations in their respective subregions for very different reasons.[23]

In the case of Nigeria, its West African subregion was littered with francophone states that looked to France, the self-appointed *gendarme d'Afrique*, for protection against the potential neighborhood bully, Nigeria. The Gallic power intervened in the region with reckless abandon, landing gendarmes in Africa at least twenty-one times between 1960 and 1990 and effortlessly shuffling regimes around in its *pré carré* (backyard).[24] Nigeria's attempts at seeking greater political influence in West Africa through economic means were also frustrated by France, which encouraged francophone states to create rival trade blocs. In its two and a half decades of existence, the Nigerian-led Economic Community of West African States (ECOWAS) has not come close to its goals of establishing a common market. Most of its trade is still tied to the West. Intracommunity trade is minute, and smuggling is rampant.[25] Nigeria did give some aid to West African neighbors, but this was insufficient to counter effectively external actors such as the United States, the Soviet Union, and France during the Cold War era. Nigeria's leadership aspirations in West Africa were, in fact, rendered a hegemonic illusion by the presence of France in the subregion.

South Africa, in contrast, was able to subdue its neighbors both economically and militarily through a policy of destabilization. Pretoria, after all, had the "apartheid nuclear bomb," a flourishing arms industry, some world-class manufacturers, and the tenth largest stock exchange in the world. Neighboring countries were also economically dependent on South Africa: cheap labor from Swaziland, Lesotho, and Mozambique flocked to South African mines. Pretoria dominated the Southern African Customs Union (SACU), which included Botswana, Lesotho, and Swaziland (Namibia joined on 4 April 1990). SACU established a common external tariff, which continues to elude ECOWAS, and managed revenue redistribution from the tariff. South Africa's exports to southern Africa were eight times more than its imports from the region. Land-locked Zambia, Zimbabwe, and Botswana depended on South Africa's ports; and the South African Gulliver's infrastructure and capital capacity proved to be irresistible magnets for regional Lilliputians.[26] Despite their attempts at lessening their dependence on Pretoria through the Southern African Development Coordination Conference (SADCC), established in April 1980, many of the subregion's states still traded covertly with, and depended on, South Africa. Pretoria sought to make the subregion safe for white minority domination through its economic and military muscle.

Despite the external constraints on Nigeria playing a hegemonic role in Africa, the country provided leadership to the anti-apartheid and decolonization struggles. Lagos gave liberation movements financial and material backing, and its contributions to the liberation struggle were aptly recognized by its invitations to meetings of the Frontline States (FLS) of southern Africa, its long chairmanship of the UN's Special Committee Against Apartheid, and its hosting of the UN anti-apartheid conference in 1977. Because South Africa was diplomatically isolated and forced to bear the brunt of many of the international community's sanctions, it was denied a global stage. Nigeria, instead, under the Organization of African Unity (OAU) and the FLS, spoke loudest for African concerns during the continent's thirty-year war against colonialism and apartheid: Nigeria was the prophet, South Africa the pariah.

By 1995, the two countries had traded places: it was Nigeria, and not South Africa, that was being considered for expulsion from the Commonwealth. It was Nigeria, under a repressive military regime, that was facing mounting criticism over its human rights record; it was Nigeria that was becoming increasingly isolated in international society; and it was

Nigeria that was considered to be possibly heading toward civil war. Having abandoned its apartheid past, South Africa was widely acknowledged to be the most likely political and economic success story in Africa.

Under the iconic leadership of Nelson Mandela,[27] South Africa had a globally revered statesman, one of the most representative political systems on the continent, arguably its best army, and Africa's largest economy. Ibrahim Gambari, Nigeria's permanent representative to the UN between 1990 and 1999 and current undersecretary-general for African affairs and adviser on Africa to Kofi Annan, the UN Secretary-General, recognized the irony of this situation when he wrote, shortly after attending Mandela's inauguration as the last chairman of the UN's Special Committee Against Apartheid in May 1994: "Would we, Nigerians, by acts of omission or commission, allow ourselves to be overtaken in the leadership role in Africa which our human resources and destiny enabled us to play in the past and perhaps entitles us to play in the future?"[28]

Under the dictatorial leadership of Nigeria's General Sani Abacha, the contrast between the two potential hegemons could not have been more stark. While military brass hats proliferated in West African countries like Nigeria, Sierra Leone, and Gambia, postsettlement South Africa provided a democratic model for its region. South Africa's government of national unity between 1994 and 1996 supported the spread or restoration of democracy in neighboring Mozambique, Lesotho, and Malawi. Mandela's South Africa set up the Truth and Reconciliation Commission to look into the injustices of an undemocratic past; Abacha's Nigeria set up the Provisional Ruling Council to bury its democratic future.

In the economic sphere, the difference between the two giants was also clear. South Africa, Africa's largest economy, has a GDP of about $130 billion, which is roughly the same size as Norway's. Nigeria's GDP is about $40 billion, while political corruption helped amass a $30 billion foreign debt, and its per capita gross national product of about $300 is about the size of Haiti's.[29] While South Africa has for years had a steel industry that feeds its arms manufacturers, Nigeria's Ajaokuta Steel Complex, planned since the early 1970s, became a white elephant mired in corruption and inefficiency. While South Africa's digital-based cellular telecommunications network is the world's second largest, Nigeria's phone system continues to be notoriously erratic. While South Africa has well-funded universities with good infrastructure, Nigeria's ivory towers are crumbling monuments to years of neglect and government closures.

General Abacha's sudden death in June 1998 greatly increased the chances of the tale of the prophet and the pariah becoming a tale of two prophets. The reformist general Abdulsaalam Abubakar turned out to be the Frederick de Klerk of Nigeria. Whereas widespread skepticism prevailed by the time he took over the reins of power from Abacha, Abubakar became instrumental in ushering in Nigeria's transition from military dictatorship to civilian rule under Olusegun Obasanjo by May 1999. In South Africa, the conservative de Klerk, who had previously been a staunch defender of apartheid, had, under severe domestic and international pressure, similarly surprised local and international observers when he reformed the very apartheid system over which his National Party had presided for over forty years. In the end, both Abubakar and de Klerk relinquished power to elected regimes.

A Tale of Two Prophets

By the middle of 1999, South Africa and Nigeria gained newly elected leaders in the form of presidents Thabo Mbeki and Olusegun Obasanjo. At home, the two leaders have focused on consolidating their fragile democracies and designing strategies to close the massive socioeconomic gaps caused by decades of white minority domination and military rule. Both countries remain deeply socially divided: South Africa specifically along racial lines, while in Nigeria the divisions are largely based on religion and ethnicity. Abroad, Mbeki and Obasanjo have worked closely at managing African conflicts through the institutions of the Southern African Development Community (SADC) and ECOWAS. Together, they have attempted to promote norms of democratic government at the OAU.

While Mbeki, an intellectual who often writes his own speeches, can be viewed as the "ideas, values, and norms" man, Obasanjo, a soldier who established one of Africa's largest farms on retirement, may be described as the "practical, institutions and organizations" man. Mbeki pursues, in large part, a normative, value-driven approach. He has stressed values and norms, such as democratization, negotiations, and peaceful resolution of disputes, sometimes modeled on South Africa's own political settlement in 1994. Obasanjo tends to pursue a more institutional approach, calling for a permanent Conference on Security, Stability, Development, and Cooperation in Africa (CSSDCA); institutional links between the SADC and ECOWAS; and a new security architecture for Africa, involving the UN and Africa's subregional organizations. The two visions—of an African renaissance and an African "Helsinki option"—complement each other. There has been a conscious effort by Pretoria and Abuja to marry the two ideas, finally culminated in the launching of the New Partnership for Africa's Development (NEPAD) in Abuja in October 2001.

There appears to be remarkable degrees of similarity, even synergy, and collaboration between the foreign and security policies of presidents Mbeki and Obasanjo. The two have a close personal relationship dating back to Obasanjo's tenure as Nigeria's military head of state between 1976 and 1979, when Mbeki served as the African National Congress (ANC) representative in Lagos. Obasanjo also met South Africa's future leaders during his visit to the apartheid enclave as co-chairman of the Commonwealth Eminent Person's Group in 1986. While Mbeki has mapped out policy pillars for an African renaissance and sought to lay the foundations for the twenty-first century as the African century, Obasanjo has focused on the establishment of a CSSDCA in Africa. Mbeki, with his apartheid-era army still being restructured, has promised to engage more with Africa in the area of peacekeeping, contributing peacekeepers to missions in the DRC and Burundi. Nigerian soldiers form the core of the UN peacekeeping mission in Sierra Leone. Before examining some of the actions and foreign policy goals of these two leaders, it is important to flesh out briefly the still skeletal concepts of the African renaissance and the CSSDCA.

Mbeki's calls for an African renaissance deserve to be taken into account in efforts to promote regional security in Africa. The renaissance may be defined as a doctrine for Africa's political, economic, and social renewal and a call for political democratization, economic growth, and the reintegration of Africa into the global economy.[30] Mbeki has called on Africans to adapt democracy to fit their own specific conditions without compromising its fundamental principles of representation and accountability. As he put it, "We want to see an African continent in which people participate in systems of government in which they are truly able to determine their destiny and put behind us the notions of democracy and human rights as peculiarly 'Western' concepts."[31]

In a rousing call for the African giant to rise from its deep slumber and take its rightful place within the community of nations, Mbeki has urged Africans both inside and outside government to mobilize and to galvanize their efforts in a sustained national and continental effort. The foot soldiers of Africa's renaissance are urged to embrace the same revolutionary zeal that freed the continent from the twin scourges of colonialism and apartheid in order to fulfill a common democratic vision. Mbeki challenges Africans to discover a sense of their own self-confidence after centuries of slavery and colonialism, which systematically denigrated their cultures and subjugated their institutions to alien rule.[32]

The African renaissance has as its central goal the right of people to determine their own future. It calls for a cancellation of Africa's foreign debt, improvement in Africa's terms of trade, the expansion of development assistance, and better access to foreign markets for African goods. While criticizing devotees of the market for failing to recognize that it distributes its rewards unevenly, Mbeki pragmatically calls for African nations to embrace the positive aspects of globalization by attracting capital and investment with which to develop their economies. The African renaissance does not naively assume, as some of its critics have maintained, that this political and economic renewal is already under way in Africa. It merely seeks to set forth a vision and prescribe the policy recommendations and actions that could create the conditions for the rebirth of the African continent. As John Stremlau noted,

> Renaissance proponents seek to convey a positive vision for Africa as a peaceful, democratic and market-oriented region. . . . No one denies the harsh realities of human deprivation and deadly conflict. Calls for a renaissance are intended to encourage all Africans to confront these realities and to take greater responsibility for reversing them.[33]

Obasanjo's proposal for a Conference on Security, Stability, Development, and Cooperation in Africa, loosely based on the Conference for Security and Co-operation in Europe, has now been adopted as a major plank of Nigeria's foreign policy. The idea was first discussed at a conference in Kampala, Uganda, in 1991 sponsored by Obasanjo's African Leadership Forum, along with the OAU and the UN's Economic Commission for Africa (ECA).[34] Its final report proposed establishing a permanent Conference on Security, Stability, Development, and Cooperation in Africa; developing a continental peacekeeping machinery; promoting conflict prevention and military self-reliance in Africa; establishing an African Peace Council of Elder Statesmen to mediate conflicts; and drastically reducing military expenditures in Africa.

In May 2000, a CSSDCA meeting held in Abuja called for a consolidation of the work between the OAU and ECA in the areas of peace, security, stability, development, and cooperation.[35] The meeting also suggested that the CSSDCA should provide a policy development forum for the elaboration and advancement of common values within the main policy organs of the OAU. Since these meetings took place, the OAU and Africa's subregional organizations have taken encouraging steps to develop security mechanisms that, in cooperation with the UN and Africa's civil society groups, can manage conflicts in Africa.[36]

Both Mbeki and Obasanjo appear to be proponents of what can be referred to as the "democratic peace" theory.[37] They promote the idea that democracy should be spread in Africa because they believe that democracies do not go to war with one another. This is what is sometimes referred to as the "democratic presumption," that democracies are inherently more peace-loving than other systems of governments, and that they are economically more prosperous than other types of government.[38] This theory is, of course, highly contentious and has been challenged in Africa and elsewhere. Both Mbeki and Obasanjo believe that Africa must be made safe for democracy, that the southern African and the West African subregions should be turned into what Mbeki has called "zones of peace."

In the area of norm-setting, Mbeki and Obasanjo have challenged the OAU's inflexible adherence to absolute sovereignty and noninterference in the internal affairs of African states.[39] Both leaders have explicitly linked autocratic misrule to the conflicts in Africa; both have spoken out against one-party and personal rule on the continent. As Obasanjo put it in 1991 at a meeting in Kampala to discuss the CSSDCA, "An urgent aspect of security need is a re-definition of the concept of security and sovereignty. . . . We must ask why does sovereignty seem to confer absolute immunity on any government [that] commits genocide and monumental crimes?"[40]

At the OAU summit in Algiers in 1999, Mbeki and Obasanjo were instrumental in advocating a doctrine against coups d'état in Africa. The two leaders strongly backed the "red card, yellow card" (a soccer analogy) approach to coups d'état. Military leaders who take power through violent means in Africa will first be cautioned and urged to return power democratically—the yellow card. Thereafter, putschists will face diplomatic and economic sanctions and possibly eventual suspension from the OAU—the red card. Mbeki, Obasanjo, and other leaders recommended the immediate reactivation of the OAU's subcommittee on Unconstitutional Changes of Government in order to finalize its work of applying sanctions against putschists. Pressured by, among others, Mbeki and Obasanjo, the OAU subsequently barred the military regimes of Côte d'Ivoire and Comoros from attending its summit in Lomé in 2000.

In 1999, African leaders decided to transform the OAU into the African Union (AU). Some of the ideas that Mbeki and Obasanjo have advocated for promoting democracy in Africa were fed into the AU process. The two leaders have argued that the AU Constitutive Act should recognize certain pretexts for intervention. They championed the idea of military intervention by regional bodies in four specific cases: first, to reverse an unconstitutional change of regime; second, to prevent genocide; third, in cases of instability that threaten to spread to engulf other states; and fourth, under gross violations of human rights.[41]

Both Mbeki and Obasanjo have stressed the importance of conflict resolution in Africa by frequently offering their personal mediation services and "good offices" for the resolution of conflicts. While Obasanjo has energetically promoted security and democracy in West Africa and sought to resolve crises in Guinea, Liberia, Sierra Leone, and Côte d'Ivoire, Mbeki has sought to make peace in the DRC, Lesotho, Comoros, Angola, and Zimbabwe. Obasanjo hosted a meeting of Commonwealth foreign ministers in Abuja that led to an agreement on peaceful land reform in Zimbabwe in September 2001, which was not implemented. Mbeki, through Mandela and Deputy President Jacob Zuma continues to lend his country's weight and resources to peace efforts in Burundi. In line with CSSDCA ideas for a Council of African Elders helping to mediate regional conflicts, Obasanjo's predecessor as Nigerian head of state, General Abdulsaalam Abubakar, currently serves as a UN special envoy to the DRC and led the Commonwealth's election-monitoring team to Zimbabwe in March 2002. Mbeki, who was particularly critical of the military regimes in Côte d'Ivoire and Revolutionary United Front rebels in Sierra Leone, was active in negotiations to restore constitutional rule to Côte d'Ivoire and undertook a successful West African tour to Nigeria, Ghana, and Senegal in October 2000.

Mbeki and Obasanjo have both stressed the need to multilateralize their foreign policies, especially with regard to peacekeeping. In the future, South African and Nigerian peacekeeping forces may serve only under the more explicit auspices of multilateral organizations such as the UN, OAU, SADC, and ECOWAS. This represents not only an attempt to legitimize such military actions but also a conscious effort to alleviate fears of aggressive regional hegemons and to share the financial burden of such military interventions more equitably.

Global Renaissance

Both Mbeki and Obasanjo subscribe to the idea that peace and security are fundamentally dependent on development. Both leaders have therefore attempted to play "bridge roles" in the *dialogue de sourds* (dialogue of the deaf) between the industrialized North and the impoverished South.[42] Pretoria and Abuja see themselves as "problem solvers" not only in Africa but in world affairs more generally. They also see themselves as pathways, even potential "building blocs," between polarized groupings of states in world affairs. Both Mbeki and Obasanjo have, for example, campaigned and lobbied the world community for greater focus on African affairs, particularly in the areas of peacekeeping and debt relief. At the annual Group of Eight (G-8) meeting in Japan in July 2000, Mbeki and Obasanjo, together with OAU chairman Algerian leader Abdelazziz Bouteflika (the "African trio"), made a formal case for the relief and forgiveness of Africa's debt.[43] Both leaders have also called for technology and resource transfers from the West to Africa, criticizing the gap between promise and delivery on the part of most Western states.

Obasanjo has attempted to serve as a bridge between Africa and the West by encouraging peacekeepers from non-African states to contribute to UN missions in places like Sierra Leone and Congo. Mbeki has increasingly spoken out against the sometimes reckless and arrogant display of power by the world's sole "hyperpower," the United States, in places like Sudan and Iraq. During a visit to South Africa by the Chinese leader Jiang Zemin, in April 2000, Mbeki called for a strategic alliance between China and the Group of seventy-seven developing countries (G-77). While on a state visit to Washington, D.C., two months later, Mbeki stressed that he was in the United States not only as South Africa's head of state but also in his capacity as the leader of the Nonaligned Movement. Obasanjo, the first African leader to visit the White House after President George Bush's inauguration in January 2001, strongly championed debt alleviation for Africa. Both Mbeki and Obasanjo have sought to act as Africa's voice in international forums and Western capitals. Both have supported the current U.S. "war on terrorism."

Between 2000 and 2001, Mbeki and Obasanjo played a crucial role in two important initiatives to enhance governance and accountability in Africa. The two initiatives were the acceleration of the OAU-mandated drafting of the Millennium Africa Recovery Plan (MAP) under the aegis of Mbeki, Obasanjo, and Bouteflika and the merger of MAP and the OMEGA Plan—spearheaded by Senegalese president Abdoulaye Wade—to form the New African Initiative (NAI).

The Millennium Africa Recovery Plan was largely authored by Mbeki and strongly supported by Obasanjo and Bouteflika. South African officials described it as a comprehensive and far-reaching global plan of action to tackle poverty and the development needs of Africa.[44] MAP was premised on the idea of Africa leading its own recovery with the support of key partners in the developed world who are requested to provide crucial assistance in confronting the challenges posed by globalization.[45] MAP singled out "a new corps of progressive African leaders" committed to the African renaissance vision of tackling poverty and underdevelopment and promoting democracy, good governance, and respect for human rights.[46] The plan foresaw industrialized countries and multilateral institutions providing debt relief, opening their markets to African products, investing in African countries, sharing their technologies and medicines with Africa, and providing military and financial support to peacekeeping missions in Africa.

Mbeki finally convinced Wade to merge his OMEGA Plan with MAP during a meeting in Pretoria in early July 2001. The formal merger of MAP and the OMEGA Plan into the New African Initiative occurred during the OAU heads of state summit of 9 to 11 July 2001, when African leaders adopted the NAI as the final working document. A careful reading of both MAP and the OMEGA Plan reveals that the NAI is largely based on MAP's main goals. The NAI refers to OMEGA's emphasis on infrastructural development, but the vision of the new initiative was clearly hatched in Pretoria, not Dakar.

According to paragraph one of the introduction to the NAI's founding document, the initiative is

> a pledge by African leaders, based on a common vision and a firm and shared conviction, that they have a pressing duty to eradicate poverty and

> place their countries, both individually and collectively, on a path of sustainable growth and development and at the same time participate actively in the world economy and body politic.[47]

NAI is further "a call for a new relationship of partnership between Africa and the international community, especially the highly industrialized countries, to overcome the development chasm that has widened over the centuries of unequal relationships."[48]

The plan is based on a straightforward bargain between Africa and its largely Western donors. In exchange for buy-in from external actors, African leaders will take responsibility for, and commit themselves to, four specific democratic, security, and economic norms and values: first, strengthening mechanisms for conflict prevention, management, and resolution at the regional and continental levels and ensuring that these mechanisms are used to restore and maintain peace; second, promoting and protecting democracy and human rights in their respective countries and regions by developing clear standards of accountability, transparency, and participative governance; third, restoring and maintaining macroeconomic stability; and fourth, institutionalizing transparent legal frameworks for financial markets.

On 23 October 2001, sixteen African heads of state and government met in Abuja, Nigeria, for the first implementation meeting of the New African Initiative. NAI was then renamed the New Partnership for Africa's Development and an implementation committee was established.[49] President Obasanjo was elected chairperson of the implementation committee, while it was agreed that South Africa would host the NEPAD secretariat.

As key members of the NEPAD implementation committee, Nigeria and South Africa have been instrumental in pushing for NEPAD members to adhere to the democratic and governance requirements of NEPAD. While Obasanjo was instrumental in pushing for a corporate and finance peer review mechanism, through which members are expected to create the conditions for private sector growth and combating corruption, Mbeki has led the Political Good Governance Initiative, through which member states commit themselves to accountable and good governance, the rule of law, protection of human rights, and term limits for heads of state and government.

Both Obasanjo and Mbeki gave notice, during the launch of the AU in Durban in early July 2002, that they intend to play a strong leadership role in implementing the goals of the new organization's Constitutive Act, notably its articles on intervention, in order to promote democracy and good governance in Africa.

Giant on the Limpopo

The promotion of the peaceful settlement of disputes has been a dominant theme running through Pretoria's Africa policy over the last eight years.[50] South Africa's "White Paper on Peace Missions" of 1999 stated that it is in its "strong national interest and experience in the peaceful resolution of seemingly intractable conflicts . . . to participate in peace missions."[51] Following King Letsie's "royal coup" in Lesotho in 1994, South Africa, under President Nelson Mandela, cooperated with Zimbabwe and Botswana to settle the ensuing constitutional crisis by helping to return the elected government of Ntsu Mokhehle to power and reinstating King Moshoeshoe II to his throne.[52] A new crisis was triggered in Lesotho after the split of the ruling Basotholand Congress Party in 1997.[53] After a disputed election in May 1998, a commission of inquiry was established comprising legal experts from Botswana, South Africa, and Zimbabwe, headed by Pius Langa of the South African Constitutional Court.[54] The principal mandate of the Langa commission was to investigate allegations of irregularities during the elections and to make appropriate recommendations.[55] After long delays, the Langa commission report was released on 17 September 1998. Its substance and recommendations only hardened the positions of the belligerent parties.[56] Violence erupted in Lesotho, with lower-ranking members of the army staging a mutiny. South Africa and Botswana sent troops to Lesotho in September 1998, and the force eventually restored order and aborted a military coup; however, the poorly executed intervention resulted in dozens of civilian casualties.

The issue of whether or not the 1998 intervention in Lesotho by South Africa and Botswana was legal and legitimate remains highly contentious. In assessing the justifications for the military intervention in Lesotho, the South African National Defense Force (SANDF) released a document in May 2000 in which it maintains the perspective that the intervention was both legal and legitimate. Titled "The SADC Intervention in Lesotho: A Military Perspective," the document emphasizes four points. First, it claims that at a meeting of SADC ministers of defense in Gaborone, Botswana, in September 1998, South Africa and Botswana, along with Zimbabwe and Mozambique, were requested to intervene in Lesotho under the auspices of the SADC, but Zimbabwe and Mozambique declined to send troops. Second, it claims that the Lesotho government lacked the capacity for law enforcement and that Lesotho's prime minister, Ntsu Mokhehle, wrote to the SADC requesting military assistance. Third, the report asserts that the situation preceding the intervention had the potential to spill into other states in the subregion and that it violated the SADC's legal principles of unconstitutional changes of government. Finally, the document contends that although the military intervention was badly executed, leading to the unfortunate loss of civilian lives and destruction of property, it succeeded in its principal goal of rolling back a coup d'état and restoring constitutional order in Lesotho.[57]

South Africa's intervention in Lesotho was, however, not launched out of sheer altruism. It was also motivated by self-interest. Two other rationales over which the SANDF document remains conspicuously silent need to be singled out here. First, Pretoria naturally wanted to prevent an implosion of land-locked Lesotho, lodged in South Africa's belly, and to stave off an influx of refugees and arms to its own country. Second, South Africa was also determined to defend and protect the Lesotho Highlands Water Project, a major source of water supply to South Africa. Khabela Matlosa further argued that

> this military intervention, which resembled a peace enforcement operation, has been fraught with controversies. It was meant to neutralize the Lesotho army and force political parties to reach a negotiated settlement. However, the South African troops immediately wreaked havoc: first around the Katse Dam in the Thaba-Teska district and then in Maseru.[58]

Until recently, South Africa was clearly more favorably disposed toward preventive diplomacy than toward keeping and enforcing peace. Under the presidency of Nelson Mandela between 1994 and 1999, the ANC-led government, which inherited a discredited apartheid army, ruled out the military option in subregional conflicts, displaying a much keener interest in brokering peace deals and promoting negotiations along the lines of its own negotiated settlement of 1994. With the 1998 military intervention in Lesotho and commitment of troops to peacekeeping missions in the DRC and Burundi, South Africa has begun to demonstrate a greater willingness to keep peace militarily in its own subregion.[59]

South Africa's efforts at promoting democracy and human rights in countries like Nigeria (when Mandela failed to obtain the support of any SADC members for sanctions against Nigeria's military regime following the hanging of nine environmental activists in November 1995), Lesotho, and Zimbabwe have met with fierce opposition from other African countries. Though Pretoria has some hegemonic attributes in the form of its preponderant military and economic power relative to its neighbors, it has often failed to convert these qualities into genuine influence, as its leadership has been challenged by Zimbabwe, Namibia, and Angola. Several of its neighbors have failed to follow South Africa's lead. Leaders like Robert Mugabe, Sam Nujoma, and Eduardo Dos Santos feel that they preceded Mbeki in the liberation struggle and complain that the ANC-led government has not repaid the sacrifices that their countries made for the liberation of South Africa. As Francis Kornegay noted, "Pretoria's African

Renaissance agenda of enlarging democracy and 'good governance' through multiparty political pluralism and civil society participation threatens the postliberation movement, one-party dominant systems that are legacies of those struggles."[60]

In the DRC, the nations of South Africa, Botswana, and Tanzania have sought to manage the conflict through diplomatic means rather than the military means employed by Zimbabwe, Namibia, and Angola in 1998 to counter the earlier invasion by Rwanda and Uganda. But South Africa's neutrality was heavily questioned by other states because of its past role of supplying arms to Rwanda and Uganda. Congolese leader Laurent Kabila, encouraged by Zimbabwe, responded not only by openly defying South African policy but also by trying to isolate Pretoria diplomatically. Three influential SADC members—Zimbabwe, Namibia, and Angola—were infuriated by South Africa's decision not to intervene militarily on their side in the DRC in 1998, accusing Pretoria of hypocrisy in intervening militarily in Lesotho while refusing to do the same in the DRC.[61]

South Africa's neighbors have also been angered by its tendency for negotiating unilateral trade agreements with external actors like the European Union (EU), its aggressive drive to secure foreign investments for itself, its protectionist trade and xenophobic immigration policies, and the ferocious drive by its mostly white-dominated corporations in search of new markets north of the Limpopo. The fact that South Africa accounts for 80 percent of SADC's GNP and has a six-to-one favorable trade balance with its smaller neighbors breeds further tension and resentment.[62]

Chastened by President Mandela's bitter experiences in promoting political change in Nigeria, Angola, and Congo, Mbeki has desisted from publicly confronting other African governments, preferring instead to seek regional consultations to settle local problems. He has consistently stressed that South Africa will engage the subregion "as a partner and ally, not as a regional superpower."[63] Pretoria's new consultative strategy was evident in Mbeki's decision to invite his Mozambican and Namibian counterparts to form part of the troika of regional leaders that engaged Zimbabwe's Robert Mugabe in talks at Victoria Falls in April 2000. This was an effort to prevent the internal conflict in neighboring Zimbabwe over the "land-grab debate" from spilling over into the subregion. Mbeki's "quiet diplomacy," almost universally lambasted by the Western press and South Africa's white media, appears to have been vindicated by the successful elections in Zimbabwe in July 2000,[64] though Zimbabwe's security situation remains highly precarious following disputed elections in March 2002. Mbeki even offered to mediate between Zimbabwe and Britain in efforts to resolve the land issue and tried to convince Saudi Arabia and Norway to fund part of the land resettlement program in Zimbabwe.

After the disputed March 2002 presidential election in Zimbabwe,

Obasanjo and Mbeki both appointed special envoys in the persons of Adebayo Adedji (Nigeria) and Kgaleme Mothlante (South Africa) to facilitate postelection dialogue between the ruling party and opposition in Zimbabwe around four key issues: ending violence, establishing a constitution-making process, developing an economic recovery program for Zimbabwe, and addressing the land question. By August 2002, Obasanjo and Mbeki appeared to be moving in the direction of a strategy of conditionality: in exchange for progress in political talks, Abuja and Pretoria would initiate, and seek to rally support for, a postconflict economic recovery plan for Zimbabwe. Progress has, however, remained stalled in Zimbabwe as political instability and land seizures continue.

In February 2000, South Africa established a $30 million African Renaissance and International Cooperation Fund to promote its foreign policy goals of democracy, development, and security in Africa. Under Mbeki's leadership, South Africa has energetically pursued an active peacemaking role in African affairs. During her first year as foreign minister, Nkosazana Dlamini-Zuma spent more time in the DRC than in any other country as she worked tirelessly to broker peace, in coordination with Zambia, Mozambique, and Tanzania. In May 2000, Mbeki dispatched his deputy director-general for African affairs, Welile Nhlapho, to the coup-prone island of Comoros to try to broker an inclusive political settlement. On the issue of Sudan, Mbeki brought together Ugandan leader Yoweri Museveni and Sudan's Omar al-Bashir, each of whom was supporting rebels in the other's country.

Former South African president Nelson Mandela has, since December 1999, attempted to broker a durable peace agreement in Burundi. The 2001 peace agreement mediated by Mandela, with the assistance of Mbeki's deputy Jacob Zuma, determined that Pierre Buyoya would remain president with a Hutu vice president for another eighteen months, starting on 1 November 2001, after which he would surrender power to a Hutu president with a Tutsi deputy for another eighteen-month period. On 28 October 2001, South Africa dispatched its first contingent of 240 peacekeepers to Bujumbura, the capital of Burundi.[65] These were the first of more than 700 peacekeepers to oversee the implementation of a three-year peace plan aimed at ending Burundi's costly nine-year civil war.[66] The UN Security Council expressed strong support for South Africa's decision to send peacekeepers to Burundi. Though there are major tensions between Mbeki and President Eduardo Dos Santos over Pretoria's refusal to become militarily involved in the Angolan crisis, Mbeki discreetly sought to coax Dos Santos to continue the peace process, though personal relations between the leaders continue to be strained. After some difficulties in its peacemaking role in the DRC, Angola, and Nigeria, South Africa has been forced to be more cautious when dealing with its African counterparts and in attempting to export its democratic model north of the Limpopo.

Through their intervention in the DRC, the nations of Zimbabwe and Angola have demonstrated their willingness to act as potential local hegemons ready to use military power, and (in the case of Angola) oil and diamond wealth, to challenge South Africa's leadership aspirations within the SADC.[67] Together with Namibia, these two states decided to intervene in the DRC conflict on behalf of beleaguered former president Laurent Kabila without South Africa's consent, at a time when South Africa was the chair of the SADC.

Given the complex and fluid nature of the southern African security architecture, Thabo Mbeki has decided on a subregional approach to conflict management that stresses the primacy of diplomatic partnerships. For example, during the SADC's extraordinary summit in Blantyre, Malawi, in January 2002, convened to address the deteriorating security situation in Zimbabwe, Pretoria and its SADC partners Botswana, Mozambique, Tanzania, and Malawi urged President Robert Mugabe to create the conditions for a free and fair election in March 2002.[68] South Africa also hosted the Inter-Congolese Dialogue for the DRC. In April 2002, Mbeki personally intervened in the dialogue after the OAU facilitator, former Botswana president Sir Ketumile Masire, had failed to produce a deal after six weeks. However, Mbeki, too, was unable to secure a broad-based deal but committed himself to staying involved in peacemaking efforts.

During the launch of the AU in Durban in July 2002, Mbeki and UN Secretary-General Kofi Annan engaged Congo's Joseph Kaliba and Rwanda's Paul Kagame in a bid to secure a peace deal between them. Days after the launch, Mbeki appointed deputy president Jacob Zuma as facilitator to promote peace between the DRC and Rwanda. In August 2002, Zuma delivered a deal that committed Rwanda to withdraw from eastern Congo within ninety days in exchange for Congo and other external actors, such as the UN, which was helping to disarm and demobilize Interahamwe militia accused of taking part in Rwanda's 1994 genocide. If implemented, this deal could help resolve Congo's protracted conflict. Encouragingly, Rwanda withdrew its troops from the DRC in fulfillment of the agreement.

West Africa's New Gendarme?

The other African giant, Nigeria, has been more militarily active than South Africa in its own subregion, though it faces similar suspicions from its neighbors.[69] In contrast to the declining French military role in West Africa, Nigeria's generals were fully committed to an activist security role in Liberia and Sierra Leone between 1990 and 1998, despite often strong opposition from the Nigerian public. An important factor that has contributed to the Nigerian-led interventions in West Africa was the changing environment of post–Cold War Africa amid the growing indifference of external actors to intervening directly in African conflicts and the growing interest of African actors in managing their own conflicts. Nigeria provided the men and money that fueled the Economic Community of West African States Cease-Fire Monitoring Group (ECOMOG) locomotive. With 75 percent of West Africa's GNP, 50 percent of its population, and a 94,500-strong army that dwarfs the combined total of its neighbors' forces, Nigeria remains the indispensable local power in West Africa.

With the interventions in Liberia and Sierra Leone, Nigeria's military brass hats were determined, at all costs, to make a success of their historical role as the protective "big brother" with special responsibilities in their subregion. However, despite Nigeria's claims of having spent about $8 billion on the interventions in Liberia and Sierra Leone, billions of dollars were diverted into the private pockets of military officials, disguised as part of the costs of the ECOMOG interventions. Under the brutal regime of General Abacha, ECOMOG also served as a bargaining tool to ward off the threat of international sanctions by implicitly threatening to withdraw Nigerian troops from Liberia and Sierra Leone.

ECOMOG was unable to pacify Liberia and Sierra Leone militarily due to the ability of local warlords to control mineral-rich parts of the countryside outside the capitals, often sheltered by dense forests. The difficulties involved in a protracted guerrilla war were unenticing for ECOMOG's ill-equipped peacekeepers. In Liberia, ECOMOG eventually needed the cooperation of local warlords, the forging of political unity within ECOWAS, as well as the provision of logistical support by the United States and the EU to disarm the warring factions, while the UN and nongovernmental-organization community provided the humanitarian relief that Nigeria and the rest of the subregion simply lacked the means to give.[70] In Sierra Leone, the UN agreed to take over the ECOMOG mission in 2000 by diversifying it to include extraregional peacekeepers and subsuming 3,500 Nigerian soldiers under its command.[71] Pax Nigeriana was in effect "hegemony on a shoestring." Nigeria simply lacked the military and financial means to impose its will on Liberia and Sierra Leone without appeasing local warlords and procuring external logistical assistance.

At the ECOWAS summit in Lomé in December 1999, West African leaders agreed to establish a standby ECOMOG peacekeeping force consisting of specially trained national units as part of its Protocol for Conflict Prevention, Management, Resolution, Peacekeeping, and Security.[72] Difficulties encountered in the ECOMOG military mission to Guinea-Bissau, which involved peacekeepers from Benin, Gambia, Niger, and Togo,[73] and had to be ignominiously withdrawn in May 1999 after just four months following factional fighting, have forced a realization in the subregion of the importance of Nigeria's financial and military resources to peacekeeping in West Africa.[74]

Like South Africa, Nigeria must, however, learn to treat its neighbors with respect and consult more closely with them if its leadership aspirations are to be realized. Most West African countries do not question the need for Nigeria's leadership, but its penchant for a unilateral diplomatic style offends the sensibilities of smaller, poorer, and weaker states. Nigeria must learn to speak softly even when it carries a big stick. As Sule Lamido, Nigeria's foreign minister, stated, "It is important that while you are playing the role of Big Brother, you have to recognize that the countries you are dealing with are sovereign nations. You have to know this and recognize that psychological feeling of independence."[75] There still remains much unease in West Africa about Nigeria's domination of the ECOMOG military high commands in Liberia and Sierra Leone.[76]

The frequent threats by Nigeria's leaders to withdraw their troops from Sierra Leone were only belatedly taken seriously when Obasanjo began a phased withdrawal of Nigerian soldiers after May 1999. As Obasanjo noted during his address to the UN General Assembly in September 1999,

> The time has come for the Security Council to assume its full responsibility, specifically in Sierra Leone and other flash points in Africa. For too long, the burden of preserving international peace and security in West Africa has been left almost entirely to a few states in our subregion. . . . Nigeria's continual burden in Sierra Leone is unacceptably draining Nigeria financially. For our economy to take off, this bleeding has to stop.[77]

Aside from these financial difficulties, there are also internal constraints on Nigeria's ability to undertake future peacekeeping missions. Nigerian troops are still involved in internal peacekeeping duties in the country's volatile oil-producing Niger delta, where armed youths have exploited the trade in weapons and environmental neglect for which the government and foreign oil companies are largely responsible. Amid fears of the social consequences, General Theophilus Danjuma, Nigeria's defense minister, shelved plans to reduce Nigeria's politicized army from 94,500 to 50,000 troops.[78] Nigeria's refusal to contribute peacekeepers to Guinea-Bissau in 1998 and its phased withdrawal of troops from Sierra Leone are clear signs of a growing wariness of the costs and frustrations of protracted peacekeeping efforts. These actions are proof of Nigeria's lack of capacity to fulfill its hegemonic ambitions in West Africa.

Giants with Clay Feet

There are significant constraints on efforts by both Nigeria and South Africa to play a hegemonic role in Africa. Presidents Mbeki and Obasanjo have lamented the devastating effects on Nigeria and South Africa of decades of apartheid and military dictatorship. Obasanjo announced in February 2000 that the Nigerian economy has yet to experience the necessary critical structural changes that could guarantee rapid economic growth and sustainable development.[79] Nigeria's infrastructure is in a state of decay, and the country remains almost entirely dependent on oil exports for its foreign exchange earnings. Nigeria is today ranked as the thirteenth poorest country in the world, while its external debt stands at $30 billion. In pursuit of a policy of "economic diplomacy," Obasanjo has set the rather ambitious target of attracting some $10 billion per annum in foreign direct investment into Nigeria. He has so far failed to come anywhere near this goal. Obasanjo has also sought to reduce Nigeria's debt through negotiations with the Paris Club of Western government creditors.

While South Africa has by far the most developed economy in Africa, with a size and scale four times that of Nigeria and three times that of Egypt, its society remains deeply divided after decades of apartheid's diabolical experiments. Over half of South Africa's population is unemployed, and Mbeki himself talks of a "South Africa of two nations."[80] One nation consists of a small white population with living standards similar to that of Spain; the other nation comprises the mainly black, chronically underdeveloped, three-quarters of the population that experiences a standard of living similar to that of Congo-Brazzaville.[81] South Africa's economy is experiencing jobless growth and shed about 1 million jobs between 1994 and 1999. The democracies of both countries are also under strain as they lack governance capacity. Several analysts have, like Yusuf Bangura, noted that the postapartheid governing elite in South Africa is not fully in control of a racially integrated military. This, as well as the continued existence of a white-dominated civil service, hampers South Africa's credibility and maneuverability in African diplomacy.[82]

The Pretoria-Abuja Axis

Despite these constraints, many of South Africa and Nigeria's leaders regard the Pretoria-Abuja axis as the vital twin-celled battery that will power Africa's renaissance. As Olusegun Obasanjo put it during a state banquet in Abuja in honor of Thabo Mbeki in October 2000, "Our location, our destiny and the contemporary forces of globalisation have thrust upon us the burden of turning around the fortunes of our continent. We must not and cannot shy away from this responsibility."[83] In October 1999, South Africa's deputy president, Jacob Zuma, and his Nigerian counterpart, Abubakar Atiku, established the South Africa–Nigeria Binational Commission, thereby formalizing the strong ties between their two countries. Zuma directly linked the commission to the African renaissance concept when he explained that "by virtue of our relative strengths, our two countries have the ability to lead the continent into the mainstream of global political, social and economic development within the broad objective of an African Renaissance."[84] Abubakar Atiku, Nigeria's vice president, echoed these sentiments when he said, "our bilateral relations transcend relations between our two countries. It is a partnership for all Africa."[85] The two countries, he hinted, would be joining forces in pursuit of their common foreign policy objectives. They would, for example, seek jointly to affect the United Nations and other multilateral institutions.

The binational commission has five concrete objectives: first, to provide a framework for collaborative and cooperative efforts to bring Africa into the mainstream of global political, social, and economic developments; second, to provide the basis for the governments and private sectors of both countries to consult with each other on their economies and investment climates with a view to promoting bilateral trade and industry; third, to improve bilateral relations in the fields of technology, education, health, culture, youth, and sports; fourth, to utilize the generous endowments of both countries in human and natural resources to maximize socioeconomic development through economies of scale, global competitiveness, and specialization based on comparative and competitive advantage; and fifth, to establish the mechanisms for putting the benefits of economic cooperation to serve peace, stability, and socioeconomic integration in other parts of Africa.[86] The binational commission was inaugurated in Abuja from 4 to 5 October 1999. The second meeting was held in Pretoria and Cape Town from 26 to 29 April 2000. The third session was held in Abuja in July 2001. The fourth meeting held in Pretoria in March 2002 proposed the creation of a free trade area between both countries.

Since Nigeria's democratic transition in June 1998, the South African corporate community has begun to view the West African giant with renewed interest. South African companies have expressed interest in exploring cooperation in the fields of infrastructure development, the financial sector, and petroleum and gas. The South African telecommunications giants Mobile Telephone Network (MTN) and M-Net/SuperSport have been listed on the Nigerian Stock Exchange. MTN spent $340 million launching its mobile telephone network in Nigeria in August 2001.[87] South Africa's electricity giant, ESKOM, has been working with Nigeria's National Electrical Power Authority. South Africa's Spoornet is working with the Nigerian Railway Corporation to revive Nigeria's railways. South Africa's Portnet is rehabilitating port facilities in Lagos. South African Airways established a short-lived alliance with Nigeria Airways. Businessmen from South Africa and Nigeria now frequently visit each others' countries in search of investment and trade opportunities. The Nigeria–

South Africa Chamber of Commerce was launched in 2000 and had 128 members in June 2002. Mbeki is taking the lead in encouraging South African corporate giants to expand their interests into Nigeria.

By June 2002, Nigeria had become South Africa's fourth largest trading partner in Africa behind Zimbabwe, Mozambique, and Zambia. In West Africa, Nigeria is already South Africa's largest trading partner, with bilateral trade increasing from $100 million in 1999 to reach $500 million in 2001. The value of Nigeria's crude oil exports to South Africa—which started in 1997—reached 1.2 billion rand in 2000. The value of South African exports to Nigeria more than doubled from 209 million rand in 1998 to 514 million rand in 1999. Oil exports have significantly boosted trade between the two countries and largely explain South Africa's large trade deficit with Nigeria. While Nigeria chiefly sends oil and, increasingly, skilled manpower to South Africa, South Africa sends wood, paper, chemicals, foodstuffs, beverages, spirits, vinegar, tobacco, vehicles, aircraft, and mechanical appliances to Nigeria. The potential for trade between the two countries is enormous.[88]

An important obstacle to the hegemonic ambitions of South Africa and Nigeria is that the relationship between the countries relies too heavily on the relationship between Mbeki and Obasanjo. There is an urgent need to institutionalize the bilateral relationship between Pretoria and Abuja so that it survives the exit of one or both leaders from the national stage. The creation of a binational commission and growing commercial ties may help to overcome this problem, but this is far from certain. The establishment of the binational commission between South Africa and Nigeria will be a positive development for Africa only if Pretoria and Abuja take the interests of other African countries into account and forge working alliances with them as well. Unless this is done, the binational commission and the broader strategic alliance between Africa's two potential hegemons could be perceived as little more than a new breed of African imperialism. South Africa and Nigeria will have to reassure other African states that their intentions are noble: to promote peace and economic integration as the public goods of constructive hegemons. Both countries should also be modest in their conduct and downplay any apparent suggestion of having ambitions to dominate their subregions for their own interests or for national aggrandizement.

Toward an African Renaissance

It would be premature to celebrate the birth of a new alliance between South Africa and Nigeria that will save Africa from itself. Aside from the need to entrench democracy in South Africa and Nigeria, both countries still have serious socioeconomic problems that could adversely affect their regional and global standing. There are some important differences in the capacities and political strengths of the two governments. While South Africa's democracy faces many socioeconomic challenges, not least that of strengthening governance capacities, South Africa has more reason than Nigeria does to feel that it can achieve domestic stability. The rules of the democratic game in South Africa are more firmly established. But South Africans should not become complacent about their alleged "exceptional democracy." Even though South Africa's democracy and future transitions from one administration to another appear to be more assured than those of Nigeria, there have recently been worrying signs. The July 2001 allegations of a plotting conspiracy against three ANC stalwarts, Cyril Ramaphosa, Tokyo Sexwale, and Mathews Phosa (the investigation of the three politicians-turned-businessmen was soon halted after strong criticism), showed that the Mbeki government sometimes behaves in a paranoid manner; this kind of behavior could have negative repercussions for future democracy. That "plot" left the distinct impression that Mbeki's crown rests uneasily on his head. It also generated a perception that the ruling party has not successfully metamorphosed from liberation movement to political party and that the line between the movement and the government has become seriously blurred.[89]

In contrast to South Africa's painstakingly negotiated democratic transition, Nigeria has had a democratic transition almost by default. The rules of the game are hard to discern. Nigeria's democracy is highly fragile because it depends so much on the centrality of one individual, Olusegun Obasanjo.[90] Obasanjo has had a difficult time trying to pass domestic legislation despite the fact that his People's Democratic Party controls both houses of parliament. The survival of his regime remains uncertain, particularly in light of the violence that has been triggered by the recent promulgation of constitutionally questionable *sharia* criminal law in a dozen states in northern Nigeria; the country has also experienced sporadic ethnic and religious clashes that have resulted in over 6,000 deaths in three years.[91] The premature departure of Obasanjo through a military coup or other unconstitutional means could have dire consequences for Nigeria and West Africa. If Obasanjo were to leave the political scene, Nigeria might witness a slide back to autocratic rule, and the bilateral relationship with South Africa would inevitably suffer, as would any dreams of an African renaissance.

Another reason for not romanticizing the relationship between South Africa and Nigeria is that even if democracy were to survive in both countries, the ties between them will not be completely free of tension. In dealing with conflict-management issues in Africa and the promotion of democracy, disputes may arise between the two powers. Even beyond

Africa, the lingering debate over the restructuring of the UN Security Council and the quibbles over a potential African permanent seat may bring some rivalries between the two states into the open. Both states agreed to seek a minimum of two African seats on an enlarged UN Security Council at the second South Africa–Nigeria Binational Commission meeting in Cape Town in April 2000. But this accord has merely papered over serious differences and sought to mask a notable area of rivalry. How Pretoria and Abuja manage these tensions will be a true test of the durability of this new alliance.

Two events in Africa have contributed significantly to the recent turn away from regional peacekeeping and the apparent reassertion of the UN's role as the primary body responsible for international peacekeeping on the continent: the emergence of black majority rule in South Africa in 1994 and the death of Nigerian dictator General Sani Abacha in 1998. Abacha's death and the election of the civilian regime of Olusegun Obasanjo led to the emergence of a regime in Nigeria that could no longer ignore public opinion on the mounting costs and casualties of regional peacekeeping. Nigeria's recent ethnic clashes and continuing instability in its oil-producing region have focused attention on events closer to home. In South Africa, Nelson Mandela's election in 1994 raised great expectations in the West that Africa's richest country would lead the charge to keep the continental peace. Mandela chose instead to alleviate poverty at home and argued that South Africa's army needed restructuring, having acquired a notorious reputation for wreaking destruction on its neighbors. After succeeding Mandela as president in 1999, Mbeki promised to engage more in ending Africa's wars. With his army now largely restructured, there are no more excuses for not contributing soldiers to peacekeeping missions in Africa.

Both Mbeki and Obasanjo have contributed peacekeepers to UN missions in the DRC and Sierra Leone. But while both leaders have committed their countries to peacekeeping in Africa, questions remain about their capacity to undertake such missions. What is needed is to turn these countries into "politically capable partners."[92] The UN and Western powers should assist in developing the capacities of subregional powers like South Africa and Nigeria to keep peace in Africa. France, previously the most interventionist external power in Africa and a staunch supporter of apartheid South Africa, has recently energetically courted anglophone Nigeria and South Africa,[93] as it has lost influence in former parts of its *pré carré,* such as Rwanda and the DRC. Paris has invited nonfrancophone states to participate in its Renforcement des Capacités Africaines de Maintien de la Paix, launched in 1997 to strengthen African peacekeeping capacity. The U.S. Africa Crisis Response Initiative could also be extended to the SADC and ECOWAS,[94] and its functions increased beyond training to focus on greater military and logistical support and building subregional capacity for conflict management.

The current UN missions in Congo and Sierra Leone could signify a new, innovative approach to UN peacekeeping in Africa based on regional pillars supported by pivotal states like South Africa and Nigeria, whose political dominance is diluted by multinational peacekeepers from outside their regions. By placing largely regional forces under the UN flag, the hope is that the peacekeepers will enjoy the legitimacy and impartiality that the UN's universal membership often provides, while some of the financial and logistical problems of regional peacekeepers can be alleviated through greater burden-sharing. These missions should also be more accountable, as the peacekeepers will have to report regularly to the UN Security Council. This might also force the council to focus more attention on African conflicts.[95]

But it would be naive of South Africa and Nigeria to expect that other regional states will stand idly by while they form an alliance to lead Africa to the promised land. Unless the two "giants" take the interests of such states into account, and consistently find ways of reassuring them of their desire for mutual benefits from regional cooperation, they should not be surprised if counter-hegemonic alliances are formed to balance their own power. Both Mbeki and Obasanjo must use their political clout to help manage conflicts and promote democracy throughout Africa. They must provide continental leadership to achieve the annulment of unpayable international debts and ensure that Africa enjoys fair benefits from global trade before other African countries can consent to their leadership role. Only then would South Africa and Nigeria be in a position to provide a beacon of democracy and engine of economic growth for Africa[96] and to embark on the arduous journey of fulfilling their hegemonic potential in Africa.

Notes

The authors would like to thank Daniel Bach and John Stremlau for their useful comments on an earlier draft of the chapter. The chapter also benefited from comments at an IPA-sponsored seminar in Botswana in December 2000, a Columbia University Africa Studies Center seminar in New York in May 2001, and a seminar at the Institute for Global Dialogue in Johannesburg in October 2001.

1. See Adrian Hadland and Jovial Rantao, *The Life and Times of Thabo Mbeki* (Rivonia, South Africa: Zebra Press, 1999); Sean Jacobs and Richard Calland, eds., *Thabo Mbeki's World* (London and New York: Zed Books, 2002); Tom Lodge, *South African Politics Since 1994* (Cape Town and Johannesburg: David Philip Publishers, 1999), 110–122; Thabo Mbeki, *The Time Has Come: Selected Speeches* (Cape Town: Tafelberg Publishers; Johannesburg: Mafube Publishing, 1998); Thabo Mbeki, *Africa: Define Yourself* (Cape Town: Tafelberg Publishers, 2002); and Mukanda Mulemfo, *Thabo Mbeki and the African Renaissance* (Pretoria: Actua

Press, 2000); and Robert I. Rotberg, "Mandela and Mbeki," in *Ending Autocracy, Enabling Democracy* (Cambridge, Mass.: World Peace Foundation, 2002), 480–496.

2. See Reuben Abati, "Obasanjo: A Psychoanalysis," *The Guardian* (Lagos), 8 July 2001, 57; Chuks Iloegbunan, "King Solomon's Dilemma," *West Africa* 4319 (1–7 April 2002): 9; Onukaba Adinoyi Ojo, *Olesegun Obasanjo: In the Eyes of Time* (New York and Lagos: African Legacy Press, 1997); and Olusegun Obasanjo, *My Command* (London, Ibadan, and Nairobi: Heinemann, 1980), *Not My Will* (Ibadan, Nigeria: University Press, 1990), and *This Animal Called Man,* (Abeokuta, Nigeria: Africa Leadership Forum Publications, 1999).

3. On prophetic leadership, see Robert Jackson and Carl Rosberg, *Personal Rule in Black Africa: Prince, Autocrat, Prophet, Tyrant* (Berkeley and London: University of California Press, 1982).

4. See, for example, Hussein Adam, "Somalia: A Terrible Beauty Being Born?" in *Collapsed States: The Disintegration and Restoration of Legitimate Authority,* ed. William Zartman (Boulder, Colo.: Lynne Rienner Publishers, 1995), 69–78; Walter Clarke and Jeffrey Herbst, eds., *Learning from Somalia: The Lessons of Armed Humanitarian Intervention* (Boulder, Colo.: Westview Press, 1997); and John L. Hirsch and Robert B. Oakley, *Somalia and Operation Restore Hope: Reflections on Peacemaking and Peacekeeping* (Washington, D.C.: U.S. Institute of Peace, 1995).

5. See, for example, Gérard Prunier, *The Rwanda Crisis: History of a Genocide* (New York: Columbia University Press, 1995).

6. We thank Daniel Bach for reminding us of this important point.

7. On the concept of "pivotal states," see Francis Deng, Sadikiel Kimaro, Terrence Lyons, Donald Rothchild, and I. William Zartman, *Sovereignty as Responsibility: Conflict Management in Africa* (Washington, D.C.: Brookings Institution, 1996), and Robert Chase, Emily Hill, and Paul Kennedy, eds., *The Pivotal States: A New Framework for U.S. Policy in the Developing World* (New York: Norton, 1999).

8. See Chris Landsberg, "Pax Pretoriana vs. Pax Nigeriana," *L'Afrique Politique* 1 (2000): 105–115.

9. Daniel Bach, "Regional Domination and Power Conversion in Africa: Soft and Hard Hegemony," paper presented at the African Studies Association meeting, Nashville, Tenn., November 2000, 3.

10. Graham Evans and Jeffrey Newnham, *The Dictionary of World Politics* (New York and London: Harvester Wheatsheaf, 1990), 153.

11. David Myers, "Threat Perception and Strategic Response of the Regional Hegemons: A Conceptual Overview," in *Regional Hegemons: Threat Perception and Strategic Response*, ed. David Myers (Boulder, Colo.: Westview Press, 1991), 5.

12. Edward D. Mansfield, "The Concentration of Capabilities and the Onset of War," *Journal of Conflict Resolution* 36, 1 (1992): 3–24.

13. Stewart Patrick, "Forging Hegemonic Consensus: America, France, and the Making of the Postwar Order, 1945–1954," Ph.D. thesis, Oxford University, 1995, 18.

14. In the domestic context, *hegemony* was used by the Italian Marxist Antonio Gramsci to refer to the complex set of ideas that rulers use to assert their legitimacy and to keep subjects in check. Gramsci also sought to redefine hegemony as a form of state domination through political consensus rather than coercion. See Antonio Gramsci, *The Modern Prince and Other Writings* (New York: International Publishers, 1959).

15. See, for example, Paul Kennedy, *The Rise and Fall of the Great Powers* (New York: Vintage, 1987), 151–158; Ali Mazrui, "Hegemony: From Semites to Anglo-Saxons," in *Cultural Forces in World Politics* (Portsmouth, N.H.: Heinemann; London: James Currey, 1990), 29–64; and James Morris, *Pax Britannica: The Climax of an Empire* (San Diego, Calif.: Harcourt-Brace, 1968).

16. See, for example, Charles Kindleberger, *America in the World Economy* (New York: Foreign Policy Association, 1977), and Joseph Nye, Jr., *Bound to Lead: The Changing Nature of American Power* (New York: Basic Books, 1990).

17. See Robert O. Keohane, "The Theory of Hegemonic Stability and Change in International Economic Regimes, 1967–1977," in *Change in the International System,* ed. O. R. Holsti, R. M. Siverson, and A. L. George (Boulder, Colo.: Westview Press, 1980), and Joshua S. Goldstein, *International Relations* (New York: HarperCollins, 1994), 80.

18. Goldstein, *International Relations*, 80.

19. Ibid.

20. Garth le Pere, "South Africa and Nigeria: A Strategic Partnership," in *Global Dialogue* 4, 3 (December 1999): 9.

21. Olu Adeniji, "The Emergence of South Africa into the Global Economy and Its Consequences for Nigeria and Africa," in *Essays on Nigerian Foreign Policy, Governance and International Security* (Ibadan, Nigeria: Dokun Publishing House, 2000), 79.

22. Henry Kissinger, *Does America Need a Foreign Policy? Toward a Diplomacy for the Twenty-First Century* (New York: Simon and Schuster, 2001), 207–209.

23. See Adekeye Adebajo, "Tale of Two Giants," *Newswatch,* 11 September 1995, 9–10, and Adekeye Adebajo and Chris Landsberg, "Trading Places: Nigeria and South Africa," *Indicator* 13, 3 (Winter 1996): 64–68.

24. See, for example, John Chipman, *French Power in Africa* (Oxford: Basil Blackwell, 1989); Guy Martin, "Francophone Africa in the Context of Franco-African Relations," in *Africa in World Politics: Post–Cold War Challenges,* ed. John Harbeson and Donald Rothchild, 2d ed. (Boulder, Colo.: Westview Press, 1995), 163–188; and Douglas Yates, *The Rentier State in Africa: Oil Rent Dependency and Neocolonialism in the Republic of Gabon* (Trenton, N.J.: Africa World Press), 1995.

25. See S.K.B. Asante, "ECOWAS/CEAO: Conflict and Cooperation in West Africa," in *The Future of Regionalism in Africa,* ed. Ralph Onwuka and Amadu Sesay (London: Macmillan, 1985), 74–95; Daniel Bach, "The Politics of West African Economic Cooperation: CEAO and ECOWAS," *Journal of Modern African Studies* 21, 4 (1983): 601–621; Olatunde Ojo, "Nigeria and the Formation of ECOWAS," *International Organization*, 34, 4 (Autumn 1980): 571–601; and Omotayo Olaniyan, "Nigeria and ECOWAS: A Role and Problem Analysis," in *Nigeria's External Relations: The First Twenty-Five Years*, ed. Gabriel Olusanya and R. A. Akindele (Ibadan, Nigeria: University Press Limited, 1986), 126–140.

26. See, for example, James Barber and John Barratt, *South Africa's Foreign Policy 1948–88: The Search for Status and Security* (Johannesburg: Southern Book Publishers; Cambridge: Cambridge University Press, 1988); Deon Geldenhuys, *The Diplomacy of Isolation: South Africa's Foreign Policy Making* (Johannesburg: Macmillan, 1994); and Joseph Hanlon, *Apartheid's Second Front: South Africa's War Against Its Neighbors* (London: Penguin, 1986).

27. See Anthony Sampson, *Mandela: The Authorized Biography* (London: HarperCollins, 1999).

28. Ibrahim Gambari, "To Pretoria and Back," *West Africa* 3999 (23–29 May 1994): 907.

29. See UNDP, *Human Development Report 1999* (New York and Oxford: Oxford University Press, 1999).

30. See Garth le Pere, Anthoni van Neuwerk, and Kato Lambrechts, "South Africa and Africa: Reflections on the African Renaissance," Occasional Paper no. 17, Foundation for Global Dialogue, Bramfontein, South Africa, October 1998.

31. Thabo Mbeki, "Prologue," in *African Renaissance,* ed. Malegapuru William Makgoba (Cape Town: Mafube Publishing and Tafelberg Publishers, 1999), xv.

32. Ibid., xiii–xxi.

33. John Stremlau, "African Renaissance and International Relations," in Makgoba, *African Renaissance,* 101.

34. See Francis Deng and William Zartman, *A Quest for Human Dignity: Towards the Development of a CSSDCA* (forthcoming); Olusegun Obasanjo and Felix Mosha, eds., *Africa: Rise to Challenge* (New York: Africa Leadership Forum, 1993); and I. William Zartman, "African Regional Security and Changing Patterns of Relations," in *Africa in the New International Order,* ed. Edmond J. Keller and Donald Rothchild (Boulder, Colo.: Lynne Rienner Publishers, 1996), 62–65.

35. See CSSDCA, draft final document, Abuja, Nigeria, 8–9 May 2000, and South African Department of Foreign Affairs, Conference on Security, Stability, Development and Cooperation in Africa (CSSDCA), Pretoria, South Africa, 21 June 2001.

36. See, for example, International Peace Academy/Council for the Development of Social Science Research in Africa, "War, Peace, and Reconciliation in Africa," Dakar and Saly, Senegal, November–December 1999, and "Southern Africa's Evolving Security Architecture: Problems and Prospects," sponsored by the International Peace Academy, Witwatersrand University, Southern African Regional Institute for Policy Studies, and African Renaissance Institute, Gaborone, Botswana, December 2000.

37. For analyses on the democratic peace theory, see Pauline H. Baker, "Conflict Resolution Versus Democratic Governance: Divergent Paths to Peace," in *Managing Global Chaos: Sources of and Responses to International Conflict*, ed. Chester A. Crocker, Fen Osler Hampson, and Pamela Aall (Washington, D.C.: U.S. Institute of Peace, 1996), 563–571; Joshua Muravchik, "Promoting Peace Through Democracy," in Crocker et al., *Managing Global Chaos*, 573–585; Miriam Fendius Elman, "Testing the Democratic Peace Theory," in *Paths to Peace: Is Democracy the Answer?* (Washington, D.C.: CSIA Studies in International Security, 1998).

38. Christopher Landsberg, "Promoting Democracy: The Mandela-Mbeki Doctrine," *Journal of Democracy* 11, 3 (July 2000): 213.

39. Adekeye Adebajo and Chris Landsberg, "The Heirs of Nkrumah: Africa's New Interventionists," *Pugwash Occasional Papers* 2, 1 (January 2000): 65–90.

40. Olusegun Obasanjo, "Africa's Rendezvous with History," in Obasanjo and Mosha, *Africa: Rise to Challenge*, 260.

41. K. Mamila, "Mbeki MAP's Out Africa's Fresh Beginning," in *Johannesburg Star*, 20 July 2001.

42. See Christopher Landsberg, "South Africa and Nigeria: Hegemons or Strategic Partners?" *Global Dialogue* 5, 2 (September 2000): 22–24.

43. During the 1999 OAU heads-of-state summit in Algiers, the OAU endorsed the idea of a troika consisting of South Africa, Nigeria, and Algeria to spearhead Africa's debt relief campaign.

44. South African Department of Foreign Affairs, "The Millennium Partnership for Africa's Recovery Program" (MAP). Draft document 3a, Pretoria, July 2001.

45. Ibid., introduction.

46. Ibid., paragraph 53.

47. NAI, "A New African Initiative: Merger of the Millennium Partnership for Africa Program (MAP) and Omega Plan," Pretoria, July 2001, introduction.

48. Ibid., 8.

49. See NEPAD, communiqué issued at the end of the meeting of the Implementation Committee of Heads of State and Government, Abuja, Nigeria, 23 October 2001.

50. See Welile Nhlapo, "South Africa and Peacekeeping: Looking to the Future," in Jakkie Cilliers and Greg Mills, eds., *From Peacekeeping to Complex Emergencies: Peace Support Missions in Africa* (Johannesburg: South African Institute of International Affairs; Pretoria: Institute for Security Studies, 1999), 127–132.

51. SANDF, "White Paper on Peace Missions," Pretoria, 24 February 1999.

52. Landsberg, "Promoting Democracy," 110; for an in-depth analysis of the early stages of the Lesotho crisis, see Khabele Matlosa, "The 1993 Elections in Lesotho and the Challenge for the New Government, Southern African Perspectives," Working Paper Series no. 28, Center for Southern African Studies, University of the Western Cape, Bellville, South Africa, October 1993; also see Khabele Matlosa, "Lesotho's Political Turmoil and Prospects for the 1998 National Election," in *Africa Insight* 27, 4 (1997).

53. See Khabele Matlosa, "The Lesotho Conflict: Major Causes and Management," in *Crisis in Lesotho: The Challenge of Managing Conflict in Southern Africa,* ed. Kato Lambrechts (Braamfontein, South Africa: Foundation for Global Dialogue, 1999), 6–11.

54. Khabele Matlosa, "The Electoral System and Election Management in Lesotho," study for the Electoral Institute of Southern Africa, Johannesburg, July 2001, 14.

55. Ibid.

56. Ibid.

57. See SANDF, "The SADC Intervention in Lesotho: A Military Perspective," Pretoria, May 2000.

58. Matlosa, "Lesotho Conflict," 9; see also Khabele Matlosa, "Military Rule and Withdrawal from Power: The Case of Lesotho," in *The Military and Militarism in Africa*, ed. Eboe Hutchful and Abdoulaye Bathily (Dakar, Senegal: CODESRIA Books, 1998).

59. See Nhlapo, "South Africa and Peacekeeping," 127–131.

60. Francis Kornegay, "Nigeria, Egypt and South Africa: A Stable Balance of Power in Africa," *South African Yearbook of International Affairs 1999/2000* (Johannesburg: South African Institute of International Affairs, 1999), 63.

61. For a perspective on South Africa's strategy toward the Congo conflict, see Claude Kabemba, "Whither the DRC? Causes of the Conflict in the Democratic Republic of Congo, and the Way Forward," *Policy Issues and Actors* 11, 6 (March 1999).

62. See David Simon, ed., *South Africa in Southern Africa* (Oxford: James Currey; Athens, Ohio: Ohio University Press, 1998).

63. See the references to southern Africa in Mbeki's speeches, "South Africa: A Workable Dream," keynote address, Europe–South Africa 1995 Business and

Finance Forum, Geneva, Switzerland, 27 June 1995, and "South Africa: A Year of Democracy," delivered at the Bruno-Kreisky Forum, Vienna, 28 August 1995.

64. For a clearheaded defense of Mbeki's policy, see Vincent Maphai, "SA Should Not Rush in Where Angels Fear to Tread," *Business Day*, 14 March 2001.

65. Maria Eismont, "Burundians Split on South African Peace Force," *Business Day*, 30 October 2001.

66. *Johannesburg Star*, 31 October 2001.

67. For a perspective on the different roles and positions of SADC member states in the DRC conflict, see Christopher Landsberg, "South Africa and the Congo War," in *The African Stakes of the Congo War*, ed. John F. Clark (New York: Palgrave, 2002).

68. *The Nation* (Malawi), 16 January 2002.

69. This section draws largely from Adekeye Adebajo, "Nigeria: Africa's New Gendarme?" *Security Dialogue* 31, 2 (June 2000): 185–199.

70. For accounts of the Liberian and Sierra Leonean civil wars, see Adekeye Adebajo, *Building Peace in West Africa: Liberia, Sierra Leone, and Guinea-Bissau*, (Boulder, Colo.: Lynne Rienner Publishers, 2002), and *Liberia's Civil War: Nigeria, ECOMOG, and Regional Security in West Africa* (Boulder, Colo.: Lynne Rienner Publishers, 2002); special issue on "Youth Culture and Political Violence: The Sierra Leone Civil War," *African Development* 22, 2/3 (1997); Stephen Ellis, *The Mask of Anarchy: The Destruction of Liberia and the Religious Dimensions of an African Civil War* (London: Hurst and Company, 1999); Robert Mortimer, "From ECOMOG I to ECOMOG II: Intervention in Sierra Leone," in *Africa in World Politics: The African State System in Flux,* ed. John W. Harbeson and Donald Rothchild, 3d ed. (Boulder, Colo.: Westview Press, 2000); Paul Richards, *Fighting for the Rainforest: War, Youth, and Resources in Sierra Leone* (Oxford: James Currey; Portsmouth, N.H.: Heinemann, 1996); and Margaret Vogt, ed., *The Liberian Crisis and ECOMOG: A Bold Attempt at Regional Peacekeeping* (Lagos: Gabumo Press, 1992).

71. See UN Secretary-General, second report pursuant to Security Council Resolution 1270 (1999) on the UN Mission in Sierra Leone, 11 January 2000, S/2000/13.

72. For details, see ECOWAS, Protocol Relating to the Mechanism for Conflict Prevention, Management, Resolution, Peacekeeping, and Security, Lomé, Togo, 10 December 1999.

73. See UN Secretary-General, report pursuant to Security Council Resolution 1216 (1998), relative to the situation in Guinea-Bissau, 17 March 1999, S/1999/294.

74. See Adekeye Adebajo, "Whither Nigeria's Foreign Policy?" *Tell,* 23 August 1999, 48–49; Comfort Ero, "The Future of ECOMOG in West Africa," in Cilliers and Mills, *From Peacekeeping to Complex Emergencies*, 61–65; Julius Ihonvbere, "Nigeria as Africa's Great Power: Constraints and Prospects for the 1990s," *International Journal* 46, 3 (Summer 1991): 510–535; and Stephen Wright and Julius Emeka Okolo, "Nigeria: Aspirations of Regional Power," in *African Foreign Policies,* ed. Stephen Wright (Boulder, Colo.: Westview Press, 1999), 125–130.

75. Sule Lamido, "I Will Surprise My Critics," interview in *This Day*, 8 August 1999, 10.

76. Personal interviews with diplomatic and military officials by Adekeye Adebajo on a research trip to Burkina Faso, Côte d'Ivoire, Guinea, Liberia, Nigeria, and Sierra Leone in July and August 1999.

77. Olusegun Obasanjo, "Nigeria, Africa, and the World in the next

Millennium," address to the Fifty-Fourth Session of the UN General Assembly, 23 September 1999.

78. See Abiodun Alao, "Security Reform in Democratic Nigeria," Working Paper no. 2, Conflict, Security, and Development Group, King's College, London, 2000.

79. Olusegun Obasanjo, speech delivered at the Commonwealth-Nigeria Investment Conference, Abuja, Nigeria, 28 February 2000.

80. Thabo Mbeki, "South Africa: Two Nations," statement at the opening of the debate on reconciliation and nation-building, National Assembly, Cape Town, 29 May 1998.

81. For further analysis of the "two nations" concept, see Nicoli Nattras and Jeremy Seekings, "Two Nations? Race and Economic Inequality in South Africa Today," *Daedalus* 130, 1 (Winter 2001).

82. Yusuf Bangura, "Comments on Regional Security and the War in Congo," in *Reflections on the Crisis in the Democratic Republic of Congo,* ed. Ibbo Mandaza (Harare, Zimbabwe: SAPES Books, 1999), 27.

83. Olusegun Obasanjo, "Nigeria–South Africa: Bond Across the Continent," in *A New Dawn: A Collection of Speeches of President Olusegun Obasanjo,* ed. Ad'Obe Obe, vol. 2 (Ibadan, Nigeria: Spectrum Books, 2001), 137.

84. *Johannesburg Star*, 6 October 1999.

85. Ibid.

86. South African Department of Foreign Affairs, communiqué from the South Africa–Nigeria Bi-National Commission, Pretoria, 6 October 1999.

87. See James Lamont, "Mobile Phone Network Opens in Nigeria," *Financial Times*, 10 August 2001, 7. On the growing bilateral trade ties, see also, "Nigeria and South Africa: Getting Down to Business," *Business in Africa,* June 2002, 34–42.

88. We would like to thank officials at South Africa's Department of Foreign Affairs for providing us with this information.

89. See Adekeye Adebajo and Chris Landsberg, "Can an Insecure Mbeki Avoid the Fate of Kwame Nkrumah?" *Sunday Independent* (South Africa), 6 May 2001, 7

90. See Adekeye Adebajo, "Into the Burning Ashes," *Times Literary Supplement*, 2 February 2001, 28.

91. See Robert Guest, "A Survey of Nigeria: Here's Hoping," *Economist*, 15 January 2000; Dan Isaacs, "Soldiers' Revenge," *BBC Focus on Africa* 13, 1 (January–March 2002): 24–25; Karl Maier, *This House Has Fallen: Midnight in Nigeria* (New York: Public Affairs, 2000); and Rotimi T. Suberu, "Can Nigeria's New Democracy Survive?" *Current History*, May 2001, 207–212.

92. John Stremlau, "Ending Africa's Wars," *Foreign Affairs* 79, 4 (July/August 2000): 117–132.

93. See Rocklyn Williams, "Beyond Old Borders: Challenges to Franco–South African Security Relations in the New Millennium," *African Security Review* 8, 4 (1999): 3–19.

94. For a comparative assessment of SADC and ECOWAS, see Anthoni Van Nieuwkerk, "Regionalism into Globalism? War and Peace? SADC and ECOWAS Compared," *African Security Review* 10, 2 (2001): 7–18.

95. See Adekeye Adebajo and Chris Landsberg, "Back to the Future: UN Peacekeeping in Africa," in *Managing Armed Conflicts in the 21st Century,* ed. Adekeye Adebajo and Chandra Lekha Sriram (London: Frank Cass, 2001).

96. See Adekeye Adebajo and Chris Landsberg, "Pax Africana in the Age of Extremes," *South African Journal of International Affairs* 7, 1 (Summer 2001): 16–19.

10

From the Organization of African Unity to the African Union

MUSIFIKY MWANASALI

The idea of "regions" has gathered renewed interest and emphasis in academic and policy circles since the end of the Cold War. The academic literature, now well supplied with studies on regions and regional security communities, largely owes this relative abundance to a shift in focus in the academic discourse on peace and security, from the bipolar structure of the international system during the Cold War to the internal and local causes of wars and violent conflicts. At the same time, perceptions of the meaning of "security" have moved beyond traditional preoccupations with the state and "national security"—the dominant Cold War paradigm—to embrace new concerns including human, environmental, food, and water security. This new emphasis on the internal roots of conflicts and extension of the concept of security beyond the Cold War paradigm has had a particular impact in Africa. It has led African political leaders to expand the mandates of the now defunct Organization of African Unity (OAU) and its newly launched successor, the African Union (AU), which came into effect in July 2002, to peace and security issues and to extend their activities into the realms of human rights, democratization, good governance, and humanitarian assistance.[1]

Despite these significant changes, the state remains the central focus of Africa's peace and security agenda, and domestic political order remains the main preoccupation of decisionmakers at both the continental and regional levels. Such a reality is to be expected from the continental organization whose raison d'être involves promoting the unity and solidarity of African states and defending their sovereignty, territorial integrity, and independence.[2]

The centrality of the state to the OAU security agenda and the OAU's principled position against interference in the internal political affairs of member states imposed serious constraints on Africa's efforts to bring an end to the scourge of internal conflicts that, paradoxically, reverberate throughout their neighborhoods and beyond. A cursory examination of Africa's political configuration shows the continent as an amorphous mosaic of overlapping communities within communities that consider themselves bound together solely by virtue of treaties signed under the OAU, which they rarely seek to implement. Members of such communities range from states with a recognizable physical base and an institutional expression of legitimacy and authority to states with no recognizable feature but a name, a flag, and a national anthem. Hence, it is legitimate to wonder if it is appropriate, from both conceptual and policy standpoints, to speak of "regions" in Africa, and if there can ever be genuine regional security communities on the continent. An added complication was the OAU's transformation into the AU in July 2002. This mutation will be a protracted political, administrative, and financial process. Its success will depend, to a large extent, on the ways in which regional economic communities (RECs) and regional security arrangements will merge into the AU.

A precise definition of "region" and "regional security community" is unnecessary for the purposes of this chapter. The discussion will focus on the efforts of one continental organization—the OAU—to construct a regional peace and security order with the assistance of its constitutive parts. We proceed from the assumption that regions and regional security communities exist in Africa because their members see themselves as part of such geographic-cum-security arrangements. This position is grounded in the recognition that despite, or due to, their variations, member states sharing geographic proximity feel united by common security concerns. These common security concerns are generated by violent intrastate conflicts with cross-boundary ramifications and conflicts occurring outside their common boundaries that impact their internal or regional security. We thus loosely apply Barry Buzan's definition of regional security complexes ("communities" in our argument) as "a group of states whose primary security concerns link together sufficiently closely that their national securities cannot realistically be considered apart from one another."[3]

This chapter aims to present, from the OAU experience, some reflections on the viability of regional security mechanisms and their effectiveness in carrying out mandates in the area of conflict management. While situating this discussion within a framework of cooperation on peace and security between the OAU and the Southern African Development Community (SADC), we wish to steer the debate toward an approach that encourages the AU to develop a comprehensive framework guiding the interactions of its security mechanism with those elaborated at the regional level.

The chapter first examines the genesis of the idea of "region" in the African context, and draws attention to the case of the SADC. It then uses the example of the war in the Democratic Republic of Congo (DRC) to illustrate the type of cooperative arrangements that could be developed between the continental organization and regional organizations in conflict management. Finally, it outlines some of the problems that will continue to impede effective cooperation between the AU and regional organizations such as the SADC. It thereby highlights proposals that have been made to correct the lack of an effective partnership between the OAU secretariat and regional peace and security organizations.

The OAU and the Five African Regions

The decision to divide the continent into regions dates back to the ninth ordinary session of the Assembly of African Heads of State and Government, which took place in Rabat, Morocco, from 12 to 15 June 1972. Southern Africa, the fifth African region, was established at the twenty-sixth ordinary session of the OAU Council of Ministers, which met in Addis Ababa, Ethiopia, from 23 February to 1 March 1976.[4] During that session, the council decided that "there shall be five regions of the OAU, namely Northern, Western, Central, Eastern, and Southern."[5] The council also gave individual member states the freedom to choose which region they wanted to belong to and requested them to communicate their choice to the OAU secretariat.

Several factors justified the OAU decision to create the five regions, including the existence of similarities in the nature and extent of problems facing particular regions; the need to encourage viable economic development projects on a regional basis; and the desire to create an equitable, geographical representation of all OAU member states on a regional basis. Organizations for economic integration were subsequently set up by each region. These were the Economic Community of West African States (ECOWAS) in 1975, the Southern African Development Coordination Conference (SADCC) in 1980, the Economic Community of Central African States (ECCAS) in 1983, the Arab Maghreb Union (UMA) in 1989, and the East African Community (EAC-new formula) in 1994.

Relationships between the OAU and regional economic organizations were later formalized and regulated by the 1991 Abuja treaty and related protocols, which established the African Economic Community (AEC) as an integral part of the OAU. The Abuja treaty was adopted by fifty-one member states on 3 June 1991.[6] Aside from the usual pronouncements regarding the equality and interdependence of member states, the signatories to the treaty committed themselves to the principles of solidarity and collective self-reliance, interstate cooperation, the peaceful settlement of disputes, the protection of human rights, and the promotion of accountability, economic justice, and popular participation. They enjoined the AEC to use these principles as a guide in the fulfillment of its mandate: a mandate chiefly concerned with the promotion of African cooperation in all fields of human endeavor. This mandate was conceived as a means of raising the living standards of African peoples; maintaining and enhancing economic stability; fostering close and peaceful relations among member states; and contributing to the progress, development, and economic integration of the continent.

The Abuja treaty also entrusted the AEC with the coordination and harmonization of policies among existing and future economic communities, with a view to fostering regional integration. African leaders determined that the community should be established gradually through the coordination, harmonization, and progressive integration of the activities of those RECs regarded as pillars of the AEC.

The responsibility entrusted to the AEC and its constitutive institutions was enormous, considering the physical diversity of the regions, their varied experience in economic cooperation, their dissimilar rates of economic growth, and their uneven capacity to organize as coherent and effective regional entities. The Abuja treaty enjoined member states to "undertake to strengthen the existing regional economic communities and to establish new communities where they do not exist in order to ensure the gradual establishment of the community."[7] By the same token, member states were requested to "take all necessary measures aimed at progressively promoting increasingly closer cooperation among the [regional economic] communities, particularly through the coordination and harmonization of their activities in all fields or sectors in order to ensure the realization of the objectives of the Community."[8]

In ratifying the Abjua treaty, OAU member states undertook

> to promote the coordination and harmonization of the activities of regional economic communities of which they are members, with the activities of the community, it being understood that the establishment of the latter is the final objective toward which the activities of existing and future regional economic communities shall be geared.

Paragraph 4 of the same article enjoins them to "undertake, through their respective regional economic communities, to coordinate and harmonize the activities of their sub-regional organizations, with a view to rationalizing the integration process at the level of each region."[9]

These decisions and resolutions provide a legal basis and an institutional framework for cooperation between the former OAU secretariat (now the AU Commission) and regional organizations such as the SADC. It has been argued that, by creating the five regions and encouraging them to develop an institutional setting for regional economic cooperation, the OAU had demonstrated its willingness to delegate to neighboring countries in the affected region the responsibility for developing a common approach toward tackling their problems in the areas of peace and security and economic cooperation and development. By the same token, the OAU appeared to have taken the position that it would intervene in regional matters only in specific conflict situations, including situations where regional efforts had been exhausted, where the credibility of the regional organization concerned may have been eroded, and where the conflict had spilled over to other regions.

This approach has led to a unique cooperative arrangement, largely determined by the regional organizations' advantage of proximity. Generally, the OAU undertook its engagements, albeit at times hesitantly and superficially, on its own initiative; occasionally it did so at the invitation of regional organizations. This had particularly been the case when internal divergences or intractable conflicts of interest among neighboring countries seemed to threaten regional cooperation, or when the concerned region requested OAU support at the United Nations.

The SADC: From Conference to Community

The above section has outlined the unwritten rules that seem to guide the relationship between the OAU and the RECs, including the SADC. The evidence suggests that these unwritten rules will continue to affect the relationship between the AU and Africa's regional communities. The commitment of SADC decisionmaking organs to the effective functioning of the AEC is noteworthy. In the final communiqué issued at the 1998 SADC summit in Grand Baie, Mauritius, SADC heads of state and government

> reaffirmed [the summit's] decision of 1995, that all the activities and policies of SADC should be carried out in the context of achieving the objectives of the African Economic Community. The summit committed SADC, as a building bloc, to play a catalytic and strategic role in the process of establishing the African Economic Community.[10]

At its launch in Lusaka, Zambia, in 1980, the SADCC was directed to coordinate economic cooperation within its geographic area. Member states were allocated areas of economic specialization and specific tasks and targets, on the basis of what they could offer the community. One of the SADCC's main objectives was to reduce the economic dependence on South Africa of countries in the region, while intensifying regional efforts, in close partnership with the OAU, to dismantle apartheid.

On 17 August 1992, in Windhoek, Namibia, the SADCC was renamed the Southern African Development Community, its current designation. Integration, rather than cooperation, was emphasized. The new mandate was expanded to include political, military, and security matters. This shift was the result of new regional dynamics generated by, among other factors, Namibia's independence in 1990 and the demise of the apartheid regime in 1994. The SADC adapted to these changes by evolving common political values and institutions, as well as the promotion of peace and security in the subregion. At the same time, the SADC began to expand further north and east, beyond its original geographic neighborhood, to include Mauritius and the DRC. At the time of writing, Uganda was due to be included in the community.

Expansion of its mandate and geographic base is not peculiar to the southern African region. This trend has been observed in nearly all the existing regions, whether defined geographically or in security terms. This trend is also observable in the establishment of new regional organizations that seek to integrate the management of economic, political, and security issues within a single cooperative framework.

The new integrative community scheme presently mushrooming at the regional level is a welcome development to the extent that it reflects a genuine commitment and stronger political will by the regions to marshal resources and coordinate initiatives in their bid to promote economic and political development. These developments conform to the letter and spirit of the Abuja treaty and the Sirte, Libya, declaration of September 1999. In Sirte, African leaders decided

> to accelerate the process of implementing the treaty establishing the African Economic Community, in particular [by] strengthening and consolidating the Regional Economic Communities as the pillars for achieving the objectives of the African Economic Community and realizing the envisaged Union.[11]

Still, the emergence of community schemes and the proliferation of regional organizations raise a host of new problems: notably, how to fit them into the existing regional arrangements and ensure effective operation and cooperation. Not only are the old regional organizations, such as the SADC, expanding beyond their geographic frontiers, they also have to cope with member states like Angola, the DRC, and Tanzania, which belong to other regional ensembles. Additionally, altered and new regional arrangements, such as the Common Market of East and Southern Africa (COMESA) or the Indian Ocean Commission grouping—the Comoros, Madagascar, Mauritius, and the Seychelles—are emerging throughout southern Africa (and the continent at large), and encroaching, as it were, on the SADC's territorial coverage as determined by the OAU.[12] The OAU's successor, the AU, needs to define the nature of these new regional schemes and organizations—particularly in the context of the five existing regions, with their mostly integrative mandate—and decide if member states should be allowed to belong to more than one regional community. Such interventions have clear potential to raise controversy, as member states may see them as an attempt by the AU to interfere in their right to choose the region or regions to which they wish to belong.

Integrated Economic and Security Management

Like other regional groupings, the SADC has established a security mechanism to deal with common security and defense matters. The Gaborone extraordinary summit created the SADC Organ on Politics, Defense, and Security on 28 June 1996, but the organ took more than two years to become operational. The delay was caused by disagreements among regional leaders, voiced particularly during the 1997 summit in Blantyre, Malawi, and the 1998 summit in Maputo, Mozambique.[13]

Following the SADC's establishment, consultations began on how to implement the provisions of the SADC treaty on defense and security, in order to enable the organization to develop an integrated defense and security framework capable of ensuring lasting peace, political stability, and a secure environment for economic cooperation and development. An SADC workshop on democracy, peace, and security was convened in Windhoek on 11–16 July 1994 to identify the principles on which the evolution of regional cooperation in security and military matters would be based. The workshop recommended, inter alia, that conflict resolution and political cooperation should become a "sector" to be allocated to one member state, for the purpose of improved coordination. The recommendations were later strengthened by the decision of the Frontline States, on 30 July 1994, to dissolve their organization and to turn it into the political and security branch of the SADC.

The Windhoek workshop submitted its proposals for the consideration of the SADC Council of Ministers, which met in Gaborone, Botswana, in August 1994. The idea of sector allocations, which received the support of South Africa, Botswana, Swaziland, Lesotho, and the SADC secretariat, was thought to be consistent with the provisions of the SADC treaty. However, the countries opposed to the idea, namely Angola, Zambia, Tanzania, and Zimbabwe, argued that peace and security were very sensitive issues and that the SADC secretariat was not institutionally strong enough to perform the duties required by such an arrangement.

Instead, these countries favored the establishment of a security mechanism that would respect the sovereignty and independence of member states. Dubbed the Association of Southern African States (ASAS), this mechanism would provide southern Africa with a framework for dealing with defense and security and conflict prevention and resolution in the region. It would function independently of the SADC secretariat and would report directly to the SADC summit. The Interstate Defense and Security Committee and a Political Affairs Unit were to be its institutional components.

The SADC Council of Ministers, which met in Harare, Zimbabwe, in March 1995, failed to reconcile the opposing proposals for an integrated economic and security management system for the region. The matter was, therefore, referred to the SADC summit due to take place in Johannesburg in August 1995. In its final communiqué, the Johannesburg summit adopted the proposal calling for the allocation of the sector on defense and security to a member state. It also directed that those ministers responsible for defense and security and those in charge of SADC matters should be consulted on the appropriate structures, terms of reference, and operational procedures for the sector.

The ministers of foreign affairs, defense, home affairs, and security of SADC member states met in Gaborone on 18 January 1996 but failed to reach a decision. Instead, South Africa and the SADC secretariat jointly proposed the creation, within the framework of the SADC treaty, of a special committee to deal with the matter of regional cooperation in the areas of peace, security, and conflict resolution. The special committee was to report to the Council of Ministers, which in turn would report to the SADC summit through the SADC chairman. This compromise was also rejected on the same basis as the ideas of sector and the ASAS—that there was a possibility that too much power and influence would be concentrated in the chairman of SADC, giving the secretariat a prominent role in security matters.

Meanwhile, Zimbabwe floated another compromise proposal that called for a SADC Organ on Politics, Defense, and Security (OPDS). The OPDS would operate at summit level and function independently of other SADC structures. It would also operate at ministerial level, and its chairmanship would rotate on a troika basis. This was the proposal that was finally accepted, despite reluctance expressed by South Africa; it was later endorsed by the SADC heads of state during their extraordinary summit in Gaborone on 28 June 1996. In the final communiqué, the summit defined the principles and objectives of the OPDS. It also affirmed that the organ constituted an appropriate institutional framework through which SADC countries would be able to coordinate their policies and activities in the areas of politics, defense, and security. The Gaborone summit also agreed to elaborate a protocol on peace, security, and conflict resolution, which would include the following provisions:

- The OPDS would operate at the summit level and function independently of other SADC structures.

- The OPDS would also operate at ministerial and technical levels.
- Chairmanship of the OPDS would rotate on an annual and a troika basis.
- The Inter-State Defense and Security Committee would be one of the institutions of the organ.
- Other structures could be established as the need arose.

President Robert Mugabe of Zimbabwe was elected as the first chairman of the OPDS. The creation of the OPDS marked a significant turn of events in southern Africa, for it enabled the regional organization to integrate its efforts and activities in the economic, defense, and security areas. However, differences of opinion persisted with respect to the status of the OPDS in the SADC structures and institutions and its legal relationship to the SADC treaty. Ultimately, it was the SADC OPDS ministerial meeting, held in Maputo on 8 May 1998, that broke the political impasse by proposing that "the most ideal structure [for the SADC organ] was to have a small Committee of Heads of State, which should have five members only."[14]

In March 2001, the heads of state and government agreed that the chair of the OPDS would rotate on an annual and troika basis. During the August 2001 SADC summit in Blantyre, the president of Mozambique, Joachim Chissano, was elected chair of the OPDS for a year.

The War in the DRC

The war in the DRC that began on 2 August 1998 put the SADC and OPDS under serious strain. Relationships between SADC members soured, and the conflict nearly undermined regional cohesion and the organization's capacity to execute its mandate in the field of peace, security, and common defense.

The differences between Zimbabwe and South Africa over the necessity of an SADC military intervention in support of the embattled DRC government have already been well documented. Suffice to say here that it was, perhaps, in order to avoid more such clashes (and the prospects of an irreparable rift within the regional organization) that the SADC collectively welcomed the OAU's involvement in the region. After the South African–led military intervention in Lesotho in 1998, it became relatively important for SADC member states to reach some sort of common position over the DRC conflict. This step was achieved at the Grand Baie summit of September 1998, during which SADC leaders "commended the governments of Angola, Namibia and Zimbabwe for timeously providing troops to assist the government and people of the DRC to defeat the illegal attempt by rebels and their allies to capture the capital city, Kinshasa, and other strategic areas." This was the strongest statement of collective SADC support for the DRC government. However, it later generated strong protests from the governments of Rwanda and Uganda, which considered it a declaration of war against them by the SADC.

As the OAU Council of Ministers convened in Algiers, the belligerents in the DRC were meeting in Lusaka, Zambia, to sign a cease-fire agreement. The draft was prepared in Lusaka from 21 to 27 June 1999, by senior officials representing SADC member states, the OAU, the UN, and the belligerents. It was then submitted for the consideration of the ministers of foreign affairs and defense, who met from 29 June to 7 July 1999. Finally, the heads of state of Angola, the DRC, Namibia, Rwanda, Uganda, Zimbabwe, and Zambia signed the agreement on 10 July 1999. The OAU, UN, and SADC signed as observers.[15]

The Lusaka cease-fire agreement was the fruit of tireless efforts by Zambian president Frederick Chiluba in his capacity as the chairman of the Regional Initiative for Peace in the DRC. The initiative was set up to coordinate efforts aimed at ending the conflict that had engulfed three African regions and a score of national and foreign interests.[16] However, by the time the Lusaka agreement came into force, the SADC's role in the DRC had become marginal compared to that of the OAU.

The shift of responsibility from the regional to the continental organization later became evident in the provisions of the Lusaka agreement. Surprisingly, the OAU and not the SADC was urged immediately to "constitute, facilitate and deploy an appropriate peace-keeping force in the DRC to ensure implementation of this agreement . . . until the deployment of the UN peace-keeping force."[17] The OAU secretary-general was also asked to appoint both a chairman of the Joint Military Commission (JMC)—which was established to facilitate the disengagement of forces—and to designate, in consultation with the parties concerned, a neutral facilitator to assist in the organization of the inter-Congolese political dialogue.[18]

Clearly, the OAU was given responsibilities that were incommensurate with its capacity to undertake and that, in the final analysis, would have been better undertaken by SADC member states.

The Lusaka agreement also set up a Political Committee comprising ministers of foreign affairs and defense and any other representatives duly mandated by the parties. The committee was mandated to assist the JMC and to deal with political issues that would arise during the implementation of the agreement. It was the Political Committee that decided that, in order to fulfill its mandate adequately, the JMC should deploy in the field. By common accord, the parties, meeting at the first JMC conference in Kampala from 11 to 12 October 1999, chose four localities that would serve as headquarters for the new JMC structures.[19] The Political Committee has met regularly in the capitals of the countries involved in the DRC vortex. Zambia, which was granted observer status at the first meeting of the Political Committee in Lusaka on 15 October 1999, serves as its headquarters.

The OAU and Regional Mechanisms

We have so far endeavored to present, from the perspective of the OAU, the principles that appeared to guide the relationship between the continental organization and the SADC. We have examined the DRC conflict to illustrate the type of cooperative arrangements that could be negotiated at the regional and continental levels for peace, security, and humanitarian assistance.

Over the years, it has been stressed that the OAU secretariat should have set up a genuine partnership and a robust complementary relationship with African regional organizations in order to implement the decisions of OAU policy organs. Although the OAU-SADC relationship gradually improved, the two organizations had once reached a point of mutual indifference that bordered on outright hostility. The SADC secretariat was conspicuously absent from key meetings convened by the OAU secretariat, while the latter invoked the fact that the SADC did not invite the OAU secretariat as a justification for its absence from meetings organized by the SADC secretariat. Various recommendations were made to remedy this lack of interaction. Proposals included those of an OAU-commissioned study, various seminars organized jointly by the OAU and Africa-based or international nongovernmental organizations, and, more recently, an address by President Alpha Oumar Konare of Mali to the thirty-sixth ordinary session of the OAU summit in Lomé, Togo, in July 2000.

The OAU secretariat realized that cooperation with all the regional organizations had suffered greatly due to the lack of adequate structures and a coherent approach within the secretariat on how best to engage the RECs. In an attempt to improve this state of affairs, the former Department of Economic, Social, and Cultural Affairs, now known as the Department of Community and Social Affairs, was tasked with dealing with the regional economic communities. This responsibility was deemed appropriate, as the department was already in charge of coordinating efforts for the institution of the African Common Market, which is envisioned as a key step toward the establishment of the AEC. In this vein, a high-level OAU-REC meeting took place in Tripoli, Libya, in February 2001, on the margins of the seventy-fourth ordinary session of the Council of Ministers.

With the development of regional security mechanisms by nearly all the RECs, the need arose for the OAU to harmonize regional peace and security instruments with the OAU Mechanism for Conflict Prevention,

Management, and Resolution, which was established by the 1993 Cairo declaration. The OAU secretariat's Political Affairs Department—whose mission includes the monitoring of political and related developments and the provision of advice on strategies for interstate cooperation to promote peace and security—was tasked with providing operational substance for the realization of the mechanism's mandate. In this capacity, it began to interact with regional security mechanisms. This emerging partnership is expected to be structured and formally defined in the newly adopted protocol relating to the establishment of the Peace and Security Council of the AU.

The AU Commission's current thinking on relations with regional organizations, particularly with regional mechanisms responsible for peace, security, and conflict management, stresses the need to strengthen the linkages within the regions in a holistic and integrated approach, without losing sight of their uniqueness and specific needs. With the exception of ECOWAS, regional security mechanisms have, in the past, generally accorded little substantive role to the OAU. However, there is an awareness that the OAU itself, or more precisely its secretariat, had shied away from taking the lead and playing an active role in regional conflicts. Frequent OAU no-shows in conflict zones, compounded by the organization's incapacity to move swiftly into action, led regional organizations to fend for themselves or to look beyond the OAU for help.

For the OAU secretariat, the OAU Mechanism for Conflict Prevention, Management, and Resolution provided the best vehicle to the legal mandate for cooperation with regional organizations in the areas of peace and security, in much the same way that the Abuja treaty did on economic matters. The Cairo declaration directed the OAU to "coordinate its activities with the African regional and sub-regional organizations and . . . cooperate as appropriate with the neighboring countries with respect to conflicts which may arise in the different sub-regions of the continent."[20]

The OAU mechanism was built around the central organ, while the OAU secretary-general and the secretariat functioned as the latter's operational arm.[21] The OAU mechanism put a strong emphasis on anticipatory and preventive action, as well as on concerted action in peacemaking and peacebuilding. This was in the letter and spirit of Paragraph 15 of the Cairo declaration that, after setting forth the objectives of the OAU mechanism, concluded:

> In setting these objectives, we [heads of state and government] are fully convinced that prompt and decisive action in these spheres will, in the first instance, prevent the emergence of conflicts, and where they do inevitably occur, stop them from degenerating into intense or generalized conflicts.[22]

For the director of the OAU Political Affairs Department, Sam Ibok, regional and subregional organizations "are the first line of defense in the search for solutions to conflicts."[23] He believes that proximity to the conflicts generates incisive knowledge about their genesis, the identity of key players, and the region's "shared culture, geography and history." These, he posits, are critical factors if "we are to have a head start in trying to forge a consensus for the resolution of a given conflict."[24]

The OAU secretariat recognized that fulfilling such a mandate adequately required a more involved and hands-on central organ and secretary-general. This is a point that the African Union should heed, as the OAU secretariat had continuously been confronted with the challenges of:

- Solving its numerous material, financial, and staff constraints in order to enhance efficiency and strengthen its linkages through the establishment of an effective network of cooperation and coordination with regional organizations.
- Streamlining the central organ's operational methods.
- Establishing a partnership with regional security mechanisms, particularly because of the multiplication and multiplicity of regional arrangements on economic-cum-security cooperation and coordination.
- Defining and delineating areas of responsibility with regional organizations in conflict prevention, management, and resolution, in conformity with the provisions of the OAU mechanism, while ensuring that the OAU did not lose its relevance or support base.

The OAU was also aware that proximity can be fraught with its own dangers. There are instances, argues Ibok, where "proximity generates tension and undermines the spirit of impartiality between neighbors, sometimes to the extent that neighbors become part of the problems." This prospect led the OAU to adopt the principle that any regional approach to conflict management would be "most effective when the participation of the neighbors sharing borders is managed properly, and at best when these are excluded from certain conflict management initiatives affecting each other."[25] The OAU's involvement in the DRC conflict illustrated this principle.

Furthermore, the OAU secretariat believed that "neighborhood" and "impartiality" should be combined in order to render more productive any regional approach to conflict management. This position came out of the realization that "at times, keeping neighbors entirely out of each other's problems carries the risk of fomenting suspicion and resentment which often complicates conflict management initiatives."[26] The OAU secretariat saw itself as a catalyst in this regard, a role that consisted primarily in ensuring that regional initiatives in conflict management were anchored in the principles of neighborhood and impartiality. Accordingly, the OAU would intervene only when a conflict appeared to jeopardize one or both of these principles. Whenever such an intervention took place, the OAU's primary task would be to coordinate the conflict-management initiatives undertaken at the regional level.

The Way Forward

Several obstacles stand in the way of achieving these objectives and operationalizing these principles. These obstacles were clearly articulated at a seminar jointly organized by the OAU and the New York–based International Peace Academy (IPA) in Addis Ababa in November 1998.[27]

While stressing the central role of the OAU mechanism in the search for peace and security in Africa, participants at the OAU/IPA seminar identified three critical areas needing urgent attention: the establishment of a legal collaborative framework; the development of a system that effectively deals with issues of "jurisdiction," "entry point," and the division of labor between the OAU and regional organizations; and a need for the OAU to provide leadership and guidance to regional peace and security mechanisms.

The seminar recognized the central mandate of the OAU mechanism and its key structures—the central organ and the secretary-general—in the maintenance of peace and security in Africa. It proposed, however, that as the OAU mechanism was not yet suitable for operational work, regional organizations would have to assist the OAU secretariat in developing it further and rendering it operational. Participants also expressed concerns about the OAU's lack of effectiveness in some regions and its lethargy in others, which they attributed to "the existence of severe organizational problems in some sub-regions, personality conflicts in others, and an occasional animosity by sub-regional organizations toward the OAU Secretariat."[28]

A study commissioned by the OAU in 1999 on the modalities for cooperation between the OAU and regional organizations reached similar conclusions.[29] This internal document extensively reviewed the experience of African regions in defense and security cooperation. It also examined the legal, institutional, and policy obstacles to effective cooperation between the OAU and the regions in the areas of conflict prevention, management, and resolution, and proposed an adjustment to existing legal, policy, and operational instruments aimed at improving cooperation and strengthening linkages with regional security mechanisms.

The authors of the study identified several hindrances impeding cooperation between the OAU and regional security mechanisms in the prevention, management, and resolution of conflicts in Africa. At the OAU level, such hindrances included:

- A lack of clarity on the division of labor and responsibilities for conflict management between the OAU and the regions.
- The physical distance between OAU headquarters and conflict theaters, which often posed serious logistical problems.
- The fact that the OAU could only become involved in conflict situations through and with the consent of member states.
- Staffing and financial constraints within the secretariat.

These are problems that the AU will now have to address. With regard to the regional organizations, the study identified several factors, including:

- The lack of a clear legal framework for cooperation with the OAU.
- The lack of agreement over—and commitment to—the definition of an appropriate institutional arrangement for political and security matters.
- The lack of human, material, and financial capacity.
- The lack of institutional experience in conflict prevention.

This study and others have proposed various measures to correct these deficiencies and bring structure and impetus to the partnership between the OAU and regional security mechanisms. According to the authors of the OAU-commissioned study, such a partnership should rest on the basic principle of "the indivisibility of continental peace and security and the need to establish a common security area spanning the entire continent."[30] It is reasonable to argue that, in the view of African leaders, the OAU mechanism was created precisely to provide the legal basis and the strategic vision for such a principle. In this regard, regional security mechanisms are expected to serve as operational instruments, or at least to operate in accordance with the vision articulated in the 1993 Cairo declaration. The secretariats of the OAU and the regional organizations would then be left with the task of elaborating a protocol or memorandum of understanding on defense and security matters, similar to the existing protocol on relations between the African Economic Community (i.e., the former OAU secretariat) and the regional economic communities.[31]

It has also been proposed that regional security mechanisms should become integral parts of the AU Peace and Security Council. The AU should ensure that the heads of the regional organizations are formally invited to attend the meetings of its policy organs and that working visits are regularly organized between the AU Commission and the secretariats of regional organizations.[32]

The centrality of the OAU mechanism in the search for peace and security in Africa was recognized and accepted by all member states. Much, however, remains to be done to render the AU Peace and Security Council more effective than the OAU mechanism and fully operational and to build and strengthen its links with regional security mechanisms.

This becomes even more problematic in light of the uncertainty surrounding the transformation of the OAU into the AU. Given the fluid relationships that existed between the OAU secretariat and RECs, the modalities of cooperation between the Peace and Security Council and regional security arrangements remain to be determined. The Constitutive Act of the AU contains a provision for a common defense policy. However, it is not sufficiently clear what type of political and security framework is required at the continental level in order to ensure the effectiveness of such a defense policy. At the moment, there is no clarity on how the security provisions contained in the act will be matched at a regional level.

This chapter has focused its discussion on a more general ground than may be suggested by its title precisely because it seeks to underscore the subsidiary and complementary relations that the AU should foster with regional security communities. Our approach reflects current thinking at the former OAU secretariat and its preference for dealing globally, at the policy level, with all the regional organizations, while taking the specificity of each individual region into account. This view is likely to persist under the aegis of the African Union.

Notes

1. This shift was accomplished in two steps. First, African leaders adopted the landmark "Declaration on the Political and Socio-Economic Situation in Africa and the Fundamental Changes Taking Place in the World," during the twenty-sixth ordinary session of the OAU summit held in Addis Ababa, Ethiopia, from 9 to 11 July 1990. Then came the other landmark declaration, the "Declaration of the Assembly of the Heads of State and Government on the Establishment within the OAU of a Mechanism for Conflict Prevention, Management and Resolution," Cairo, Egypt, June 1993 (hereafter referred to as the Cairo declaration). The Cairo declaration is discussed below.

2. OAU, *The OAU Charter and Rules of Procedure*, Article II, Paragraph 1; African Union, *Constitutive Act of the African Union,* Article 3.

3. Barry Buzan, *People, States, and Fear: An Agenda for International Security Studies in the Post–Cold War Era,* 2d ed. (Boulder, Colo.: Lynne Rienner Publishers, 1991), 190.

4. It stipulates that "the 26th ordinary session of the Council of Ministers decided [on] the establishment of a 5th political region of the Organization of African Unity, to be called Southern Africa." See also OAU, "Report of the

Plenary," Twenty-Sixth Ordinary Session of the Council of Ministers, Addis Ababa, Ethiopia, 23 February–1 March 1976 (CM/Plen/Rept. I (XXVI) Rev.1).

5. OAU, Resolution CM/Res.464 (XXVI), Twenty-Sixth Ordinary Session of the Council of Ministers, Addis Ababa, 23 February–1 March 1976.

6. The OAU had fifty-three member states, including the Sahrawi Democratic Arab Republic. The Kingdom of Morocco withdrew from the organization in 1981, in protest against the admission of the Sahrawi Democratic Arab Republic. At the time that the Abuja treaty was concluded, the Republic of South Africa was not yet a member.

7. Chapter IV, Article 28, Paragraph 1 of the Treaty Establishing the African Economic Community (the Abuja treaty) deals with regional economic communities.

8. Ibid.

9. Ibid. The Abuja treaty has been ratified by forty-four OAU member states.

10. SADC, final communiqué of the SADC Summit of Heads of State or Government, Grand Baie, Mauritius, 13–14 September 1998, Paragraph 38, 13–14.

11. The Sirte declaration was adopted by the OAU heads of state and government during their fourth extraordinary session, in Sirte, Libya, which was held from 8 to 9 September 1999. The declaration is generally considered as renewing the ideal of an African Union that was so dear to the OAU's founding fathers and several generations of pan-Africanists. The African Union was "born" in Lomé, Togo, in July 2000, with the adaptation of the Constitutive Act of the AU by the thirty-sixth ordinary session of the assembly of heads of state and government. It was officially consecrated at the fifth extraordinary session of the heads of state and government, held in Sirte, Libya, on 1 March 2001. The act, which has been signed by all fifty-three member states, entered into force on 26 May 2001, after its ratification by two-thirds of the member states. In Lusaka in July 2001, the thirty-seventh ordinary session of the OAU assembly of heads of state and government officially inaugurated the one-year transition from the OAU to the AU. The latter was finally launched in Durban in July 2002.

12. Some of these issues were raised by the Council of Ministers during its seventy-second ordinary session held in Lomé, Togo, from 6 to 8 July 2000, after the request by the states members of Cen-Sad (the community of Sahelo-Saharian states) to be recognized by the OAU as a regional organization. President Alpha Oumar Konare of Mali raised similar concerns in his address to the closed session of the Lomé summit.

13. The lack of consensus resulted from a disagreement over the nature and relationship of the new organ to the existing regional integration structures. Southern African leaders were at first divided over whether there should be two SADC summits or whether the SADC organ should be distinct from the existing SADC institution. See also SADC, "Report on the Ministerial Meeting of the SADC Organ on Politics, Defence and Security," Maputo, Mozambique, 8 May 1998.

14. Ibid., Paragraph 2.1.

15. It is said that the ministers amended substantively the draft proposed by the experts and that the final agreement was substantively different as a result. Owing to the breakup a few weeks earlier of the main rebel group, Rassemblement Congolais pour la Democratie (RCD), into two rival factions, the Congolese rebel leaders signed only after intense persuasion by regional leaders. The head of the Congolese Liberation Movement was the first to sign on 1 August 1999; all of the approximately fifty founders of both RCD factions were eventually allowed to sign on 31 August 1999.

16. The Lusaka cease-fire agreement is frequently referred to as the outcome

of regional efforts to bring peace to the DRC. In reality, the idea of a regional initiative for peace in the DRC was proposed by the OAU secretary-general in a bid to bring together a variety of individual, sometimes competing, peace initiatives. There were, at the time, at least three major initiatives. Former South African president Nelson Mandela, then SADC chairman, convened talks among the Congolese belligerents in Durban and Pretoria, South Africa. There were also talks in Victoria Falls, Zambia, and a peace process initiated in Libreville, Gabon, by central African heads of state. Representatives of the governments of Gabon, Kenya, Rwanda, and Uganda also attended the meeting of SADC defense and foreign affairs ministers, which took place in Lusaka on 26 October 1999.

17. See Article III, Paragraphs (a) and (b) of the Lusaka Cease-Fire Agreement for the Democratic Republic of the Congo.

18. The Lusaka-based regional JMC was set up on 16 November 1999, pursuant to Chapter 7 of the agreement's modalities, to facilitate the disengagement of forces and to prepare the modalities for locating, disarming, and regrouping armed groups in the DRC. Subsequently, and in application of the decision of the OAU central organ, the OAU deployed officers from Algeria (5), Malawi (10), Nigeria (10), and Senegal (5). The deployment took place from 16 to 23 November 1999, under very difficult conditions, and OAU observers were provided with very minimal equipment. Assistance expected from the UN came very late and was insufficient to meet the needs of the OAU team in the field.

19. The four localities are Boende (Equateur Province), Kabalo (Katanga Province), Kabinda (Eastern Kasai Province), and Lisala (Equateur Province). Deployment of OAU observers in Kabalo has been delayed owing to a lack of adequate infrastructure. Called "local JMCs," these new structures comprise representatives of the parties and a number of neutral OAU military observers whose tasks include observing troop disengagement and investigating allegations of cease-fire violations. OAU observers and investigators were deployed—and continue to operate—amid serious financial and material constraints. Of the nearly U.S.$5 million pledged to the OAU Peace Fund, only $2 million has so far been disbursed. The balance at the end of the third quarter of 2000 was estimated to be under $100,000. See OAU, "Report of the Secretary-General on the Situation in the Democratic Republic of the Congo," June 2000.

20. OAU, Cairo declaration, Paragraph 24.

21. Ibid., Paragraphs 15 and 17. On the composition and rules of procedures of the central organ, see Paragraphs 18–20.

22. Ibid., Paragraph 15.

23. S. B. Ibok, "The Effectiveness of African Regional and Sub-Regional Mechanisms to Prevent Ethnic and Racial Conflicts," paper presented at the regional seminar of experts on the prevention of ethnic and racial conflicts, Addis Ababa, 4–6 October 2000, 7–9.

24. Ibid., 8.

25. Ibid., 8, 9.

26. Ibid., 8.

27. OAU and IPA, "Report of the Second OAU/IPA Seminar on Peacekeeping and Peacemaking in Africa," Addis Ababa, 28 November–3 December 1998.

28. Ibid., 9.

29. OAU, "Interfacing the OAU Mechanism for Conflict Prevention, Management and Resolution with Africa's Sub-Regions and Arrangements: Elements of a Partnership Program," Addis Ababa, July 1999. The study was funded by the United Nations Development Programme Capacity-Building Project at the OAU, and conducted by a team of international consultants.

30. Ibid., 24.

31. Among the RECs, the OAU (on behalf of member states), COMESA, SADC, the Intergovernmental Authority on Development, and ECOWAS signed the protocol on 25 February 1998. ECCAS signed it on 11 October 1999. The UMA has not signed it. This protocol entered into force on 25 February 1998. Another protocol relating to the establishment of the Peace and Security Council of the African Union was adopted by the first ordinary session of the Assembly of the AU in Durban on 9 July 2002 and signed by twenty-seven member states. It will enter into force on the deposit of the instruments of ratification by a simple majority of the member states of the AU. The Peace and Security Council of the AU shall replace the OAU Mechanism for Conflict Prevention, Management and Resolution.

32. OAU/IPA, "Report," 8. The OAU has already begun to implement the first measure, at least at the level of the council and the summit.

11

The Intergovernmental Authority on Development and the East African Community

Monica Kathina Juma

A changed international political climate following the end of the Cold War era, the correspondingly diminished significance of Africa in East-West relations, and the pangs of democratization and internal change have combined to generate dynamics that present new challenges for security in most of Africa today.[1] Nonetheless, one can identify several positive trends, the most significant manifested in renewed attempts by Africa to seek security for itself. The 1990s will be remembered as the decade when the continent sought to devise home-grown initiatives as the way out of the quagmire in which it finds itself. Interest has burgeoned in revamping, creating, or strengthening mechanisms aimed at achieving subregional and continental security.

This chapter tracks the developing desire to secure both states and people within the Greater Horn of Africa (GHA), which comprises two overlapping subregions. The first subregion, the Horn of Africa, consists of Djibouti, Sudan, Ethiopia, and Somalia. The second is East Africa, traditionally comprising Kenya, Uganda, and Tanzania, but increasingly and alternatively called the Great Lakes region associated with Rwanda, Burundi, and the eastern parts of the Democratic Republic of Congo (DRC).

Plagued by conflicts of varying intensity and magnitude that were exacerbated by superpower interests and rivalry during the Cold War era, this region has, for the past five decades, been rendered insecure for both its states and peoples. Prior to the 1990s, states in this region tended to act in isolation and sought security at each other's expense. Unable to secure consensus in areas of "high" politics such as security, cooperation was confined to "soft" arenas, including agriculture, drought, and disease control. In the last decade, the region has witnessed a dramatic shift, as states have striven to establish common security arrangements. This development is rooted in an unprecedented level of political consensus and commitment to cooperate in seeking collective security and, more significant, a people-centered security.

The chapter traces and examines this shift from cooperation in areas of soft security to matters of high politics, such as conflict resolution, security, and defense, on which states have traditionally remained hesitant to cooperate. This shift has great potential to facilitate the attainment of regional security. The chapter then highlights the challenges of conceiving a regional security framework and draws lessons for the GHA region and other regional organizations, in particular the Southern African Development Community (SADC).

Material is organized in six sections. After an introduction that establishes the scope of the discussion, the second section gives an overview of the security situation in the GHA region. Section three looks at conflict resolution mechanisms and peace initiatives in the Horn of Africa using illustrations from two peace processes, the Sudan peace process and the Somali Djibouti-led peace process. The opportunities and challenges specific to each are highlighted. The church-sponsored People to People Peace (PPP) initiative in southern Sudan is used to examine the role of nonstate actors in complementing state action in conflict management, resolution, and prevention. Section four addresses attempts by members of the Intergovernmental Authority on Development (IGAD) to develop a subregional conflict early warning and response (CEWARN) mechanism and details attempts to promote a culture of peace in the region. In this regard, the initiative toward addressing the proliferation of small arms and light weapons is analyzed. Section five looks at attempts to revitalize the East African Community (EAC) as a strategy for enhanced economic integration and conflict prevention. Section six presents and discusses lessons derived from these two subregions.

Security in the Greater Horn of Africa

Academic debates on security indicate a concept characterized by inherent contradictions. Analysis of these contradictions, while potentially stimulating, will not detain us here.[2] Historically, nation-states have tended to form groupings to counter common threats. The agenda and thrust of such cooperation is determined by the nature of the perceived threat. This logic fashions security, which always involves high levels of interdependence among actors attempting to secure themselves.

Our starting point is that common security constitutes the pursuit of freedom from threat.[3] This definition underscores Barry Buzan's observation that security, whether individual, national, or international, ranks prominently among the problems facing humanity today.[4] From this perspective, one may safely argue that the GHA region is an insecurity-prone region. In recent times, most of Somalia; all of northern Kenya; north and western Uganda; western Tanzania (particularly refugee camps in Ngara); most of southern Sudan; much of Burundi; and, until lately, the border between Eritrea and Ethiopia have been zones characterized by intense conflict and insecurity. Capturing the pervasiveness of insecurity in the region, Ambassador Bethwell Kiplagat observes, "in the last 50 years, there has not been a single day of peace throughout the entire IGAD subregion."[5]

Insecurity within the GHA region exists in a variety of forms, the most prevalent being military confrontation, in one of two forms. The first is intrastate conflict (essentially internal or domestic in character), examples of which include the civil war in Sudan, the Somalia civil war since 1990, the so-called banditry situation in northern Kenya, and tensions within Burundi and the DRC. The second involves interstate conflict (pitting one or more states against each other), examples of which include the recently ended Ethiopia-Eritrea war, the ongoing tensions between Sudan and Eritrea, the historical Kenya-Somalia tensions, the uneasy relations between Uganda and Sudan, and the military occupation of the DRC by Rwanda and Uganda.

A second manifestation of insecurity is the weakening state. Although states remain significant protagonists in this theater of insecurity, their survival has increasingly come under threat. As a result of failure in the state-building project, this region exhibits a range of state types, from strong states to weak disintegrating states. At one end of the scale is Kenya, viewed as a strong, security-conscious state; at the other end is Somalia, which presents a case of substantial state collapse. In between these two extremes are Sudan, Burundi, and to some extent Ethiopia, states experiencing varying degrees of internal conflict that have polarized them and threatened to tear them apart. Then there is Uganda, defined for most of its independence history as pathological, but currently restructuring, as is Eritrea, which is making a good attempt to stand as an independent state. Finally, the best-case scenario is epitomized by Tanzania, lauded as a relatively stable state. However, the October 2000 election exposed some unnerving cracks in a nation historically envied in this region for its peace.

None of these states can boast of having all the requisite attributes of a state. In particular, none can claim the monopoly of the means of coercion. With the possible exception of Tanzania, the above states are in direct competition with nonstate actors, in terms of owning and using arms. In most cases, nonstate actors are often better equipped and possess substantial skills and means to wage war. Even Kenya, defined as a strong state, is not immune to this problem. Unconfirmed estimates indicate its North Eastern Province to have the largest per capita illicit ownership of arms in the country.[6] This story is replicable in northern Uganda, southern

Sudan, and Ethiopia, where states are in constant engagement with insurgence groups.

Governments in this region have reacted to the increase in arms among nonstate actors by acquiring more arms, ostensibly to curb security threats. This has engendered an arms race that has accelerated the proliferation of illegal small and intermediate arms. However, arms have neither improved security nor generated peace; they have instead contributed to increased tensions and insecurity. Of concern to security analysts is the tilting balance in the acquisition and control of arms in favor of nonstate actors. This is paralleled by a steady decline in the ability of states to subdue these actors or demand accountability for arms in their possession. States have no capacities to move and track arms within their territories. Apart from accentuating state insecurity, this development has critical implications for power alignment and realignment in the region.

As Somalia continues to be a conduit for arms, the Kenya-Ethiopia defense axis is threatened by, among other factors, the presence and activities of the Oromo Liberation Front within some parts of Kenya. In addition, the ability of states to continue accumulating arms is being curtailed by factors such as international pressure to reduce military expenditure.[7] Meanwhile, insurgents are able to extract resources from the international economy in the form of three critical elements: armaments, food,[8] and external remittances.[9] An increased sense of insecurity may partly explain states' growing enthusiasm for seeking peaceful resolution of disputes at both the internal and interstate levels.

In addition to the negative effects resulting from direct military confrontation between state and nonstate actors, insurgency has destabilizing effects on a society that can be extremely difficult to eradicate, as illustrated by the legacy of the liberation wars in Angola and Mozambique. Besides the proliferation of weapons, prolonged insurgency inevitably multiplies the numbers of people skilled in their use. This, in turn, translates into increased insecurity in urban areas and escalation of violence in rural areas. Such violence has taken the form of banditry and cattle rustling in the Rift Valley Province of Kenya and the Karamojong region in Uganda. In short, it leads to a breakdown in the rule of law and extensive disruption of normal lives.

Dependent largely on agriculture, the economies of this region have suffered a double blow, from insurgent activity as much as from shifting government policies. As experience in northern Uganda indicates, insurgent activities render production difficult, if not impossible. Further, the agricultural sector has borne the brunt of shifting government support, as states increase military expenditure in an attempt to secure themselves. Comprising some of the world's poorest countries, the GHA region has seen a steady decline in economic performance. This has accelerated state incapacity. As Christopher Clapham has remarked, given the poor basic economy in this region, states face critical difficulties in trying to extract resources for their maintenance.[10] The result is a steady fragmentation in the institutional basis of state power, an outcome that threatens the state's ability to function.

Another disturbing manifestation of insecurity in this region takes the form of forced displacement within and across borders. More than a quarter of Africa's 6 million registered refugees are generated and hosted within this region.[11] With the exception of Tanzania, the other states in this region including Somalia, Uganda, Kenya, Rwanda, Burundi, and Ethiopia have, in addition to generating refugees, been theaters of internal displacement. Sudan alone has generated some 4 million internally displaced persons. In all cases, this displacement is rooted in prolonged abuse by governments of citizens' human rights.

Summing up the situation in this region, the U.S. ambassador in Kenya, Johnnie Carson, captured the impact of insecurity as follows:

> The collapse of the Somali state, more than 15 years of civil war in the Sudan, the on-going conflict between the Lords Resistance Army and Ugandan authorities, the unfortunate (but hopefully now concluded) war between Ethiopia and Eritrea, have combined to cause enormous destruction and have set back economic development in the IGAD area. These conflicts have also increased the flow of arms in the region, created an enormous refugee crisis, increased tension and instability along borders and created a political climate that says open conflict is acceptable to resolve problems.[12]

This state of affairs has put immense pressure on actors, particularly states, to seek collective security.

Conflict Resolution and Peace Initiatives in the Horn

If the GHA region has been characterized by conflict and insecurity in the 1990s, it has also seen concerted efforts toward resolving conflict and promoting peace and regional security. Actors, both state and nonstate, are engaged in initiatives seeking to establish common security at various levels. At the interstate level, collective security is pursued within the frameworks of IGAD and the East African Community.

The IGAD Conflict Resolution and Peace Initiative

Conceived in 1986, the Intergovernmental Authority on Drought and Desertification (IGADD) had a narrow mandate that provided for cooperation in areas of "soft" security, in which consensus was easily built. Cooperation was principally conceived in areas of drought and desertification. Within this framework, security was viewed as the prerogative of individual states and therefore as falling outside the arena of collective action.[13] Consequently, there was no mechanism for common security. The emergence in the 1990s of a consensus among member states in favor of establishing a regional mechanism for collective security was a major paradigm shift.

Defining insecurity as the main obstacle to economic development in the Horn of Africa region, member states expressed a commitment to confront insecurity together as a bloc. This desire generated political will that transformed IGADD. On 21 March 1996, member states signed an agreement establishing IGAD. This agreement expanded the mandate of IGAD to include peace and security, economic cooperation, infrastructural development, and political and humanitarian affairs. Its principles and aims were stated as the maintenance of regional peace, security, and stability in the Horn of Africa region. Article 7 of the agreement provided for the creation of subregional mechanisms for the prevention, management, and resolution of inter- and intrastate conflicts through dialogue. Conflict prevention and promotion of peace were prioritized areas of activity, viewed as prerequisites for economic cooperation and social progress. Demonstrating hitherto unknown political commitment, states pledged themselves to resolve outstanding security problems and conflicts and to preserve peace, security, and stability in the region. On top of IGAD's transformative agenda was the call for the creation of a mechanism for security, not envisaged in the previous structure.

The revitalization of IGAD was a momentous development for the Horn of Africa. It provided an opportunity to deal with insecurity collectively. A security mechanism was conceived within the Office of Political and Humanitarian Affairs[14] and structured into two divisions: Conflict Prevention, Management, and Resolution (CPMR) and Humanitarian Affairs. In shaping common security, the CPMR has identified five output areas. It seeks to build the relevant capacity on conflict prevention, management, and resolution; to document peacemaking initiatives in the region; to promote a culture of peace and tolerance; to develop an early warning mechanism; and, finally, to establish a peace fund to complement the activities of other actors engaged in humanitarian and peacebuilding work.

Numerous factors have slowed the pace in attaining some of these outputs, but IGAD has registered remarkable advances in three areas: conflict management and resolution; establishment of early warning mechanisms; and the creation of a culture of peace and tolerance within IGAD. To illustrate this claim, we examine the Sudan peace process, the Somalia

Djibouti-led peace process, and attempts to address the problem of proliferation of small arms and light weapons in the region.

The Sudan Peace Process

The Sudan peace process seeks to address the conflict between the government of Sudan and the Sudan People's Liberation Army/Movement (SPLA/M).[15] Expressing the position that insecurity in the Sudan in many ways causes regional instability, IGAD member states have, since the mid-1990s, felt uniquely placed to resolve Africa's longest civil war. Prior to the 1996 treaty, several failed attempts were made to address this conflict. In November 1993, IGAD held its first summit of the IGAD Heads of States Peace Committee in Kampala, Uganda, and set up a standing committee on the Sudan conflict. Comprising the foreign ministers of Kenya, Uganda, Ethiopia, and Eritrea, this committee was mandated to draw up an agenda and program of work for a negotiated settlement to the Sudan conflict.[16]

The first session of the standing committee, held in March 1994, deliberated the principles that would underpin the framework for the search for peace, interim arrangements, and the establishment of a humanitarian committee. In May 1994, a second session adopted a draft Declaration of Principles as a basis for resolving the conflict. Four key elements were identified: commitment by all parties to using peaceful means in resolving conflicts; respect for the right to self-determination; separation of religion from state; and recognition of the heterogeneous nature of the Sudan and the promotion of Sudan as a democratic, secular state. A third session met in July 1995 to discuss the draft Declaration of Principles. However, disagreement emerged on two critical issues: the question of separation of state and religion, and self-determination of the south, about which the government of Sudan expressed reservations. When the fourth session of the standing committee was held in September 1994 to try and resolve these differences, the positions of both parties continued to polarize and harden. This led to an adjournment of the negotiations to allow for further consultations. Absence of authority to ensure compliance and the apparent inability of the regional states to enforce basic conditions for negotiations were to become the main obstacles to the progress of the Sudan process.

Committed to move the peace process forward, a summit of the IGAD Heads of States Peace Committee met shortly after this adjournment to review the process and decide on a future course of action. Out of this summit came two decisions that were to form the basis for later action. Consensus was reached that the IGAD initiative should continue and that the Declaration of Principles should be adopted to form the basis for negotiations. Arguing that it was "duty bound to 'Islamize' and 'Arabize' the whole of Sudan,"[17] the government of Sudan rejected these decisions and withdrew from the negotiations, stalling the talks for more than thirty-three months. Following the 1996 treaty, pressure was exerted on Sudan to comply with the spirit of IGAD. Eventually, an extraordinary summit of IGAD member states on the Sudan problem was held in July 1997. At this meeting, the government of Sudan accepted the Declaration of Principles as the basis for discussion and withdrew its reservations on the issues of state and religion, and the self-determination of the south. While this move provided the much-needed impetus to advance the peace process, the need for a structured approach to guiding it became apparent.

To provide continuity, an IGAD ministerial subcommittee on the Sudan peace process was constituted. At its first session, held in September 1997, it mandated the IGAD secretariat to seek external financial assistance to aid negotiations; requested IGAD members to provide financial assistance; and recommended the establishment of a peace fund to sponsor the peace talks. Meanwhile the government of Sudan and SPLA/M agreed to cooperate fully in the search for a negotiated solution. Despite increasing eagerness to get the process going, it stalled after a meeting scheduled for October 1997 failed to take place. After intense lobbying, the second ministerial subcommittee was convened in May 1998. During this meeting, the issue of self-determination for the south was agreed on for the future, with a qualification: it would be supervised in the interim period by international observers. Shortly after this, the third session was held in Addis Ababa in August 1998, during which an agreement was reached that the borders of the south would be determined as they stood on 1 January 1956. The parties also agreed to observe a three-month cease-fire to facilitate the delivery of humanitarian relief. However, the issue of Islam remained contentious, as religion is deeply entrenched in the constitution of May 1998 and the October 1999 laws.

After connections were drawn between the attacks on U.S. embassies in Kenya and Tanzania and Sudan's support for Osama Bin Laden, the relationship soured between Sudan and the region; Sudan's relations with Kenya, a prime mover of the process, were particularly affected. Talks stalled for a year until July 1999, when the fourth session was convened. This lull reinforced the realization that moving the process forward required a permanent structure, beyond the ad hoc arrangements that had characterized previous attempts, to engage on a continuous basis with all parties concerned. It was also agreed that a ministerial organ lacked the time, leverage, and capacity to sustain the momentum required for the peace process. To overcome these shortcomings, IGAD member states established a permanent IGAD secretariat on the Sudan peace process in July 1999. Chaired by Kenya and based in Nairobi, the secretariat was placed under Ambassador Daniel Mboya, an IGAD special envoy. It was mandated to create and coordinate technical committees to help move the peace process forward on a regular basis, within the framework of the Declaration of Principles.

The secretariat identified four primary areas for negotiations: the right to self-determination for the people of southern Sudan; self-administration for southern Sudan; delinking the various peoples of the Sudan (i.e., the Arab north and the African south) and secularizing the constitution; and equitable sharing of resources among all Sudanese people. Four committees were constituted and are operating to address the issues of self-administration; self-determination; religion and state; and the sharing of subterranean wealth. In addition to the secretariat, the SPLA/M leadership has proposed the formation of an African IGAD Partners Forum, to operate alongside the donor-constituted IGAD Partners Forum. Such a structure, it is argued, would provide an opportunity to draw lessons beyond the immediate subregion. Proposed members of such a forum are Nigeria, Egypt, and South Africa, all seen as having the requisite experience to inform the Sudan peace process. Further, these states are viewed as having the muscle to compel the government of Sudan to engage in a "critical dialogue" about the war.

While there has been significant development in structures and processes toward the settlement of this conflict, several issues remain unresolved. Principal among them is the question of self-determination for the south, about which the Sudanese government remains ambiguous. There are also disagreements related to the definitions of fundamental issues. In particular, parties have adopted different interpretations of the southern border. The government of Sudan argues that the Abiei region falls in the north, while SPLA views it as a Dinka homeland, and therefore as being in the south. The marginalized regions of the Nuba Mountains and the southern Blue Nile region have also not been dealt with. These border disputes must be understood within the context that most of Sudan's subterranean wealth lies on this belt. Further, the government holds *sharia* law as supreme throughout Sudan, a matter that generates great unease within certain quarters. There are also criticisms that negotiations taking place concentrate on two parties, excluding a number of key stakeholders. A combination of these factors raises the risk of this process suffering a crisis of legitimacy.

Despite these difficulties, political developments in Sudan have provided opportunities for the peace process. Power struggles between Umar Al-Bashir of Sudan, and his former ally, Hassan Al-Turabi, with the formation of the National Democratic Alliance by a number of political opposition parties in the north, has somewhat changed the course of the conflict. Once defined in terms of north versus south, this conflict has evolved into a series of conflicts with varying epicenters. There is conflict between the government and SPLA/M, SPLA/M and some splinter groups, and between the government and opposition elements in the north. The sacking of Al Turabi and his placement under house arrest in early 2001 created splinters within the government. Diverse views on, and proposed solutions to, the conflict have slowed and at times bogged down negotiations within IGAD.

Four members of IGAD—Kenya, Uganda, Ethiopia, and Eritrea—agree that the regime in Sudan poses a security risk to the region and should thus be brought under control. SPLA/M, under John Garang, has therefore become a unifying factor among leaders in this region. They allow SPLA/M to operate from their territories and support its leadership. While this support has put pressure on the government of Sudan to seek peace, states that offer it risk appearing partial.[18] Concerned about IGAD's partiality, and afraid that it could be isolated internally and internationally, particularly after the UN imposed sanctions and the United States blacklisted it as a terrorist nation, the government of Sudan sought to direct the peace process from Khartoum. So far, it has normalized relations with its neighbors, including Eritrea, Ethiopia, and Uganda. Increasingly, it is involving Arab States such as Egypt, Libya, and Qatar in the search for peace. This has produced the Egyptian-Libyan initiative, whose main principle is the unity of the Sudan. Egypt and Libya have sought involvement in the Sudan conflict, citing historical, cultural, and, more important, security concerns, in particular protection of the Nile waters.[19]

Beyond its neighbors, Sudan is presenting a softer and more acceptable face through diplomatic efforts. This campaign culminated in the lifting of the UN sanctions against it in October 2001. At the domestic level, it has pledged constitutional changes and has held sporadic talks with SPLA/M.[20] Internationally, pressure has been mounting on the Sudan. In the U.S. Congress, there is a growing coalition between those who define this conflict in religious terms; the black caucus (which it views in terms of race and slavery) and human rights proponents (who view it as a manifestation of the failure of governance and the rule of law) are also increasing pressure on the U.S. government to take the lead. In response, the United States, in August 2001, appointed a special envoy on Sudan to begin dialogue with the government on these and other issues. Although such developments have the potential to increase the momentum toward peace, they risk marginalizing and probably scuttling regional peace initiatives, particularly if they continue to be pursued outside its framework. The latest in the negotiations between the government of Sudan and SPLA/M culminated in the Machakos declaration, signed on 20 July 2002, between the two. Other than bringing together El Bathir, the president of Sudan, and John Garang, the leader of SPLA/M, for the first time, the declaration out of this meeting agreed on a framework for peace.

The Djibouti-Led Peace Process on Somalia

This is perhaps the most unusual peace process in Africa to date. A people-led experiment, with limited international support, resuscitated Somalia, a state that since its collapse in 1991, had been reduced to a "ghostly presence on the world map." For nearly a decade, Somalia sustained life without a government, the longest duration of state collapse in the modern era.[21] Between 1991 and 1998, a dozen failed attempts were made to restore peace and a functional state in Somalia. The first of these, led by the Djibouti government in 1991, aimed at halting the chaos before total collapse ensued. It led to the election of Ali Mahdi Mohamed as interim president, alongside the formation of a government; the government, however, was unable to function. Eleven other conferences were organized, the last of which was a national reconciliation meeting concluded in Cairo in December 1997. These failures led to a marked sense of despair among the Somali population and reluctance among the international community to engage with the peace process. After the harrowing experience of U.S. marines under the banner of the UN peacekeeping force in Somalia, international opinion coalesced into an unspoken belief that Somalia was irredeemable. The implications of this situation for peace were clear. If peace were to be brokered, action must concretize within the region.

In October 1998, in cooperation with the IGAD Forum Partners Liaison Group, IGAD member states created a standing committee on the Somali peace process, chaired by Ethiopia. Mandated to steer peace and reconciliation in Somalia, this committee, like the one on the Sudan, provided an ideal forum for negotiations. In spite of this demonstration of regional commitment, most actors within the international community remained unenthusiastic and expressed disinterest about Somalia. This lethargy had the effect of strengthening the regional resolve to seek a solution.

It was in this context of international despondency about Somalia that President Ismail Omar Guelleh of Djibouti, the then-chairman of IGAD, delivered a substantive and far-reaching statement on Somalia to the Fifty-Fourth General Assembly of the UN in New York in September 1999. In his statement, President Guelleh outlined a phased approach to peace in Somalia whose key element was the shift in focus from warlords to the Somali civil society. Immediately, the UN expressed support for the initiative, encouraging other international actors to rethink their stance on Somalia. Shortly thereafter, the IGAD standing committee met to review the situation in Somalia, in light of Guelleh's proposals. In October 1999, Djiboutians organized a march to express support for the Somali process and encouraged their government to take the lead role. Under Guelleh's tutelage and funded by the Djibouti coffers, without any significant external support, the Djibouti-led peace process was initiated and generated a historical momentum that culminated in the restoration of a government for Somalia. As argued elsewhere, a compilation of experiences related to this process could prove an invaluable document and guide toward securing lasting peace in Somalia.[22]

The Djibouti-led process adopted a two-track approach. First, it encouraged intense consultations with state actors, including IGAD member states, the Arab League, the Organization of African Unity (OAU), and the UN. In this regard, the IGAD summit held in Djibouti in November 1999 was critical. It reinforced the adopted approach and declared its commitment to push forward with "a bottom-up approach in which the role of warlords is contained and that of civil society enhanced." Further, the heads of states agreed that "peace in Somalia and the welfare of its people cannot be allowed to continue to be held hostage to the narrow and personal interests of those who have failed to save Somalia from calamity." Finally, it called for "an end to the political tourism carried out by Somali warlords" and underlined "the need for countries not to cooperate with those in Somalia that hinder the peace process."[23]

The second, and perhaps most crucial, track involved extensive consultations with Somalis. Drawing on cultural and social similarities, the government of Djibouti brought together Somalis from all walks of life, including clan leaders and warlords, in a series of conferences. Deliberations in these meetings sought modalities for restoring a government in Somalia. They also gave the peace process a broad-based character, in effect legitimizing it.

With support from neighboring countries, the UN, Somalis in Somalia and the diaspora—and steered personally by a highly committed President Guelleh—the peace process generated its own dynamics. From March to May 2000, a series of meetings organized in Djibouti initiated a process of consensus-building among and between Somali populations. A group of sixty Somali intellectuals, professionals, and seasoned former politicians was the first to meet in this series. The president then met with Somali elders to seek advice on issues crucial to Somalia and how best to tackle them. In addition, representatives from the business community, which is a very powerful social category, were invited. In attendance at the last consultative meeting, held in May 2000, were more than 200 Somali traditional leaders and 100 women delegates. In addition to these meetings, Djibouti sent missions to various parts of Somalia to increase its knowledge of the crisis and obtain a wide cross-section of views on the political situation.

Having established a great desire to restore peace and order, President Guelleh took the next step. On 4 June, he opened the main conference, dubbed the Somali National Peace Conference, in Arta, Djibouti. In attendance were some 1,200 delegates from all walks of life in Somalia, and some 1,500 observers. Lasting until 13 August 2000, the conference identified four main areas of concern: arms control, the disarmament of the militia, looted property, and the status of Mogadishu. Special committees were set up to look into each of these issues comprehensively. Monitoring this process closely, President Guelleh kept it on course and diffused tensions as they arose.[24] Finally, on 13 August 2000, the conference formed a Transitional National Assembly composed of 245 members.[25] A week later, Abdallah Deerow Isaak was elected speaker of the National Assembly and Abdul Kassim Salat Hassan was elected president of Somalia. After his inauguration in Djibouti, Salat appointed a prime minister with whom he later moved to Somalia. Shortly thereafter, a new Legislative Assembly and cabinet were established and are functional despite the great challenges associated with security and legitimacy.

Several factors make this peace process a classic case for study and adaptation. First, the demonstration of commitment by all neighboring states, and Djibouti in particular, to support and aid this peace process was crucial. Complementing the support of state actors was that of a wide spectrum of the Somali population, both at home and abroad. The outcome was a process that underscored the potential of civil society and the significance of involving the real stakeholders in a peace process. Fragile as this peace is, and despite follow-up having stalled, it is clear that local, national, and regional actors have played a critical role in providing a basis to sustain it.

A major challenge for Somalia's fragile peace is one of legitimacy. Peace has yet to crystallize. A number of Somali warlords have expressed opposition to Salat's government and dismissed the peace initiative as an imposition from Djibouti. The extent to which Salat's government will be able to withstand such opposition is still unclear. Furthermore, the deep polarization along clan lines that characterizes Somali society threatens the chances of sustainable peace. If no means of countering interclan loyalties is found, the potential for establishing order, security, and the rule of law will remain elusive—a problem illustrated by the assassination of a close aide of the president within weeks of his arrival in Mogadishu. The situation calls for sustained campaigns to help entrench a culture of peace and tolerance and long-term political commitment to support this process.

While IGAD continues to support the reconciliation process, there is a need to interpret peacebuilding in a wider perspective that embraces the provision of material support, as a means to jump-start the economy and disengage state operations from acts of war. Such an approach was echoed by the UN Secretary-General's report on Somalia in 1999, in which he argues that "re-establishing of a functioning state in Somalia, will require . . . not only an enormous effort of political will on the part of the Somali people and their leaders, a massive rebuilding operation will also be a necessary accompaniment of any peace process in Somalia."[26]

This proposition is as valid now as it was then. If peace and security are to be sustained, IGAD and other "friends" of Somalia need to extend their engagement beyond peace activities and support the rehabilitation and reconstruction of Somalia.

People to People Peace Initiative

Among nonstate actor initiatives for peacebuilding is the People to People Peace program. Conceived within the New Sudan Council of Churches (NSCC) in 1997, it grew out of consultations between the SPLM and NSCC in Yei County, which recognized and endorsed the role and contribution of the church in the peace process. The initiative had two main objectives: to create a chaplaincy for the SPLA and to provide continuous dialogue between the SPLA/M and the people. Focusing on resolving conflicts at the local level, the PPP initiative trains people in leadership skills, conflict resolution and peace, and reconciliation methods. It uses traditional methods of conflict resolution based on dialogue, mutual forgiveness, and compensation in its efforts to promote a culture of peace and tolerance.

After consultations with, and advice from, chiefs and elders, the NSCC started with the Nuer and Dinka communities on the West Bank. In March 1999, it organized the Wunlit meeting, which led to the Dinka/Nuer Wunlit accord. Since the signing of the accord, hostilities have ceased and trade between the Nuer and the Dinka has resumed. In August 1999, another agreement was signed in Chukudum between the Dinka and the Didinga. These activities have transformed once hostile relationships into relations of mutual understanding and respect.

Encouraged by the success achieved in the West Bank, the PPP initiatives turned to intercommunal conflicts in the East Bank, in the Bor areas of the Upper Nile. Consultations with leaders of various communities saw a breakthrough that led to the Liliir peace conference, 9–15 May 2000. This meeting endorsed the Wunlit accord and discussed issues related to access to animal grazing areas, water points, and the return of abducted women and children. An amnesty for previous offenses against people and property was declared, a public covenant between all ethnic groups made, and a comprehensive document, pledging peace and reconciliation, signed.[27]

This initiative provides the potential to nurture peace from the grassroots level. The extensive church network provides an invaluable structure upon which long-term peace can be anchored. Further, this initiative accords the IGAD process an opportunity to tap local knowledge and expertise. In an attempt to participate in the state-led peace process and expand its activities, the NSCC is seeking observer status within IGAD. This challenges IGAD to facilitate the participation of nonstate actors in the peace process.

Establishment of Early Warning Mechanisms

The second output where IGAD has had some measure of success relates to the establishment of an early warning mechanism. In recognition of the difficulties and challenges associated with conflict management and resolution, IGAD member states have identified the need to engage in preventive action as a means of diffusing tensions before they escalate into open conflicts. Following a decision by the summit held in April 1998, member states agreed to the creation of an early warning and response mechanism for the IGAD region. Shortly thereafter, they mandated the IGAD secretariat to explore ways of establishing such a mechanism.

The IGAD Conflict Early Warning and Response Mechanism

Seizing the opportunity accorded by the agreement of the heads of states in April 1998, IGAD engaged the participation of a range of nonstate actors in the process of establishing its CEWARN mechanism.

In March 2000 the secretariat contracted the Forum for Early Warning and Early Response (FEWER)[28] as its partner in the establishment of an early warning mechanism for the IGAD subregion. At the first workshop, held in April 2000, FEWER was commissioned to undertake a feasibility study on the design of a conflict early warning and response mechanism for the region. In their write-up, the FEWER team raised conceptual matters related to such a system, which were discussed at the first CEWARN workshop in July 2000. Drawing participants from a wide range of state and nonstate actors in the region, the workshop provided critical feedback on the FEWER report.[29] This meeting resulted in twenty-eight recommendations and a decision to commission national consultants in all IGAD member states to reflect on these recommendations within their national contexts. Contracting local expertise added value in terms of harnessing local knowledge and experiences at an early stage of the process.

Seven national consultants were contracted and mandated to identify in-state systems in early warning and conflict management, to assess their strengths and weaknesses, and to assess the possibility of linking such systems with similar mechanisms at subregional, regional, and international levels. Their reflections were discussed at the second CEWARN workshop in September 2000. Among the significant outputs of this meeting was the identification of, and deliberation on, four entry areas for early warning: pastoral communities and cattle rustling, small arms and environmental security, peace processes, and civil society. It was agreed that the ministry of foreign affairs was best placed to become the focal point for every country's CEWARN and the link between intrastate CEWARN systems and regional and international mechanisms. From deliberations on the nature of the desirable system, participants underscored the need for the IGAD CEWARN system to go beyond the OAU mechanism, which is based on a security intelligence system.[30] Participants at CEWARN II proposed an in-between model for the IGAD CEWARN system. Preference was expressed for an open early warning system, described as a "disinterested intelligence model." Defined as a collaborative mechanism, the key characteristic of this system is the participation of state, nonstate, and traditional actors.

This workshop also discussed the legal and institutional arrangements of CEWARN. An examination of the treaty establishing IGAD revealed several bottlenecks in the envisaged system. First, the treaty does not contemplate the establishment of CEWARN and, therefore, lacks an anchor for a CEWARN mechanism. Its establishment within the current framework would make it dependent entirely on the goodwill of states. Second, the treaty does not address any conflict that may arise between CEWARN and other regional institutions, such as the AU, the East African Community (EAC), and the like. Effective operation of an early warning system calls for networking with such agencies, a function that calls for a clear delineation of relationships. Third, there is a problem of access to, processing, and sharing of information, which is critical for the operation of a CEWARN system. Fourth, there is the question of how decisions should be made within CEWARN, what lines and levels of accountability would be created, and how, if at all, these could impact its work. In view of the need for quick action, how would the mechanism deal with state bureaucracies? Finally, there is the question of the institutional relationship between the IGAD secretariat and CEWARN. What lines of command would be established?[31]

A consensus was reached to examine these issues further. As a result, it was recommended that IGAD, with the assistance of FEWER, engage a team of legal experts to look at other regional early warning mechanisms and sensitize IGAD states to the legal and institutional issues that relate to the establishment of CEWARN. Such consultations, it was argued, could ensure state participation in CEWARN's formation, and implant a sense of ownership in it. It was agreed that a declaration of general principles on the establishment of CEWARN be drafted for presentation to the heads-of-state summit in November 2000. A related recommendation urged the constitution of a legal committee, to begin consultations toward the drafting of legal instruments of cooperation in this area. In particular, this meeting called for a protocol in the area of early warning.

Phase three of this process began with a high-level meeting to deliberate both the draft declaration of principles and the draft protocol on CEWARN, held in October 1999. During this meeting, a bureau was established to facilitate the adoption of the CEWARN program and agenda and a draft declaration and protocol on CEWARN.[32] Article 4 of the protocol defines its functions as including collection, processing, and analyzing information; establishing networks of cooperation including memoranda of understanding with various other actors; and creating, managing, and disseminating databases of information on early warning. In terms of operations, Article 5 provides for cooperation between members and the mechanism in access, collection, analysis, and dissemination of information. Aware of the sensitivity surrounding information, the protocol proposes a supplementary technical protocol on the collection, sharing, and dissemination of information.[33]

Outstanding Issues and Challenges

While still in its formative stages, the CEWARN system faces potential challenges. Two of these—political will and technical capacity—have a direct impact on its functioning. Given that a CEWARN system will be based on the availability of information, some of which is sensitive, there is no provision for dealing with a state that is unwilling to facilitate the collection of relevant information. If the prevailing political will slackens, the chances of the mechanism falling dormant are real. Even if the existing level of political will were to remain, an early warning mechanism presupposes a certain level of infrastuctural support and technical capacity to collect relevant information, undertake competent analysis, and disseminate such information to critical actors. In a region where investment in infrastructural development is less than average, the optimal operation of a CEWARN system will require substantial investment in support systems and communications-related capacity.

Addressing the Proliferation of Small Arms and Light Weapons

A third output is the attempt to create a culture of peace and tolerance through activities aimed at combating the proliferation of small arms and light weapons. IGAD has, in cooperation with other stakeholders, supported activities that seek to nurture a culture of peace. Noting that the easy availability of illicit small arms and light weapons escalates conflicts, undermines political stability, and has a devastating negative impact on human and state security, IGAD has embraced the agenda of dealing with the problem of the proliferation of small and intermediate arms in the region.[34] To address this problem, foreign ministers from the GHA region met and signed the Nairobi Declaration on the Monitoring and Control of Illegal Circulation of Small Arms and Light Weapons in the region and beyond, in March 2000.[35] This declaration was to form the basis of the African position at the UN meeting on small arms held in New York in July 2001. The Nairobi declaration makes a link between the proliferation of arms and insecurity and political strife and notes the role of extreme poverty in exacerbating the use of arms for survival. More significant, it recognizes the growing practice of conscripting children into armed groups.

An important outcome of this meeting was the creation of the Nairobi Initiative on Small Arms and Light Weapons, which sought to work toward achieving greater state and human security by combating the proliferation of illicit arms and small weapons. To actualize this initiative, the Nairobi Secretariat on Small Arms and Light Weapons was established and mandated to coordinate regional action in addressing this problem. This development was the first step toward a moratorium on small arms in the region. In addition, it set regional standards to deal with small arms and created a momentum around which Africa formulated its common position during the UN Conference on Illicit Trade in Small Arms and Light Weapons in the Great Lakes Region and the Horn of Africa.

Following the signing of the declaration, a group of African experts met and identified seven activity areas. The first comprised a coordinated agenda for action and focuses on the institutional framework necessary to support activities in this area. A proposal was made for the establishment of country focal points to deal with the problem of small arms and light weapons and to oversee the implementation of the coordinated agenda.

Second, the meeting resolved to utilize regional cooperation and coordination frameworks to ensure long-term sustainable commitment in the pursuit of the objectives enshrined in the Nairobi declaration. Participants sought to develop, implement, and sustain a comprehensive strategy to combat the illicit proliferation of small arms and light weapons, taking into account the linkages between arms proliferation and all aspects of human security, as well as the long-term objective of attaining peace, stability, and development in the region. To implement these, a series of national and regional workshops and seminars were proposed, together with the exchange of information with other subregional organizations such as the EAC, IGAD, ECOWAS, and the SADC.

Third, proposals were made to promote legal uniformity and minimum standards to govern the manufacture, possession, import, export, transfer, and control of small arms and light weapons within the territories of the signatories. Fourth, operational issues including capacity building to deal effectively with the issues within the region were discussed. Fifth were issues of control, seizures, forfeitures, distribution, collection, and destruction of arms by states. Here, action aims at boosting state effectiveness and accountability in verifying the stock of small arms and light weapons, safe storage under the state's control, and monitoring weapons owned by private security companies and dealers. Sixth were concerns relating to publicizing policies, regulations, and laws relating to small arms and light weapons. Finally, the meeting proposed the promotion of a culture of peace through education, awareness-raising campaigns, and the promotion of tolerance. To achieve this, it emphasized the involvement of, and cooperation with, all sectors of society in preventing and reducing the problem of illicit small arms and light weapons. In pursuit of the objectives of this declaration, IGAD and the EAC produced in May 2001 a draft joint protocol on the control and monitoring of small arms and light weapons.

While this development has great potential, its greatest challenge lies in its dependence on the goodwill of states. There is no telling how long the prevailing positive political will in the region will last. A sustained regional approach to addressing the problem of the proliferation of small arms and light weapons needs to go beyond the assumed goodwill of states. A move by IGAD and the EAC to develop a collaborative protocol to address this problem is commendable and needs support from member states to facilitate its incorporation into municipal law. In August 2002, the Nairobi secretariat arranged the first ministerial review meeting. The meeting deliberated on the mandated functions and operations of the secretariat.

A related difficulty is the initiative's inherent assumption that states in this region are in control. States are neither necessarily the only nor the most significant actors. Addressing this problem requires involving insurgency groups as well as civilians, who are key players. In a region where warfare has become a means of livelihood, these initiatives have to address themselves to the related problem of child soldiers and the phenomenon of the multiplication of militia groups. Intervention with these groups would have to be broader and support such groups to engage in other ways and means to earn livelihoods. Finally, initiatives toward combating the proliferation of arms need to deal with the challenge of accessing accurate information, which is difficult to obtain in regions that fall outside state control.

Regional Integration as a Conflict-Prevention Strategy

Although not entirely new, the East African Community is the youngest of the African regional blocs.[36] The signing of the East African Treaty on Cooperation in 1999 revitalized the EAC, which had collapsed in 1977. Elsewhere in Africa at this time, as in the other parts of the world, states were initiating or strengthening regional blocs such as IGAD, the SADC, and ECOWAS, as a means of enhancing common security. At the same time, there was an expanding internal desire among the peoples of this region to forge a regional framework for addressing issues of common concern. This desire has yet to be met by current arrangements. Also, the scope provided within the 1984 Mediation Agreement on Sharing the Assets and Liabilities of the Community encouraged the reconstitution of the EAC. Article 14.02 of this agreement urged states to explore and identify areas for future cooperation and to make arrangements for such cooperation. It was on this provision that negotiations on the reestablishment of the East African Co-operation was built.

While the East African region is not as conflict prone as most of Africa, consensus among policymakers and practitioners in the region is that potential for conflict is real. To curb this threat, Kenya, Uganda, and Tanzania conceive regional cooperation as a strategy for preventive action. It is seen as a means of increasing mutual benefit and a vehicle for socioeconomic development and regional peace. This preventive perspective is embodied in the thrust of the treaty, which is to create a single market and investment area.[37] Notably, the first protocol to this treaty is one on the East African Customs Union, to be followed by a common market and finally a political federation. The rationale behind this is to create a wide economic space that will encourage competition and innovation, in addition to attracting local and foreign investors. To facilitate such development, the treaty identifies the development of economic infrastructure as an essential prerequisite in the creation of an economic space. It is envisaged that economic prosperity and regional integration will reduce the chances for conflict and thus enhance security.

This proactive position forms the backbone of the EAC treaty, which defines cooperation as an agent for regional peace and security. Based on the same premise as IGAD, the EAC sees regional peace and security as the foundation on which development can be attained. Among the fundamental principles of this community are peaceful coexistence and good neighborliness (Article 6[b]), peaceful settlement of disputes (Article 6[c]), and good governance (Article 6[d]). In this regard, there are memoranda of understanding on foreign policy and regional peace and, more significant, on common defense and security issues, which is currently under revision. This memorandum is expected to build on an already established tradition of undertaking joint maneuvers and military exercises between these three countries. In recognition of the security implications of forced migration—one of the main challenges facing the region—these states are moving toward the harmonization of refugee and immigration policy and practice.

Despite the potential advantages of this regional bloc in terms of promoting progress and, by extension, security, concerns have arisen about the impact of membership of other regional organizations, such as the SADC (Tanzania) and IGAD (Kenya and Uganda), on the commitment of members to the EAC. In particular, Tanzania's withdrawal from the Common Market of Eastern and Southern Africa (COMESA) has caused unease in Kenya and Uganda that Tanzania may feel more inclined toward the SADC than toward the EAC. In a region faced with scarcity of resources and an increasing problem of government debt, multiple membership of regional organizations runs the potential risk of minimal commitment in their contributions and other forms of support.

Another concern arises out of the unclear role of nonstate actors in this regional bloc. The EAC has no express framework for the involvement of civil society in conflict prevention. This generates fears that it may fall into the same trap as the earlier treaty, where states were the sole stakeholders.

Enhancing Regional Security: Lessons for the SADC

Developments in the IGAD and EAC subregions suggest a variety of lessons; the next section outlines six conclusions that we consider to have direct implications for the SADC region.

Process-Based Regional Security

As illustrated by experiences in the IGAD and EAC subregions, sustainable security is process-based, as opposed to being a quick fix, deliverable product. Devoting attention to process is of the utmost importance because it forms the building blocks of trust, a critical prerequisite for all conflict resolution measures. In the context of interstate conflicts, process acquires even greater significance because of the psychopolitical dynamics involved. As observed by Michelle Parlevliet, "to overcome negative feelings and perceptions so that structural issues can be addressed, protagonists have to develop trust in the process and in those who guide it."[38] Thus, whether security is sought in a conflict-ridden environment (IGAD), or as conflict-preventive action (EAC), it is a process that is based on consensus-building, trust, and networking between various sectors of society at the local, national, and regional levels. At the local level, it means harnessing capacities and engaging in wide dissemination of conflict-management skills. As the PPP initiative in the Sudan indicates, local knowledge and skills have great potential as support bases for broader processes. At the national level, process takes the form of legal administrative and policy environment that facilitates the pursuit of security. Regionally, process involves strong collaboration between actors within a subregion. Networking at all three levels calls for long-term investment in building and sustaining relations among and across actors.

Citizens as Main Stakeholders

Conventional perceptions of security are tied to a state-centric perspective that privileges the state at the expense of citizens. If peace is to be sustainable and security ensured, then regional security mechanisms must open up to the participation of the peoples of these regions. Perhaps this understanding can be incorporated into the SADC-led initiative in the DRC. Difficult and uncertain as the Somali peace process may seem, it offers a critical lesson for other conflict-ridden regions. Citizen participation offers crucial support and legitimacy to a peace process. Once people feel they own a peace process, even when the peace is fragile, there is great enthusiasm to protect and nurture it. The principal lesson to be derived from the Somali and Sudan peace processes has to do with the value added by civilian actors in search of peace. Both processes vindicate the role of civil society in bottom-up movements toward peace and security. The pressure to have the EAC conceived and nurtured as a people-driven process can also be seen in this light. Broad-based participation adds value to processes by ensuring the local ownership, and hence sustainability, of peace. An inescapable recommendation to emerge from these experiences is the importance of involving all stakeholders, especially nonstate actors, in peace processes.

Political Commitment to Regional Security

Regional security presupposes a level of confidence-building among states within a region. In a region where, historically, suspicion and tension have governed state relations, pursuit of common security is a great challenge. The Horn of Africa experiences not merely conflict but conflict systems with shifting epicenters and is characterized by the predominance of the use of force. Moreover, leaders in the region commonly and repeatedly break peace agreements. A paramount challenge lies in this history—how to ensure that such agreements are honored, how to sustain and to translate into action the emerging desire of leaders to address their differences and engage in greater cooperation on matters of security and economic development. This challenge calls for consensus-building at a regional level. A similar challenge confronts southern Africa, where states still remain wary of each other's interests. The case of South Africa and Zimbabwe in the DRC conflict is a clear example of what disagreement can do to a regional mechanism. Erratic state relations and a history of tension are likely to affect mutual trust, which is the prerequisite for a mechanism for resolving and preventing conflict.

Institutional Framework

In the GHA region, as in southern Africa, security mechanisms are developing as appendages to the main instruments of regional cooperation. For instance, the basic treaty documents promulgating the EAC, like those of the SADC, do not provide explicitly for a security mechanism. Even IGAD, which came closest to such a provision, leaves it as a statement of intent. No provision is made for institutional arrangements within, for example, the IGAD secretariat. This means that agreement on the pursuit of regional peace is sought outside the main institutional arrangements and remains a matter of consensus with limited or no means of enforcing compliance. As illustrated by the Sudan peace process, this holds the pursuit of security hostage to unpredictable political interests.

Explicit frameworks are needed to promote and safeguard regional security. Such frameworks would also provide for the structural links between core units including the secretariat, heads of state, and relevant ministries, such as those of foreign affairs. If there is a protocol, as has been proposed by IGAD and the EAC, it should address these relationships. Further, optimal functioning of such a protocol remains subject to the development of national mechanisms that embody the collective regional spirit. Thus, the incorporation of regional treaties into domestic law and frameworks is of paramount importance. The utility of such an institutional arrangement lies in checking political interests and enforcing compliance once a member has signed up to a security arrangement treaty. It would also minimize the role of powerful actors in subverting the mechanism for their own interests.

In addition, such frameworks need to recognize the interests of each state and allow for the differences in levels of development across members. Thus far, regional mechanisms have tended to assume an identity of character and interests in states, failing to address their individual and deep-seated fears. Small states, for example, perennially fear larger, more powerful states. Administratively, the institutional framework needs to provide for structures to support the implementation of programs of action. As things stand, good intentions often fail to be translated into action for lack of a clear modus operandi. Finally, institutional development must take account of the role of nonstate actors and provide for their involvement. Given that these actors are not members of regional organizations, there is a need to clear a space for their participation. This could be done through the creation of a nongovernmental organization (NGO) desk within regional bodies or by forming a regional forum for all NGOs, which would be represented in some of the organs of regional bodies, such as the Council of Ministers. Although the EAC treaty provides for NGO participation, structures for incorporating NGOs are not clearly delineated.

Enabling Environment

To pursue security as a process, to ensure participation, and to enhance networking and positive political will require an enabling environment. This calls for investment in expertise and support systems, both material and human. For instance, for a CEWARN system to operate, the dominance and control of government structures in areas concerning information needs to be addressed. There is a need to liberalize airwaves and to draw up agreements on CEWARN information-sharing. Given the sensitivity associated with such a development, a big question is, who should fund security? So far, much security funding has been sourced from outside the affected regions. A valuable lesson to be drawn from this experience is that such funds have interests attached to them and may not necessarily hasten peace processes and the achievement of security. The Somali peace process is a case in point. While outside funding is significant, the environment under which a peace process is being pursued is as critical as foreign support. The question must be addressed of how to apply local, national, and international assistance to a peace process without overwhelming it or undermining the chances of its survival.

Developmental Perspective

The emerging consensus that security is linked to development provides a critical impetus for states to rethink their development strategies and priorities. The advantage of a developmental perspective on security is that it reduces the chance of disagreements between state actors, focuses on issues of preventive action that are less controversial, and is less likely to destroy trust and cooperative spirit. Experiences from the Horn of Africa indicate the usefulness of a strategy of identifying various noncontroversial entry points within a region. Such an approach is holistic and provides for the crucial interlinkage between security and other issues, such as respect for human rights, good governance, and economic and social development.

Notes

1. Arguing that conflicts will increase rather than decline in the third world, Augustus R. Norton predicts a situation of "lebanonization," or the breakdown of

the state. States, he argues, are under threat from increasing internal tensions caused by the challenges of building coalescent societies, winning legitimacy, and meeting the basic needs of the constituents, as well as the failure of the Western pluralist democratic project and the impact of global communication on citizenry. See A. R. Norton, "The Security Legacy of the 1980s in the Third World" in *Third World Security in the Post–Cold War Era,* ed. T. G. Weiss and M. A. Kessler (Boulder, Colo.: Lynne Rienner Publishers, 1995). This position underscores the need to search beyond state actors in the quest for security and promotion of freedoms.

2. For a comprehensive definition and exposé of security, see, for example, B. L. Job, *Insecurity Dilemma: National Security of Third World States* (Boulder, Colo.: Lynne Rienner Publishers, 1992), and Barry Buzan, "People, State, and Fear: The National Security Problem in the Third World," in *National Security in the Third World: The Management of International and External Threats,* ed. Edward E. Azar and Chung-In Moon (Aldershot, U.K.: Edward Elgar, 1988).

3. This conception of security is derived from Ole Waever in Waever et al., *Identity, Migration, and the New Security Agenda in Europe* (London: Pinter, 1993).

4. Buzan, "People, State, and Fear," 1.

5. Ambassador B. Kiplagat headed the FEWER team that was assisting IGAD in the establishment of a CEWARN mechanism for the region.

6. This situation is explained in terms of the breakdown of state mechanisms in Somalia but also in terms of the inability of the government in Kenya to control arms inflow. Professor John J. Okumu (scholar of governance issues and security), interviewed by the author, Nairobi, Kenya, 11 September 2000. An ISS report released to the Kenyan media on 29 July 2002 indicates that Nairobi alone is swamped with more than 500 illicit small arms.

7. By 1988, the Ethiopian government was spending some 50 percent of its revenue and 15 percent of gross domestic product for military purposes. See Christopher Clapham, "The Political Economy of Conflict in the Horn of Africa," *Survival* 32, 5 (September/October 1990): 410–411. In the same vein, one of the stickiest areas in Uganda-donor relations today is Uganda's rising military expenditure. Since 1997, the World Bank and International Monetary Fund have consistently argued that Uganda's military expenditure is disproportionate to its resources and affects allocation to other sectors.

8. Principally this takes the form of relief aid. Research in the Horn of Africa is increasingly linking such assistance with the economies of war.

9. Remittances come from a growing number of exiles from insurgent regions who have found employment abroad. In addition to amounts that they send home to relatives, exiles are regularly taxed by "their" governments, insurgent or otherwise. In an April 2000 interview with an Eritrean who lives and works in Washington, D.C., it came out that when war broke out between Eritrea and Ethiopia in 1998, Eritreans met and collected some U.S.$5 million. This money was used to purchase arms in support for the war effort.

10. Clapham, "Poltical Economy of Conflict," 403–419.

11. In addition, there are substantial numbers of unregistered refugees not included in this figure.

12. Johnnie Carson, address to the first CEWARN meeting, Nairobi, 5 July 2000.

13. Security cooperation remained at the bilateral level with signing of military alliances and pacts, such as the Kenya-Ethiopia defense pact. However, these arrangements remained fluid and often suffered violation of one kind or another.

14. Activities were grouped into three areas in order of their priority as fol-

lows: political and humanitarian affairs; economic development; and agriculture, food policy, and environmental protection.

15. At the beginning of the conflict, the SPLA and the government of Sudan were the two main protagonists, hence the initial definition of this conflict as being one between the north and the south. However, over time splinter groups have developed from the SPLA/M, such as the group under Riack Machar; splinters have also occurred in the north, which has seen the coalition of opposition parties such as the Umma Party. For a comprehensive analysis of these developments, see Gérard Prunier, *Identity Crisis and the Weak State: The Making of the Sudanese Civil War* (Geneva: WRITENET, 1996).

16. There were several attempts to resolve the conflict prior to this, the most significant being the 1972 Addis Ababa accord, which delivered peace until it broke down in 1989. For details of the Addis Ababa accord, see ibid.

17. This period corresponds with Sudan's support for Saddam Hussein. On the ground, this anti-American logic translated into an anti-African ideology whose banner was carried by Hassan Al-Turabi. In 1995, Sudan was also implicated in the assassination attempt on President Hosni Mubarak of Egypt; in the same year, it broke diplomatic ties with Eritrea, whom it accused of supporting Sudanese rebels. For a detailed analysis of this, see ibid., 24.

18. For instance, during the IGAD ministerial meeting held in Khartoum on 20 November 2000, the foreign minister of Kenya had to take time to calm fears within Sudan that Kenya was partisan in this conflict.

19. Some analysts predict an escalation of tensions over the Nile waters. So far, Egypt has been attempting to hold its Nilotic neighbors in check, but this has not been without challenges. For instance, in 1995, following the failed attempt on the life of the Egyptian president, Sudan was accused of links with the terrorist act. Sudan's response was swift. It called off the Nile treaty, after which Hassan Al Turabi declared that Sudan had the full control of the Nile. This prompted Egypt to threaten war. The conflict between the government and the SPLA has also complicated the question of the control of the Nile. In addition, the Ethiopian opposition to the Egyptian plan to harness more than its share of the Nile waters carries the potential of sparking off tensions between these two countries. For a comprehensive analysis of potential conflicts, see, for example, Jeroen Warner, "Conflict on the Nile," in *Conflict Trends, Special Feature: Water Wars* (Umhlanga Rocks, South Africa: Creda Communications, 2000).

20. Africa Peace Forum, *Dispatch* (Nairobi), 2000, 9.

21. Mohamed-Said Douleh, "The Djibouti-Led Process. A People-Led Experiment: Towards the Making of a New Somalia," concept paper for the CEWARN II meeting, Kampala, Uganda, 11–12 September 2000, 1.

22. Ibid., 3.

23. See IGAD, "Declaration of the Seventh IGAD Summit of Heads of States and Governments," Khartoum, Sudan, 26 November 1999.

24. In one such situation where disputes over political representation threatened to derail the process, President Guelleh intervened personally. Demonstrating immense political skills, using a sense of drama, and engaging his knowledge of Somali psychology, he challenged the participants to seize the moment and act as expected by those whom they represented at the conference. Several analysts have attributed the formation of the Transitional National Assembly to this powerful intervention. See, for example, Doualeh, "Djibouti-Led Process."

25. Ibid., 6, 10.

26. UN Secretary-General, "Report of the Secretary-General on the Situation in Somalia," 16 August 1999, S/1999/882, 16.

27. From the Liliir peace conference, press release, obtained from the New Sudan Council of Churches, Nairobi.

28. This is a consortium of NGOs, research centers, and international agencies that work in the conflict-prevention field. FEWER has as its objectives the provision of an institutional framework to facilitate cooperation and synergy among the providers and users of country and region-specific early warning information and analyses, and the development of regional capacities for contributing to early warning and early intervention strategies.

29. Participants at this meeting debated the conceptual models of early warning presented by the FEWER team, discussed their appropriateness, and identified how IGAD could effectively engage in early warning and response activities.

30. During his presentation at the CEWARN I workshop in Nairobi (July 2000), Howard Adelman distinguished between the intelligence model of early warning and the transparency model. See IGAD, "Report on the CEWARN II Workshop." Kampala, Uganda, 11–12 September 2000.

31. For a comprehensive analysis of the legal and institutional aspects of the establishment of CEWARN, see Makumi Mwagiru, "IGAD Conflict Early Warning Mechanism: Legal and Institutional Aspects," background paper for the CEWARN II meeting.

32. Alier Deng Ruai of Sudan and Teumezghi of Eritrea were unanimously elected to the positions of chairperson and rapporteur, respectively.

33. See, for example, Article 5 (7) of the draft protocol on CEWARN.

34. UN General Assembly, "Report of the Group of Governmental Experts on Small Arms," 19 August 1999, A/54/258, 24. distinguishes small arms from light weapons. Small arms are defined as weapons designed for personal use, including revolvers and self-loading pistols, rifles and carbines, submachine guns, assault rifles, and light machine guns. Light weapons are designed for use by several persons serving as a crew and include heavy submachine guns, hand-held under-barrel and mounted grenade launchers, portable anticraft and antitank guns, recoilless rifles, portable launchers for antiaircraft and antitank rockets and missile systems, and mortars of caliber of less than 100mm. Ammunition and explosives form an integral part of small arms and light weapons used in conflicts, and include cartridges for small arms, shells, and missiles for light weapons, antipersonnel and antitank grenades, land mines, explosives, and mobile containers with missiles for single-action antiaircraft and antitank systems.

35. See the "Nairobi Declaration on the Problem of the Proliferation of Illicit Small Arms and Light Weapons in the Great Lakes Region and Horn of Africa," Nairobi, 15 March 2000.

36. The roots of this cooperation can be traced to the construction of the Kenya-Uganda Railway (1897–1901). For various reasons, colonial administration promulgated policies that nurtured regional cooperation in various sectors. After independence, the three states of Kenya, Uganda, and Tanzania legalized this cooperation by signing the Treaty for East African Co-operation in 1967. This treaty provided for a joint East African commission, a common services organization, and the East African Community. For the historical milestones in this cooperation, see Sam Tulya-Muhika, "Revival of the East African Co-operation and Its Institutional Framework," in *EAC, Perspectives on Regional Integration and Co-operation in East Africa* (Arusha, Tanzania: EAC, 2000).

37. Francis Muthaura (secretary-general, East African Community), interview by author, Eldoret, Kenya, November 2000.

38. Michelle Parlevliet, "The Role of Civil Society in Preventing Deadly Conflicts in Africa," paper presented at the Fifth Meeting of the Independent International Commission on Kosovo, South African Institute of International Affairs, University of the Witwatersrand, Johannesburg, 25–26 August 2000, 15.

PART 3

Extraregional Actors

12

The United Nations

IBRAHIM A. GAMBARI

The post–Cold War era and the globalizing world in which we live pose enormous challenges for those actors seeking to promote global peace, security, and development. In the preamble of the United Nations Charter, the founders declared:

> We the peoples of the United Nations determined to save succeeding generations from the scourge of war . . . [pledge] to reaffirm faith in fundamental human rights, in the dignity and worth of the human person, in the equal rights of men and women and of nations large and small, and . . . to promote social progress and better standards of life in larger freedom.[1]

Fifty-five years after these worthy goals were espoused, though they have not been abandoned, they have not been fully realized. It is now for successive generations to make the UN live up to the high expectations of its founders and thereby help to translate these noble ideals into concrete achievements.

African states need to develop innovative home-grown strategies to cope with the new security challenges of the post–Cold War era. The goal is not simply to find "African solutions to African problems," however desirable that may be. Rather, the prospects for obtaining international support for solving many of Africa's problems will be greatly enhanced when Africans themselves make serious and sustained efforts to address these difficulties. Africa's case for international collaboration and assistance becomes both credible and achievable if Africans are spearheading such efforts. In any case, given the multiplicity of the challenges of peace and security in the new millennium, it is only through genuine international collaboration that African security mechanisms can become stronger.

Although the Southern African Development Community (SADC) and the UN face similar challenges in promoting peace, security, and development, there are also particular challenges for each organization. How can these two organizations work together to promote common goals while emphasizing the strengths of each organization in order to establish an effective division of labor? After outlining the major security challenges confronting the SADC and the UN, this chapter will analyze the security challenges faced by both organizations and briefly assess five case studies of UN peacekeeping and peacemaking in SADC states: Namibia, Angola, Mozambique, South Africa, and the Democratic Republic of Congo (DRC). The chapter concludes by suggesting ways in which the UN and the SADC can work together to promote peace and security in southern Africa.

The SADC's Security Challenges

With the end of the Cold War and the negotiated settlement in South Africa in 1994, one major challenge faced by the SADC was, and continues to be, that of building or consolidating a security community in southern Africa.[2] In this regard, SADC leaders recognize the need to work on a concept of security different from the one that prevailed in the region during the apartheid era. Moreover, there is an increasing realization within the SADC that in order to succeed in establishing an effective security architecture in southern Africa, countries in the region will need to collaborate more closely.

During the apartheid era, security in southern Africa was synonymous with defense, an issue that was dealt with exclusively by the region's military establishments. Large armies and large defense budgets and expenditures were regarded as essential for security; their absence was seen as a sign of insecurity. Military expenditure in southern Africa as late as 1990–1991 was as high as 20 percent of the gross domestic product (GDP) in some SADC states.[3] However, during the Cold War era and the height of apartheid, Botswana was among the countries that had the smallest army in the region (although Botswana has increased such spending in recent years) and the lowest military budget. Yet the state and people of Botswana enjoyed a high degree of stability and prosperity. Botswana's *pula* has been one the most stable currencies in the region, and the country has witnessed lower crime rates than most other states in the region. Botswana's economy is also one of the fastest growing in the world.[4] There are important lessons to draw from Botswana's experience. Perhaps the most relevant lesson is that security cannot simply be equated with military activities or remain an exclusive preserve of the military. There are serious nonmilitary threats to the security of the states and peoples of southern Africa that are just as important. We will now briefly assess four of the security challenges facing southern Africa: continuing armed conflicts, the impact of HIV/AIDS on security, the effects of transnational crime and the proliferation of small arms, and the failure of economic development to bring prosperity and peace to southern Africa.

Curbing Conflicts

The demise of apartheid in South Africa in 1994 removed an important military threat to the security and development of the countries of southern Africa, most of which had united under the banner of the Frontline States in a bid to balance the destructive and destabilizing forces of apartheid South Africa's powerful army.[5] This is not to suggest that there is no longer a need for military forces in southern Africa, as regional armies still have an important role to play in the overall maintenance of peace and security in the region.

Until the death of Angolan rebel leader, Jonas Savimbi, in February 2002, there were currently two major conflicts in the SADC region: the ongoing war in the DRC, in which three SADC members—Zimbabwe, Angola, and Namibia—were militarily involved; and the twenty-six-year-old conflict in Angola, which brought death, destruction, and plunder to the long suffering people of that unfortunate country. In addition, violence occurred between May and June 2000 in Namibia's Caprivi strip; skirmishes between white farmers, their workers, and veterans of the liberation struggle in Zimbabwe moved that country toward chaos and confusion. And the security situation in Mozambique, considered to be a major success story of UN peacekeeping in Africa, remains precarious eight years after the UN forces departed. Moreover, following the refusal by the opposition party to accept the result of the 1998 elections, a volatile situation emerged in Lesotho, which resulted in military intervention by South Africa and Botswana.

All these conflicts require southern African armies to remain alert in order to maintain security. However, the conflicts in Angola, the DRC, Zimbabwe, Mozambique, and Lesotho illustrate the limits of military solutions to the problem of peace and security in the subregion. Military actions need to be aligned with political, social, and economic programs to improve the material condition of the peoples in these countries. The role of the military must be to protect the achievements and values that other political, social, and economic institutions have acquired. This broader definition of peacebuilding is essential for promoting security in southern Africa. If military activities take place in the absence of good governance and sound political, economic, and social policies and institutions, they are likely to have negative consequences, including the oppression of certain groups and the erosion of the military's raison d'être (i.e., to defend a constitutional order as well as the territorial integrity of the state).

The Impact of HIV/AIDS

Conflict is not, however, the only source of human insecurity in southern Africa. Epidemics such as HIV/AIDS pose a serious threat to the very existence of communities in the region. The impact of this epidemic is already visible in many African states. In some countries, when we visit villages, we see the elderly and children under fifteen, but we see no youth. In other villages, we see women and children but no men, and when we ask after the men, we are shown graveyards. It is clear from these experiences, garnered during my official travels in southern Africa as special adviser to the UN Secretary-General, Kofi Annan, that HIV/AIDS should be a matter that concerns us all.[6]

The situation is reaching epidemic proportions. In 1998 alone, HIV/AIDS and related illnesses killed ten times more Africans than the conflicts in the continent.[7] An estimated 24.5 million people in sub-Saharan Africa remain infected with the virus. Yet the majority of Africans still lack access to treatment, even as AIDS threatens to reverse the negative impact of the gains of development. According to a Joint UN Programme on HIV/AIDS report, the pandemic will reduce South Africa's economic growth rate by 0.3 percent to 0.4 percent annually, resulting by 2010 in a GDP that will be 17 percent lower than it would have been without AIDS. Indeed, the United Nations Development Programme estimates that in twenty years, Africa's GDP will be reduced by one-third as a consequence of the HIV/AIDS pandemic. The UN also estimates that in the next decade, 25 to 50 percent of personnel in the health, education, security, and civil service sectors will die as a result of HIV/AIDS. These sobering statistics demonstrate the urgency of linking the fight against the scourge of AIDS with the SADC's security policies.

In January 2000, the UN Security Council declared HIV/AIDS a threat to international security. The pandemic is particularly devastating in southern Africa.[8] Government projections indicate that 35 percent of Botswana's population and 60 percent of Zimbabwe's is infected with the HIV virus. In the worst-affected cities of southern Africa, 40 percent of pregnant women are estimated to be HIV positive. To face up to this global crisis, UN Secretary-General Kofi Annan has proposed a strategy to contain and reduce the spread of HIV/AIDS: this strategy is aimed at young men and women between the ages of fifteen and twenty-four and focuses on providing better care for those living with the illness.

Transnational Organized Crime and the Proliferation of Small Arms

During the last four decades of the twentieth century, significant technological advances were made, especially in the area of transport and telecommunications, which facilitated the flow of information and circulation of goods, services, people, and capital. These developments have led corporations increasingly to operate transnationally. However, the very developments that facilitate the circulation of people, goods, services, and money also facilitate the transportation of drugs, arms, illicit money, and illegal immigrants. Globalization has had the undesirable consequence of facilitating the expansion of networks of organized crime and of black markets, which pose challenges for the maintenance of domestic law and order and international security. This situation has been particularly pronounced in southern Africa.[9] Many of southern Africa's weak states do not possess the expertise to conduct proper investigations and devise mechanisms to counter transnational organized crime. Regional states have very low levels of law enforcement; as a result, their domestic environment facilitates the operation of criminal groups, while much criminal activity goes unchecked.

The end of the Cold War has also been accompanied by a surplus of weapons in international arms markets, even as the normal legal arms markets have shrunk. This has resulted in increasing competition among arms producers. The decline in prices for arms has facilitated the sale of weapons to nonstate actors, particularly in countries such as Angola, Mozambique, and South Africa, with a resultant expansion of criminal activity that allows the establishment of regular markets through indirect and illegal channels. General insecurity permits greater transfer of resources from the public sphere to illegal activities, thus facilitating protracted social conflict that feeds on itself and reproduces and spreads conflicts throughout southern Africa.

The Failure of Economic Development

Although the end of apartheid in 1994 led to an improvement in diplomatic relations in southern Africa, the political change has not been matched by significant economic dividends for the region's peoples. South Africa's economy, by far the largest in the region, has experienced low growth rates since the end of apartheid;[10] yet trade has continued to be largely one-way, from South Africa to its neighbors. Like the UN, the SADC faces the challenges of placing people, and not just states, at the center of its activities. Within the SADC, South Africa remains the regional magnet, as, following increasing unemployment rates in Zimbabwe, Mozambique, Malawi, and Lesotho, the nationals of neighboring states continue to regard South Africa as a potential employer. However, South Africa has its own massive unemployment problems, and the closure of its gold mines following the drop of gold prices in 1999 has worsened the region's economic decline.

The UN's Security Challenges

At the beginning of this chapter, we referred to the ideals of the UN Charter and the organization's commitment to peace and security, the promotion of human rights, fundamental freedoms, and socioeconomic development. The fundamentals of security include the assurance that the value, achievements, and gains of humanity are not jeopardized and that there will be predictable, peaceful relations in the future. These are the main challenges facing the UN and the SADC. We next analyze the changing nature of UN peacekeeping with particular reference to Africa. We then assess the UN's peacemaking and peacekeeping efforts in five SADC member states: Namibia, Angola, Mozambique, South Africa, and the DRC.

Peacemaking and Peacekeeping

If this is the season for international peacekeeping operations, it is a season of anomie with respect to Africa, as demonstrated by the difficulties of United Nations peacekeeping operations in Sierra Leone (UNAMSIL), the Democratic Republic of Congo (MONUC), and Western Sahara. Unlike the peacekeeping operations of the Cold War era, current UN operations are usually integrated, multifunctional undertakings that include civilian administration, peacemaking, election monitoring, disarmament, demobilization, restructuring of security forces, and human rights monitoring. These new peacebuilding operations are increasingly undertaken to manage conflicts that are within rather than between states. These intrastate conflicts usually have no clear front lines and are often fought by armed militias with little discipline and, in most cases, ill-defined chains of command.[11]

In view of the proliferation of civil wars in Africa, efforts to obtain international support for managing these conflicts can only be enhanced if African leaders make serious efforts to address their own peace and security challenges. It will be a pity if, when African actors take collective action through "coalitions of the willing" or through regional arrangements such as the SADC, the Economic Community of West African States, the Intergovernmental Authority on Development, and the African Union (AU), the international community and the UN fail to come up with the financial and logistical support to complement these efforts.

However, the starting point for the UN is to put its own peacekeeping and peacemaking machinery in order. The debacle of UNAMSIL in Sierra Leone in May 2000 (when UN peacekeepers were disarmed and kidnapped) and the dilemma of deploying more MONUC peacekeepers to the DRC[12] illustrate the urgency of addressing the issues of mandate, financing, equipment, and logistical support, as well as cooperation between the UN and regional organizations in Africa.

In this regard, in early 2000 Secretary-General Kofi Annan charged a panel of experts to assess the shortcomings of the existing UN system for addressing peace and security issues and to make frank and specific recommendations aimed at correcting these flaws.[13] The panel of experts produced what became known as the "Brahimi report," published in August 2000. The report made recommendations that could strengthen the UN's capacity to undertake future peacemaking, peacekeeping, and peacebuilding operations.[14] These recommendations include the necessity for clear and realistic mandates for UN peacekeeping operations, and clear and robust doctrines and means with which to undertake such missions once the UN Security Council has approved them. The Brahimi report also recommends strengthening the capacity of the UN to develop peacebuilding strategies and to implement programs in support of these strategies. The implementation of the Brahimi panel's recommendations remains a major challenge for the UN and the wider international community.

UN Peacemaking Efforts in Southern Africa

Two of the UN's most notable successes occurred in southern Africa: the world body oversaw the withdrawal of Cuban and South African troops from Angola and Namibia and organized Namibia's transition to democratic rule by 1989; the UN also oversaw the end of the two-decade civil war in Mozambique and monitored that nation's first democratic elections in 1994. Despite these successes, how to do more with less has become a major challenge confronting the United Nations. The organization suffered two spectacular failures in Angola in the 1990s and is currently struggling to monitor a peace agreement in the DRC, another SADC country. The 1990s saw resources available for UN peace operations in Africa decline markedly after the UN's two peacekeeping debacles in Angola that led to the withdrawal of its peacekeepers from that country in 1992 and 1998, and particularly after the withdrawal of UN peacekeepers from Somalia following the killing of eighteen U.S. peacekeepers in October 1993. The slogan "African solutions for African problems" became an excuse for the most powerful members of the UN Security Council to avoid large-scale UN involvement in Africa. This was tragically evidenced by the Rwandan genocide in April 1994, which occurred under the noses of an ill-equipped UN force, as, in stark contrast, majority rule was arriving in South Africa in the presence of UN civilian observers.

The United Nations and Namibia

In 1919, after the settlement of World War I, the League of Nations granted the Union of South Africa a mandate to administer the territory of South West Africa, which South Africa had wrested from the Germans during the war. That mandate formally ceased in 1946.[15] In October 1946, General Jan Smuts, prime minister of South Africa, submitted to the United Nations a case for incorporating South West Africa (Namibia) in the Union. The application was opposed by India and subsequently turned down by the UN. South Africa refused to accept this decision and, during the 1950s and 1960s, the question of South Africa's occupation was debated at every UN session.

In October 1966, the UN General Assembly resolved unanimously to end the mandate and cancelled South Africa's right to administer the territory. Pretoria defied the UN and instead masterminded the balkanization of Namibia into twelve self-governing provinces. In 1971, the International Court of Justice backed the UN's decision to revoke South Africa's mandate over the territory. Following this decision, the UN in 1971 adopted a resolution declaring the South West African People's Organization (SWAPO) the "sole, authentic voice of the people" of Namibia.

In 1978, the UN Security Council adopted resolution 435, requiring free and fair elections to be held in Namibia under UN supervision. The plan determined that, prior to the polls, South Africa would withdraw all its forces from the territory and release all political prisoners, a cease-fire would be declared, and an interim administrator-general for Namibia would be installed to administer the territory.[16]

Two obstacles stalled the implementation of the UN peace plan. First, Pretoria was unwilling to give up the territory's Walvis Bay, which it considered strategic to its own interests. Second, South Africa insisted that it have a key role in maintaining security over the territory during any transition period and that the UN deploy only a small force. SWAPO began to engage in fierce armed struggle, as it launched its campaign from neighboring Angola and Mozambique. By 1985, South African and Cuban troops were fighting fierce battles in the Angolan town of Cuito Cuanavale, and the white-ruled republic suffered major casualties for the first time. In May and June 1988, Angola, Namibia, and South Africa agreed to international mediation over the Namibia peace process.

On 20 July 1988, Angola, South Africa, and Cuba signed what came to be known as the New York accord through the mediation efforts of the United States. With the thawing of the Cold War, Washington played an important peacebrokering role, as an agreement was reached for South Africa to implement resolution 435 in exchange for a withdrawal of Cuban forces from South West Africa/Namibia.

The UN peacekeeping mission in Namibia helped to confine South African and SWAPO troops to their bases, and UN Secretary-General Javier Perez de Cuellar unveiled a plan for a UN force of 6,150 personnel: 4,650 troops, 500 police officers, and 1,000 civilian observers. A budget of $416 million was approved for the operation. Finnish diplomat Marthi Ahtisaari and his UN peacekeepers successfully oversaw the implementation of resolution 435. On 21 March 1990, South Africa's flag was lowered and a new flag was hoisted over the new state of Namibia.

The UN and Angola

We next turn to the UN's role in Angola. During the 1980s, Angola's civil war was inextricably intertwined with the conflict in South West Africa/ Namibia. South Africa refused to withdraw its troops from southern Angola and continued to support Angola's National Union for the Total Independence of Angola, (UNITA) rebels. This position was offset by the support of Cuban troops on the side of the Popular Liberation Movement of Angola (MPLA) government in Luanda. After years of acrimony, a series of internationally brokered talks between the belligerents led to Cuba's decision to withdraw some 50,000 troops from Angola; South Africa also withdrew 2,000 of its troops from southern Angola.[17]

In April 1990, the withdrawals from Angola and Namibia started to take place under UN monitoring and verification. The linkage of the Angolan and Namibia conflicts meant that the resolution of one would have positive spillover effects for the other. Thus, the willingness of external powers to withdraw from Angola and Namibia meant that the stage was set for the possible resolution of both conflicts.

Following Namibia's independence in 1990, the MPLA and UNITA signed the Portuguese-sponsored Bicesse Peace Accords in May 1991. The accord called for even stronger UN involvement in the Angolan peace process.[18] The Bicesse accords made provision for the establishment of a joint Political-Military Commission and the UN contributed 300 unarmed UN observers to implement it. But these observers proved too few and too weak and demobilization, notably of UNITA, turned out to be negligible.

The first United Nations Angola Verification Mission (UNAVEM I) was a small mission to verify the withdrawal of Cuban troops from Angola. The mission started with the signing of the peace accords by South Africa, Angola, and Cuba on 22 December 1988, and was mandated to run for thirty-one months. The mission was straightforward: unarmed observers were to "verify the redeployment northwards and the phased and total withdrawal of Cuban troops from the territory of the People's Republic of Angola."[19]

The estimated cost of the operation was $18.8 million. UNAVEM I successfully completed its tasks because the Cuban troop withdrawals occurred ahead of schedule and because UNAVEM officials had access to fixed aircraft, helicopters, and ground transportation to verify the withdrawal of the troops. The goodwill of Angola and of Cuba was therefore vital to the success of the mission.

Fighting between the MPLA and UNITA continued after the withdrawal of foreign troops, until the two parties signed the Bicesse accords on 31 May 1991, brokered chiefly by the United States, Soviet Union, and Portugal.[20] The accords called for a UN-monitored cease-fire; the demobilization of the two armies estimated at 200,000 troops; the creation of a new, unified 50,000-strong army; UN-supervised elections; and the establishment of a Joint Monitoring Commission, involving both parties and the UN, to implement the agreement.

But, despite mandating the deployment of UNAVEM II and its 700 peacekeepers, the UN Security Council failed to provide the mission with the necessary financial and logistical backing.[21] Further exacerbating the situation was the mutual suspicion between UNITA and the MPLA that continued to affect peace efforts. Preparations for the elections remained poor.[22] Logistics and transportation also remained poor as the communications infrastructure in Angola had been heavily damaged by the twenty-five-year war. With such a small peacekeeping force, the UN relied entirely on the goodwill of the parties to implement the accords and was unable to prevent a return to war when such goodwill was lacking. Further fueling the war was the fact that the MPLA controlled the country's oil resources, while UNITA plundered its diamond wealth.

The UN's electoral role in Angola was soon rendered impossible when its observers faced violence and intimidation. Voting took place in September 1992, with the UN deploying 400 electoral observers. Incumbent president, José Eduardo dos Santos, narrowly won the first round of presidential elections but was just short of a 50 percent majority. A runoff with UNITA leader Jonas Savimbi was therefore required to determine the outcome. Savimbi refused to conclude the electoral process and failed to disarm his fighters. He continued his guerrilla war, and the UN Security Council eventually imposed economic sanctions on UNITA in October 1997.

UNAVEM III occurred after the Lusaka protocol of November 1994. It was a conscious effort to correct the mistakes of the Bicesse accords by providing 7,000 peacekeepers and offering UNITA posts in a transitional government. Both the MPLA and UNITA refused to implement the agreement, and by 1998 a devastating war had returned to Angola. In response, the UN withdrew its military mission from Angola. In August 2000, the UN reestablished a political office in Luanda.

With the defeat of UNITA and the death of its leader, Jonas Savimbi, on 22 February 2002, the Angolan Armed Forces established contacts with

UNITA in order to reach an agreement on the cessation of hostilities and end the war in Angola. The agreement was subsequently formalized in a memorandum of understanding (MoU) signed in Luanda on 4 April 2002 and witnessed by the UN and the troika observer nations (Portugal, Russia, and the United States), among others. The MoU is intended to replace the Lusaka protocol on military matters and to complement the protocol on political matters. Under the MoU, the UN has the role of an observer in the Joint Military Commission but expects to chair the Joint Commission (when it is reestablished) to mediate between the government and UNITA in addressing the remaining issues under the Lusaka protocol.

According to the Secretary-General's report on Angola, submitted to the Security Council in August 2002, the MoU "marked a new era in the Angolan peace process and presented new challenges for the United Nations presence in Angola." In his view, "the prospects for long-term peace are better today than at any time before." In this regard, more than 84,000 UNITA troops have been quartered with their weapons, and the cease-fire continues to hold. Moreover, there is now a single national army with the incorporation of 5,000 UNITA soldiers into the armed forces of Angola at a ceremony on 31 July 2002.

However, reintegration into society of the remaining almost 80,000 UNITA ex-combatants remains a major challenge. Dealing with the humanitarian situation is another challenge. Kofi Annan is gratified that the government and UNITA have taken responsibility for managing the peace process, but he observed that "they will need the active support of the international community to overcome the political, security, humanitarian, and socio-economic challenges and to consolidate peace in the country."

The UN and Mozambique

The role of the UN and other international actors in bringing an end to Mozambique's war was decisive. Between 1975 and 1990, the Front for the Liberation of Mozambique (FRELIMO) government and the Mozambique National Resistance (RENAMO) rebels were locked in a brutal civil war.[23] From 1988, intermediaries from the Community of Sant' Egidio, a Catholic international lay association, began to facilitate informal negotiations between the warring parties.[24]

The first of a series of direct meetings between FRELIMO and RENAMO was held at the Covenant of Sant' Egidio in Rome in July 1990.[25] At further talks in November 1990, a joint verification committee was established, with Botswana and Zimbabwe playing prominent mediation roles.[26] A month later, a cease-fire was agreed.

The two warring parties signed the "basic principles" of the Mozambican Peace Agreement in October 1991, covering six key areas: the law on political parties, the electoral system, military issues, security guarantees, a cease-fire, and an international donor conference.[27] A year later, FRELIMO and RENAMO signed a comprehensive peace agreement that included agreements on the establishment of a new Mozambican army, the creation of a commission to supervise and monitor the peace process, and the recognition of all political parties in Mozambique.[28]

In December 1992, the UN Security Council approved a peacekeeping mission to Mozambique (ONUMOZ). ONUMOZ was mandated to monitor the cease-fire, undertake disarmament and demobilization, facilitate the return of 2 million refugees from neighboring countries,[29] oversee the coordination of humanitarian assistance, and verify national elections.[30] The ONUMOZ mission experienced several difficulties. It took the UN almost six months to establish the mission. Soon after the UN's arrival, RENAMO's leader, Afonso Dhlakama, refused to demobilize his troops unless more funds were provided for transforming his guerrilla movement into a political party. On the eve of elections, he threatened a boycott of the poll.

The mediation role played by UN Special Representative Aldo Ajello was crucial in securing the success of the mission. He effectively used the cease-fire commission to resolve military issues, secured funds for implementing the agreement, and effectively coordinated the UN's political and humanitarian tasks.[31] ONUMOZ disarmed and demobilized 64,130 FRELIMO and 22,637 RENAMO fighters between January and August 1994.[32] UN electoral observers oversaw parliamentary and presidential elections in October 1994, which FRELIMO won. ONUMOZ deployed nearly 6,000 peacekeepers, 130 civilian police, and cost $332 million a year.

The UN and South Africa

Throughout the apartheid period, the UN pressured South African governments to end white minority domination. By the 1960s, apartheid united the UN in a way that few issues had ever done. In 1962, the UN Special Committee against Apartheid was created, institutionalizing punitive action against South Africa by member states. In 1963, the UN Security Council agreed to a voluntary arms embargo against South Africa by member states, and, in the ensuing years, the world body appealed to governments and international organizations to tighten oil and arms embargoes, as well as sports and cultural boycotts against Pretoria.[33]

In 1974, the UN General Assembly denied South Africa access to all UN meetings. In 1977, the UN Security Council imposed a mandatory arms embargo on the government in Pretoria, the first time it had taken such an action against a member state. By 1978, more than half the meetings of the

UN Security Council were devoted to southern Africa, particularly the apartheid issue in South Africa.

The white minority government in Pretoria was delegitimized and the national liberation movements popularized at the UN as "the authentic representatives of the peoples as a whole."[34] Apartheid was defined as a unique form of international aggression and the UN passed an avalanche of resolutions branding it a "crime against humanity" and a "threat to international peace and security."[35] During the volatile 1980s, the UN repeatedly urged the end of the apartheid government's state of emergency, the release of Nelson Mandela and other political prisoners, and negotiations to establish a nonracial and representative government in Pretoria.[36]

By 1990, the UN was in the forefront of efforts to support a negotiated settlement in South Africa,[37] and I frequently traveled to the country between 1990 and 1994 in my role as the last chairman of the UN Special Committee against Apartheid, to encourage both sides to pursue a durable peace settlement. The collapse of the negotiations process in 1992, however, raised fears within the UN. The African National Congress called for a more direct UN role and specifically requested that the UN begin monitoring the violence in the country. By 1993, the UN Secretary-General, Boutros Boutros-Ghali, had appointed a special representative to South Africa, Angela King, to support the democratic transition in the country.[38]

The UN Observer Mission in South Africa (UNOMSA) sent civilian observers to monitor political rallies and acted primarily within the parameters of South Africa's National Peace Accord structures. UNOMSA observers regularly reported to the UN Secretary-General; actively supported local efforts to resolve disputes and promote reconciliation; and established and maintained contact with all parties and facilitated contact between the parties, intervening when appropriate.[39]

Toward the end of the UN mission, the former Algerian foreign minister, and peripatetic and skillful diplomat Lakhdar Brahimi, succeeded Angela King as the Secretary-General's special representative in South Africa. During the historic elections of 26 to 29 April 1994 in which Nelson Mandela became president,[40] the UN and other international bodies were responsible for administering and verifying the polls. The UN General Assembly had approved a budget of $40 million for UNOMSA's operations.

The UN and the DRC

After decades of autocratic rule by Mobutu Sese Seko, the balance of forces in Zaire was radically altered by the mid-1990s. Laurent Kabila's

Alliance of Democratic Forces for the Liberation of Congo-Zaire mounted a rebellion against Mobutu. By 1997, Zaire was plunged into a bitter civil war and the turbulence spilled over into neighboring states.[41] With the help of Uganda, Rwanda, and Angola, Kabila's revolt grew into full-scale rebellion against Mobutu. On 16 May 1997, the Mobutu era came to an end when the autocrat fled the country.

Laurent Kabila's rule was marked by difficulties before his assassination by his bodyguard in January 2001 and his succession by his son, Joseph Kabila. Barely one year after helping to deliver him to power, Uganda and Rwanda sponsored Congolese Rally for Democracy (RCD) rebels in their bid to topple Laurent Kabila. A countervailing pro-Kabila alliance was formed when Zimbabwe, Namibia, and Angola intervened on the side of the beleaguered ruler of the DRC. The three SADC states condemned what they regarded as an invasion of the DRC by Uganda and Rwanda.

Relations between the Kabila regime and the UN quickly soured, as Kabila continually placed obstacles in the way of the UN mission, which attempted to investigate allegations of human right abuses. In September 1997, Kabila demanded the withdrawal of the UN team from his country.[42] In July 1999, Congo's warring parties signed the Lusaka peace accord, which committed all the warring parties to a cease-fire.[43]

Shortly after the signing of the accord, African states began to canvass the UN for an international peacekeeping operation in the DRC. On 24 February 2000, the UN Security Council agreed to send 5,537 UN observers and troops to Congo to observe the 1999 Lusaka accord.[44] This figure was later reduced to 3,000. MONUC costs an estimated $142 million per annum. Like UNAVEM II in Angola, MONUC seems inadequate to oversee the disarmament of over 100,000 troops and relies heavily for its success on the goodwill of the parties.

The DRC has recently experienced continued instability and some progress in the implementation of the Lusaka agreement. Fighting in Kisangani between rival factions of RCD-Goma resulted in over one hundred deaths and disappearances in May 2002. RCD-Goma has accused the UN of bias and announced that Namanga Ngongi, the special representative of the UN Secretary-General, was "banned" from visiting territories under its control. Though other foreign armies remain in the Congo, Namibia withdrew its contingent in 2001, while Angola and Uganda (which maintains a presence in the northeast) have reduced their presence.

The UN Security Council delegation, with the participation of all fifteen members, visited the Great Lakes region from 27 April to 7 May 2002 and proposed the establishment of a "curtain" of troops along the Congo's borders with Rwanda, Burundi, and Uganda as a way of facilitating the withdrawal of all foreign troops. This proposal is still under review and, if implemented, it could help build the confidence necessary for foreign troop withdrawals. The UN currently has 3,804 troops in the DRC, though their logistics backup remains a major challenge. One sign of optimism is that the cease-fire has generally held among most of the Congo's factions.

The Inter-Congolese dialogue, involving 358 delegates of the DRC's warring parties, political parties, and civil society representatives, took place in Sun City, South Africa, between 25 February and 18 April 2002, under the chairmanship of Sir Ketumile Masire. It resulted in the adoption of thirty resolutions on political, legal, economic, security, and cultural issues, and it proposed a power-sharing agreement under which Joseph Kaliba would continue as president with a Congolese Liberation Movement–nominated prime minister until elections are held after thirty months. The Rwandan-backed RCD refused to sign the agreement. The government in Kinsasha, however, signed the accord with other rebel groups. The signatories of this agreement control about 70 percent of the Congo's territory.

In July 2002, a potentially groundbreaking deal was brokered in South Africa by President Thabo Mbeki (with the blessing of Secretary-General Kofi Annan) between Rwanda's Paul Kagame and Joseph Kaliba. Under the deal, Rwanda withdrew its forces from the DRC in exchange for the disarming of Hutu militias by the Kinshasa government, with the UN monitoring the agreement's implementation. The successful implementation of this agreement could resolve one of the most intractable issues of the DRC conflict, allowing the UN an opportunity to oversee the end of the Congo's destructive civil conflict, which, by some estimates, has claimed over 2.5 million lives. In addition, the Secretary-General established a new mission to succeed the UN Office in Angola. The new mission has two main components: one for political, military, and human rights and the other for humanitarian and economic recovery and development tasks. Both components are coordinated and headed by a special representative of the Secretary-General. Between September and November 2002, I served in this capacity.

Toward a SADC/UN Security Partnership

It is clear from the SADC's changing security role and the UN's experiences in southern Africa that, though the SADC and the UN have not worked closely in the security field, there is a basis for such collaboration between the organizations. The legal basis for such cooperation is enshrined in Chapter VIII of the UN Charter, which is dedicated to regional security arrangements. Article 52 of Chapter VIII of the charter encourages the development of regional organizations for the purpose of maintaining international peace and security, provided that such arrangements or agencies and their activities are consistent with the purposes and principles of the UN. In the same article, the UN Security Council is mandated to encourage the development of pacific settlement of disputes through regional arrangements. These are underutilized provisions of the charter. In order to enhance effective cooperation between the UN and the SADC in the framework of peacekeeping and peacemaking, we offer three policy recommendations.

First, the UN should put in place mechanisms for enhancing the capacity of regional organizations like the SADC to undertake peacekeeping operations. The UN possesses experience and expertise that can be passed on to regional organizations, including training courses, workshops, and seminars on relevant aspects of peacekeeping operations.

Second, there should be better and more systematic coordination between the UN and regional organizations like the SADC. Under normal circumstances, the UN and regional organizations have very little regular contact; only during crises does cooperation increase. Recent examples of cooperation include the joint deployment of UN and Economic Community of West African States Cease-Fire Monitoring Group military personnel in Liberia and Sierra Leone, and UN and OAU personnel in Rwanda and Ethiopia-Eritrea. This cooperation has often taken place after hostilities have erupted. Ideally, there should be regular contact between the UN and Africa's regional organizations in order to develop common early warning mechanisms and to devise preventive strategies and planning for military operations.

In this regard, a number of organizations and state entities in the SADC region have undertaken initiatives to prepare their nationals to participate in peacekeeping operations through seminars and courses. These include the Zimbabwe Staff College, the SADC Peacekeeping Training Centre, the African Centre for the Constructive Resolution of Disputes, and the Center for Peace Initiatives. It is important that the knowledge acquired and suggestions made during these regional meetings are linked to policy implementation. This is an area that merits further exploration by the UN and the SADC so as to promote positive and mutually rewarding collaboration.

The third recommendation to strengthen UN/SADC security cooperation would involve regional organizations such as the SADC playing important roles with the UN in efforts to control the proliferation of illicit arms and in the disarmament of armed combatants. The UN and the SADC must assess the experiences of disarmament, demobilization, rehabilitation, and reintegration in countries like Angola, Mozambique, and Namibia and make recommendations to guide their future actions. This is certainly an area of common interest in which close partnership between the UN and the SADC can help achieve substantial results.

Conclusion

The UN, SADC, and other regional organizations in Africa should develop a common understanding of the interrelatedness of the challenges of peacemaking, peacebuilding, and preventive diplomacy beyond strictly peacekeeping operations in Africa. Keeping the peace does not start with the arrival of a peacekeeping force, nor does it end with its departure. Peacekeeping forces have the function of securing a minimal condition of peace to allow parties space and time to work together to rebuild their countries. This effort, however, needs to continue even after the departure of peacekeeping forces. Moreover, efforts at restoring peace in Africa are unlikely to succeed unless the root causes of conflicts are properly addressed.[45]

This point was highlighted in the Secretary-General Kofi Annan's report on "The Causes of Conflict and the Promotion of Durable Peace and Sustainable Development in Africa" of April 1998, which explicitly noted the link between peace and development.[46] The most serious disenchantment with the existing political order in many African countries emanates from problems of power sharing, religious intolerance, ethnic chauvinism, political marginalization, and the mismanagement of national resources. The Secretary-General's report of September 1999 therefore recommended that "good governance," the promotion of public health priorities, and a focus on social justice and human rights, are essential ingredients for promoting durable peace and security in Africa. Kofi Annan also urged the international community to support the efforts of African governments by providing more development aid and debt relief.

In concluding this chapter, it is important to note that there is a growing belief, in the UN and elsewhere, that the concept of security is far more than a military or police exercise or an exclusive preserve of the military. With particular reference to Africa, security can only be achieved through a combination of efforts in the military, political, social, economic, and environmental spheres. This is why the UN will remain engaged in all these spheres of social interaction to build synergies particularly between the global body, the SADC, and civil society actors in southern Africa. There can be no durable peace and security without both justice and development, and at the heart of this imperative is "good governance." The SADC and the UN have complementary roles to play in promoting good governance, development, peace, and security for the benefit of the peoples of southern Africa.

Notes

1. Charter of the United Nations, 26 June 1945.

2. See Jakkie Cilliers, *Building Security in Southern Africa: An Update on the Evolving Architecture*, ISS Monograph Series no. 43, Institute for Security Studies, November 1999, and Cedric de Coning, "Breaking the SADC Organ Impasse: Report of a Seminar on the Operationalisation of the SADC Organ," ACCORD Occasional Paper no. 6, African Centre for the Constructive Resolution of Disputes, 1999.

3. See key economic, social, and environmental indicators, military expenditure (as a percentage of GDP) for 1990–1991 published in SADC, "Subregional Report Implementation of Agenda 21: Review of Progress Made Since the United Nations Conference on Environment and Development, 1992," UN Commission on Sustainable Development, fifth session, New York, 7–25 April 1997 [available at: www.un.org/dpcsd/earthsummit].

4. See Steven Friedman, Chris Landsberg, Zondi Masiza, and Maxine Reitzes, "State of Anxiety? Reconstructing the State, Democratisation and Economic Growth in Southern Africa," Centre for Policy Studies, Johannesburg, April 1999, 16.

5. See, for example, Deon Geldenhuys, *The Diplomacy of Isolation: South Africa's Foreign Policy Making* (Johannesburg: Macmillan, 1994); also see James Barber and John Barratt, *South Africa's Foreign Policy 1948–88: The Search for Status and Security* (Johannesburg: Southern Book Publishers; Cambridge: Cambridge University Press, 1988), and Joseph Hanlon, *Apartheid's Second Front: South Africa's War Against Its Neighbours* (London: Penguin Books, 1986).

6. See UN Secretary-General Kofi Annan's report, "We the Peoples: The Role of the United Nations in the 21st Century," presented at the millennium summit, New York, 6–8 September 2000, on the eve of the first UN General Assembly of the new millennium [available at: www.un.org/millennium/sg/report/].

7. For a perspective on the HIV/AIDS debate in southern Africa see Prega Ramsamy, "SADC: The Way Forward," in *Regional Integration in Southern Africa, Comparative Perspectives,* ed. Christopher Clapham, Gregg Mills, Anna Morner, and Elizabeth Sidiropolous (Johannesburg: South African Institute of International Affairs, 2001), 33–42.

8. See Beverly Peters, "HIV/AIDS: Uniting and Dividing South Africa and the United States," in *The Reality Behind the Rhetoric: The United States, South Africa, and Africa,* ed. Greg Mills and John Stremlau (Johannesburg: South African Institute of International Affairs, and Washington, D.C.: Centre for Strategic and International Studies, 2000), 97–110.

9. See Mark Shaw, "Organised Crime and State Responses in Southern Africa," in Christopher Clapham et al., *Regional Integration,* 115–120.

10. See Anthony Ginsberg, *South Africa's Future: From Crisis to Prosperity* (Basingstoke, UK, and London: Pan Macmillan, 1998).

11. See Christopher Clapham, "The United Nations and Peacekeeping in Africa," in *Whither Peacekeeping in Africa?* ed. Mark Malan (Halfway House, South Africa: Institute for Security Studies, 1999), 25–44; also see Oliver Furley and Roy May, eds., *Peacekeeping in Africa* (Aldershot, UK: Ashgate, 1998); Marrack Goulding, "The United Nations and Conflict in Africa Since the Cold War," *African Affairs* 98, 391 (April 1999): 155–166; and Agostinho Zacarias, *The United Nations and International Peacekeeping* (London: I. B. Tauris, 1996).

12. See Adekeye Adebajo and Chris Landsberg, "Back to the Future: UN

Peacekeeping in Africa," in *Managing Armed Conflicts in the 21st Century,* ed. Adekeye Adebajo and Chandra Lekha Sriram (London: Frank Cass, 2001).

13. UN General Assembly, "Report on the Panel on UN Peace Operations," document A/55/305, New York, 17 August 2000.

14. International Peace Academy and Center on International Cooperation, "Refashioning the Dialogue: Regional Perspectives on the Brahimi Report on UN Peace Operations," regional meetings in Johannesburg, Buenos Aires, Singapore and London, February–March 2001.

15. See Peter Katjavivi, *A History of Resistance in Namibia* (London: James Currey; Paris: UNESCO; Addis Ababa: OAU, 1988).

16. John Barratt, "Outlook on Namibian Independence: Some Domestic Constraints," *International Affairs Bulletin* 7, 1 (1983).

17. See Margaret J. Anstee, "Angola: The Forgotten Tragedy, a Test Case for UN Peacekeeping," in *International Relations* 11, 6 (December 1993); also see Virginia Page Fortna, "United Nations Angola Verification Mission I," in *The Evolution of UN Peacekeeping,* ed. William Durch (New York: St. Martin's, 1993), 376–405.

18. Moisés Venâncio and Carla MacMillan, "Portuguese Mediation in the Angolan Conflict in 1990–91," in *Mediation in Southern Africa,* ed. Stephen Chan and Vivienne Jabri (London and Basingstoke, UK: Macmillan, 1993), 105.

19. "The Blue Helmets Return," *Africa Confidential* 40, 24 (December 1999).

20. Alex Vines, "Angola: 40 Years of War," *Track Two* 9, 2 (2000).

21. UN Department of Public Information, "The UN and the Situation in Angola, May 1991–June 1994," reference paper, New York, 1994.

22. See Margaret Anstee, *Orphan of the Cold War: The Inside Story of the Collapse of the Angolan Peace Process, 1992–93* (Basingstoke, UK: Macmillan, 1996).

23. See, for example, William Finnegan, *A Complicated War: The Harrowing of Mozambique* (Berkeley and Los Angeles: University of California Press, 1992); and Alex Vines, *RENAMO: Terrorism in Mozambique* (Bloomington and Indianapolis: Indiana University Press, 1991).

24. Moisés Venâncio, "Mediation by the Roman Catholic Church in Mozambique, 1988–91," in Chan and Jabri, *Mediation in Southern Africa,* 147.

25. See Andrea Bartoli, "Mediating Peace in Mozambique: The Role of the Community of Sant'Egidio," in *Herding Cats: Multiparty Mediation in a Complex World,* ed. Chester Crocker, Fen Osler Hampson, and Pamela Aall (Washington, D.C.: U.S. Institute of Peace, 1999), 245–273.

26. Hasu P. Patel, "Zimbabwe's Mediation in Mozambique and Angola, 1989–91," in Chan and Jabri, *Mediation in Southern Africa,* 119.

27. UN Department for Public Information, "The United Nations and Mozambique 1992–95," New York, 1995, 4; Chris Landsberg, "Directing from the Stalls? The International Community and South Africa's Multi-Party Negotiations Forum," in *The Small Miracle: South Africa's Negotiated Settlement,* ed. Steven Friedman and Doreen Atkinson (Johannesburg: Raven Press, 1994), 287.

28. Venâncio, "Mediation by the Roman Catholic Church," 166.

29. UN Department for Public Information, "United Nations and Mozambique," 4.

30. Philip Sibanda, "Lessons from UN Peacekeeping in Africa: From UNAVEM to MONUA," in *From Peacekeeping to Complex Emergencies: Peace Support Missions in Africa,* Jakkie Cilliers and Greg Mills (Johannesburg: South

African Institute of International Affairs; Pretoria: Institute for Security Studies, 1999), 123.

31. See Aldo Ajello, "Mozambique: Implementation of the 1992 Agreement," in Crocker, Hampson, and Aall, *Herding Cats,* 619–642.

32. Chris Alden, "Bullets, Ballots and Bread," paper presented at the International Workshop on Southern Africa After Democratization, Tokyo, January 1996, 34.

33. Chris Landsberg and Mark Suzman, "South Africa's Quest for Democracy," *Oxford International Review* 11, 3 (1992): 27.

34. Ibid.

35. See Chris Landsberg, "Exporting Peace? The UN and South Africa." *Policy: Issues and Actors* (Center for Policy Studies, Johannesburg) 7, 2 (April 1994): 2.

36. Ibrahim A. Gambari, "Apartheid and Current Developments Inside South Africa: The Role of the United Nations," lecture given to the African Studies Group, Fletcher School of Law and Diplomacy, Medford, Massachusetts, 30 April 1993, 7.

37. UN General Assembly, "Declaration on Apartheid and Its Destructive Consequences in Southern Africa," New York, December 1989.

38. UN Secretary-General, "Report on the Question of South Africa," UN General Assembly and Security Council, New York, 10 January 1994.

39. See Mark Shaw, "Crying Peace Where There Is None? The Functioning and Future of Local Peace Committees of the National Peace Accord," Transition Series Research Report no. 31, Centre for Policy Studies, Johannesburg, August 1993.

40. For an eyewitness account, see Ibrahim Gambari, "To Pretoria and Back," *West Africa*, 3999 (23–29 May 1994): 906–907.

41. Claude Kabemba, "Whither the DRC? Causes of the Conflict in the Democratic Republic of Congo, and the Way Forward," *Policy: Issues and Actors* (Center for Policy Studies, Johannesburg) 11, 6 (March 1999).

42. See Musifiky Mwanasali, "Peacebuilding in the Democratic Republic of Congo," Policy Briefing Series, International Peace Academy, New York, April 1998.

43. International Crisis Group (ICG), "The Agreement on a Ceasefire in the Democratic Republic of Congo: An Analysis of the Agreement and Prospects for Peace," ICG Democratic Republic of Congo Report no. 5, Brussels, 20 August 1999.

44. UN Secretary-General, Report on preliminary deployment in the Democratic Republic of Congo, 15 July 1999, S/1999/790.

45. See Elizabeth Cousens and Chetan Kumar, eds., *Peacebuilding as Politics* (Boulder, Colo.: Lynne Rienner Publishers, 2001), and Olara Otunu and Michael Doyle, eds., *Peacemaking and Peacekeeping for the New Century* (Lanham, Md.: Rowman and Littlefield, 1998).

46. Kofi Annan, "The Causes of Conflict and the Promotion of Durable Peace and Sustainable Development in Africa," Report of the Secretary-General, United Nations, New York, 1998; also see Kofi Annan, "Durable Peace and Sustainable Development in Africa," in *South African Journal of International Affairs* 7, 1 (Summer 2000).

13

The United States

JENDAYI E. FRAZER

The relationship between the United States and the Southern African Development Community (SADC) turns on questions of political purpose, policy process, and programmatic resources. At the second SADC–U.S. forum, held in Maputo, Mozambique, in May 2000, the president of Mozambique, Joaquim Chissano, hailed the forum as a "shining example of partnership between the United States and SADC."[1] Indeed, regular dialogue forums have become measures of progress rather than assessments of concrete actions that "enhance the welfare of the people of SADC and the United States." Advancing the U.S.–SADC relationship beyond symbolic dialogue requires articulation of an explicit strategic rationale for partnership, commitment to organizational change, and provision of adequate resources from all sides to establish strong institutional linkages. What explains the current gap between rhetoric and action in building a U.S.–SADC partnership?

First, the Frontline States' loose security alliance has not been replaced with the functioning security framework provided by the SADC Organ for Politics, Defense, and Security Cooperation (OPDSC). The failure of SADC member states to act with collective purpose on security was dramatically illustrated by their division on whether to intervene militarily or pursue a diplomatic approach in the Democratic Republic of Congo (DRC) war. U.S. officials and constituents opposed to the funding of African subregional organizations point to intra-SADC divisions over the OPDS and the DRC as evidence of the futility of investing in capacity-building for African subregional cooperation and collective action on security. U.S. critics often conveniently ignore evidence of positive regional security coordination provided, for example, by the SADC Inter-State Defence and Security Committee (ISDSC).[2] The ratification by the SADC heads of state and government summit in August 2001 in Blantyre, Malawi, of the recommendation that the OPDSC would account to the heads of state and government summit, and the election of President Chissano of Mozambique to chair the OPDSC with President Benjamin Mkapa of Tanzania as his deputy, will hopefully go a long way toward proving the critics wrong.

Second, many SADC members remain suspicious of U.S. intentions in southern Africa. This is largely due to the U.S. history of supporting the British and Portuguese colonial regimes in Rhodesia, Mozambique, and Angola in the 1960s and 1970s; the minority government in South Africa during apartheid; and the National Union for the Total Independence of Angola insurgents through the 1980s. As a result, U.S. failure to back its rhetorical commitments and programs with adequate resources is often interpreted as reflecting some hidden motives or sinister imperialist purpose. SADC officials and constituents opposed to U.S. influence in the subregion ignore the fundamental change in the United States' Africa policy away from colonial "spheres of influence" and Cold War "communist containment" orientations. Regional critics approach the U.S. government as a unitary actor whose every action reflects an intended purpose rather than acknowledging that, like that of all other governments, U.S. policy is the (often incoherent) product of multiple competing interests and their actions. These sometimes reflect the failed or partial execution of policy directives. This chapter clearly demonstrates that the U.S. government is not monolithic in carrying out its Africa policy.[3]

The chapter focuses on closing the gap between U.S. intentions, actions, and resources in building a strong security partnership with the SADC. It highlights, in particular, the U.S. intragovernmental political-military dynamics shaping its security engagement with the SADC. It also emphasizes peacekeeping operations as the "hard test" for building a U.S.–SADC partnership in the future.

The chapter moves from a discussion of U.S. interests in the subregion to an analysis of the institutional constraints on achieving a coherent policy approach and engagement strategy backed by sufficient resources to advance U.S. goals and objectives in southern Africa. It outlines U.S. interests in subregional security. It identifies areas of commonality and disagreement with SADC members that must be addressed in order to lay a solid foundation or rationale for a U.S.–SADC strategic partnership. It then examines the policy formulation process during President Bill Clinton's administration, revealing the competing institutional interests that must be managed in order to establish a coherent and sustainable approach in southern Africa. Finally, it details the Clinton administration's resources and U.S. security and military engagement programs. It suggests that the Bush administration must realistically align its expectations to shape the region with the resources it will actually invest.

The chapter concludes with a recommendation that the political and military infrastructure for security cooperation be established through confidence-building measures, regulatory mechanisms, and peace enforcement capability. While every "partnership" is two-sided, this chapter scrutinizes the U.S. policy process in order to enhance understanding and advance U.S.–SADC relations beyond the often unspoken, yet pervasive historical mistrust and suspicion that block the development of constructive, mutually beneficial relations.

U.S. Interests: A Strategic Rationale for SADC Partnership

U.S. foreign policy during the Clinton administration was guided by the White House's National Security Strategy. This identified U.S. national interests, core objectives, and regional priorities. During the Clinton administration, U.S. national security interests were divided into three categories or tiers: vital interests, important national interests, and humanitarian and other interests. In practice, *vital interests* referred to the core security objective of protecting U.S. national survival and the physical defense of the homeland and of North Atlantic Treaty Organization allies. European stability was prioritized in the National Security Strategy as vital to U.S. security. *Important national interests* largely referred to the core economic objective of promoting U.S. prosperity through efforts at home and abroad. Europe and Asia Pacific were prioritized as key regions for U.S. trade and commercial activities. The promotion of democracy, human rights, and respect for the rule of law were core objectives dictated by U.S. *humanitarian interests*. Africa largely fell within this category, with U.S. engagement driven by some sense that U.S. national values demand action. Although this was not explicitly stated, Africa ranked last in the five regional listings in the security strategy: Europe and Eurasia; East Asia and the Pacific; the Western Hemisphere (Latin America, Caribbean, Canada); the Middle East, North Africa, Southwest Asia and South Asia; Africa.[4]

The fact that Africa historically comes last in U.S. geostrategic regional priorities is essential to understanding the internal U.S. policy process determining the type and level of its engagement on the continent, specifically in southern Africa. Explaining U.S.–Africa policy requires three levels of analysis:

1. The overall approach to sub-Saharan Africa (low priority, low resources).
2. Distinct subregional strategies (of which southern Africa is the most integrated).
3. Individual policies toward specific African countries (South Africa

and Nigeria are prioritized as pivotal states) and SADC members (the U.S. focus is on South Africa, Botswana, Zimbabwe, and Angola).

U.S. Security Interests in Africa

African nations provide little or no direct military threat to the United States, but various transnational threats do exist to U.S. interests from organized crime, narcotics and small arms trafficking, terrorism, disease, and degradation of critical natural resources. In addition, political and social instability, ethnic strife, and other sources of conflict sometimes threaten U.S. nationals and property interests in Africa. Multinational terrorist organizations clearly have the capacity and will to threaten and strike at U.S. interests in Africa. For some U.S. officials, the August 1998 embassy bombings in east Africa signaled the growing futility of treating any region as entirely outside the United States' vital national security objective of protecting its citizens and facilities (see Box 13.1). However, the real issue is not recognizing that vital (Tier 1) U.S. security interests are threatened globally, but understanding the way in which regional rankings dictate the type of response. In Africa, the United States protects its citizens mainly through noncombatant evacuation operations, and most of its strategic oil resources in Africa come from offshore (more secure) drilling. Thus, preventing and responding to Africa's transnational security threats supports broader American objectives to promote democracy and free trade on the continent.

U.S. Interests in the SADC

The United States has a compelling concrete self-interest in the progress of the SADC. First, regional integration offers the promise of access to a large commercial market sustained by politically stable member states. Realizing this trade potential rests on fostering a more secure environment—especially ending the wars in Angola and the DRC; containing escalating social tensions in Zimbabwe; and preventing them in South Africa. Second, investing in the capacity of African national armies and subregional organizations to prevent, manage, and resolve conflicts and to carry out peace operations will reduce pressure on U.S. forces to conduct reactive noncombatant evacuation and humanitarian relief operations. Third, combating transnational threats—deadly diseases, environmental degradation, organized crime, terrorists, and arms proliferation—necessitates a collective regional and global approach.

Box 13.1 U.S. Security Goals in Africa

U.S. values compel humanitarian action in Africa by assisting countries in responding to man-made and natural disasters, environmental degradation, contagious disease epidemics, and refugee flows.

U.S. global vital interests mirrored in Africa:

- Protecting U.S. citizens and nationals and, as appropriate, U.S. facilities. Includes planning for the conduct of noncombatent evacuation.
- Combating terrorism and international crime (and its sponsors) directed against the United States and its citizens.
- Protecting access to strategic natural resources vital to the United States, especially oil resources that supply over 13 percent of U.S. demand (compared with 17 percent from the entire Middle East).
- Preventing the proliferation of nuclear, biological, and chemical weapons and their delivery; deter their use or threatened use against the United States or its vital interests; and being prepared to counter the use of such weapons through a combination of offensive and defensive measures, including counterforce, active defense, and passive defense.
- Maintaining freedom of access to international water and airways.

The core U.S. security objective is promoting regional stability:

- Developing apolitical professional militaries under civilian authority that respect human rights and the rule of law.
- Enhancing African military peacekeeping and conflict-management capabilities by improving the capabilities of countries and regional organizations to conduct peace operations and respond to humanitarian disasters.
- Building capable security partners and cooperative security arrangements to defuse cross-border tensions while addressing the underlying, legitimate security concerns of neighboring states.

Cooperative Security Against Transnational Threats

During the second SADC–U.S. forum in May 2000, the deputy secretary of state in the Clinton administration, Strobe Talbott, articulated the above interests in calling for U.S.–SADC progress in four areas:

1. Promoting the SADC's regional economic integration.
2. Strengthening the region's ability to address security challenges.
3. Tackling the scourge of HIV/AIDS.
4. Building the capacity to prepare for and manage disasters.[5]

One year later, in May 2001, the U.S. secretary of state, Colin Powell, also stated that the United States would champion the SADC's efforts to promote stabilizing economic integration, establish a free trade area among its members, develop a greater indigenous peacekeeping capability, promote good governance and economic reform, and help fight HIV/AIDS.[6]

This list of common goals reflects an emerging consensus that African societies and the international community must adopt a more integrated political, economic, and security approach to collectively address transnational threats to security, national development, and global peace. U.S. and SADC officials can agree that the halting progress toward democracy and sustainable development in the region directly undermines regional stability and that most wars in Africa are, at their core, conflicts over material resources and political access. A key element of a strategic rationale for U.S.–SADC partnership is the understanding that the long-term collective security of the subregion depends on SADC countries—in concert with international actors—building institutions and regional security arrangements to prevent and settle conflicts without resorting to violence. However, while the U.S. and SADC members can agree on both Talbott's and Powell's lists of general mutual interests, translating these into operational plans is far more difficult. For example, the early planning and implementation of the African Crisis Response Initiative (ACRI) resulted in much confusion, miscommunication, and suspicion and ultimately in the SADC (except Malawi) rejecting the United States' major African peacekeeping training program.[7]

African Solutions to African Problems

Mutual interests alone cannot provide a strategic basis for a U.S.–SADC partnership. Instead, a clear understanding is needed of what all sides concretely or materially gain from cooperation and what all are willing to sacrifice to forge a sustainable relationship (i.e., what the burden-sharing compact involves). The United States seeks to limit its military exposure or peacekeeping deployments in the subregion by supporting the SADC's regional conflict management, prevention, and response capabilities. SADC members largely seek U.S. diplomatic support and material resources for the goals and objectives set by the region, rather than by Washington.

Peacekeeping is the issue of greatest potential contention between the United States and the SADC. The current state of affairs entails the United States offering financial assistance and, where appropriate, logistical support, especially airlift and communications, but not ground troops for African regional peacekeeping efforts.[8] African officials believe that the United States has a global responsibility, as a UN member, to fully support peace operations (including combat troops) on the continent as elsewhere.[9] For a strategic partnership to work, the United States must sacrifice the level of diplomatic influence it expects to exercise over regional decisions and the SADC must sacrifice the amount of military and financial support expected from the United States. Essentially, both sides must come to a common understanding of what "African solutions to African problems" actually means. As a first step to meaningful strategic partnership, the SADC must continue with efforts to operationalize the OPDS, and the Bush administration should target limited resources in support of the SADC's homegrown initiatives that are consistent with U.S. interests and objectives.

U.S. Focus on Select SADC Member States

Both Africa's large size and limited U.S. financial assistance necessitate the UN and U.S. trans-Atlantic allies working together to leverage scarce resources. In addition, a selective U.S. engagement strategy in Africa's subregions is widely recognized as a way to concentrate U.S. resources effectively. However, with the exception of South Africa and Nigeria, there was no full agreement within the Clinton administration on which countries should receive focused attention. The State Department's African Affairs Office has never developed an operational strategy to guide its (and other agencies') allocation of resources. The African Affairs Office of the Department of Defense (DOD), which sets U.S.–Africa security policy for the Office of the Secretary of Defense, prioritized South Africa, Angola, Zimbabwe, and Botswana for focused attention in southern Africa. The U.S. European Command (USEUCOM), which is responsible for planning, organizing, and overseeing operational military engagement activities for most African countries, selected South Africa, Botswana, and Zimbabwe as focus countries "based on an assessment of how they support broad US and USEUCOM policy objectives."[10] The Bush administration's engagement strategy in the subregion has yet to emerge fully, except the continued understanding of South Africa's strategic importance.

A strategy of focused or selective engagement has its critics. First, some U.S. officials argue that universal coverage is the best way of ensuring U.S. influence across Africa, especially where governments and institutions are unstable and can change almost overnight. Second, selecting countries for "special" attention can contribute to intra-SADC tensions and divisions, as members vie for leadership and compete for external funding and resources. U.S. officials are especially sensitive to how a close diplomatic relationship with South Africa could raise suspicion and resentment with the unintended potential consequence of undermining South Africa's subregional leadership. Neither objection addresses the fundamental strategic premise that maximizing limited resources requires a U.S. security policy that engages subregional organizations and selected "anchor" or "focus" states in coordination with multilateral international initiatives.

The Bush administration should establish explicit and transparent criteria for determining anchor countries based on:

1. Their impact on the subregion (size of their population, territory, and economy and their military and democratic record).
2. U.S. strategic interests (size of the resident U.S. citizen population, the amount of U.S. commercial investments, access to oil, and whether the countries are stable democracies).

Under this scheme we can expect South Africa, Angola, Zimbabwe, and Botswana to stand out among the SADC's fourteen members as candidates for focused U.S. engagement. Angola and Zimbabwe are currently the most problematic countries for advancing U.S. core objectives—democracy, prosperity, and security. South Africa is the United States' largest trading partner in sub-Saharan Africa and has the armed forces and appropriate military capability to play a lead role in regional peace operations. Botswana is viewed as an island of democratic political and economic stability in the subregion. Angola's promise as a major oil producer has only grown with new oil discoveries off its coast. Zimbabwe has the second largest diversified economy in southern Africa and remained an attractive destination for U.S. citizens and commercial investments until the 2000 postelection political turmoil and a declining, war-burdened economy. The criteria should be applied flexibly with, for example, Mozambique deserving substantial support for its positive political and economic reform record over the past ten years. The overall goal remains to pursue a foundation level of engagement across the continent but also to maximize resource efficiency and policy effectiveness by pursuing focused strategic engagement with countries clearly well positioned on the continent to have a long-term stabilizing regional and subregional influence.

The Clinton Administration: A House Divided

The Bush administration can, and should, learn some important lessons from the Clinton administration's Africa policy. The Clinton administration's foreign policy has been widely criticized as ad hoc and reactive, responding to new emergencies on the basis of "best lessons" from past crises. Somalia (1992–1994) and Rwanda (1994) are the two experiences that most colored policy discussions on U.S. military engagement in Africa. Since Somalia, and despite the Rwanda genocide, the Clinton administration did not establish a coherent Africa security policy. The problem persisted beyond the post-Somalia paralysis and reflected unresolved internal policy divisions within the Clinton administration and resource constraints on the conduct of U.S. foreign affairs. Both problems are illustrated here by reference to the fashioning of U.S. policy in the UN peace operations in Sierra Leone and the DRC. This section can help to build realistic expectations between the United States and SADC members on the evolution of U.S. policy and concrete actions and assistance available for strengthening regional security cooperation in southern Africa.

Bureaucratic Policy Divisions

The African Affairs and Global Affairs bureaus within the State Department, Defense Department, and National Security Council (NSC) learned different "best lessons" from the peacekeeping debacles in Somalia and Rwanda. Somalia seems to have fundamentally shaped the global affairs bureaus' approach to UN peacekeeping, especially in Africa. Rwanda crystallized an African subregional capacity-building orientation for the regional bureaus. The primary lesson from Somalia for the global affairs bureaus—the DOD's Peacekeeping Office, the State Department's International Organization Affairs Bureau, and the NSC's Multilateral Affairs Office—was "to avoid overextending the UN where it is not in a position to do the job and to pick up the pieces."[11]

African operations were considered the most likely to overexpose the UN in situations where there is no peace to keep and the UN does not have the combat ability to enforce peace on the warring parties. The global affairs bureaus fulfill their "mission" to protect UN peacekeeping—especially in the face of strong congressional opposition—by applying strict criteria set out in Presidential Decision Directive 25 (PDD 25) before approving any operations as a member of the UN Security Council.[12] In effect, the global bureaus' post-Somalia posture was a predisposition to oppose or barely support UN peace operations on the continent, and the de facto starting point for U.S. decisionmakers was "no U.S. boots on African soil."

The African Affairs bureaus, especially in the State Department and NSC, were less concerned with "protecting" the UN from "messy" operations and more concerned with coming to terms with "best lessons" from the international failure to respond to the Rwanda genocide in 1994. They viewed their mission as fulfilling the "never again" pledge that Clinton made during his 1998 visit to Kigali. The African Crisis Response Initiative was developed in this spirit in 1996, when many feared an impending genocide in Burundi. The ACRI became the U.S. government's flagship African peacekeeping training program and was funded at an annual cost of approximately $20 million. It expended some $75 million since its inception in

1997 and trained approximately 6,000 peacekeepers from eight African militaries, mainly from West Africa. The ACRI's battalion and command post training exercises were intended to increase African capacity to participate in peacekeeping. However, the original concept was to establish a rapidly deployable Africa Crisis Response Force capable of peace enforcement. The Clinton administration was divided over whether and how to transform the ACRI program to provide the combat training and security assistance to create the type of units needed for peace enforcement in any future genocidal contingencies, and in Sierra Leone, where the Revolutionary United Front (RUF) violated the terms of the Lomé peace agreement and attacked peacekeepers with the UN Mission in Sierra Leone (UNAMSIL).[13]

In addition to building the ACRI program, the State Department, DOD, and NSC African Affairs bureaus pushed for U.S. leadership to build regional and multinational coalitions that could marshal properly trained, equipped, and funded troops to keep or enforce the peace in Africa. Internationally, peace operations led by subregional organizations and ad hoc regional coalitions constitute an emerging trend for places like Sierra Leone and the DRC, where mass communal violence and widespread human rights abuses occur.[14] Indeed, a bipartisan consensus is slowly emerging within the U.S. government that international and regional coalition-building is the key to effective peacekeeping, especially where U.S. vital strategic interests are not at stake. One senior official responsible for U.S. global peacekeeping policy in the Clinton administration stated the dilemma thus:

> How do we confront the consequences of political violence and its aftermath (violent aftermath) where [the U.S. government is] reluctant to commit U.S. forces to peace-enforcement exercises based on appropriate vital interests calculations? The options are as follows:
>
> 1. Since we are not involved in classic peacekeeping in most of Africa we might walk away and disguise this as something else (and there are many ways to dress it up). Basically, we could leave conflicts like Sierra Leone to their own fate.
>
> 2. In failed states and ongoing conflicts where the protagonists are not clearly defined, the United States can play a continued role in deterring or pressuring the protagonists and dealing with domestic political constituents. Basically, the pursuance of a diplomatic engagement approach.
>
> 3. Where the United States is not prepared to commit resources to ensure we prevail, we need to marshal international resources rather than walk away from it. . . . Chapter VII is the key question today and involves the international community imposing its will on the parties. Basically, "blue hatting" regional peace enforcers is crossing a Rubicon that we may need to do.[15]

Again, the Bush administration should note that the evolution of U.S. policy through these three options has been played out in Sierra Leone since 1998. The United States—preoccupied with Kosovo for much of 1998 and 1999—essentially walked away from Sierra Leone under cover of timely official statements from the president and secretary of state denouncing the violence and human rights abuses. In fact, the U.S. assistant secretary of state for African affairs, Susan Rice, testified that the entire fiscal year's allotted voluntary peacekeeping operations (VPKO) budget of approximately $17 million had, by mid-1998, been spent on Sierra Leone.[16] Diplomatic engagement revolved around the three trips of the special envoy, Jesse Jackson, to the region and his slightly more frequent phone calls to regional leaders to broker a cessation of hostilities agreement in May 1999. The final Lomé agreement, signed on 7 July 1999, made the Revolutionary United Front leader Foday Sankoh the vice president and offered the RUF extensive political and economic concessions in order to end the fighting, including four ministerial posts and Sankoh's placement in charge of a new commission to oversee Sierra Leonean diamond areas.

The policy divisions between the global affairs and African affairs bureaus surfaced most sharply in fashioning U.S. policy to support the implementation of the Lomé agreement. The global affairs bureaus initially prevailed to push the U.S. government to resist "blue helmetting" Nigerian/Economic Community of West African States Cease-Fire Monitoring Group (ECOMOG) troops already engaged in Sierra Leone peace operations, in preference for UN troops operating under a Chapter VI mandate from India, Jordan, Kenya, and Ghana. The global affairs bureaus feared Nigerians might act violently or commit extensive human rights abuses, thereby tarnishing the UN's reputation in the course of implementing the Lomé agreement. From the beginning, the African affairs bureaus argued in support of a robust subregional effort, as Nigeria and ECOMOG had already demonstrated the requisite experience and interests to stay the course in Sierra Leone. The African affairs bureaus at the State Department and the NSC argued that "blue helmetting" Nigerian troops would provide ECOMOG with critical international resources to sustain its efforts in the face of newly elected president Olusegun Obasanjo's threat in early 1999 to withdraw all Nigerian troops from Sierra Leone. The bureaus' position, which favored supporting ECOMOG operating under UN authority with a robust mandate and a funding assessment, was tragically vindicated after 500 of the newly deployed UN peacekeepers, with no operational experience in Sierra Leone, were ambushed and held hostage in May 2000.

After UNAMSIL was pinned down by the RUF, the United States rapidly moved to option three, providing $100 million training assistance in support of Nigerian peacekeeping in Sierra Leone. President Clinton asked Secretary of Defense William Cohen to provide the resources needed to equip and train up to seven West African battalions for effective service in UNAMSIL. The U.S. government quickly framed the new policy direction as consistent with its global approach to build regional peacekeeping coalitions with lead regional states, as it did with Australia in the case of East Timor. Both U.S. president George Bush and former vice president Al Gore supported this new regard for building regional capacity. Both are on record saying their administration would rely on regional lead states and subregional military coalitions for peacekeeping, such as Nigeria and ECOMOG for West African peace operations.[17]

What does this mean for U.S.–SADC relations? The Bush administration is already more open to requests for critical resources and assistance (e.g., logistics, airlifts, communications) to strengthen the capacity of regional leaders and functioning subregional collective security organizations. However, limited resources and low expectations for the success of UN peace operations in Africa will persist. The failure of SADC members at the time to establish a functioning security organ and to cooperate to end the regional war in the DRC, the civil war in Angola, and Burundi's insurgency provided a ready rationale to limit U.S. concrete (as distinct from rhetorical) support. The positive movements during 2001 toward operationalizing the OPDSC could go a long way toward helping to build confidence in the SADC. U.S. support for the UN mission in the Democratic Republic of Congo (MONUC) illustrates the point. The former U.S. ambassador to the UN, Richard Holbrooke, clearly stated in a speech in Pretoria, during his December 1999 ten-nation trip to southern and central Africa, that even very limited resources and diplomatic support were contingent on regional progress in conflict resolution:

> Let me turn now to what is perhaps the biggest challenge we may face in Africa in the coming year. I speak of course of the Democratic Republic of the Congo. Last week, the United States joined the other members of the Security Council in approving a resolution that authorizes the UN to begin preparations for deployment of 500 military observers. Preparing for a peacekeeping mission in the Congo, getting it right, is our main focus for the remainder of the trip. The task is truly daunting, as President Mbeki warned us yesterday. But, as he also said, we—the U.S., the United Nations, the international community—must not turn away from this responsibility. . . . But peacekeeping requires more than words, more than paper agreements. The parties to the Lusaka Agreement must respect their commitments if peace is to return to the troubled Congo. The international community cannot simply impose peace in the Congo. What most stands in the way of international efforts to assist the Congo right now—and I say this with great regret—is the actions of some of the parties themselves. The UN cannot alone bring peace to this troubled nation, as we have seen so tragically in three historic failures of the United Nations, in the decade since the end of the Cold War: Somalia, Bosnia, and Rwanda. Two in Africa and one in Europe. And I would add Angola. . . . If the par-

> ties in Congo truly want the international community's involvement and support, such violations of these commitments are simply unacceptable.[18]

U.S. public diplomacy clearly and rightly placed the responsibility for slow progress in implementing the Lusaka accord and establishing MONUC on the shoulders of the parties to the agreement. This included the DRC's SADC coalition partners, Zimbabwe, Angola, and Namibia.[19]

U.S. actions pushing for conflict resolution in the DRC were led by the African affairs offices at the State Department and NSC and involved several fronts:

- Diplomatic support for the efforts of former Zambian president Frederick Chiluba and the SADC summit to reach the Lusaka cease-fire accord.
- Approving the UN Security Council Resolution 1258 to deploy up to ninety military liaison officers to the subregion, and UNSCR 1291 establishing the 500 member MONUC cease-fire observer mission.
- Providing the Joint Military Commission with its first allocation of $1 million (out of $5 million pledged) in financial assistance after gaining congressional approval in December 1999—six months after the cease-fire was signed.

However, many in the United States never expected the parties to the Lusaka accord actually to sign the cease-fire agreement in July. They resisted any serious support planning until after the fifty leaders of the Congolese Rally for Democracy (RCD) signed on 31 August. The global affairs planners at the State Department, DOD, and NSC eventually helped to develop the UN's staged or phased operation concept for the DRC, anticipating that the signatories would be unable to maintain the cease-fire on the ground. The idea was to prevent the need to move beyond MONUC Stage 1, which would involve the deployment of ninety liaison officers. The implementation of either Stage 2 (500 observers and 5,000 international troops) or Stage 3 (15,000-strong peacekeeping force) would have required a more substantial international commitment, including ground force deployments. Skepticism remained throughout the U.S. government about the viability of a UN peacekeeping operation in the DRC because of the huge size of the territory and difficult terrain, the evident lack of political will to end fighting by the signatories, and the robust peace-enforcement mandate needed to deal with the nonsignatories. In the words of one senior Clinton administration official responsible for peacekeeping policy:

> Peace enforcement would require 100,000 troops, and this is not going to happen. No one will contribute the necessary troops. We are working on

> the basis of some willingness on the part of the protagonists/parties to "keep the peace." UN forces and monitors are not in a position to deliver the peace, but they can keep the parties' feet to the fire by monitoring compliance and pressuring them if/when the agreement begins to unravel. The UN will send in many monitors backed up by force.[20]

Resource Constraints

The phased concept of operation was both prudent (consistent with PDD 25) and defensive (slowing U.S. contribution to another UN peacekeeping operation). By mid-1999, U.S. peacekeeping planners and the Contribution to the International Peacekeeping Account (CIPA) were stretched thin, with new UN operations planned for Sierra Leone, Ethiopia-Eritrea, East Timor, and the DRC, and U.S. troops deployed to Bosnia, Kosovo, the Persian Gulf, and Asia.[21]

In 1999, the total global CIPA budget was $219 million, of which African affairs were allocated $29 million; the anticipated cost of UN peacekeeping operations globally in 1999 was $539 million. The MONUC liaison operation was expected to cost between $84 and $120 million in 1999, while the African affairs' combined CIPA and VPKO budget was $48 million in 1999. The 2000 fiscal year request for MONUC was estimated at $4 million in the 150 international affairs budget,[22] perhaps reflecting the judgment of administration officials that the signatories would not provide the environment needed to deploy more UN peacekeepers. The Clinton administration's budget request anticipated an increase in the CIPA to $605 and $739 million in fiscal years 2000 and 2001 to support ongoing UN peacekeeping operations. African UN peace operations were expected to cost $142–190 million in 2000 but only $85 million of combined CIPA and VPKO funds were budgeted for Africa (see Table 13.1).

During the Clinton administration, U.S. resources available to forge new security relations with Africa were very limited and therefore unable effectively to match the scope and magnitude of security threats on the continent.

U.S. Military Engagement in Southern Africa

U.S. national security strategy during the Clinton administration stated that a key U.S. security goal in Africa was to "promote regional stability through engagement with subregional organizations and key African states, using carefully harmonized U.S. government programs and initiatives."[23] The goal was to move away from reactive noncombatant evacuation and humanitarian relief operations to more "shaping engagement" aimed at

Table 13.1 U.S. State Department African Affairs Budget for the 150 International Affairs Account (U.S.$ in millions)

150 International Affairs Account	FY 1998 (actual)	FY 1999 (estimated)	FY 2000
AID-DFA	700	711	745
PL 480 , Title II	421	221	134
PL 480 , Title III	19.8	14.9	0
ESF	26	98	73
MRA	131	136	145
VPKO	17	19	28
CIPA	46	29	57
IMET	8	8	8.5
FMF	17	10	10
NADR	9.6	14.7	16
Total[a]	1,395	1,262	1,217

Notes: FY: fiscal year; AID-DFA: USAID–Development Fund for Africa, development assistance; PL 480: food assistance; ESF: economic support funds; MRA: migration and refugee assistance; VPKO: voluntary peacekeeping operations; CIPA: contributions to international peacekeeping; IMET: international military education and training; FMF: foreign military financing; NADR: nonproliferation, antiterrorism, demining.

a. Total figures do not add up exactly due to rounding.

enhancing security, bolstering prosperity, and promoting democracy.[24] How did these objectives translate into engagement programs and dollars?

Response Activities

Sub-Saharan Africa remained the region most likely to involve commitment of U.S. forces in a contingency situation. In some respects the internal debate about "no U.S. boots on African soil" was misguided, since in the five years preceding the Bush administration the United States deployed military personnel to participate in three to five humanitarian relief operations, including aid to the government of Mozambique during the Cyclone Connie floods in February 2000, and seven noncombatant evacuation operations (see Table 13.2). Rapid response to crisis situations is one of USEUCOM's regional objectives;[25] the essentially reactive nature of the command's engagement may protect the lives of U.S. citizens but is operationally dangerous and represents an inefficient use of resources. It also reflected ineffective policy and was costly in terms of lives lost in Africa.

Shaping Activities

The United States under Clinton had two flagship security programs to build African capacity to respond to conflict and conflict prevention—the

Table 13.2 U.S. Government Military Operations in Africa, 1990–2000

Noncombatant Evacuation Operations	Humanitarian Operations	Other Operations
Sharp Edge, 1990–1991 (Liberia)	Provide Hope, 1992 (Somalia)	Provide Transition, 1992 (Angola)
Eastern Exit, 1991 (Somalia)	Restore Hope, 1992 (Somalia)	United Shield, 1995 (Somalia)
Quick Lift, 1991 (DRC)	Sustain Hope, 1993 (Somalia)	Assured Lift, 1997 (ECOMOG support)
Silver Anvil, 1992 (Sierra Leone)	Support Hope, 1994 (Zaire/Rwanda)	Eagle Vista, 1998 (POTUS Trip)
Distant Runner, 1994 (Rwanda)	Atlas Response, 1998 (Mozambique)	Response, 1998 (Kenya/Tanzania)
Assured Response, 1996 (Liberia)	Noble Response (food), 1998 (Kenya)	POTUS Trip 2000 (to Nigeria and Burundi)
Quick Response, 1996 (Central African Republic)	Mozambique (floods), 2000	
Noble Obelisk, 1997 (Sierra Leone)		
Guardian Retrieval, 1997 (Zaire)		
Shepherd Venture, 1998 (Guinea-Bissau)		
Shadow Express, 1998 (Liberia)		
Autumn Shelter, 1998 (DRC)		

ACRI (funded at approximately $20 million per year), and the Africa Center for Strategic Studies (ACSS), an educational initiative to increase officer professionalism and enhance civilian control (funded at $40 million over five years). Both these projects continued in the Bush administration, while ACRI is undergoing transformation. In addition, the United States continues to provide bilateral security assistance and conducts military-to-military engagement programs—primarily through the International Military Education and Training (IMET) programs; democratization seminars; regional exercises; Joint Combined Exchange Training (JCET); ship visits; and General Officer/Flag Officer visits (see Appendix, p. 294). The total Clinton administration "shaping engagement" amounted to approximately $8.5 million annually in IMET for African military officer education in the United States, and three to four military education teams conducting one- to two-week democracy seminars in Africa; one or two annual West African Training Cruise ship visits for Seabee engineering exercises; fewer than twenty JCET exercises for small unit tactical training by U.S. special forces; and one or two medically related and mass casualty exercises (see Table 13.3).

Table 13.3 U.S. Military Education Training in Africa (U.S.$ in thousands)

Country	FY 1998 (actual)	FY 1999 (estimated)	FY 2000 (required)
Angola	0	0	100
Botswana	540	500	450
Democratic Republic of the Congo	0	0	70
Lesotho	81	75	75
Malawi	284	335	335
Mauritius	63	50	50
Mozambique	178	80	180
Namibia	203	175	175
Seychelles	79	75	75
South Africa	804	850	800
Swaziland	93	75	75
Tanzania	185	150	200
Zambia	143	150	150
Zimbabwe	336	300	300
Total	2,989	2,815	3,035

Source: Data derived from the U.S. State Department, "Foreign Military Training and DOD Engagement Activities of Interest, Volume 1," joint report to Congress, Washington, D.C., 1 March 2000.

Note: FY: fiscal year.

Most U.S. security assistance and military-to-military engagement activities were bilateral programs. More important for U.S.–SADC relations are regional exercises that occur only once or twice annually, such as Natural Fire in East Africa, and Blue Hungwa and Blue Crane in southern Africa. Such regional exercises were essential for bringing together SADC member militaries to train together as a common force. External participation was also important for building common expectations, sharing doctrine, facilitating interoperability, and establishing multinational command and control experiences with the United States and others who were asked to provide airlift, communications, and logistical support to future regional peace operations. For example, in the Blue Crane exercise conducted 7–30 April 1999, the United States, Belgium, and Germany provided C-130s for the air movement of SADC forces deploying to South Africa. The United States also sent a four-person team to serve on the International Advisors and Monitors Group. The Department of Defense viewed the ACRI, the ACSS, and regional exercises as the three legs of its regional approach to African peacekeeping. To date, the ACRI has been an unsuccessful tool for engagement with the SADC. The United States needed to take the next step to seek SADC input on how the ACRI program transformed or replaced with another flagship engagement program could have met the needs of the subregion.

Security assistance funds for African conflict-prevention activities will remained limited and increased the importance of focused engagement. In addition to promoting the development of subregional organizations and key anchor states, U.S. forces required reorganization to establish an African subcombatant command able to harmonize U.S. security assistance and military engagement programs across the continent. An Africa Command might have helped to achieve greater operational coherence and meaningful engagement in Africa. Currently, all SADC members, except Seychelles and Mauritius, are part of USEUCOM. Thus, the main benefit of this reorganization of forces for the SADC would have been a greater devotion of resources to peacetime engagement than was the case at the time; African countries were ranked last in the European Command area of responsibility under Clinton. A subcombatant command would have been able to move beyond emergency-response deployments to more concerted and sustainable shaping activities with senior military leaders, combined forces, and appropriate equipment—exclusively dedicated to African contingencies and exercises.

Conclusion

A fundamental challenge for constructive U.S. military engagement with SADC countries under the Bush administration is overcoming historical distrust and building common strategic purpose, planning, and operations. The United States is still viewed with great suspicion within the region. The SADC has been quite wary of U.S. military training programs, but member states have accepted bilateral security assistance, mainly IMET and ACSS educational opportunities. At home, interested U.S. parties and Africa activists generally oppose U.S. military engagement, except in emergencies, at which time they pressure the administration to deploy U.S. forces in peacekeeping and humanitarian relief capacities. Political leadership and open dialogue are needed to inform domestic and foreign constituents of U.S. military and security goals and objectives in the subregion. A case must be made that peacetime engagement improves the likelihood that the U.S. military will deploy to familiar terrain for peace support operations. Future engagement in support of U.S. and SADC goals for greater peace and security in the region should focus on establishing:

- Confidence- and security-building measures aimed at building political trust and understanding.
- Monitoring and regulatory agreements to fight transnational threats such as crime and arms proliferation.
- An implementation and enforcement capacity in order to carry out

successful crime interdiction, peacekeeping, and peace-support operations (see Box 13.2).

In conclusion, an interesting case study to judge concrete progress in U.S.–SADC relations may be made by tracking the development of the U.S.-sponsored International Law Enforcement Academy for Africa (ILEA). The academy, jointly established in Gaborone, Botswana, in July

Box 13.2 Cooperative Security Arrangements Between the SADC and the United States

SADC countries and the United States can cooperate on a bilateral, subregional, and multilateral basis as appropriate. The arrangements can reinforce overall peace operation capacity, especially logistics, communication, and airlift, in addition to the fundamental objective to strengthen professional, capable national armies and security forces.

Develop confidence- and security-building measures:

- Encouraging joint military activities including training, regional exercises, and attendance at each other's military academies.
- Regularly notifying immediate neighbors of major military exercises and invite regional and international observers.
- Developing collective understanding of possible sources of threat to Africa's security.
- Undertaking joint fact-finding missions and joint mediation exercises to deescalate emergent conflicts.

Monitoring mechanisms and regulatory agreements:

- Establishing nonaggression treaties that set out common principles and prescribe behavior in defined fields.
- Developing intelligence- and resource-sharing capacities with key governments to penetrate and combat narcotics, crime, and terrorist activities and to track the illegal small arms trade.
- Ensuring, in concert with South Africa and other parties, effective controls on the transfer of sensitive or destabilizing conventional arms and dual-use technologies, and establish regional arms registers.
- Enhancing national custom controls and harmonize export regulations.
- Establishing shared databases on known or suspected drugs or arms traffickers and illicit end users.

Implementation and enforcement capabilities:

- Holding joint planning and military exercises for Chapter VI and VII peacekeeping operations.
- Establishing common doctrines and command and control capability and build interoperability for peace operations.

2000 by the U.S. and Botswana governments, will address U.S. and SADC common interest in stemming the growing crime menace in southern Africa that is threatening both social and economic well-being. In the three areas of cooperation outlined above, the academy aims to foster relationships and understanding between U.S. law enforcement agencies and their counterparts in the region. Regulatory mechanisms will be established as U.S. police and customs officials work with the Southern African Regional Police Chiefs Cooperation Organization (SARPCCO) on customs and border control to counter small-arms trafficking. Enforcement capability will be enhanced through ILEA courses that will cover a wide range of law enforcement skills, including police survival, forensics, fighting organized crime, supervisory police training, police strategy, narcotics identification, evidence handling, and customs interdiction.[26] At the May 2000 U.S.–SADC forum, the bilateral efforts of the United States and Botswana, in consultation with SARPCCO, to establish the ILEA were recognized as a potential concrete contribution to the law enforcement agencies of SADC member states. Continued open dialogue to establish common strategic purpose and sufficient provision of resources is essential to build the policing and military linkages that are a necessary component of broader U.S.–SADC democracy and development efforts.

Appendix: U.S. Military and Humanitarian Programs in Africa

USEUCOM Engagement Activities in Africa

Combined Exercises. The U.S. Navy, Army, and Air Force conduct combined exercises and combined training with African nations in order to enhance U.S. combat readiness, gain area expertise, maintain access, and gain familiarity with the host nation's military. Training includes amphibious landing exercises, dissimilar air combat training, command post training, naval passing exercises, navy salvage and diving training, and small unit exercises.

Joint Combined Exchange Training. JCET activities provide a dual payoff to USEUCOM through enhanced engagement opportunities and improved training for special operations forces. The program focuses on the conduct of unit training exchanges with armed forces of host countries. JCET objectives support USEUCOM's regional strategy by promoting military professionalism; improving language, cultural, and interpersonal skills; and developing rapport with allies.

Exercise-Related Construction (ERC). The ERC program is designed to support chairman of the Joint Chiefs of Staff exercises to enhance safety, save resources, and enable U.S. operations in a host nation. It can be used to train engineer troops or foster host nation relations (though it cannot be considered nation building). This program benefits both militaries by providing U.S. forces with usable facilities when they deploy, and allowing continued use for host nation military training and exercises.

African Crisis Response Initiative. USEUCOM uses the ACRI as a key tool in shaping the African environment by promoting professional apolitical militaries, respect for human rights, and the role of a military in a democracy. The ACRI enhances existing African military capabilities for possible peacekeeping and humanitarian assistance operations in either a subregional or pan-African context. It prepares both African and U.S. soldiers for possible operations in Africa and provides knowledge and relationships that will facilitate response to crisis and humanitarian situations in Africa.

Military medical exercises in Africa (MEDFLAG). USEUCOM has organized and executed military medical exercises in Africa, known as MEDFLAGs, since the 1980s. A MEDFLAG is a joint military exercise where U.S. military components comprise medical crisis-response teams and deploy into African countries. In addition to valuable training for U.S. forces, MEDFLAG team members provide health care to the local population alongside their African colleagues during the exercise.

Port visits. Port visits are high-visibility, multifaceted engagement tools. Benefits include hosting high-level nationals, performing local "goodwill" projects, and training with the host nation across a broad spectrum of shipboard specialties.

International Military Education and Training. The objective of IMET is to influence future leaders through formal training in U.S. military schools and to create a better understanding of the United States in the international military community. The "Expanded IMET" component exposes select countries to U.S. democratic ideals and principles, assists in the management of defense resources, helps to develop military judicial systems based on the principle of internationally recognized human rights, and imparts the principle of civilian control of the military.

Chaplain engagement activities. USEUCOM chaplains participate in the chiefs of chaplain conferences, which provide a forum for the chiefs to learn about each country's military chaplaincies, examine the religious and social problems common to each military in order to find possible solutions, and determine how best to implement these solutions. It also allows them to discuss ways of building a working relationship between the military chaplaincies to these countries and to discuss how U.S. military chaplaincies can assist their chaplaincies.

Civil affairs engagement activities. Civil affairs units conduct seminars that address the "role of the military in a democracy" and "disaster preparedness." These seminars provide a means for USEUCOM to support both emerging democracies and established countries in Africa. The democracy seminar is a viable tool for enhancing democratization and enforcing the legitimate role of the military in a democracy, while the disaster preparedness seminar enhances a country or region's ability to respond to natural or man-made disasters.

The Joint Military Commission (JMC). The JMC provides a forum for discussion between senior U.S. and key African national defense personnel on security assistance, combined exercises, policy issues, mapping and hydrography, and other items of mutual interest.

Security assistance program. Security assistance primarily involves foreign military sales, excess defense articles, foreign military financing, and IMET. The U.S. security assistance program will continue to stress sustainability, logistical improvements, and a modest amount of new equipment purchases.

Humanitarian Assistance Programs (HAPs)

Humanitarian and Civic Assistance (HCA). HCA is an adjunct to the combined exercise program. HCA projects are limited in scope and added to already scheduled combined exercises. These projects may include rudimentary construction of a basic sanitation facility, school or clinic, well drilling, and basic medical and dental assistance.

Other humanitarian assistance (HA). The HA program provides funding to carry out humanitarian projects. The only restriction is that a project must be of primary benefit to the civilian population. Projects can include actions such as deployment of military medical teams, engineering teams, construction of medical clinics or schools, operator and maintenance training for HAP-EP-delivered equipment, and disaster preparedness.

DOD Humanitarian Assistance Excess Property Program (HAP-EP).

Nonlethal DOD excess property is donated to foreign nations for civilian use.[27]

Notes

1. U.S. State Department, "Confidence and Security Building Measures: Communiqué, Second SADC-US Forum Maputo, Mozambique, 11 May 2000," Bureau of Political-Military Affairs, U.S. State Department, Washington, D.C., May 2000.

2. E. Berman and K. E. Sams, *Peacekeeping in Africa: Capabilities and Culpabilities* (Geneva: UN Institute for Disarmament Research, 2000), 151–191; G. Cawthra, "Subregional Security: The Southern African Development Community," *Security Dialogue* 28, 2 (1997): 207–218; H. Solomon and J. Cilliers, "Southern Africa and the Quest for Collective Security," *Security Dialogue* 28, 2 (1997): 191–205.

3. Graham Allison's classic foreign policy decisionmaking book, *Essence of Decision,* addresses the common practice of "black boxing" other nations' decisionmaking processes with the problematic result of treating their actions as rational intended outcomes rather than the result of organizational routines, political competition, and bureaucratic politics. See G. Allison and P. Zelikow, *Essence of Decision: Explaining the Cuban Missile Crisis* (New York: Addison-Wesley Longman, 1999).

4. U.S. White House, *A National Security Strategy for a New Century* (Washington, D.C.: U.S. Government Printing Office, October 1998).

5. U.S. State Department, "Confidence and Security Building."

6. See Colin Powell, remarks at the University of the Witwatersrand, Johannesburg, South Africa, 25 May 2001.

7. J. E. Frazer, "The African Crisis Response Initiative: Self-Interested Humanitarianism," *Brown Journal of World Affairs* 4, 2 (Summer/Fall 1997): 103–118.

8. L. D. Kozaryn, "U.S. Will Offer Logistics Support to Congo Mission," U.S. Department of Defense News Release, American Forces Press Service, 18 February 2000.

9. Lakhdar Brahimi, Algeria's former foreign minister and chairman of the 2000 panel on UN Peace Operations (the Brahimi Report), puts it bluntly: "You can't have a situation where some people contribute blood and some contribute money." This is exactly what we have today, with developing countries contributing more than 75 percent of the nearly 30,000 UN troops taking part in fifteen missions around the world, while the United States, Japan, and European countries were billed for more than 85 percent of the $3 billion cost of UN peacekeeping in 2000. See C. Lynch, "Providing UN's Peacekeepers," *Washington Post*, 15 November 2000, A36; UN, "Report of the Panel on United Nations Peace Operations," New York, 21 August 2000.

10. USEUCOM, "United States European Command Support to U.S. Policy in Africa," theater engagement plan, Stuttgart, Germany, 2000 [available at: www.eucom.mil/Africa].

11. Interview with senior Clinton administration official responsible for coordinating U.S. peacekeeping and humanitarian affairs policy, Washington, D.C., 22 May 2000.

12. The 1994 Presidential Decision Directive 25 (PDD 25) sets out the president's policy guidance and criteria for supporting UN peace operations and seeking congressional approval.

13. The ACRI training program exposes the host military to the full range of UN Chapter VI peacekeeping tasks, from convoy escorts, logistics, protection of refugees, and security for relief workers to negotiations, command and control, and liaisons with civil and nongovernmental organizations; J. Fisher-Thompson, "UN Important to US-Africa Peacekeeping Goals, US Official Says," *Washington File*, 11 January 2000.

14. E. Greco, "New Trends in Peacekeeping: The Experience of Operation Alba," *Security Dialogue* 29, 2 (1998): 201–212.

15. Interview with senior Clinton administration official responsible for coordinating U.S. peacekeeping and humanitarian affairs policy, Washington, D.C., 22 May 2000.

16. S. E. Rice (Assistant Secretary for African Affairs), "U.S. Policy Towards Sierra Leone," testimony before the Senate Foreign Relations Committee's Subcommittee on African Affairs, Washington, D.C., 11 October 2000.

17. See "Vice President Gore and Governor Bush Participate in Second Presidential Debate," *CNN/AllPolitics* presidential debates transcript, 11 October 2000.

18. R. C. Holbrooke, "Conflict in Africa: The Search for Peace in the Congo," *Vital Speeches of the Day* 66, 6 (1 January 2000): 165–168. This was an address by Ambassador Holbrooke, the U.S. permanent representative to the UN, which was delivered in Pretoria, South Africa, on 6 December 1999.

19. The Congolese Rally for Democracy parties signed the Lusaka accord on 31 August 1999, seven weeks after the other parties. President Kabila has persistently denied access to MONUC by refusing to provide security guarantees and allow UN military liaison officers to deploy to locations identified by UN headquarters as suitable. Between 1 September and mid-November, MONUC headquarters apparently registered twenty-six cease-fire violations involving all the main belligerents, including Rwandan and Ugandan forces turning against each other. During the same period, the DRC used the lull in military operations to refurbish its war effort, including training and rearming Interahamwe and the Front de Défense de la Démocratie nonsignatory armed groups. In the last two weeks of November, the DRC government launched a major offensive, which amounted to an outright abrogation of the Lusaka accord.

20. Interview with senior Clinton administration official responsible for coordinating U.S. peacekeeping and humanitarian affairs policy, Washington, D.C., 22 May 2000. In fact, DOD only supported UNSCR 1528 based on the understanding that no U.S. military would participate in any potential DRC peacekeeping operation.

21. Kozaryn, "US Will Offer Logistics Support."

22. The 150 Account funding categories are AID-DFA (USAID—Development Fund for Africa, development assistance); PL 480 (food assistance); ESF (economic support funds); MRA (migration and refugee assistance); VPKO (voluntary peacekeeping operations); CIPA (contributions to international peacekeeping); IMET (international military education and training); FMF (foreign military financing); NADR (nonproliferation, antiterrorism, demining).

23. U.S. White House National Security Strategy draft document 2000, 60.

24. U.S. Joint Chiefs of Staff, "National Military Strategy of the USA: Shape, Respond, Prepare Now: A Military Strategy for a New Era," U.S. Department of Defense, Washington, D.C., September 1997.

25. Sub-Saharan Africa is divided across three combatant commands: the European Command, the Central Command, and the Pacific Command.

26. R. Boone (Deputy Assistant Secretary for International Narcotics and Law Enforcement Affairs), "Remarks at the Signing of the ILEA Agreement with the Government of Botswana," Gaborone, Botswana, 24 July 2000.

27. USEUCOM, "USEUCOM Engagement Activities in Africa," European Command J-5 Strategic Plans and Policy Africa Division, Stuttgart, Germany, 2000 [available at: www.eucom.mil/hq/ecj5_africa.htm].

14

The European Union

Talitha Bertelsmann-Scott

Over the last couple of decades, our understanding of security concerns has been reinterpreted to reflect the realities in which societies and states operate. Unique definitions of security as they pertain to the developing world have also been developed. Referring to southern Africa, for example, one commentator holds that:

> A holistic approach to the management of security underpins most South African security policy and finds expression in key Southern African Development Community and Organization of African Unity (OAU) documents. This approach rests on the concept of a broader definition of security, which is multifaceted and multidimensional: economic, social and even environmental issues have all been put onto the security agenda.[1]

The traditional focus on military concerns, borders, and access to weapons has been adapted to accommodate an understanding of security that highlights the security of the individual. Jakkie Cilliers, from the Institute of Security Studies (ISS) in South Africa, has identified a number of key areas that impact particularly on the security of southern African states and their citizens. They include the illegal proliferation of drugs, migration, the environment, population growth, global economic changes and poverty, light weapons proliferation, and the need to reform the United Nations.[2]

However, other analysts and organizations have their own definitions of what constitutes "security" in today's world. The "new" definition, often invoked by the European Union (EU), focuses on democratization, press freedom, good governance, and socioeconomic development. A "peaceful state" is no longer seen as a state in which no military conflicts are occurring but as a state that shows a commitment to, and tradition of, democracy. If the link between peace and democracy is taken as a given, peacebuilding necessarily becomes a long-term project rather than a one-time event.

This conceptual broadening of the field of security has not brought a uniform understanding of the security concerns that face the southern African region. The region remains predominantly troubled by "traditional" security threats. Cross-border wars and civil conflicts continue to exacerbate the threats posed to individuals. Such threats include human rights abuses, HIV/AIDS, and water scarcity. While wars, concerns about borders, and the proliferation of weapons threaten millions in sub-Saharan Africa, leaders simultaneously have to pay attention to a multitude of issues that international organizations and analysts have identified as key to security. The difficulty of problem solving in southern Africa is aggravated by the multitude of actors in the area, each possessing their own priorities and agendas.

Foreign actors are increasingly seeking alternatives to military interventions. The United States withdrew all its troops from African soil after October 1993 in the aftermath of the Somali debacle. The UN Security Council, of which the United States is a key member, has also become increasingly reluctant to send peacekeeping missions to areas of conflict. *The Economist* captured these sentiments early in 1999: "To send foreign soldiers, whether African or not, to intervene in any of the continent's manifold disputes looks ever more hopeless, ever more foolish."[3]

The EU as International Actor

EU Foreign Policy

In terms of economic commitment, the largest external actor active in the southern African region is the European Union. Given that southern African states united in their efforts toward regional integration and development with the formation of the Southern African Development Community (SADC) in 1992, and that all the SADC's member states are former European colonies, these two regional organizations boast a longstanding political relationship.[4]

It is important to have a clear understanding of what is meant by *European Union,* as the term is often used incorrectly to refer to the sum of European states rather than the supranational organization. Until 1993, the EU had no mandate to act in the field of foreign policy. It is often incorrectly assumed that the EU has been involved in military interventions or peacekeeping missions on the African continent. European military involvement in Africa has occurred solely on a *bilateral* level.

> "Actorness" in the world is something which most non-theoretical observers automatically assume that the European Community possesses,

> but which on closer examination might be seriously doubted, on the grounds that the EC in foreign policy is solely intergovernmental, and is therefore no more than the sum of what the Member States severally decide.[5]

Given Europe's own war-torn past, agreeing on foreign policy objectives directly after World War II would have been impossible. The issue was therefore avoided by excluding it altogether from the EU agenda. This reluctance to become involved was so widespread that mention of the term "collective foreign policy formulation" was eschewed:

> For almost forty years of European construction the very expression "common foreign policy" remained taboo. Although the Member States of the European Community endeavored to co-operate on major international policy problems and accepted that their respective national diplomatic services would meet and conduct dialogue, they never incorporated in any treaty the objective of a "common foreign policy," which is that of the European Union.[6]

In the absence of a unified EU foreign policy, the member states created an intergovernmental approach to foreign policy through European Political Cooperation (EPC). With the EPC, the individual states endeavored to reach consensus on foreign policy issues. The EPC, however, never facilitated any EU action and most often only released statements.

Security concerns in southern Africa were never included on any EU agenda. It was left to individual member states to interact binationally with SADC states regarding stability, unless consensus could be reached through the EPC. Aspects of security were only included on the EPC agenda in 1983. Cooperation on security matters was difficult to achieve, and this hampered European action in southern Africa. For example, the EPC struggled with opposing views on instituting sanctions against apartheid South Africa, with Britain opposing this course of action and most other countries favoring it.

This approach to foreign policy proved unsatisfactory for most EU member states, and many years of negotiation between European diplomats finally resulted in the Maastricht Treaty.

> The Common Foreign and Security Policy (CFSP) was established by the Maastricht Treaty and came into force on 1 November 1993. The European Union can now make its voice heard on the international stage and express its position on armed conflicts, human rights and any other subject.[7]

Since the CFSP's inception, the EU's foreign policy has become more coherent, although it will take Brussels a number of decades to establish a tradition of foreign policy for the EU. Although that foreign policy is still somewhat inconsistent, certain trends are discernible, the most important of these being the promotion of democracy and human rights. The CFSP operates chiefly through three different mechanisms:

- "Joint action," through which the EU physically becomes involved in specific situations.
- "Common positions," where no action is required but an EU position would influence the situation.
- "Statements," which have only limited impact.

The CFSP remains an intergovernmental institution of the EU; unanimity is required for action to be taken. Member countries can also abstain from participating in joint actions.[8]

Table 14.1 records the attention that the EU has given to African matters in recent years. It is clear that Africa, and southern Africa in particular, receives only limited attention through the CFSP. EU aid to the SADC is decided and allocated within five-year plans. According to a 2000 EU-SADC briefing note, the EU-SADC Regional Indicative Program funds projects in the SADC to the tune of some 121 million euros. Beyond aid, direct engagement in the region is rarely undertaken. Despite 1999 being a turbulent year in southern Africa, the EU did not become involved in the region through any joint action. J. Petersen and E. Bomberg argue that

Table 14.1 EU Action in Africa

Year	Joint Action in Africa	Common Position on Africa
1996	Two joint actions were initiated: one for Zaire and one for the Great Lakes region.	No common positions were reached, but a a special envoy was sent to the Great Lakes region.
1997	Thirteen joint actions were initiated, of which only two were on Africa: the Great Lakes and the Democratic Republic of Congo (DRC).	Thirteen common positions were reached, of which only seven were on Africa, including Nigeria, Angola, and Sierra Leone.
1998	Africa was the focus of only three joint actions out of the twenty that the EU undertook.	Only six of the twenty-two common positions focused on Africa.
1999	No joint actions were undertaken in Africa in this year, as opposed to twelve joint actions taking place elsewhere.	Only four out of twenty-two common positions focused on Africa.

Source: Compiled from G. Edwards and G. Wiessala, "The European Union: Annual Review," *Journal of Common Market Studies* (1996–1999).

despite the emergence of a coherent EU policy after the CFSP, the EU still lacks the instruments to act on that policy, particularly as it does not command a military force:

> The EU already does a credible job . . . of taking decisions on matters of foreign policy, and doing it collectively. . . . However, in foreign policy more than in other EU policy sectors, common "decisions" do not necessarily produce effective action or policy. The CFSP's central and most serious problem is a lack of policy instruments, which can be deployed to support or enforce policy decisions.[9]

This dilemma is exemplified by the EU's response to the 2000–2001 Zimbabwean crisis. The union initially strongly condemned the widespread intimidation in the run-up to the country's elections toward the end of 2000. In the months prior to the elections, the EU recommended that nonhumanitarian aid be cut, mainly because of the unlawful occupation of white-owned farmland and Zimbabwe's involvement in the crisis in the Democratic Republic of Congo (DRC). The EU committed 1.83 million rand (approximately $300,000) to an election monitoring project and sent hundreds of observers to regions throughout Zimbabwe. These observers eventually declared the elections "unfree and unfair" due to the widespread incidence of violence and intimidation.

After the parliamentary elections, the situation in Zimbabwe deteriorated: land occupations continued; violence and intimidation were widespread; and the independent media were frequently silenced. During the first part of 2001, the EU attempted to engage Zimbabwe on several occasions. Talks were initiated through political dialogue within the African-Caribbean-Pacific (ACP) grouping, with threats of expulsion from the group. The EU participated in a combined mission to Zimbabwe with the UN and the World Bank, aimed at dissuading President Robert Mugabe from his current policies under the threat of sanctions and the suspension of aid. However, these efforts had little impact on Mugabe. Significantly, the threats were never implemented.

A resolution on Zimbabwe by the EU Parliament, which exemplified the difficulty that the organization has in dealing with foreign policy, was released in September 2001.[10] The resolution applauded the bilateral suspension of aid by Denmark and Norway, while questioning France's increased engagement with the country. It called on the European Commission to review its food aid program and suspend all development cooperation assistance to Harare. It further called on the EU Council to invoke measures under the Cotonou agreement to suspend Zimbabwe and take joint action against Mugabe. It also called on the European Investment Bank to review its loans to Zimbabwe. Not only was bilateral action juxtaposed against collective action, but the various arms of the organizations within the EU structure also proved incapable of agreeing on a unified course of action.

The EU's Development Cooperation Policy

The EU's inability to reach consensus on Zimbabwe does not mean that it was oblivious to the security threats in the southern African region; nor was it entirely incapable of acting on them. Any action, however, had to take the guise of promoting socioeconomic development through the commission's development cooperation policy. The limits of engagement through development assistance were often stretched in order to address issues like apartheid, internal instabilities, and transitional governments. Considerable focus was placed on regional integration and the promotion of democratic principles, as this approach had secured lasting peace and stability on the European continent.

The EU is the world's largest contributor to development aid, and it has invested billions in the development of southern Africa over the last several decades. (The EU contributes around 0.51 percent of its gross national product to development aid, compared to a 0.32 percent contribution by Japan and 0.15 percent by the United States.) It has used two institutional avenues to channel this aid (apart from interactions with individual states), namely the SADC and the recently expired Lomé convention. It was hoped that the SADC's regional integration efforts would result in greater harmony in southern Africa, while the Lomé convention would promote economic development, which in turn would lead to greater stability in the region.

Although the EU remains southern Africa's largest donor and continues to spend large sums on development aid, there is growing concern among EU member states that this money is being wasted and that aid has not achieved its aims. This has resulted in the EU tying stricter conditions to its aid and disbursing funds only in a limited number of project areas.

New conditions tend to focus on the basic elements of peace and stability, as identified by the EU. These include respect for human rights, good governance, and the democratization of the state apparatus. If a recipient state fails to show that it is adhering to these basic elements, the EU will refrain from funding development projects there. (Although this is true in theory, the EU has suspended aid in only a limited number of countries.) In South Africa, for example, the EU implements development aid exclusively in the following areas: basic social services; private sector development; good governance, democratization, and human rights; and regional cooperation.[11]

This chapter will now take a closer look at the relationship between the EU and southern Africa by focusing on the two instruments the EU has hitherto used to promote peace and stability in the region, namely the SADC and the Lomé (Cotonou) convention. The EU's involvement in the SADC and the Lomé convention has not been without its own contradictions, and this could result in additional insecurities for the region.

The EU and the Southern African Development Community

In the years prior to South Africa's transition to democracy in 1994, the European Economic Community (EEC) played a leading role in trying to reverse apartheid. It had a comprehensive strategy for ending apartheid, which included sanctions, sporting isolation, and the suspension of full diplomatic ties with the pariah state. It pursued this strategy through the EPC. The EEC also provided support for the Southern African Development Coordination Conference (SADCC) in its efforts to lessen dependence on the dominant South Africa. This was done through development cooperation.

The EEC attempted to reduce southern Africa's dependence on South Africa and actively encouraged and subsidized the SADCC.[12] This approach was informed by its firm belief in regional integration as a vehicle for stability and development. To a lesser extent, the Lomé convention—geared toward promoting economic development and political cooperation—was also used to help South Africa's neighbors counter Pretoria's destabilization policies.

During this period, the SADCC followed a purely functionalist approach to integration, which included cooperation in the formulation and execution of joint projects aimed at overcoming underdevelopment-related deficiencies in production and infrastructure. The EEC and its individual member states largely funded these projects. There was no explicit focus on security in the region.

Political analysts deemed SADCC a success when judged against the projects it implemented. While the expectations of the organization were minimal, it made real contributions toward the development of infrastructure in the region. However, in the realms of security and regional integration, the SADCC had very limited success. Dependence on South Africa never really diminished, and Pretoria continued to dominate the region.

The Southern African Development Community was born after heads of state and government in the region met in Windhoek, Namibia, and signed a declaration and treaty in August 1992. With the demise of the apartheid government and South Africa's conversion to democracy in 1994, the SADC faced a new era. The emergence of a democratic South Africa changed the region's economic outlook; the SADC would now attempt to harness the republic's comparative economic strength to foster regional development.

The policy of excluding the former apartheid regime was abandoned for one of incorporating the new South Africa as the core around which regional integration and development would coalesce and be sustained.

South Africa acceded to the community in 1994 and took over the chairmanship in 1996. Despite dominant South African participation in the organization, the EU's role in southern Africa was not scaled down. With its own economic problems at home, South Africa could not take on the funding burden in the region, despite the fact that its democratization coincided with the establishment of the CFSP. While these two developments created the expectation that substantial changes could be realized in the region, such expectations were quickly dashed and the region continued to rely on external assistance.

Neither did the end of apartheid spell the end of conflicts in southern Africa. Two of the largest SADC members in terms of geographic coverage—Angola and the DRC—are still trying to implement peace agreements. Zimbabwe, previously seen as the seat of economic stability in the region, is slipping into complete economic and political collapse. The acceptance of the CFSP has not meant greater direct participation in either conflict resolution or peacekeeping for the EU. Brussels continues to operate through development assistance, although with a slight change in focus. That new focus holds that:

> [The] Commission has started to review EC assistance to the [SADC] states to take account of the broader peace-building objective. And this does not simply mean to add on to the traditional development agenda specific projects of peace-building and conflict prevention, such as mediation training for local leaders or academic seminars, important though these may also be. . . . Peace-building is not simply a sectoral policy such as health or infrastructure. Peace-building is . . . an approach, a concept, a yardstick that can help to guide the right priorities for development assistance. Every single development project, be it in the field of agriculture, health, education or any other, has the potential to be a peace-building project—provided it is designed and implemented in a way that it contributes to addressing the root-causes of violent conflicts in a targeted manner.[13]

Most important, the CFSP has enabled Brussels to comment and act on security developments within the region through means other than direct, physical engagement. Although no action has yet been agreed to, official dialogue forums have finally been established. However, with the tilt to the CFSP, a shift in understanding of southern African security threats has also been noted. Previously the focus was exclusively on economic development and integration; today, a far greater focus is placed on the essentials of peace and stability. Each and every project implemented by the EU is viewed as a potential promoter of peace and stability. In short, a far more holistic approach is taken to security concerns in the SADC region. This approach argues that:

> If the root causes of conflict are to be tackled successfully, then political and socio-economic imbalances, insufficient respect for democratic principles, human rights, media freedom and the free flow of information need to be addressed. I would like to underline that development cooperation, including the programs within the framework of the Lomé convention, has an important role to play in assisting countries address such issues and in support for the peaceful reconciliation of divergent interests.[14]

The EU has been very involved with the SADC since its inception and has maintained its historic and current links with the organization. It is through the SADC-EU ministerial conference that security concerns over the region are now finally being raised. These conferences were initiated in Berlin in 1994 (after the EU's adoption of the CFSP) through Germany's foreign minister, Klaus Kinkel. In September of that year a very ambitious cooperation agreement was signed between the EU and the SADC. It contains references to the two civil and regional wars that are currently raging in southern Africa. This is a substantial shift away from the broad-brush approach of the old Lomé convention. For example:

> It was agreed that ministers of member states of the two communities would meet every two years. Current affairs would be dealt with by a common EU-SADC steering committee of high ranking public officials, meeting every six months. The two bodies have given special emphasis to the following issues of mutual interest:
>
> - the development of the SADC;
> - the future of the Lomé Convention;
> - human rights and democracy;
> - the conflicts in Kosovo, Angola, and the DRC;
> - the EU's Agenda 2000;
> - the EU's opening towards new member countries in the East; and
> - the fight against drugs and HIV/AIDS.[15]

Despite the ambitious agenda and the number of conferences that have been held to date, these meetings have amounted to little more than talk-shops about security concerns in the southern African region. The only tangible involvement in issues of security by Europeans has been through contact between individual EU member states and the SADC. A good example here is Operation Blue Crane, in which troops from all SADC states—except the Seychelles and the DRC—participated in a subregional peacekeeping training exercise in April 1999. The project was largely funded by EU member states.

The Lomé Convention and the Cotonou Agreement

Founded in February 1975, the Lomé convention governed relations between seventy African, Caribbean, and Pacific countries—all former colonies of European Union members. The convention grew from its initial forty-six member states into a seventy-state-strong instrument of North-South cooperation. Apart from receiving development aid from the EU, the member states also enjoyed preferential access to EU markets. The convention made special provisions for the ACP countries in two areas, namely, trade and financial cooperation. Under trade, it offered unrestricted, nonreciprocal, and duty-free access for industrial products (including coal, steel, textiles, clothing), duty reductions, and quantitative access for agricultural products. Under financial cooperation, Lomé provided for massive aid packages: it offered more aid than all the other EU states collectively. Aid was channeled through the European Development Fund and the European Investment Bank.[16]

Why the Lomé Convention Expired

In the twenty-two years that the Lomé convention governed relations between the ACP and the EU, the Lomé countries have had access to a vast amount of development aid and preferential bids. However, most of these countries have not benefited from them as Europe had hoped. Some of the ACP countries remain among the least developed economies in the world. (In southern Africa these include Lesotho, Swaziland, and Malawi.) It is increasingly felt in Europe that development aid is a waste of money, as past projects have not succeeded in alleviating poverty or in developing adequate infrastructure. The EU, therefore, wanted to restructure the convention so that the development aid and trade it offered would begin to show some concrete results.

The renegotiation of the Lomé convention began in September 1999 and a new agreement was reached between the EU and the ACP in June 2000. Although the convention expired in February 2000, it will, for practical purposes, continue to exist until its projects have been completed. The successor agreement will be known as the Cotonou agreement.

There are a number of key differences between the Lomé convention and the Cotonou agreement. Importantly, political dialogue now forms the core of the agreement. It is, for example, determined that "the dialogue will be deeper and wider than at present. It will cover a broad range of political issues that fall outside of traditional development cooperation."[17] This means that greater political attention will be paid to regional conflicts, the arms trade, and migration.

Cotonou replaces the aid aspect of the Lomé convention and prepares the way for new trade agreements between the ACP and the EU that will eventually replace the nonreciprocal benefits that Lomé offered. However, the change from Lomé to the Cotonou agreement has not been without controversy, especially with regard to the outstanding trade arrangements. There are fears that the end of nonreciprocal benefits will result in severe economic hardships in the ACP countries, which in turn could exacerbate security concerns.

Although this has been fiercely denied, the EU–South Africa Trade, Development and Cooperation Agreement (TDCA) has been seen as a precedent for trade agreements between the developed and the developing world, and for the future trade relationship between the EU and the SADC in particular. When negotiations were initiated between the EU and South Africa, Pretoria applied for full membership in the Lomé convention. This request was, however, denied, apparently due to South Africa's economic sophistication relative to its SADC partners. Instead of the nonreciprocal trade benefits offered by Lomé, South Africa had to settle for a free-trade agreement that would place substantial burdens on its economy. The fact that the negotiations took almost five years to conclude is indicative of the difficulties that South Africa had in negotiating and accepting such a complex trade deal.

A number of elements of the EU–South Africa TDCA are of great importance with regard to the Cotonou agreement and the outstanding trade negotiations.

• *South Africa was offered partial accession to the Lomé convention.* South Africa was permitted to join the convention as a political member: no aid or nonreciprocal trade benefits were available to it, but Pretoria participated in all political aspects of the convention. This demonstrates that the EU is keen to keep the political fold of the ACP together, while seeking individual trade arrangements with ACP states or regions. Reaching a separate agreement with the economic powerhouse of the SADC, leaving the rest of the states in the region to conclude their own, separate agreements, is perhaps the most controversial aspect of the TDCA. Many analysts have expressed the concern that the TDCA will have severe negative impacts on SADC member states, particularly Botswana, Namibia, Lesotho, and Swaziland. Increased economic hardship in these countries will only exacerbate security concerns.

• *The liberalization of trade, or free trade, is the main component of the TDCA.* The ACP countries should expect to lose out on most of their previous trade preferences; this could have serious repercussions for socioeconomic security, given that such a large number of ACP states built their economies on these preferences in the past. A number of UN agencies have found, in separate studies, that trade liberalization has had profoundly negative impacts on developing countries. In conjunction with International Monetary Fund and World Bank structural adjustment programs, developing states are increasingly kept from playing the social role needed to cushion citizens from the negative fallouts of trade liberalization. Economic hardship—especially food insecurity—contributes directly to the instability in the region.

• *Development aid is included as a contractual part of the agreement.* This is aimed at ensuring greater control over where development money goes and on which projects it will be spent, in order to limit the corruption normally associated with development grants. In the case of the Cotonou agreement, it means that the aid budget will favor "good" performers over "bad." However, many of the international development agencies are calling for decisionmaking to move closer to the communities that need the support. Cotonou remains vague on how to incorporate nongovernmental organizations and civil society, yet their successful integration and utilization is key to mitigating the negative impacts of trade liberalization and security fallouts.

• *The nature of the negotiations was itself a contested terrain.* The talks between the EU and South Africa were protracted, costly, and eventually threatened the political relationship between the two parties. Whether the ACP will have the necessary funds and skill to negotiate in a similar fashion is doubtful.

Future Trade Arrangements Under the Cotonou Agreement

The EU has suggested that the old agreement of nonreciprocal, beneficial access to EU markets for ACP countries could make way for regional free trade agreements. It is still unclear which ACP regions would be eligible for a regional economic preference agreement (REPA) with the EU. In order to conclude a regional agreement, one would expect the region at least to be organized into a community for the purposes of economic integration. The Pacific states, for instance, are not organized into any regional organization. And other regions that might have regional integration schemes might not be aiming at a customs union—a prerequisite for a REPA. In addition, most regions consist of both developing and least developed countries. At this point it is not foreseen that the least developed will be included in the REPAs, which makes the feasibility of these agreements questionable.

The SADC is a case in point. South Africa is classified by the EU as an "economy in transition," whereas its immediate neighbors in the Southern

African Customs Union (SACU) are classified as "developing" and "least developed" countries. South Africa—and legally, therefore, the SACU—has reached a separate agreement with the EU. If the least-developed countries of the SADC were excluded from the REPA, it would only leave Zimbabwe, Zambia, Mauritius, and the Seychelles to reach agreement with Europe. From an ACP perspective, the meager efforts by African states to promote regional integration on their own terms are being steamrolled by Europe. And from a practical point of view, the REPAs do not appear to be feasible.

However, by the time the REPAs are implemented, there may be few tariffs remaining in the world. At least three World Trade Organization rounds of negotiations are expected to be held by 2015, and this could erode tariffs for most products, including those in the agricultural sector.[18]

Trade liberalization has not brought increased economic growth to southern Africa in the past and has had virtually no positive effect on poverty alleviation. It is doubtful whether increased trade liberalization will finally yield the neoliberal promises of prosperity. Can we, therefore, expect further economic decline and hardship and an increase in wars and civil conflicts in the region? And will the EU be willing to become involved under such circumstances?

The Limits of EU Involvement: A Source of Instability?

It is clear that the EU prefers nonactive means of contributing to peacekeeping in southern Africa: it prefers dialogue, sanctions, and financial support for programs with potential to promote peace and security. The EU's main contribution to peace and stability in the SADC is through its support for socioeconomic development.

The EU, which funds more than 80 percent of all SADC projects, remains its largest donor.[19] Without this support it is questionable whether there would be enough commitment from SADC member states to support the African regional organization. With the shift in ideology away from development aid toward liberalization, one has to question whether the EU will be willing to support the SADC indefinitely. In addition, the overlap between regional organizations in southern Africa is also of concern to the EU donors, especially the overlap between the SADC and the Common Market of Eastern and Southern Africa (COMESA), which appears to be hampering regional integration efforts. Some analysts have suggested that the EU could withdraw support from one organization in order to let it die a natural death and allow the other to thrive. Should this occur, it could have dangerous repercussions for both regions, as they have both become dependent on the development projects funded by the EU. This possibility is becoming increasingly likely, given the EU's preference for REPAs. The overlap between the SADC and COMESA would hamper the creation of a REPA for southern Africa.

Also, the changing trade preferences under the Cotonou agreement could place a number of SADC states' economies at risk if they face open competition both at home and on the European market. Having based their economies on EU preferences and established trade routes between the former colonies and Europe, it will be difficult for these developing economies to diversify or to find alternative trading partners. Although the EU is mostly blamed for causing these concerns, southern Africa should realize that it will have to stand on its own feet if it ever wants to be considered a truly peaceful and stable region. Overdependence on foreign actors makes the region vulnerable.

Conclusion

As the EU is not involved in traditional peacekeeping mechanisms on the African continent, the pertinent role the organization plays is often overlooked. Despite some new thinkers concentrating on the broader issues when dealing with peace and stability in southern Africa, many analysts still tend to focus on military forces and arms. It is crucial to understand the EU's approach to stability and to recognize the potential threat that the region's dependence on Brussels poses, but it is also important to acknowledge the potential for using EU aid to create an enabling environment for peace and stability in southern Africa.

The threat lies, first, in an overdependence on EU funding for regional development projects and, second, in an overdependence on nonreciprocal trade preferences for SADC states on the EU market. These two mechanisms have hitherto formed the gist of the EU's approach to building lasting peace and stability in southern Africa. Yet the contribution of this approach toward creating the essential elements for peace and stability is doubtful. Southern Africa still faces a myriad of security threats, ranging from the HIV/AIDS epidemic to severe food shortages and other environmental disasters. Poverty is still endemic to southern Africa and in such an atmosphere, democracy struggles to survive.

Instead of Europe stepping up its efforts in southern Africa, it would seem as if its commitment to the region is slowly eroding. The EU development-aid pool is shrinking and trade preferences will soon be a thing of the past. The EU is expecting developing states to accept these changes and will not be willing to spend much more on adjustment programs. This could have serious repercussions for the less-developed members of the SADC.

South Africa might well benefit from this approach at the expense of some of the smaller states, and this could threaten the SADC's stability.

Although not explicitly stated in any CFSP directive, it is also clear that the EU will not be involving itself physically in any peacekeeping mission in the near future. The CFSP as yet controls no military force, and, even if this were to change, it is doubtful whether such a force would ever be sent to southern Africa. Southern African solutions for regional instability need to be found as a matter of urgency.

Notes

1. G. Cawthra, "Towards a Holistic Approach to Security Management at Regional Security Level," *African Security Review* 6, 5 (1997).

2. See Jakkie Cilliers and Greg Mills, eds., *From Peacekeeping to Complex Emergencies: Peace Support Missions in Africa* (Johannesburg: South African Institute of International Affairs; Pretoria: Institute for Security Studies, 1999), 4. Population decline may in fact also become a serious security threat.

3. "Africa's Wars," *The Economist,* 14 January 1999.

4. SADC states include Angola, Botswana, the Democratic Republic of Congo, Lesotho, Malawi, Mauritius, Mozambique, Namibia, Seychelles, South Africa, Swaziland, Tanzania, Zambia, and Zimbabwe. The EU member states are Austria, Belgium, Denmark, Finland, France, Germany, Greece, Ireland, Italy, Luxembourg, Netherlands, Portugal, Spain, Sweden, and the United Kingdom.

5. C. Hill, "The Capability-Expectations Gap, or Conceptualising Europe's International Role," *Journal of Common Market Studies* 31, 3 (1993), 308–309.

6. EU, "The Council of the European Union and the Common Foreign and Security Policy," Brussels, Belgium [available at: http://ue.eu.int/pesc/pres.asplang=en].

7. Ibid.

8. J. Peterson and E. Bomberg, *Decision-Making in the European Union* (London: Macmillan, 1999), 11, 228–232.

9. Ibid., 12.

10. "European Parliament Urgency Resolution on the Situation in Zimbabwe," *AllAfrica,* 9 April 2001 [available at: http://allafrica.com/stories/printable/200109040316.html].

11. In total, 500 million euros were committed to the European Programme for Reconstruction and Development in South Africa for the period 1996–1999. Of this amount, 20 percent was spent on good governance, democratization, and human rights.

12. SADCC members were Angola, Botswana, Lesotho, Malawi, Mozambique, Swaziland, Tanzania, Zambia, and Zimbabwe.

13. J. De Deus Pinheiro, "Can EU Development Assistance Contribute to Peace and Security?" paper presented at a CESD/ISIS conference on "The Future of the EU's Common Foreign and Security Policy," Brussels, Belgium, 24 September 1998.

14. J. De Deus Pinheiro, commissioner's address, EU/SADC Ministerial Conference, Vienna, Austria, 3 November 1998.

15. K. Von der Ropp, "The Challenge of Change: Comparative Lessons from the Experiences of the EU and SADC," *ISS African Security Review* 2, 9 (2000): 21.

16. M. Mayer and L. Kritzinger-van Niekerk, "Towards a South African Position on the Lomé Convention," paper presented at the Development Bank of Southern Africa, Johannesburg, 1997.

17. ECDPM, "Innovations in the Cotonou Agreement," Cotonou Information Kit 4, European Centre for Development Policy Management, Maastricht, Netherlands, January 2001, 1.

18. ECDPM, "The EC's Impact Studies on Regional Economic Partnership Agreements," Lomé Negotiating Brief no. 5, Maastricht, Netherlands, February 1999, 22.

19. SADC, *SADC Statistics: Facts and Figures 1999*, SADC Secretariat, Gaborone, Botswana, 1999.

15

The Commonwealth

KAYE WHITEMAN

The notion of security in international politics is more often related to power, order, and, by extension, the furtherance of peace, than to democracy per se. While none can doubt that both nationally and internationally this narrow definition of security has powerful resonance, it has its downside. At its most negative, it can be used to mask authoritarianism and worse. National security is too often a justification for secrecy and cover-ups, and it is most frequently used by national intelligence and police organizations of varying repute. Internationally, it tends to be attached to institutions representing higher ideals such as the United Nations Security Council or the Organization for Security and Cooperation in Europe and is more closely related to procuring peace, even if it is associated with military operations in pursuit of that objective.

The end of the Cold War at the close of the 1980s opened up discussions on security beyond the struggle against communism. These discussions focused on the prosecution of the democratic agenda and, in particular, on issues of conflict resolution, one of the growing themes of the post–Cold War world. As Chief Emeka Anyaoku said in 1989, shortly before becoming secretary-general of the Commonwealth: "Security in our interdependent world is multi-faceted and can no longer be simply defined in terms of its military aspect."[1]

Nowhere has the word *security* evolved more in meaning than in southern Africa, especially in South Africa. For many, it was incarnated in South Africa's notorious Bureau of State Security (BOSS),[2] but when BOSS's reputation was utterly disgraced, its name was changed. The State Security Council, established in 1972, continued with many of the same excesses. Many other organizations bore the tag, and all the armed organizations, from armed forces to police, were generically referred to as "security forces." During apartheid, security was one of the principal justifications used to defend the apartheid crimes perpetrated against the South African people; and while usage of the term was not dropped after 1994, it was subtly reinterpreted, for instance, in the Security and Defense Committee. National and international security were still vital issues, but they underwent conceptual changes that saw them encompassing wider areas, even as the role of the security forces itself evolved. The current South African minister of safety and security does not only oversee police affairs. A computer search of post-1994 studies on security in southern Africa revealed a rapid growth in studies on agricultural and food security; the growth of the security organ of the Southern African Development Community (SADC) and its potential role in bringing stability to the region; and more tolerant and sympathetic associations as a precondition for "freedom" and "development."[3]

The Commonwealth and International Security

In the past, the Commonwealth often discussed security in the international context, especially in relation to the Cold War, and from the point of view of those (notably its influential nonaligned member countries) trying to ease international tensions. The 1983 Goa Declaration on International Security and the 1985 Nassau Declaration on World Order both focused strongly on these preoccupations, especially in the wake of the U.S. invasion of Grenada in November 1983, which seriously divided the 1983 Delhi Commonwealth Heads-of-Government Meeting (CHOGM). The Goa declaration has particular relevance for the Commonwealth because it has increased advocacy on behalf of the small and vulnerable states that form the majority of its members.[4] Although the Goa declaration was focused on the political vulnerability of small states rather than their economic vulnerability—the locus of current Commonwealth advocacy—it remains relevant.

Both the Delhi and Nassau declarations focused on apartheid in South Africa, yet neither mentioned the threat that the country posed to security in the region. The latter notion would have challenged the apartheid regime's image of itself as the guardian of security in a region faced with a "communist threat."

In its modern context, the Commonwealth has rarely, if ever, been connected with military operations. The "Commonwealth troops" in the Korean War had no central structure or actual Commonwealth endorsement—it was merely a useful piece of nomenclature.[5] William Gutteridge, in an interesting essay on Commonwealth military ties, acknowledges that from the time the Commonwealth secretariat was set up in 1964–1965, even the coordination of military assistance through the Commonwealth office was abandoned and became a purely bilateral matter.[6] Bodies such as the Commonwealth War Graves Commission and the British Commonwealth Ex-Services League still function, but they tend to be associated with the "old" or even the "white" Commonwealth.[7] Unbelievably, it was only in November 2000 that the cenotaph observance in London for the first time included representatives of religions other than Christianity and Judaism in acknowledgment of the large numbers of war dead from all over the Commonwealth.[8] The contribution of Commonwealth countries to United Nations peacekeeping operations has been significant and frequently lauded. Countries such as India, Nigeria, Ghana, and Canada have all played prominent roles in this regard.

A major exception to the reluctance of the new Commonwealth to involve itself in military matters was its dispatch of a 1,300-strong Commonwealth monitoring force to Rhodesia/Zimbabwe to supervise the congregation of guerrilla forces at assembly points before and during the March 1980 election that paved the way for independence. This force was largely British in inspiration, funding, composition, and command (non-British members hailed from Australia, Fiji, Kenya, and New Zealand). However, that the force operated under the Commonwealth umbrella was psychologically important, and it still stands as testimony to the Commonwealth's achievements and potential capacities. Such an exercise has never been repeated in quite the same way in Africa.

The Commonwealth and Security During the Cold War

This chapter is centrally informed by the overarching and profoundly democratizing role played by the Commonwealth in the liberation process in southern Africa from 1961 to 1994, when South Africa became a multiracial democracy. A defining moment for South Africa came at the prime ministers' conference in 1960. Previously, South Africa had been protected by the principle of noninterference, but at the 1960 conference it was told that if it wanted to be a republic it would have to reapply for membership in the Commonwealth; this inevitably set the scene for its departure. Then South African prime minister Hendrik Verwoerd came to London in 1960 (having spurned the previous summit, at which South Africa was in the dock as a result of the Sharpeville Massacre) to put the country's case himself. South Africa was forced out of the Commonwealth in 1961, after intensive pressure from African and Asian states. This development occurred against the background of a rapidly evolving international situation in which some kind of major commitment was being sought for decolonization. Western powers, led by the British and the French, were pushing ahead rapidly with decolonization in Africa; at the same time, there was concern in the West that African opinion could be alienated as a result of the Congo crisis. Patrice Lumumba had been murdered two months prior to the 1960 prime ministers' conference, and the crucial decolonization and breakup of the Central African Federation had not yet occurred.

The Commonwealth was itself in the full flux of change. From a cozy club of white dominions that had been initiated almost as an extension of the empire in 1931, it had been revolutionized by the decolonization that began after World War II. The defining moment in this process was the deal between Pandit Nehru and Clement Attlee at the 1949 meeting in which India's republican status was accepted as a constitutional form within the Commonwealth framework; King George VI remained, however, the symbolic head of the Commonwealth.[9] This effectively changed the Commonwealth from a white man's club of dominions and gave it, from 1949 onward, an ideology of independence that included formal backing for the decolonization process.

But this new ideology took some time to prosecute, particularly because the new member countries, still feeling the weight of past practice and experience, took time to flex their muscles. The Commonwealth was seriously split over Britain's Suez fiasco in 1956, which proved a climacteric of the end of the empire, demonstrating Britain's reduced status in the world. By 1960, the balance of membership of the Commonwealth was beginning to tilt decisively, with Ghana, Malaysia, Singapore, and Nigeria joining the South Asian members. Before 1960, Ghana had been the only African Commonwealth member; by 1961, the influence and weight of Nigeria, and the moral influence of the leader of the soon-to-be-independent Tanganyika, Julius Nyerere, also played a part in pushing the decolonization agenda. This was a period of great confidence in Africa, despite the Congo debacle and other divisions in the continent, and there was widespread belief that decolonization heralded a bright African future.

Rhodesia and South Africa: 1961–1975

There was, however, one overwhelming security issue that the Commonwealth was compelled to deal with over the next thirty years or so—the thorny issue of white minority rule in South Africa and Rhodesia. The 1961 crisis in the Commonwealth over South Africa's membership set the scene for the conflicts over southern Africa for the next thirty years or more.[10] Canada's support (even under the conservative John Diefenbaker) for the Afro-Asian position was crucial, obliging British prime minister Harold Macmillan and Australian prime minister Robert Menzies (one of white South Africa's most ardent supporters) to acquiesce. The subsequent rantings from right-wing newspapers in London against "what the Commonwealth was becoming," were symptomatic of a deep end-of-empire malaise.

The pattern of the score was set for the next thirty years, and it reached a crescendo in the furious but ultimately impotent attempts to bury the Commonwealth during the "Thatcher versus the rest" confrontations of the 1980s.[11] The agitation in the British media over Zimbabwe in 2000 was but a pale echo of the acrimonious furor over Suez, the Congo, South Africa, and Rhodesia. But over the years this underlying conflict and hostility in the Commonwealth became key ingredients within the crucible where the modern association was forged.

The crisis over South Africa's departure from the Commonwealth saw the battle lines being drawn within the association. It also set the scene for the battle over what was then known as Southern Rhodesia; this dispute came to a head four years later with a unilateral declaration of independence by Ian Smith's white-run government. Smith's government resisted even lukewarm proposals from the British to move in the direction of wider suffrage. In retrospect, there are those who believe that military action by the British might have been effective and possibly even bloodless, given the power of loyalty to the Crown that existed in Southern Rhodesia. But then British prime minister Harold Wilson and most of his government opposed the use of force, partly owing to political anxieties rooted in the Labour government's extremely small majority. Thus, Wilson famously surrendered this important alternative by publicly stating his opposition to the use of force.

One great "if" of history is what Sir Alec Douglas-Home of the Conservative Party would have done if he, instead of Wilson, had won the British election, given the relatively benign record of the conservatives as decolonizers. Politically, it would have been easier for him than for Wilson to send the British military into Rhodesia, but it would still have required great courage and imagination. If troops had been sent in, thousands of lives would have been saved in Zimbabwe, sparing Britain much international aggravation. But it was not to be, and the inaction was widely perceived as having a racist element, an imputation the British took a long time to live down.[12]

The concept of security favored by Smith and his South African backers was to "tough it out," and for a time they persuaded the U.S. government (with the UK, France, and Germany broadly following suit) that minority regimes, which included the Portuguese colonial administrations in Angola and Mozambique, could survive. The United States, at this point, saw the military presence of France and Portugal (a North Atlantic Treaty Organization ally) as useful in warding off "communist expansionism" in Africa. The Portuguese revolution in 1974, which triggered full and immediate decolonization of Portugal's anachronistic African empire, considerably diminished confidence in that view. The failed South African attempt to introduce a pro-Western regime in Angola in November 1975 (stopped in its tracks by the crucial Cuban intervention of that month) was also a decisive factor in determining the balance of power in southern Africa. This brought the Commonwealth into play once more, after it had for several years resisted intervention.

The British failure of nerve proved, paradoxically, to be the making of the Commonwealth because of the fifteen years of friction over Rhodesia that ensued in the forum.

Ironically, Rhodesia's unilateral declaration of independence occurred just after the establishment of the Commonwealth secretariat in London, following a decision at the 1964 summit.[13] This marked the definitive emancipation of the Commonwealth from British governmental control, and the Rhodesia question was the issue that demonstrated the change. The Rhodesia issue, which increasingly came to be known as the Zimbabwe issue as the liberation movements—the Zimbabwe African Peoples' Union and its rival, the Zimbabwe African National Union (ZANU)—became better known, featured prominently at each Commonwealth summit. From the summit in Lagos (January 1966) through to that in Lusaka (July 1979), Rhodesia dominated the agenda. But the organization grew and defined itself in spite of these often agonizing frustrations.

Although Wilson was unwilling to use troops, there were others who were ready to do so, notably Rhodesia's neighbors in the Commonwealth. Tanzania hosted the Organization of African Unity (OAU) Liberation Committee, and Zambia committed itself in ways that were to prove damaging: not only did it apply sanctions, but it also offered military support to the liberation movements, thus inviting reprisals.[14] The association of the Frontline States—Angola, Botswana, Mozambique, Tanzania, Zambia, and Zimbabwe—was conceived to counter the threat to their security. Once Zimbabwe became independent in 1980, the Southern African Development Coordination Conference (SADCC) provided an additional answer to South African intransigence. While the SADCC had clearly stated economic aims, it also had a strong political bias and thus a security subtext. The racist regimes' efforts at destructive destabilization of their neighbors, which continued through the whole Zimbabwean independence struggle (particularly after Angola and Mozambique gained independence), constituted a pattern of behavior that presaged the reckless counteroffensives carried out by South Africa. Attacks on Harold Wilson by Commonwealth figures, such as the prime minister of Sierra Leone, Sir Albert Margai, and the vice president of Zambia, Simon Kapwepwe, at the September 1966 London meeting considerably irked the Wilson government. Although summits had been held in 1964, 1965, and 1966, Wilson postponed holding another for as long as possible, and the next was only held in January 1969.

After Edward Heath and the Conservative Party came unexpectedly to power in 1970 on a ticket that in part supported the resumption of arms sales to South Africa, he engaged in some brinkmanship with African leaders that seriously threatened to break up the Commonwealth.[15] Up to the last minute there was even uncertainty about whether Heath would attend the Singapore summit of January 1971, and long confrontations at the summit led to an uneasy compromise that eventually meant no significant British arms were sold to the apartheid regime. By the next CHOGM in Canada in 1973, Heath had modified his line further, albeit truculently, and, by the time he left office in 1974, his relations with Africa had almost normalized.

The confrontations over southern Africa led several leaders to reform Commonwealth structures in order to make them more effective policy instruments, while trading on strengths such as the Commonwealth's informality. Leaders from the "old Commonwealth," most notably Canada's premier Pierre Trudeau, regularized the holding of meetings at the Singapore and Ottawa summits (calling them CHOGMs for the first time because so many of the heads of state were presidents rather than prime ministers) and introducing the "retreat" concept,[16] which proved to be beneficial in encouraging the special "Commonwealth spirit." The Singapore summit also saw the first of an important series of Commonwealth declarations. The Singapore declaration provided a "mission statement" on the Commonwealth's basic values, most notably Paragraph 6 on racial equality, which was declared to be at the heart of the association's values and was to guide its actions for the next twenty years.

Eight years later, racism was to be the subject of a declaration all its own at the 1979 Lusaka CHOGM, a summit better known for cutting the Gordian knot on Rhodesia. Significantly, there was no actual written commitment to democracy in the Singapore declaration (or in any successive declaration until the Harare summit in 1991). This was possibly due to the fact that with so many one-party states and military regimes, and no agreement even on the nature of democracy in the African Commonwealth, the word might have caused embarrassment and political problems, especially given the imperative for political consensus at Commonwealth meetings. The Singapore summit's emphasis on racial equality with its subtext of majority rule, however, sent a clear signal to Rhodesia and South Africa.

There is no doubt that in these formative years the personality of the Commonwealth's first secretary-general, Arnold Smith of Canada, played an important part in holding the international grouping together. As Derek Ingram has written, "this tough, resilient and amiable diplomat inevitably had many critics over the years, but his persistent faith in the Commonwealth, in sometimes appallingly difficult circumstances, coupled with adroit diplomatic skills, showed that Commonwealth governments had made a wise choice."[17] Certainly, the backing of the Canadians was crucial in helping many of the new members retain the belief that the Commonwealth really was an entity devoted to the welfare of its members and had ceased to represent solely British interests.

Rhodesia/Zimbabwe and South Africa: 1975–1990

At a vital moment in the history both of the Commonwealth and of southern Africa, there was a change in the secretary-generalship. The association unanimously appointed the foreign minister of Guyana, Sir Shridath Ramphal. An outgoing and fluent lawyer-politician, he had won his international spurs in the long negotiations (1973–1975) over the Lomé convention between the African-Caribbean-Pacific Group (ACP) and the European Economic Community. He was thus well versed in the politics and language of the new international economic order. The advent of a third world political figure taking the helm of the Commonwealth was a significant element in the 1970s atmosphere, redolent with possibilities of change. Ramphal, according to an official who worked closely with him in Marlborough House (headquarters of the Commonwealth), "made the modern Commonwealth" and had "breadth of vision, and an ability to see the connectivity of things."[18] Events were on his side, but he had the political flair and judgment to take advantage of them.

Ramphal amply lived up to expectations, especially in relation to the action that was needed to speed up decolonization in southern Africa. Although he was appointed in 1975 at the Commonwealth's first Caribbean summit in Kingston, Jamaica, his first CHOGM was in London in 1977. The conclusion of the Gleneagles agreement on breaking sporting links with South Africa achieved a spectacular coup. A sympathetic Labour Party government under Jim Callaghan in London doubtless helped in realizing this, but it was still seen as something of an achievement for Ramphal.

The summit was an important move by the Commonwealth toward recognizing the legitimacy of the armed liberation struggle in South Africa. The declaration, after stating that "the independence of Zimbabwe must be achieved on the basis of majority rule," and recognizing that maximum pressure on the "illegal Smith regime" was necessary, noted that "the armed struggle has become complementary to other efforts, including a negotiated settlement" and agreed that its maintenance was "inevitable." For a grouping like the Commonwealth, this acceptance of the unavoidability of the armed struggle was a major commitment.[19]

The configuration among Western powers—the end of the Kissinger era, and the Carter-Callaghan meeting of minds—combined with persistent guerrilla activity (particularly by Mugabe's ZANU), to set the scene. Henry Kissinger's brief incursion into southern Africa bequeathed a half-cocked election, which brought Bishop Abel Muzorewa briefly to power as a circumscribed prime minister in March 1979. But this proved to be a hollow victory and certainly was not going to end the war. As Ramphal noted in his report to the heads of government for 1977–1979, Commonwealth members realized that the 3 March 1979 internal settlement bought time and maintained minority rule.

Western opinion increasingly accepted the Nyerere-Kaunda line that peace could only return to the country through accommodating the freedom fighters.[20] Surprising some commentators, Margaret Thatcher reluctantly accepted the advice from her foreign secretary, Lord Carrington, that she "bite the bullet" on Rhodesia/Zimbabwe because maintaining the internal settlement would risk a "break up of the Commonwealth."[21] Biting the bullet meant engaging with the Commonwealth at its biennial CHOGM in Lusaka. She tried to wriggle out of the event and to prevent the Queen from attending, but she was finally forced to commit to the compromises hammered out in Lusaka, which provided, among other things, for Rhodesia/Zimbabwe to return to British constitutional rule under temporary British stewardship while pre-independence elections were held in which all parties would participate.

To some extent, because the Lusaka agreement anticipated a brief return to British control, this was easy for her to do and accorded with her own instincts to be shot of the problem early and for good.[22] Her advisers, however, were also keen to retain Britain's place in the world, its prestige with its allies, and its influence in Africa. The Lusaka CHOGM was critically important to subsequent events.

The true role of Ramphal and other Commonwealth officials has never been properly recorded. Ramphal, for example, has never written his memoirs,[23] and only he knows exactly how much he did, when, where, and how. It is certain that with other African leaders, he was very influential in keeping the various Zimbabwean parties at the conference table, and the formula for settling the land issue was very much his initiative. This formula was never implemented, and the land question has consequently come back to haunt Zimbabwe.

In spite of the "writing being on the wall" after the Lusaka summit, many, including Ian Smith, still went to Lancaster House believing that the share of power he had wanted from the bogus "internal settlement" might still be negotiated in London. Smith now claims that the South African government under B. J. Vorster engaged in a "great betrayal" at Lancaster House, to please the Americans. There were indeed strong indications that the South Africans considered the Rhodesia/Zimbabwe war to be an increasing liability that could compromise their own security (as well as the hopes they entertained of limited international acceptance).

This mutual interest was evident from the time Vorster met Kissinger in 1976. The South Africans had sought to preempt the ascension of Robert

Mugabe—considered by them as the most dangerous of the freedom fighters—to power. But even that was ultimately of limited concern, as long as they were secure within their own borders. By the time Mugabe and his party confounded expectations and foiled British intrigues (among other attempts) to influence the election in February 1980,[24] the panic and machinations of the past year seemed trivial and inconsequent. Democracy had spoken, and much had been put into perspective. Zimbabwe went on to enjoy at least fifteen years of progress and prosperity. The Commonwealth was consistent in the way in which it prosecuted its cause and in the determination of its leaders not to have half-measures, of the kind desired by British government, foisted on them.

Zimbabwe's independence provided the space for renewed activity within the conference; but this time the target was South Africa. Dropping Rhodesia as an agenda item "freed the front line states of the burden of the struggle in Zimbabwe and enabled them to join the new state in joint moves towards regional self-reliance"[25] (a reference to the establishment in 1980 of the SADCC, with which the Commonwealth had, from the beginning, a close and useful relationship). The enthusiasm with which the new state joined the Commonwealth facilitated a Commonwealth role alongside the European Community in helping to underpin the new grouping; the South Africans took a dim view of this. South West Africa/Namibia also took on greater international focus (including being featured on the Commonwealth agenda) as a weak link in South Africa's armor, as it technically involved a decolonization issue, thus necessitating United Nations involvement. A decade went by before forces were internationally mobilized.

The main matter in hand, however, was South Africa itself. Because of its unusual history, the issue in South Africa was perceived to be more about liberation than about decolonization. Commonwealth summits in the 1980s became increasingly engaged with the South African issue. Ramphal had stated clearly at the beginning of the decade, "For the Commonwealth to remain true to the multiracialism which is part of its credo . . . its role in the 1980s must also encompass the effort to bring apartheid to an end in South Africa."[26] What had begun with the Gleneagles agreement of 1977 developed, through the Melbourne and Delhi CHOGMs, to the 1985 Nassau CHOGM at which Thatcher was confronted by the rest of the Commonwealth.

This important breakthrough led to the adoption of sanctions, albeit limited and resisted by Thatcher. This Commonwealth action occurred against the backdrop of an international wave of financial and economic sanctions by the UN and others in 1985 and 1986, in reaction to the increasing brutality of P. W. Botha's regime in South Africa, which was especially evident in its military scourging of the Frontline States. Sir Robin Renwick, who was Britain's ambassador in Pretoria during the late 1980s and early 1990s, said that Botha "did more than anyone to turn the South African regime into a Latin American style junta—complete with death squads."[27] As important as the adoption of sanctions in Nassau was the pioneering act of sending to South Africa an eminent persons group (EPG) jointly led by former Nigerian head of state General Olusegun Obasanjo and former Australian prime minister Malcolm Fraser. This was, arguably, the most influential of all Commonwealth initiatives on South Africa, offering for the first time, as the report of the group *Mission to South Africa* said, a blueprint for a negotiated settlement.[28] In his official biography, *Eye of Fire*, Chief Anyaoku says that British attempts at disinformation almost caused it to abort before it began but, once produced, it made essentially moderate proposals, which, even if rejected by the Botha regime, "planted a seed that grew and had many branches."[29]

Botha's rejection of the EPG led to an even tougher approach at the next CHOGM in Vancouver in 1987, where the Okanagan declaration produced one of the most comprehensive statements ever made by the Commonwealth. An isolated Thatcher dissociated herself completely from the declaration and provoked still greater dismay by referring to the ANC as "terrorists." The Okanagan declaration also situated the conflict fully in the context of the Frontline States, most of which were already in the Commonwealth. It heightened the priority accorded the region by elevating the Commonwealth South Africa Committee into a committee of foreign ministers, which became the Commonwealth's main guiding organ for the South African issue until the transition ended in 1994.

The Kuala Lumpur summit in 1989 was less bitter than Vancouver, perhaps because the replacement of Botha by the more emollient F. W. de Klerk and the progress in the Angola/Namibia talks presaged more serious changes. It was not without the usual Thatcher contretemps, but six months after Kuala Lumpur, Nelson Mandela was released and the ban on the ANC was lifted, measures recommended by Nassau, the EPG, and most of the international community. In his memoirs, de Klerk gives the impression of not knowing where matters would end; he had clearly been hoping for a different solution.[30] Few had thought that everything would happen so soon. This was a period of profound change that saw the fall of the Berlin Wall; Mandela's release and the subsequent "negotiated revolution" were part of a wave of changes. Yet, for anyone engaged in the long battle, they represented a great deal more. For the Commonwealth, these were the glory years, and, after decolonization, the organization conceived ending apartheid as the last great good cause.

This is perhaps the moment to ask what role the Commonwealth really played. If the key internal player was the ANC, which had been willing to take up arms, and the key external player the United States (for the beginning of U.S. disinvestment in the mid-1980s really set the red lights flashing), and if the UN was the major theater for much of the international diplomacy, still the Commonwealth helped significantly to determine the international climate and to set the agenda. The formation of the EPG was one of the defining moments on the road to a negotiated settlement, and its recommendations were eventually used as the basis for the final settlement in 1994.

Throughout this period, Commonwealth initiatives had been developing alongside a parallel process at the UN, as the former's diplomacy moved from rhetorical support of the armed struggle to a more planned form of engagement.[31] Moreover, the Australian initiative[32] at the Kuala Lumpur CHOGM in 1989, which set up an agency to examine financial flows to South Africa, reportedly led to U.S. state banks refusing to deal with South Africa, and this seriously affected the economic situation within the apartheid state. But if the deus ex machina was unavoidably de Klerk himself, a multitude of factors combined to bring about the fundamental change. Patti Waldmeir in her account of the end of apartheid writes, "De Klerk had been pushed to the edge of the cliff by the combined forces of history, economics, demography and mortality; by sanctions, and disinvestments, by sporting boycotts, and Nelson Mandela; by the process of decline which began the day apartheid was invented."[33]

At a certain period, the conflicts between Margaret Thatcher and the rest of the Commonwealth exposed the Commonwealth to attacks that, in turn, only helped forge for it a more solid identity. This was, in a sense, a preparation for the changed scenario of the 1990s, in which the deepening of democracy became the focus of international efforts. The involvement of the Commonwealth in the southern African drama was, arguably, the making of the Commonwealth as an international force and was crucial in its transformation from a postcolonial club into a purposive grouping in its own right. But the dramas at the international level were merely a backdrop for internal events, from Sharpeville to Soweto to the mounting antigovernment campaigns of South Africa's United Democratic Front in the 1980s and to the increasingly desperate attacks by the South African regime on neighboring African states.

Because of the regional nature of the South African crisis, the Commonwealth mounted a series of programs for capacity building, as almost all the Frontline States under threat were Commonwealth countries and members of the SADC. Technical assistance and other support given to the SADC helped it transform into an economic community in 1994, after South Africa joined, and this assistance was developed and expanded as the organization expanded.

The Commonwealth and Security in the Post–Cold War Era

Namibia

Particularly important in the Commonwealth's history is the Namibian crisis. Throughout the 1970s South West Africa/Namibia figured in Commonwealth deliberations, even as the international campaign for its independence through a UN trusteeship developed. In the 1980s, the extent to which the Namibian situation prefigured possible outcomes in South Africa became apparent, and the United States used it both to get the Cubans out of Angola, thereby appeasing a domestic constituency, and to put pressure on the Pretoria regime. Although diplomatic moves for Namibian independence had already begun when he came to power in 1988, de Klerk was a willing partner in the enterprise, and Namibian independence followed closely on Mandela's release. By then, the Cold War had ended and the Cuban presence in Luanda was no longer an issue. Through facilitating Namibian independence, the Commonwealth built up an important constituency in Namibia, and the Namibians still show immense gratitude for this. The Commonwealth further consolidated this relationship by, for example, providing training to almost the entire Namibian foreign ministry, under the Commonwealth Fund for Technical Cooperation.

Mozambique

A parallel example of strategic thinking by the Commonwealth occurred in Mozambique. Commonwealth links began almost immediately after Mozambican independence in 1975 and were originally championed by Michael Manley, the socialist prime minister of Jamaica. The British government also sanctioned this strategy because the UK was developing its own ties with Mozambique, partly because of its proximity to Rhodesia. The connection paid off during the Lancaster House conference in 1979, as Samora Machel was one of the main influences in convincing Mugabe to stay at the conference table. Machel was tired of the war and was particularly irritated by the way the Rhodesian Special Branch had virtually invented the Mozambique National Resistance Movement, originally a bogus guerrilla movement, in opposition to the authentic liberation movement in Mozambique, Front for the Liberation of Mozambique.

Ironically, Machel's role at Lancaster House earned him the gratitude of Thatcher, who later invited him on a state visit to Britain and awarded him one of Britain's highest honors. From the 1980s onward, Mozambique was provided with a program of Commonwealth technical assistance similar to that for Namibia. From 1988 to 1993 there was even a "special fund for Mozambique"—an indication of the priority it enjoyed. Relations were so good that when South Africa rejoined the Commonwealth, President Mandela pressed enthusiastically for Mozambique to join, despite its lack of a colonial British past. The British experience with Mozambique was, arguably, a remarkable example of forward-thinking diplomacy.

Mozambique's membership of the Commonwealth was accepted in 1995 (South Africa having been accepted as a member in May 1994).[34] This exceptional membership was supported by other SADC members.[35] Mozambique's own evolution into a multiparty democracy obviously helped substantially, as the criterion that membership of the Commonwealth should be granted only to democracies gained ground in the post–Cold War era. Ultimately, however, it was Nelson Mandela's endorsement that tipped the balance.

South Africa

Upon Mandela's release and the lifting of the ban on the ANC, the central issue became the process of a negotiated settlement. The South African transition became more subtle and complex during this "diplomatic phase" because there were many imponderables and obstacles to holding a proper democratic election, including the continuing existence of the Bantustans, violence, and the presence of a sinister "third force" that allegedly fomented violence among black South Africans. There was clearly a useful role for the Commonwealth to play because of its informal manner of operating, personal contacts with de Klerk, and "a special interest, special familiarity, and knowledge of South Africa."[36]

Chief Emeka Anyaoku, who became secretary-general in July 1990, used his diplomatic skills to full advantage in this period. He established an important role for a Commonwealth observer group to assist in the transition. The Commonwealth Observer Mission in South Africa went to South Africa in three phases between 1992 and 1994: the first included senior Commonwealth police officers, a retired Nigerian general, and other prominent personalities. Its presence, alongside a similar UN exercise, with a mission to curtail violence, reconcile communities, facilitate the return of refugees, and begin the socioeconomic rebuiling process undoubtedly influenced behavior and had a moderating influence, especially in KwaZulu-Natal, where the risks of civil war were greatest. Resources from the Commonwealth were also committed to improving police-community relations and to the electoral structures, as well as in the sectors of media and broadcasting.

The international monitoring exercise amounted to a peacekeeping operation, and the Commonwealth involvement, which on occasion entailed brokering peace deals,[37] pointed the way to a future role for the association. Never had the link between benevolent security policies and democracy been more clearly established. For example, when it came to observing the election itself, the Commonwealth team was reinforced by the Commonwealth Peacekeeping Assistance Group, which was to provide training, advice, and assistance to the National Peace Keeping Force, an organ that was supposed to have a special role in the elections (although it was never formally deployed).

The sparse resources provided by Commonwealth member governments, a factor that has held back Commonwealth operations on many occasions, inhibited full observation of the election. The Commonwealth Observer Group of 100, led by the former prime minister of Jamaica Michael Manley, was smaller and arrived much later than either the UN or the European Union (EU).[38] Arguably, the quality of its observers was superior (Mandela himself has said "the Commonwealth teams proved to be especially well qualified and effective in their role"[39]), but in view of pre-election violence and other uncertainties, an earlier arrival would have been useful. At least the Commonwealth, unlike the EU, promptly published a good, crisp report,[40] and its contribution on the ground to the creation of a favorable climate for the elections was widely respected.

When President Mandela came to office in May 1994, one of his first acts was to bring South Africa back into the Commonwealth, and he played a significant and constructive part in the summits in Auckland and Edinburgh. Mandela's foreword to *Eye of Fire* (the biography of Chief Anyaoku) observed, "the Commonwealth has become increasingly known for its various programs to promote and consolidate democracy, including in South Africa."[41]

The Commonwealth and Democracy Since 1990

Having assisted in the liberation of southern Africa, the Commonwealth turned its attention to questions of democracy, which became more closely linked to regional security and the survival of autocratic rule. In this regard, the prioritization given by Chief Anyaoku to the South African project, which he said was one of the two most significant developments during his ten-year period as secretary-general, was paralleled by the campaign, which he personally spearheaded, to bring more democracy to the Commonwealth. The objective was partly consistency—that the Commonwealth should not preach democracy in South Africa without practicing it.

As Anyaoku said in his report to the Durban CHOGM in 1999, "Commonwealth unity was . . . directed to combating the evil of apartheid. But the price of thus diverting the Commonwealth effort was to compel the association to live with a contradiction—professing a democratic vocation but containing within its ranks governments which could not be described by any definition as democratic."[42] At the end of his period in office, he noted on several occasions that there had been nine military regimes or one-party states in Commonwealth Africa when he took office; by the end of the decade there were none.

His first CHOGM, in Harare in 1991, had seen a full Commonwealth declaration by the heads of government on democracy, human rights (as part of a number of preoccupations that a little later in the decade would come to be grouped as "good governance"), and sustainable development. It was a clarion call only made possible by the changes that had swept the world in the previous two years. It was certainly the most comprehensive and groundbreaking statement made so far by the same Commonwealth that a few years before had been too nervous even directly to broach the word *democracy* in its declarations. The inclusion of "human rights" was also a major breakthrough, taking full advantage of the new opportunities.

It was vitally important for the Commonwealth that the dramatic changes, especially those involving South Africa, took place as a major world climacteric—the end of the Cold War—offered the first real chance to take Commonwealth values beyond the South African struggle. Shridath Ramphal, at the end of his fifteen momentous years in office, had seen the historic opportunity and had initiated the High Level Appraisal Group, in order for the Commonwealth to undertake a first-ever self-examiniation. This review produced the bones of material later fleshed out in the Harare declaration. Chief Anyaoku, who continued with the High Level Appraisal Group, was reportedly particularly insistent that the CHOGM be held in Harare because of the historic and emotional link between Zimbabwe and the Commonwealth, which went back to 1965. The fact that this was the furthest south the Commonwealth had ever met cannot be sufficiently emphasized. Zimbabwe was territory that for a long time had been taboo for such a meeting. The choice of Zimbabwe for such a major declaration had an inspirational impact on the whole southern African region.

Chief Anyaoku was, perhaps, smartly surfing the post–Cold War international tide, but it was clearly time to prioritize efforts to make the Commonwealth relevant, a subject of persistent pressure. Chief Anyaoku's own personality was an interesting mixture: a reserved and conscientious civil servant who had risen to the top from within the Commonwealth,[43] he also showed (perhaps by virtue of his long familiarity with the political balancing act involved with such a variegated multitude of states) an astute and highly political instinct when it came to making important decisions. It was very significant that an African held the office of secretary-general at this time, not only because of the Commonwealth's involvement in the South African transition but also because of the need to sell the newly reasserted democratic values of the organization elsewhere on the continent. Where once there had been a risk of the Commonwealth breaking up over African questions (division threatened on several occasions over the Rhodesia/Zimbabwe and the South Africa issues), the presence of Africa in the association was now properly cemented.

Anyaoku's cooler approach was perhaps needed after the flamboyant Ramphal years; he was able deftly to assist at different delicate negotiating stages in South Africa's transition. Mandela's personal tribute to Anyaoku in the foreword to *Eye of Fire*, cited above, and his keenness to see South Africa a Commonwealth member as quickly as possible both bear testimony to this. If Ramphal was the "architect of the present Commonwealth," Anyaoku, especially as one who had worked a long time with Ramphal, was its builder and consolidator.

Destiny later called Anyaoku to play a particularly difficult role in his own country, Nigeria. Although in some respects his Nigerian origins were a disadvantage, there were few who could have walked the tightrope as well as he did. He was, at the time, subjected to heavy criticism from the Abacha government in Nigeria and its mouthpieces, such as Foreign Minister Tom Ikimi. However, there were a number of "hawks" in the Commonwealth who felt that he had not been tough enough on the Abacha regime, suspecting that this was precisely because it was his home country.

It was a source of great pain and difficulty to him that Nigeria's membership of the Commonwealth was suspended over human rights abuses, notably the execution of the writer-politician Ken Saro-Wiwa and eight Ogoni activists in 1995, on the very eve of the Auckland summit, and that the positions he was obliged to take earned him obloquy at home. Mandela, who had staked much on counseling caution, felt the arrogant defiance of General Sani Abacha as a betrayal, provoking his furious reaction during the summit. Mandela's support for the suspension was almost certainly what tilted the conference in this direction, although it was an unprecedented action. Previous departures from the Commonwealth—South Africa, Pakistan, and Fiji—had been self-propelled, if only to avoid inevitable expulsion.

The suspension was accompanied by the Millbrook declaration, which gave teeth to the principles set out in the Harare declaration and involved setting up the Commonwealth Ministerial Action Group (CMAG) that has served as a democratic watchdog ever since. The action group first served as a watchdog on Nigeria, then Gambia (where there had been a coup in 1994), and then on Sierra Leone, Pakistan, and Fiji. Even if it is argued that the Commonwealth played no part in the near-miraculous demise of the Abacha regime, its experience ensured that when the regime fell, the Commonwealth was well positioned to assist its democratic recovery in 1999. This engagement was accompanied by the observance, throughout the decade, of over thirty elections in Commonwealth countries, many of them in Africa,[44] as well as a program for "deepening democracy." It was increasingly felt that if the Commonwealth commitment to democracy and governance was serious, simply observing elections, however important an activity, was not enough.

By the end of the decade, the problem of Zimbabwe had begun to loom again in southern Africa. By a curious irony, the tensions in Zimbabwe over the land issue, regrettably still unsettled twenty-one years after Lancaster House had attempted to broach the issue in 1979, came to a head in April 2000. This occurred just as the new secretary-general (Don McKinnon, former foreign minister of New Zealand) assumed office. The resurgence of the land issue was perhaps symptomatic of deeper political tensions, amounting to a *crise de regime* for Mugabe, twenty years after independence. Matters became highly sensitive when the issue of race was raised and McKinnon found himself under pressure to "do something" from a resuscitated "kith and kin" lobby allied to pro-democracy campaigners. The difficulty of arriving at the traditional Commonwealth consensus was dispensed with, as many African Commonwealth countries, especially neighbors like South Africa, were nervous about public opinion. They felt that the issue was best dealt with by privately engaging Mugabe, a course of action, according to some, that did not necessarily pay off, even if there was a widespread opinion in Africa that this was a private war between Britain and Zimbabwe. In March 2002, Zimbabwe was suspended from the Commonwealth for one year.

The prestigious position of Zimbabwe and its leader in the Commonwealth did not make the case any easier; Harare was, after all, the home of the 1991 declaration on democracy. Provocative utterances from British ministers Robin Cook and Peter Hain also worsened the situation. They sought cover from the Commonwealth by trying to invoke the CMAG, by now a seasoned "fire-fighting" body. It is worth noting that the southern African region was involved in the eight-member CMAG from the beginning; South Africa was a member from 1995 to 1997, when it was replaced by Botswana,[45] which now holds the chair in the person of General Mompati Merafe. Botswana has been very dedicated to CMAG objectives as a reflection of its own long attachment to democracy.

An attempt by the British to get the Zimbabwe issue onto the CMAG agenda at the beginning of May 2000 was diverted, if not entirely quelled. The main strategy for McKinnon, in a situation in which the Commonwealth appeared disadvantaged in every course of action, was to emphasize the need for elections and for the Commonwealth to send observers. Mugabe duly acceded to this. Although the run-up to the election was still marked by serious violence and intimidation, the Commonwealth was thus seen to be playing a proactive role. The Commonwealth observer team was led by former Nigerian head of state

General Abdulsalami Abubakar. In difficult circumstances it produced a report that was both objective and honorable, despite the fact that the exercise on the ground appeared somewhat overshadowed by the bigger EU observer mission.

The Commonwealth line on the holding of an election had been well justified as the opposition, while not winning, did remarkably well. The opposition, for the first time, became a serious parliamentary force for Mugabe to reckon with, and this had occurred without fully plunging the country into crisis. Both democracy and security were tenuously preserved, although the situation remains uncertain. Any future Commonwealth role is imponderable and has been made more difficult by the lack of a clear definition of CMAG's role. The issue was not even raised, let alone placed on the agenda, at the CMAG meeting in New York in September 2000. There is still a feeling in parts of the Commonwealth that the secretariat should be deployed to assist on the land issue.

The Zimbabwe crisis highlighted the real dilemma of the Commonwealth in its pursuit of democratic standards for its members. This was seen at the Durban CHOGM in the postponement, without serious discussion, of structured guidelines and thresholds for the operation of CMAG. Durban had looked cozy and under control for both the Commonwealth and Africa. This was because of the special position of the host, South Africa, in Commonwealth mythology and the welcome return of a democratic Nigeria. Continuing contradictions were somehow swept under the carpet, and the Pakistan coup of October 1999 was only a "specter at the feast"; most important, the African democratic front had been maintained.

In 2000, the Zimbabwean crisis began to cause new problems for the association, and a host of questions were raised about the future of the Commonwealth itself. Already, the report on the future of the Commonwealth issued on the eve of the Durban summit by a private think tank, the Foreign Policy Centre (suspected, despite denials, of being inspired by New Labour), had highlighted the contradictions of CMAG and called into question the "London-centricity" of the Commonwealth.[46] It hinted at a number of things that have subsequently happened, such as the introduction of a Commonwealth chairperson.

The Commonwealth and the Security of Southern Africa

Although the Commonwealth has kept clear of the military aspects of the SADC, there are those who would like to see a higher profile for the association in the field of conflict resolution. At present there is no unit in the Commonwealth secretariat specifically dedicated to this purpose—it tends to fall under what are loosely described as "the secretary-general's good offices" and, too often, to the overstretched Political Affairs Division. In Africa these "good offices" have been used extensively in Sierra Leone, where a personal representative of the secretary-general attended all the peace talks leading up to the aborted Lomé accord of July 1999, as a "moral guarantor."

In the SADC region, these good offices have been used in Zanzibar to facilitate a deal between parties following disputes in the 1995 elections,[47] and in Lesotho (for the last ten years) in a patient and not unproductive long-ranging effort to broker a deal between political parties. Both cases form part of the association's facilitation of democracy, which is seen by the Commonwealth as a means of stabilizing and enhancing security in the region. There may well be a case in the near future for invoking these good offices in Swaziland as growing democratic forces struggle to establish themselves. Obviously, the Commonwealth has not been and cannot be directly involved in the Congo war. But it has watched over the present crisis there with concern, as many Commonwealth members have been affected on both sides of the conflict. The porous nature of borders in the region makes it difficult to confine threats to democracy within a single country; this reinforces the need for a regional approach to the subject.

The informal family atmosphere of the Commonwealth and its multiple civil society networks put it in an ideal position to meet the demands of the twenty-first century. There are increasing calls for the "rolling back of big government" and for the Commonwealth to become more involved in conflict resolution, either as a backup for the UN or in disputes where it has special advantages. These advantages include its involvement in both the Zimbabwe elections and the South African transition. Unfortunately, the Commonwealth has very limited resources, so many of its tasks have to be performed by proxy, as in Sierra Leone in 1998, where a highly praised Commonwealth Police Task Force with members from Barbados, Britain, Canada, Sri Lanka, and Zimbabwe was almost entirely funded by the British. The provision of advice and expertise has always been a Commonwealth forte, and there is no reason why it cannot apply in the security field.[48] Capacity building in both the security forces and civil society is increasingly seen as part of governance support. This carries the advantage that few would argue against good governance as an objective, and good governance reinforces stability and security. The equation governing this situation is that security is essential for democracy to flourish.

South Africa continues to be a major component in the association's twenty-first-century history. Mandela was an enthusiastic and significant participant in Commonwealth affairs (especially on the Nigerian question); his successor has also taken on the Commonwealth mantle, partly because other members have expected much of the "new South Africa" as a key player in helping to keep the association relevant. Thus, President Thabo Mbeki hosted the Durban summit some five months after his inauguration, and South Africa took the chair. South Africa also took on direction of the High Level Review Group, which was due to produce new directions for the Commonwealth in the twenty-first century, at the CHOGM in Brisbane in October 2001. It remains to be seen how much influence South Africa's chairing has had on the way the Commonwealth is run.

The fact that an African is no longer secretary-general could give significance to having another African in the chairperson's role, but so far this has had limited impact, and ends after two years. We may suppose that some South African effort has been concentrated on the High Level Review Group, but it is clear that unless that group makes a breakthrough on the political front, it is in danger of disappointing. No amount of commitment on HIV/AIDS and other subjects will compensate for the lack of a commitment so far to spell out the mandate of CMAG in the manner proposed, and postponed, in Durban, which would have reinforced its role as a pioneering democratic watchdog. This is a serious test for the next CHOGM. There could, nevertheless, be further CMAG activity on the conflict-resolution side, using the comparative advantage deriving from the Commonwealth's "family atmosphere" and unofficial contacts. Although these matters tend to be demand-driven and often depend very much on personal diplomacy by the secretary-general, if the Commonwealth can demonstrate an ability to deliver, there will be continuing calls for its services in this respect.

Conclusion

Some may question the significance of the Commonwealth's role in southern Africa and whether this chapter inflates its importance. Noncomprehension or misunderstanding of the Commonwealth's role is prevalent and often leads to an over- or underestimation of its impact. There is additionally always some ambiguity involved in trying to chart the different areas where the Commonwealth has played a part in the evolution of southern Africa, especially in relation to moves toward full multiparty or nonracial democracy. While not to be exaggerated, the Commonwealth's role cannot be ignored.

One key factor to recognize when assessing the curious international position of the Commonwealth is that it has always "punched above its weight." The secretariat has a staff of only 300 and a budget of £35 million—including the funding for the programs of the Commonwealth Fund for Technical Cooperation. This paucity of means serves to emphasize the fact that its successes have arisen from its influence rather than its muscle power. As Chief Anyaoku was wont to say, the Commonwealth has been a "force for good" in the world. But a skeptic might ask, to paraphrase Joseph Stalin's question of the Pope, "how many divisions has the Commonwealth?" Its individual member states self-evidently have considerable military power and have made significant contributions to peacekeeping in different parts of the world, either under the UN umbrella or independently. But it is hard for the Commonwealth to claim this as anything but a surrogate form of power.

In the area of international economic relations, an increasingly important arena of international diplomacy, the Commonwealth has engaged, over some years, in significant advocacy on behalf of the heavily indebted poor countries.[49] Currently the secretariat is engaged in advocacy on behalf of small states faced with a diktat from the Organization for Economic Cooperation and Development (OECD—commonly perceived as the rich nations' grouping) against offshore financial centers engaged in "harmful tax competition." This is in spite of the fact that donors have encouraged small states to diversify into developing these same offshore financial centers that are now so shocking to the OECD. On this sort of issue, the Commonwealth's role as a bridge between developing and developed countries is invaluable. This arena is, however, limited, and the small number of member governments who actually finance the Commonwealth is also more than capable of intimidating it.

The Commonwealth can provide assistance to countries in need of diplomatic know-how to facilitate their relations with the EU or the World Trade Organization.[50] And the demand for such services is bound to increase because of mounting concerns over globalization,[51] which, in many ways, can threaten the security of the whole southern African region. But the Commonwealth is still struggling to make its mark when there are so many bigger organizations, including the World Bank and International Monetary Fund, as well as different UN agencies that are already active in this area. Given its size and meager resources, it is impossible for the Commonwealth to be involved in everything: some feel it must identify niches—areas where it does well and has earned appreciation. It should then focus on filling these niches until such time as its members wish to increase its resources.

On the other hand, there are powerful arguments for keeping broader ambitions in view. It may sometimes look as if the Commonwealth "punches above its weight," but its special nature dictates that it should be a big player; with sufficient resources, it could certainly tackle a larger role.

The Commonwealth has over the years shown enormous resilience in the face of skepticism and disillusion, even derision, and countries still wish enthusiastically to join it, as South Africa, Mozambique, and Cameroon did in 1995. There were some, during Nigeria's suspension, who worried that Nigeria would walk out of the Commonwealth altogether. It did not, and instead put a high priority on returning as a democracy once it had undergone political change. Many of the Commonwealth's smaller members are keen to use it as their advocate, even while complaining of its limitations.

The Commonwealth's lack of focus may in part result from the strong civil society roots in so many of its member states; strong civil societies are, perforce, diverse and difficult to coordinate. The civil society dimension of the Commonwealth can be turned to considerable advantage in modern times, for, as we have already noted, big government is under attack from those who want to see it rolled back and decentralized. In southern Africa, especially given the South African concern with civil society, the Commonwealth can play a pertinent role both in the maintenance of democracy and in conflict resolution.

To be relevant and responsive to the needs of its members, the Commonwealth must capitalize on its advantages. Great issues, such as those that put the Commonwealth on the map from the 1970s to the 1990s, will become increasingly rare. The Commonwealth should not attempt to overreach its capacities, but it is still uniquely placed to engage in creative and experimental diplomacy and advocacy in tough situations; this could give it a role in issues of democracy and security in southern Africa. How it walks this tightrope will test it as a major constructive force in world diplomacy in the twenty-first century.

Notes

1. Emeka Anyaoku, speech given at the "Professions for World Disarmament and Development" conference, London, 18 March 1989; reprinted in *The Missing Headlines* (Liverpool, UK: University Press, 1997), 392.

2. See G. Winter, *Inside BOSS: South Africa's Secret Police* (London: Passim, 1981). Winter was an agent who defected, and some of his assertions are specious and unreliable, but the book still contains much source material.

3. Thabo Mbeki, interview, *Time,* 9 September 2000, 44: "All of us have an obligation to de-racialize our society. It guarantees our security, and addresses the possibility of a savage explosion down the line. To tackle racism we have to end the socio-economic divisions in our society."

4. The Commonwealth's formal commitment to small states came two years later at the Nassau CHOGM.

5. A "Commonwealth brigade," a survivor of the Korean War, comprising Britain, Australia, New Zealand, and Malaysia, existed in Hong Kong until 1972. See W. Gutteridge, "Military Ties," in *The Commonwealth in the 1980s,* ed. A.J.R. Groom and P. Taylor (London: Macmillan, 1984), 116–124.

6. Ibid. Gutteridge also mentions two organizations that may or may not still be in existence but are certainly unknown to the Commonwealth secretariat. These are the Commonwealth Committee on Defence (Clothing and Operational Equipment) and the Commonwealth Defence Science Organisation. Both, he says, were set up after World War II but involved members of the new Commonwealth

like India and Malaysia and were still meeting in the early 1980s. Later in the decade the names were changed to "defense agencies"; the bodies still exist.

7. Records show that the notion of the "British" Commonwealth was officially buried in 1947, even before the birth of the modern Commonwealth at the London conference of 1949.

8. A 114-year-old Ugandan veteran was included in the 2000 procession.

9. I am grateful to Derek Ingram for the following elucidation of this particular point: "The London declaration of 1949 accepted the 'British monarch' as head in accepting 'the King as the symbol . . . and as such, the head of the Commonwealth.' The 'headship' was vested in the person of the King and subsequently passed to the Queen. Only at the Edinburgh CHOGM in 1997 was the criterion changed to the 'British monarch'; this point was skated over in the communiqué and appears only in the endorsed criteria. My own view is that most countries never spotted the change."

10. P. Robertson, "A Common Purpose: the Commonwealth's Support for AAM," in *The Anti-Apartheid Movement: A 40-Year Perspective* (London: AAM Archives Committee, 2000), 46–49. Robertson notes that during the 1950s the principle of noninterference permitted South Africa to resist pressure from the new members on the subject of apartheid, but at the 1960 prime ministers' meeting, it was told that if it wanted to be a republic it would have to submit its membership of the Commonwealth anew, which inevitably set the scene for its departure.

11. This was a period during which the then-prime minister of Britain, Margaret Thatcher, virtually stood alone in her support or opposition of certain positions within the Commonwealth. Her opposition to economic sanctions against South Africa was one position.

12. The issue of the use of force was discussed extensively at the "Rhodesian UDI," a public record office witness seminar held at the Public Record Office in Kew, London, on 6 September 2000. The author participated in this discussion.

13. A. Smith, *Stitches in Time* (London: Andre Deutch, 1977), 4–5. He says that President Kwame Nkrumah of Ghana first proposed this, with support from President Milton Obote of Uganda and Eric Williams of Trinidad and Tobago. It had crucial backing from Australia and Canada, and the British premier, Sir Alec Douglas-Home, was persuaded there might be some electoral advantage for him.

14. Zambia's difficult struggle is chronicled very effectively in R. Hall, *The High Price of Principles* (New York: Africana, 1969).

15. See D. Ingram, *The Imperfect Commonwealth* (London: Rex Collings, 1976), 59–70.

16. The retreat was very much Trudeau's own notion, the first being held at Mont Tremblant, Canada, in 1973.

17. Ingram, *Imperfect Commonwealth*, 17.

18. Private interview with the author, London, October 2000.

19. Commonwealth, "Commonwealth Heads of Government: The London Communiqué," London, June 1977, xx.

20. Cyrus Vance, *Hard Choices* (New York: Simon and Schuster, 1983). Former U.S. secretary of state Cyrus Vance writes, "We recognized that identifying the United States with the cause of majority rule was the best way to prevent Soviet and Cuban exploitation of southern Africa." All parties paid lip service to majority rule from 1976 onward.

21. P. Carrington, *Reflect on Things Past* (London: Collins, 1983).

22. S. Chan, *The Commonwealth in World Politics, 1965–1985* (London: Lester Crook, 1988), 35–46.

23. He published two volumes: *Inseparable Humanity*, an anthology of reflections, and *An End to Otherness*, a collection of speeches.

24. The British were trying to ensure that Joshua Nkomo and Abel Muzorewa formed a coalition that would win the elections.

25. Commonwealth Secretary-General, "Eighth Report to Heads of Government," Commonwealth Secretariat, London, 1981, 8.

26. Ibid.

27. Robin Renwick, "Rational Explanation for a Miracle," book review, *The Financial Times,* 8 May 1997, 15.

28. See Commonwealth, *Mission to South Africa: The Findings of the Commonwealth Eminent Persons Group on Southern Africa* (London: Penguin, 1986).

29. P. Johnson, *Eye of Fire—Emeka Anyaoku* (Trenton, N.J.: Africa World Press, 2000), 43–46.

30. See F. W. de Klerk, *The Last Trek—A New Beginning: The Autobiography* (London: Macmillan, 1998).

31. A point made by Christopher Landsberg, "Exporting Peace? The UN and South Africa,"*Policy Issues and Actors* (Centre for Policy Studies, Johannesburg) 7, 2 (April 1994): 9.

32. I am grateful to Derek Ingram for drawing my attention to this initiative.

33. P. Waldmeir, *Anatomy of a Miracle* (London: Penguin, 1997), 109.

34. The "instant membership" of South Africa was decided in a special resolution at the Limassol summit in Cyprus in 1993.

35. Eight of the then ten members of the SADC were in the Commonwealth—Botswana, Lesotho, Malawi, South Africa, Swaziland, Tanzania, Zambia, and Zimbabwe. The SADC now has twelve members, including another Commonwealth country, Mauritius.

36. Johnson, *Eye of Fire,* 84.

37. Ibid., 88–89. Johnson cites the example of Moses Anafu, who brokered a peace deal in the Port Shepstone area of KwaZulu-Natal.

38. Manley played a vital part in several CHOGMs and is counted as one of the major figures in a Commonwealth gallery of heroes.

39. Johnson, *Eye of Fire,* vi.

40. COGSA (Commonwealth Observer Group), "Report on the South African Elections," Commonwealth Secretariat, London, 1994.

41. Johnson, *Eye of Fire,* vi.

42. Commonwealth Secretary-General, "From Kuala Lumpur to Durban," report, London, October 1999.

43. In this his career strongly resembled that of the present UN Secretary-General, Kofi Annan, who also rose to the top from within the organization.

44. Elections observed in Africa during the decade were Zambia (1991); Seychelles, Ghana, and Kenya (1992); Lesotho and the Seychelles (1993); South Africa, Malawi, and Namibia (1994); Tanzania (1995); Sierra Leone and Ghana (1996); Cameroon (1997); Seychelles and Lesotho (1998); Nigeria, Malawi, and Mozambique (1999); and Zimbabwe and Tanzania (2000).

45. The other members of the CMAG are Australia, Barbados, Bangladesh, Canada, Malaysia, Nigeria, and the UK.

46. K. Ford and S. Katwala, *Reinventing the Commonwealth* (London: Foreign Policy Centre, 1999).

47. The Commonwealth's attempts to broker peace between the government and opposition forces in Zanzibar resulted in an agreement, signed in June 1999.

Unfortunately this agreement came unstuck during the October 2000 elections, which the Commonwealth team in Zanzibar described as a "fiasco."

48. In 1999, the Solomon Islands brought in Commonwealth mediation to help resolve a breakdown of security in the country. In November 2000, an eminent persons group was dispatched to Papua New Guinea to advise on the restructuring of the security forces.

49. Commonwealth Finance Ministers meetings, notably those in Trinidad (1989) and Mauritius (1997) and Ottawa (1998), have produced important initiatives on debt.

50. In November 2000, the Commonwealth signed a memorandum of understanding with the ACP in Brussels, giving the EU observer status at ACP meetings. Since the late 1970s, the Commonwealth has given technical assistance to the ACP in their repeated negotiations with Brussels.

51. Two relevant documents are the "Fancourt Declaration on Globalisation" and the "Durban Communiqué," both from the Commonwealth Secretariat, 1999.

Part 4

Conclusion

16

Southern Africa's Security Architecture: Challenges and Prospects

MWESIGA BAREGU AND CHRISTOPHER LANDSBERG

This volume has assessed the major security, trade, and political challenges faced by the southern African subregion. It has also assessed the role that the Southern African Development Community (SADC), the subregion's main multilateral organization entrusted with coordinating regional economic and political integration, as well as peace and security in particular, has played in managing these challenges. The volume has argued that southern Africa's security not only involves developing a coherent security architecture to manage military conflicts in states like Angola, Zimbabwe, the Democratic Republic of Congo (DRC), Lesotho, and Swaziland. It also must grapple with issues of trade, governance and democracy, HIV/AIDS, and social justice issues like land reform and redistribution.

The diverse issues addressed by this volume include the role and prospects of the SADC Organ on Politics, Defense, and Security (OPDS), now the Organ on Politics, Defense, and Security Cooperation (OPDSC); the link between trade and security; the role of civil society actors in managing conflicts; the link between democratization and security; social justice questions; the critical land debate; comparative lessons for the SADC from other African subregions; and the legitimacy crises facing South Africa and Nigeria as they try to assume the roles of regional hegemons in their respective areas. It further investigates the SADC's relationship with important external actors such as the United Nations, the former Organization of African Unity (OAU), the African Union (AU), the Commonwealth, the United States, and the European Union (EU) and the SADC's relations with and ability to learn lessons from the Economic Community of West African States (ECOWAS), the Intergovernmental Authority on Development (IGAD), and the East African Community (EAC).

The volume will hopefully make a modest contribution to addressing the problems, and meeting the challenges, of southern Africa's regional security architecture. At the very least, it should generate further debate and discussion about the future of southern African regional security. Let us now highlight some of the observations and recommendations that emerge from these chapters.

The volume's primary theme is the conceptual shift from an emphasis on state security, with its military and national security implications, to a broader human security paradigm, which focuses on the challenges posed by social justice issues such as poverty; land possession, dispossession, and repossession; and economic exclusion of significant segments of indigenous populations. The human security and social justice paradigm is supported by emerging evidence of the complex links between inter- and intrastate conflicts in southern Africa (and throughout the continent). This is a conflict terrain in which socioeconomic and politico-human rights problems spill over from one country to the next and where societal tensions become shared challenges for neighboring states, as well as for an entire subregion searching for ways and means to institutionalize conflict prevention and management.

The authors of this volume identify the key challenges of a viable and effective regional security architecture. The first challenge is the absence of this broader human security perspective from the official SADC agenda. Perhaps, now that the heads of state have resolved the modalities of the SADC organ's relationship to the SADC proper, human security can begin to be factored into its framework alongside a more prominent role for civil society organizations and nongovernmental organizations (NGOs) in operationalizing the SADC organ, including the Protocol on Politics, Defense and Security Cooperation.

The second challenge is developing the capacity to cope with globalization and the security implications it poses for governance not only in southern Africa but also in the region as a whole, where it erodes the ability of states to deal with critical social justice questions. Third, this volume has also highlighted just how important the distinction is between, on the one hand, formal or procedural democracy (free and fair elections, the protection of civil liberties, separation of powers, and the role of opposition parties) and, on the other hand, the strengthening of substantive democracy (the ability of the state to be responsive to the needs of the citizenry, to eradicate poverty, and to ensure the effective participation in decisionmaking and addressing pressing issues of poverty, land dispossession, and economic justice). Formal democracy, while crucial, can never be a sufficient condition for responding to the particular needs of African societies. This means that in southern Africa, as elsewhere in Africa, the prospects for democracy and its consolidation depend on addressing major economic challenges, which relate to redressing historical imbalances, regulating resource distribution, and promoting broader social justice. Otherwise, even the reversibility of formal (and largely donor-driven) democracy and development cannot be ruled out, a prospect that carries serious long-term security implications.

While land reform controversies in southern Africa reflect the salience of social justice concerns for the realization of political stability, an examination of international, regional, subregional, and major country actors and interests reveals a whole range of other issues that must be addressed. These issues include arriving at viable working relationships between subregional actors such as the SADC, ECOWAS, IGAD, and the AU, while factoring in a credible role for major actors such as South Africa and Nigeria. Partnership building in southern Africa's evolving security architecture must start within Africa and the subcontinent itself. However, external actors such as the UN Security Council and the Western powers must own up to their responsibilities as critical actors with interests in the region.

Indeed, apart from the UN, which has actively but hesitantly been involved in conflict resolution and peacekeeping initiatives in Angola and in the DRC, other extraregional actors have kept a relatively low profile. This emerges clearly in the survey of extraregional actors, whether these are major powers such as the United States, regional intergovernmental and economic blocs like the EU, or international organizations such as the Commonwealth, as well as the World Bank and International Monetary Fund. Whether or not the Brahimi report on UN peace operations, which recommends centralization of peacekeeping operations, will make a difference in generating higher profile commitments remains to be seen.

These points generate several observations and recommendations. The traditional understanding of security—meaning, in large part, the security of sovereign states, their borders and governments—needs to be expanded to cope with the current problems faced by southern Africa, such as displaced persons, immigration, HIV/AIDS, and drought, and to address critically the desperate social justice challenges that are often put on the back burner by regional and external actors. This has been the case particularly in the peace agreements that brought about the settlements in Zimbabwe, Namibia, and South Africa. Security, viewed through the realist paradigm's military lens of threat perception, has often led to high defense expenditures and confrontation rather than negotiation; it has tended to be state-centric rather than people-centered. To address the changing security needs of the southern African subregion, conflict prevention and conflict management involving civil society actors with a stress on formal peace and, more critically, social justice, should be the primary goal of any new security architecture within the SADC. But the nature of civil society itself can be flawed. Externally funded NGOs often parade as civil society while they actually have limited connectedness with the poor and the destitute. Also, it should be emphasized that the proliferation of NGOs that parade as civil society may erode the capacities of civil societies to help address security challenges and influence policy.

Security is intimately linked to issues of poverty, disease, the environment, and ethnic and political conflict. Poverty and inequality of resource distribution, including issues related to land reform, remain a principal source of instability in the whole of southern Africa. HIV/AIDS presents a particular threat, as the UN Security Council recently noted.[1] There is a direct link between the prevalence of HIV/AIDS and social exclusion and poverty; this is the essence of Thabo Mbeki position in the HIV/AIDS debate and should be the debate's focus. Regional and subregional economic integration, in addition to its importance in overcoming poverty, is a precondition for advancing peace and security in southern Africa. It is essential, however, to ensure that institutions in southern Africa are designed to fit the problems they confront rather than the political convenience of the day.

Southern Africa's principal multilateral organization remains the SADC. Within the SADC, the body responsible for security is the new SADC Organ on Politics, Defense, and Security Cooperation. Within the OPDSC is the Inter-State Defence and Security Committee (ISDSC), a successor institution of the disbanded Frontline States. While much has been said about the lack of political will in efforts to operationalize the OPDS, there are ongoing efforts by SADC members to establish a functioning decisionmaking process.

That process was substantially advanced by the August 2001 Blantyre summit's ratification of the special summit in Windhoek in March 2001, which resolved the question of the modality of relationship between the OPDSC and the SADC proper. This issue decided in favor of a compromise between centralized, integrated authority and a decentralized, autonomous process falling under the heads-of-state summit. There was also a change of leadership from Zimbabwe's Robert Mugabe to Mozambique's Joaquim Chissano, with both Mugabe and Tanzanian president Benjamin Mkapa as his deputies. Although these changes represent progress, they still do not resolve concerns about the lack of transparency and the need for greater civil society involvement. It remains to be seen how the SADC organ will interact with the AU, in which the principle of state sovereignty is being challenged, and with the New Partnership for Africa's Development (NEPAD) stressing the politics of accountability and peer review among heads of state.

It should be understood that the OPDSC itself cannot be effectively operationalized without the proper operationalization of the SADC Protocol on Politics, Defense, and Security Cooperation. The effective institutionalization and ratification of the protocol should now become a primary focus of individuals, organizations, and governments, including the SADC. However, a challenge here is for the SADC to address the status of the Luanda Mutual Defense Pact between Zimbabwe, Angola, Namibia, and the DRC and to finalize the process of an SADC common defense pact, leading eventually to an SADC common security community.

A major challenge confronting governments and civil society actors throughout southern Africa is institutional bridge-building to close the gaps between rhetoric and action and between policy and practice. The conflict and the peace process in the DRC highlights the ongoing challenges facing the SADC. The challenge facing peacemakers in southern Africa and the Great Lakes region is how to institutionalize a process of conflict management in a region of complex inter- and intrastate conflicts, taking into account the range of actors and interests involved. A more immediate challenge is determining how the SADC can contribute to the work of the United Nations Mission in the Congo or, to state it properly, how the UN mission should be altered and expanded to respond to the priorities and demands of the leadership and people of the region, especially in the aftermath of the South Africa–brokered DRC–Rwanda agreement of July 2002, as well as the breakthrough in Angola. The peace process in the DRC further faces the challenge of the meaningful engagement of actors and interests in the Inter-Congolese Dialogue (ICD). Indeed, the Sun City process of the ICD, which commenced in February 2002, revealed the complex interconnections between the internal and external interests and actors in the DRC.

Organizationally, an appropriate division of labor between the SADC and the UN must take account of the different challenges facing each organization. For the SADC, this includes addressing the impact of HIV/AIDS, transnational organized crime, the proliferation of small arms, economic development, and above all social justice. For the UN, it includes ensuring that globalization benefits people in all parts of the world, not only the rich industrialized nations, as well as both strengthening the UN's role and focusing it on peacemaking and peacekeeping in the region. Cooperation between the UN and subregional organizations like the SADC can bring together UN experience and expertise and local understanding of specific issues such as the control of illicit arms and the disarmament of former combatants in states like Mozambique. But experience teaches us that the modalities of divisions of labor between the UN and subregional organizations in Africa should be properly worked out, and the UN Security Council in particular cannot be allowed to shirk its responsibilities on the continent. There is also a need to extend diplomacy and partnership beyond the liaison between the SADC and the UN. Equally urgently, a more effective relationship must be developed between international, regional, and subregional organizations, including the SADC, the UN, ECOWAS, the EAC, the IGAD, and the AU. Building an effective relationship between the SADC and the conflict management and prevention mechanisms of these institutions is an issue that has received insufficient scholarly attention.[2] A good place to start is for the UN to clarify its stance on the position and role of regional initiatives in peacekeeping operations, such as the interventions in the DRC and Lesotho by SADC states.

There are promising signs of interregional cooperation involving Africa's regional and subregional organizations, based on cooperation among some of their leading member countries. South Africa's cooperation with the ECOWAS states of Nigeria, Ghana, and Senegal in a peacekeeping mission in Burundi is an indication of the potential cross-regional engagements that could develop. The challenge still remains how to involve neighboring countries more directly in peace processes in which they have vested interests.

Multilateral organizations must develop a common understanding of the connections between preventive diplomacy, peacemaking, and peacebuilding that goes beyond peacekeeping. Keeping the peace does not start or stop with the arrival or departure of a peacekeeping force; efforts to restore peace in Africa are unlikely to succeed unless the root causes of conflicts are properly addressed and the means found of effective peacebuilding to prevent the rekindling of conflicts.[3] Here again, a proactive role for civil society must be factored into operationalizing southern Africa's peace and security architecture. Recent events in the subregion underline the importance of civil society actors. The role of the churches, labor movement, and progressive NGOs in Zambia in reversing the campaign to change the constitution to allow the incumbent to seek another presidential term is indicative, as is the church's increasing activity in Zimbabwe and Angola.

The idea of subregional actors, such as South Africa and Nigeria, promoting hegemonic stability in partnership with others so as to manage African conflicts more effectively will remain controversial and contested for as long as these states do not address the legitimacy crises associated with their giantism and, in South Africa's case, the destructive role it played during the era of white-minority domination and its legacy of apartheid. It is vital that this hegemonic potential be harnessed into multilateral frameworks involving subregional organizations (the SADC and ECOWAS), regional organizations such as the African Union, and international organizations like the UN. Nigeria and South Africa (along with Senegal, Egypt, Botswana, Tanzania, and others) were in the forefront of the drafting and marketing the New Partnership for Africa's Development. NEPAD needs to focus on the following areas:

- Democracy, governance, and peace and security.
- Economic and corporate governance.
- Infrastructure and information technology.
- Human resource development (notably health and education).
- Agriculture and market access.[4]

A subcommittee on peace and security to focus on conflict management, prevention, and resolution has been set up, with South Africa as chair and also including Algeria, Gabon, Mali, and Mauritius. The active involvement of SADC member states like South Africa and Mauritius in the activities of NEPAD has led them to push for a process in which southern African security concerns and issues would be streamlined along NEPAD's priority areas. But NEPAD can only succeed if it becomes part of a larger pan-continental agenda and framework that enjoys the support of all African countries and sorts out its relation with the AU. The issue is not NEPAD's relationship to the SADC but to the AU.

External actors like the UN, the United States, the EU, and the Commonwealth can play an important role in supporting the SADC's efforts to strengthen its security capacity. These external actors will, however, need to consult better with the SADC and AU to determine these organizations' own needs and priorities, and they must recognize that such assistance requires both resources and continued commitment on their part. Indeed, the type of partnership between Africa and the northern industrial powers of the G-8 that emerged after the G-8 summit in Canada in June 2002 will not provide the needed framework for building more viable partnerships between extraregional actors and the SADC, beyond the UN. There is a glaring absence of reciprocity and mutual accounting in that partnership.

While the G-8 endorsed NEPAD at its summit in Genoa in July 2001 and committed itself to working with the NEPAD secretariat task force in drafting the terms of reference for a NEPAD/G-8 to be launched at the Canada summit, they failed to live up to their own promises and the expectation of the Africa partners.

Turning to the question of the SADC's capacity to deal with internal challenges faced by its members, let us take the case of Zimbabwe. The January 2002 Blantyre summit mandated the establishment of a task force on Zimbabwe, including SADC states Malawi, Tanzania, South Africa, Botswana, and Mozambique (which has succeeded Zimbabwe in its head of state chairing the OPDSC). The broad terms of reference of this task force to engage all members of Zimbabwean society represented an unprecedented intervention into the affairs of a member state. Moreover, it was justified at the summit by a consensus that the situation in Zimbabwe affected its neighbors, an acknowledgment, in turn, reinforced by the recognition that the AU can intervene in the affairs of states in situations of instability, coups d'état, or genocide that threaten the peace and security of other states. The task force concerned itself primarily with the social justice issue of land and said that the question needs to be addressed as a matter of urgency. Despite that, the SADC had failed to prevail on the situation in Zimbabwe, a stabilization of Zimbabwe is unlikely if the land question is not addressed. In early 2001, SADC leaders also impressed upon President Robert Mugabe the urgent need to put in place the conditions for a credible election. That election subsequently took place in March 2002 and was controversially free and fair according to the majority of regional and continental actors but judged unfree and unfair by the Commonwealth and EU missions.

Angola after the death of UNITA's Jonas Savimbi and the DRC in the midst of a complex ICD also present the OPDSC with not only challenges but opportunities to foster credible peace in two of the region's most important states. Growing tensions in Swaziland over the perceived stubbornness of the monarchy to democratize the polity persist. On an encouraging note, the fears of a disputed election in Lesotho in May 2002 did not materialize. But the country now needs urgent postconflict stabilization.

The expectations that the end of apartheid would usher in a smooth transition from hostility to solidarity and from war to peace were clearly optimistic. Both intra- and interstate conflicts persist in southern Africa, suspicions and tensions between states, though not unique to the subregion, remain a key feature of regional politics, while the dominant issue of social justice remains dormant.

To conclude, this volume has argued that the SADC OPDSC security architecture has been evolving, albeit confronted with a variety of security challenges. All of the above suggests that southern Africa's security architecture remains fluid and contradictory, and the challenges for the OPDSC are clear. Despite encouraging steps to break the impasse over the OPDSC, the organ's achievements in promoting collective security in southern Africa are not well known to the public. Its strategic vision on how to address the insecurity facing the subregion is still unclear. A key difficulty in translating vision into concrete policies derives from the captivity of the security planners to old security paradigms. Security in southern Africa is still largely seen in terms of being an exclusive preserve for the military and this state-centric paradigm does not allow for a process that promotes human security and protects the rights of individuals and addresses social justice.

Reconceptualizing the SADC's evolving security architecture will require aligning the organization with a new security thinking around a set of "assured shared values" and establishing the rules of the game, such as democratic freedoms, human rights, nonviolent means of resolving disputes, security cooperation, and, essentially, addressing the vast social justice challenges of the region. Involving civil society actors in conflict management in southern Africa will also be essential in efforts to establish a "people-centered" approach to security. Nontraditional security issues like HIV/AIDS, which disproportionately affects the SADC subregion, must be put on the agenda. There has also not been a level of institutional reform capable of facilitating the implementation of a new security thinking.

The OPDSC should spearhead the transformation of the security agenda by adopting a structure that can ensure the promotion of democratic order; good governance; and economic, social, and operational issues in the context of social justice and substantive democracy. There must be a linkage between activity at the national level and regional policies. The advantage of the OPDSC is that it is well positioned to draw expertise and ideas from other sources, such as research institutions, think tanks, and, above all, civil society organizations. The OPDSC is well suited to develop thinking that can influence policy and action in southern Africa and contribute to strengthening capacity—especially in the civilian sectors dealing with security, such as parliaments and defense-related ministries.

Putting a new security concept into practice implies the establishment or improvement of legal frameworks that can facilitate action by appropriate actors. The signing of collective and nonaggression pacts—notably the SADC Common Defense Pact—human rights protection acts, moratoria to limit arms smuggling, and pacts for environmental protection and the protection of the rights of children and vulnerable groups in conflict could be the first step. The SADC will need to embark on institutional development, both at the national and the regional level, to implement and monitor the various accords established. The organization must establish priorities and a program of action agreed to by national institutions. There is a need to examine critically the role of the defense industry in the region and whether or not it can play a role in meeting the region's defense needs, especially in supplying equipment, and in servicing training, research, and development. However, none of these tasks is likely to be effectively performed if some of the sovereignty of member states is not pooled to address common security concerns.

It is hoped that the forgoing observations and recommendations will highlight the nature of the challenges faced by southern Africa's regional security architecture, make a modest contribution to the much-needed discourse between SADC leaders and the subregion's intelligentsia and civil society in addressing the subcontinent's challenges, and help build a more stable, secure, and prosperous subregion in which social justice and human security, alongside democratic governance and peace, define the security agenda.

Notes

1. See UN Security Council resolution 1308, 17 July 2000.

2. See Monde Muyangwa and Margaret A. Vogt, "An Assessment of the OAU Mechanism for Conflict Prevention, Management and Resolution, 1993–2000," International Peace Academy, New York, November 2000.

3. See Elizabeth Cousens and Chetan Kumar, eds., *Peacebuilding as Politics* (Boulder, Colo.: Lynne Rienner Publishers, 2001), and Olara Otunnu and Michael Doyle, eds., *Peacemaking and Peacekeeping for the New Century* (Lanham, Md.: Rowman and Littlefield, 1998).

4. International Peace Academy, "NEPAD: African Initiative, New Partnership?" 16 July 2002, New York.

Acronyms and Abbreviations

ACCORD	African Centre for the Constructive Resolution of Disputes
ACP	African-Caribbean-Pacific
ACRI	African Crisis Response Initiative
ACSS	Africa Center for Strategic Studies
AEC	African Economic Community
AFRA	Association for Rural Advancement
ANC	African National Congress
ARI	African Renaissance Institute
ASAS	Association of Southern African States
BFTU	Botswana Federation of Trade Unions
BOSS	Bureau of State Security
CBOs	community-based organizations
CEWARN	conflict early warning and response
CFSP	Common Foreign and Security Policy
CFU	Commercial Farmers' Union
CHOGM	Commonwealth Heads-of-Government Meeting
CMAG	Commonwealth Ministerial Action Group
COMESA	Common Market of Eastern and Southern Africa
CONSAS	Constellation of Southern African States
COSATU	Confederation of South African Trade Unions
CPMR	Conflict Prevention, Management, and Resolution division (IGAD)
CSCE	Conference for Security and Co-operation in Europe
DBSA	Development Bank of Southern Africa
DESTIN	Development Studies Institute
DLA	Department of Land Affairs (S.A.)
DOD	Department of Defense (U.S.)
DRC	Democratic Republic of Congo
EAC	East African Community

ECA	Economic Commission for Africa
ECCAS	Economic Community of Central African States
ECOMOG	ECOWAS Cease-Fire Monitoring Group
ECOWAS	Economic Community of West African States
EPC	European Political Cooperation
EPG	eminent persons group
ESAP	Economic and Social Adjustment Program
ESTA	Extension of Security of Tenure Act
FEWER	Forum for Early Warning and Early Response (IGAD)
FLS	Frontline States
FRELIMO	Front for the Liberation of Mozambique
FSPs	farmer support programs
GEAR	Growth, Employment, and Redistribution
GoZ	government of Zimbabwe
ICD	Inter-Congolese Dialogue
ICJ	International Court of Justice
IGAD	Intergovernmental Authority on Development
IGADD	Intergovernmental Authority on Drought and Desertification
ILEA	International Law Enforcement Academy for Africa
IMCRD	Inter-Ministerial Committee on Resettlement and Rural Development
IMET	International Military Education and Training
IMF	International Monetary Fund
IPFP	Inception Phase Framework Plan
IPLRAD	Integrated Programme of Land Redistribution for Agricultural Development in South Africa
ISDSC	Inter-State Defence and Security Committee
ISPDC	Inter-State Politics and Diplomacy Committee
JMC	Joint Military Commission
LAPC	Land and Agricultural Policy Centre
LSCF	large-scale commercial farms
LRPPs	land reform pilot projects
LRRP	Land Redistribution and Resettlement Program
MAP	Millennium Africa Recovery Plan
MDC	Movement for Democratic Change
MoU	memorandum of understanding
NAFU	National African Farmers Union
NAI	New African Initiative
NATO	North Atlantic Treaty Organization
NCA	National Constitutional Assembly (Zimbabwe)
NDA	National Department of Agriculture (S.A.)
NECF	National Economic Consultative Forum
NEOs	noncombatant evacuation operations
NEPAD	New Partnership for Africa's Development

NGOs	nongovernmental organizations
NLC	National Land Committee
NLWVAZ	National Liberation War Veterans Association of Zimbabwe
NSCC	New Sudan Council of Churches
OAU	Organization of African Unity
OECD	Organization for Economic Cooperation and Development
OPDS	Organ on Politics, Defense, and Security
OPDSC	Organ on Politics, Defense, and Security Cooperation
PCIAs	peace conflict impact assessment tools
PLAAS	Programme for Land and Agrarian Studies (Univ. of Western Cape)
PPP	People to People Peace program
PTOs	permissions to occupy
RCD	Congolese Rally for Democracy
RDP	Reconstruction and Development Program
RECs	regional economic communities
RENAMO	Mozambique National Resistance Movement
REPA	regional economic preference agreement
RUF	Revolutionary United Front
SACU	Southern African Customs Union
SADC	Southern African Development Community
SADCC	Southern African Development Coordination Conference
SADT	South African Development Trust
SAPs	structural adjustment programs
SARIPS	Southern African Regional Institute for Policy Studies
SARPCCO	Southern African Regional Police Chiefs Cooperation Organization
SLAGs	settlement/land allocation grants
SPLA/M	Sudan People's Liberation Army/Movement
TDCA	Trade, Development and Cooperation Agreement (EU-SA)
UMA	Arab Maghreb Union
UN	United Nations
UNAIDS	Joint UN Programme on HIV/AIDS
UNAMSIL	UN Mission in Sierra Leone
UNAVEM	United Nations Angola Verification Mission
UNDP	United Nations Development Programme
UNITA	National Union for the Total Independence of Angola
UNOMSA	UN Observer Mission in South Africa
USEUCOM	U.S. European Command
VPKO	voluntary peacekeeping operations (U.S.)
ZANU(PF)	Zimbabwe African National Union (Patriotic Front)
ZCTU	Zimbabwe Congress of Trade Unions
ZNLWVA	Zimbabwe National Liberation War Veterans Association

Bibliography

Abati, Reuben. "Obasanjo: A Psychoanalysis." *The Guardian* (Lagos), 8 July 2001.

ACCORD (African Centre for the Constructive Resolution of Disputes). "Trends in Preventive Action." ACCORD online publications, 2001 [available at: www.accord.org.za/publications/ct-2001/preventive.htm].

Adam, Hussein. "Somalia: A Terrible Beauty Being Born?" In *Collapsed States: The Disintegration and Restoration of Legitimate Authority,* edited by William Zartman. Boulder, Colo.: Lynne Rienner Publishers, 1995.

Adams, M. *Breaking Ground: Development Aid for Land Reform.* London: Overseas Development Institute, 2000.

Adams, M., B. Cousins, and S. Manona. "Land Tenure and Economic Development in Rural South Africa: Constraints and Opportunities." In *At the Crossroads: Land and Agrarian Reform in South Africa into the 21st Century,* edited by Ben Cousins. Bellville, South Africa: PLAAS; Johannesburg: NLC, 2000.

Adebajo, Adekeye. *Building Peace in West Africa: Liberia, Sierra Leone, and Guinea-Bissau.* Boulder, Colo.: Lynne Rienner Publishers, 2002.

———. "Into the Burning Ashes," *Times Literary Supplement,* 2 February 2001.

———. *Liberia's Civil War: Nigeria, ECOMOG, and Regional Security in West Africa.* Boulder, Colo.: Lynne Rienner Publishers, 2002.

———. "Nigeria: Africa's New Gendarme?" *Security Dialogue* 31, 2 (June 2000).

———. "Tale of Two Giants." *Newswatch,* 11 September 1995.

———. "Whither Nigeria's Foreign Policy?" *Tell,* 23 August 1999.

Adebajo, Adekeye, and Chris Landsberg. "Back to the Future: UN Peacekeeping in Africa." In *Managing Armed Conflict in the 21st Century,* edited by Adekeye Adebajo and Chandra Lekha Sriram. London: Frank Cass, 2001.

———. "Can an Insecure Mbeki Avoid the Fate of Kwame Nkrumah?" *Sunday Independent* (South Africa), 6 May 2001.

———. "The Heirs of Nkrumah: Africa's New Interventionists." *Pugwash Occasional Papers* 2, 1 (January 2000).

———. "Pax Africana in the Age of Extremes." *South African Journal of International Affairs* 7, 1 (Summer 2000).

———. "Trading Places: Nigeria and South Africa." *Indicator* 13, 3 (Winter 1996).

Adedeji, A., ed. *South Africa and Africa: Within or Apart?* African Centre for Development and Strategic Studies. Cape Town: SADRI Books; London: Zed Books, 1996.

Adeniji, Olu. "The Emergence of South Africa into the Global Economy and Its Consequences for Nigeria and Africa." In *Essays on Nigerian Foreign Policy, Governance and International Security.* Ibadan, Nigeria: Dokun Publishing House, 2000.

"Africa's Wars." *The Economist,* 14 January 1999.

Ajello, Aldo. "Mozambique: Implementation of the 1992 Agreement." In *Herding Cats: Multiparty Mediation in a Complex World,* edited by Chester Crocker, Fen Osler Hampson, and Pamela Aall. Washington, D.C.: U.S. Institute of Peace, 1999.

Ake, Claude. "The New World Order: A View from Africa." In *Whose World Order? Uneven Globalization and the End of the Cold War,* edited by H. Holm and G. Sorenson. Boulder, Colo.: Westview Press, 1995.

Ala, Jacqui. "Gender Biases: Stumbling Blocks to Effective Development Policies." *Discussion Papers in International Relations* 1, 4 (September 1997).

Alao, Abiodun. "Security Reform in Democratic Nigeria." Working Paper no. 2, Conflict, Security, and Development Group, King's College, London, 2000.

Alden, Chris. "Bullets, Ballots and Bread." Paper presented at the International Workshop on Southern Africa After Democratization, Tokyo, January 1996.

Alexander, Jocelyn. "The Unsettled Land: The Politics of Land Redistribution in Matabeleland, 1980–1990." *Journal of Southern African Studies* 17, 4 (1991).

Allison, G., and P. Zelikow. *Essence of Decision: Explaining the Cuban Missile Crisis.* New York: Addison-Wesley Longman, 1999.

ANC (African National Congress). "Land Manifesto for ANC Policy Conference." Endorsed final draft, Johannesburg, 1992.

Annan, Kofi. "The Causes of Conflict and the Promotion of Durable Peace and Sustainable Development in Africa." Report of the Secretary-General, United Nations, New York, 1998.

———. "Durable Peace and Sustainable Development in Africa." *South African Journal of International Affairs* 7, 1 (Summer 2000).

———. "South Africa and the United Nations." Address delivered to the South African Institute of International Affairs, Johannesburg, 21 March 1997.

———. "We the Peoples: The Role of the United Nations in the 21st Century." Report presented at the Millenium Summit, United Nations, New York, 6–8 September 2000 [available at: www.un.org/millenium/sg/report/].

Anstee, Margaret J. "Angola: The Forgotten Tragedy, a Test for UN Peacekeeping." *International Relations* 11, 6 (December 1993).

———. *Orphan of the Cold War: The Inside Story of the Collapse of the Angolan Peace Process, 1992–93.* New York: St. Martin's Press, 1996.

Anyaoku, Emeka. Speech given at the "Professions for World Disarmament and Development" conference, London, 18 March 1989. Reprinted in *The Missing Headlines.* Liverpool, UK: University Press, 1997.

Asante, S.K.B. "ECOWAS/CEAO: Conflict and Cooperation in West Africa." In *The Future of Regionalism in Africa,* edited by Ralph Onwuka and Amadu Sesay. London: Macmillan, 1985.

Axworthy, L. "Human Security: Safety for People in a Changing World." Department of Foreign Affairs and International Trade, Ottawa, Canada, 29 April 1999.

Bach, Daniel. "The Politics of West African Economic Cooperation: CEAO and ECOWAS." *Journal of Modern African Studies* 21, 4 (1983).

———. "Regional Domination and Power Conversion in Africa: Soft and Hard

Hegemony." Paper presented at the African Studies Association Meeting, Nashville, Tenn., November 2000.

Baker, Pauline H. "Conflict Resolution Versus Democratic Governance: Divergent Paths to Peace." In *Managing Global Chaos: Sources of and Responses to International Conflict,* edited by Chester A. Crocker, Fen Osler Hampson, and Pamela Aall. Washington D.C.: U.S. Institute for Peace, 1996.

Bangura, Yusuf. "Comments on Regional Security and the War in Congo." In *Reflections on Crisis in the Democratic Republic of Congo,* edited by Ibbo Mandaza. SARIPS Series no. 4. Harare, Zimbabwe: SAPES Books, 1999.

Banks, Michael. "Four Conceptions of Peace." In *Conflict Management and Problem Solving: Inter-Personal to International Applications,* edited by Dennis Sandole and Ingrid Sandole-Staroste. London: Pinter, 1987.

Barber, James, and John Barratt. *South Africa's Foreign Policy 1948–88: The Search for Status and Security.* Johannesburg: Southern Book Publishers; Cambridge: Cambridge University Press, 1988.

Baregu, Mweisiga. "Preventive Diplomacy and Peace-Building in Southern Africa." SARIPS Peace and Security Series no. 2, Harare, Zimbabwe, 1999.

Barratt, John. "Outlook on Namibian Independence: Some Domestic Constraints." *International Affairs Bulletin* 7, 1 (1983).

Bartoli, Andrea. "Mediating Peace in Mozambique: The Role of the Community of Sant'Egidio." In *Herding Cats: Multiparty Mediation in a Complex World,* edited by Chester Crocker, Fen Osler Hampson, and Pamela Aall. Washington, D.C.: U.S. Institute of Peace, 1999.

Bayley, B. *A Revolution in the Market: The Deregulation of South African Agriculture.* Oxford: Oxford Policy Management, 2000.

Beinart, W., ed. Special issue: "The Politics of Colonial Conservation." *Journal of Southern African Studies* 15, 2 (1989).

Beinart, W., and C. de Wet. "Resettlement of Land Reform in South Africa." *Review of African Political Economy* 61 (1994).

Beinart, W., and R. Kingwill. "Eastern Cape Land Reform Project: Pre-planning Report." Working Paper no. 25, LAPC, Johannesburg, 1996.

Berman, E., and K. E. Sams. *Peacekeeping in Africa: Capabilities and Culpabilities.* Geneva: UN Institute for Disarmament Research, 2000.

Bernstein, H. "The Political Economy of the Maize Filière." *Journal of Peasant Studies* 23, 2 (1996).

Binswanger, H., and K. Deininger. "Are Large Farms More Efficient Than Small Ones? Government Intervention, Large-Scale Agriculture and Resettlement in Kenya and Zimbabwe." World Bank conference, Mbabane, Swaziland, November 1992.

———. "The Evolution of the World Bank's Land Policy." *World Bank Research Observer* 14, 2 (August 1999).

———. "South African Land Policy: The Legacy of History and Current Options." *World Development* 21, 9 (1993).

Binswanger, H., K. Deininger, and G. Feder. "Power, Distortions, Revolt, and Reform in Agricultural Land Relations." World Bank Working Paper Series no. 1164 (1993). In *Handbook of Development Economics*, ed. J. Behrman and T. N. Srinivasan. Vol. 3. Washington, D.C.: World Bank, 1995

Bisseker, Claire. "Botswana and Uganda Lead the Way in the Battle." *Financial Mail,* 15 June 2001.

———. "It's Worse Than You Thought—Unless Behaviour Changes." *Financial Mail*, 15 June 2001.

"The Blue Helmets Return." *Africa Confidential* 40, 24 (December 1999).

Bond, Patrick. *Elite Transitions: From Apartheid to Neoliberalism in South Africa.* London: Pluto Press, 2000.

Boone, R. "Remarks at the Signing of the ILEA Agreement with the Government of Botswana." Gaborone, Botswana, 24 July 2000.

Brammer, Horst. "In Search of an Effective Regional Security Mechanism for Southern Africa," *Global Dialogue* 4, 2 (August 1999).

Bull, Hedely, and Adam Watson. *The Expansion of International Society.* Oxford: Oxford University Press, 1985.

Bush, Kenneth. "A Measure of Peace: Peace and Conflict Impact Assessment (PCIA) of Development Projects in Conflict Zones." Working Chapter no. 1, International Development Research Center, Ottawa, Canada, 1998.

Buzan, Barry. *People, States, and Fear: An Agenda for International Security Studies in the Post–Cold War Era.* 2d. ed. Boulder, Colo.: Lynne Rienner Publishers, 1991.

———. "People, States, and Fear: The National Security Problem in the Third World." In *National Security in the Third World: The Management of International and External Threats,* edited by Edward E. Azar and Chung-In Moon. Aldershot, UK: Edward Elgar, 1988.

Buzan, B., M. Keltrup, et al. *The European Security Order Recast.* London: Pinter, 1990.

Carim, Xavier. "Strategic Perspective for Southern Africa in the 1990s: Theoretical and Practical Considerations." Southern Africa Perspectives, Centre for Southern African Studies, University of the Western Cape, Bellville, South Africa, August 1993.

Carrington, P. *Reflecting on Things Past: The Memoirs of Peter Lord Carrington.* London: Collins, 1983.

Carson, Johnnie. Address by the U.S. Ambassador to Kenya to the first Conflict Early Warning and Response Mechanism (CEWARN) meeting, Nairobi, 5 July 2000.

Cawthra, G. "Subregional Security: The Southern African Development Community." *Security Dialogue* 28, 2 (1997).

———. "Towards a Holistic Approach to Security Management at Regional Security Level." *African Security Review* 6, 5 (1997).

CFU (Commercial Farmers' Union). Land reform proposal. Harare, Zimbabwe, 1998.

Chan, S. *The Commonwealth in World Politics, 1965–1985.* London: Lester Crook, 1988.

Chase, Robert, Emily Hill, and Paul Kennedy, eds. *The Pivotal States: A New Framework for U.S. Policy in the Developing World.* New York: Norton, 1999.

Cheater, Angela. "Women and their Participation in Commercial Agricultural Production: The Case of Medium-Size Freehold in Zimbabwe." *Development and Change* 12 (1981).

Chenje, Munyaradzi, and Phyllis Johnson, eds. *Water in Southern Africa.* Maseru and Harare, Zimbabwe: SADC/IUCN/SARDC, 1996.

Chipman, John. *French Power in Africa.* Oxford: Basil Blackwell, 1989.

Cilliers, Jakkie. *Building Security in Southern Africa: An Update on the Evolving Architecture.* ISS Monograph Series 43, November 1999.

Cilliers, Jakkie, and Greg Mills, eds. *From Peacekeeping to Complex Emergencies: Peace Support Missions in Africa.* Johannesburg: South African Institute of International Affairs; Pretoria: Institute for Security Studies, 1999.

Clapham, Christopher. "The Political Economy of Conflict in the Horn of Africa." *Survival* 32, 5 (September/October 1990).

———. "The United Nations and Peacekeeping in Africa." In *Whither Peacekeeping in Africa?* edited by Mark Malan. Halfway House, South Africa: Institute for Security Studies, 1999.

Clapham, Christopher, Greg Mills, Anna Morner, and Elizabeth Sidiropolous, eds. *Regional Integration in Southern Africa: Comparative Perspectives* Johannesburg: South African Institute of International Affairs, 2001.

Clarke, Walter, and Jeffrey Herbst, eds. *Learning from Somalia: The Lessons of Armed Humanitarian Intervention*. Boulder, Colo. Westview Press, 1997.

Claassens, A. "Land Rights and Local Decision Making Processes: Proposals for Tenure Reform." In *At the Crossroads: Land and Agrarian Reform in South Africa into the 21st Century,* edited by Ben Cousins. Bellville, South Africa: PLAAS; Johannesburg: NLC, 2000.

COGSA (Commonwealth Observer Group). "Report on the South African Elections." Commonwealth Secretariat, London, 1994.

Coker, Christopher. "South Africa: A Military Role in Southern Africa, 1969–92." In *Southern Africa Regional Security: Problems and Prospects*, edited by Robert Jaster. London: Gower, 1985.

Commonwealth. "Commonwealth Heads of Government: The London Communiqué." London, June 1977.

———. "Harare Commonwealth Declaration," Harare, Zimbabwe, 16–22 October 1991.

———. *Mission to South Africa: The Findings of the Commonwealth Eminent Persons Group on Southern Africa*. London: Penguin, 1986.

Commonwealth Secretary-General. Eighth Report to Heads of Government. Commonwealth Secretariat, London, 1981.

———. "From Kuala Lumpur to Durban." Report, London, October 1999.

Cook, L. "Land Affairs Is Now 'a Sick Department.'" *Johannesburg Business Day,* 15 August 2000.

Cousins, Ben. "Didiza's Recipe for Disaster." *Johannesburg Mail and Guardian,* 18 August 2000.

———. "Land Reform at the Crossroads." *Reconstruct,* 20 February 2000.

———. "Who Will Benefit from Land Reform?" *Johannesburg Mail and Guardian,* 15 September 2000.

Cousins, Ben, Dan Weiner, and Nick Amin. "Social Differentiation in the Communal Lands of Zimbabwe." *Review of African Political Economy* 53 (1992).

Cousens, Elizabeth, and Chetan Kumar, eds. *Peacebuilding as Politics: Cultivating Peace in Fragile Societies*. Boulder, Colo. Lynne Rienner Publishers, 2001.

Cowen, M. "Commodity Production in Kenya's Central Province." In *Rural Development in Tropical Africa,* edited by J. Heyer, P. Roberts, and G. Williams. London: Macmillan, 1981.

Crewe, Mary. "A Grim Prognosis as Paralysis Grips Education Chiefs: Effects of Pandemic Underestimated or Ignored." *Financial Mail,* 28 January 2000.

Cross, Catherine, et al. "Making a Living Under Land Reform." In *Land, Labour and Livelihoods in Rural South Africa, Volume Two: KwaZulu-Natal and Northern Province*, edited by Michael Lipton, Frank Ellis, and Merle Lipton. Durban, South Africa: Indicator Press, 1996.

Dashwood, Hevina. "Social Welfarism, Poverty Alleviation, and Political Stability in Zimbabwe." *Canadian Journal of Development Studies* 3 (1999).

———. *Zimbabwe: The Political Economy of Transformation.* Toronto: Toronto University Press, 2000.

de Coning, Cedric. "Breaking the SADC Organ Impasse: Report of the Seminar on the Operationalisation of the SADC Organ." ACCORD Occasional Paper no. 6, 1999.

De Klerk, F. W. *The Last Trek—A New Beginning: The Autobiography.* London: Macmillan, 1998.

Deng, Francis, Sadikiel Kimaro, Terrence Lyons, Donald Rothchild, and I. William Zartman. *Sovereignty as Responsibility: Conflict Management in Africa.* Washington, D.C.: Brookings Institution, 1996.

Desmond, C. *The Discarded People: An Account of Forced Resettlement in South Africa.* Harmondsworth, UK: Penguin, 1971.

de Wet, Chris. "Land Reform in South Africa: A Vehicle for Justice and Reconciliation, or a Source of Further Inequality and Conflict?" *New Routes* (Uppsala, Sweden) 2, 2 (1997).

———. "Resettlement and Land Reform in South Africa." *Review of African Political Economy* 61 (1994).

Douleh, Mohamed-Said. "The Djibouti-Led Process. A People-Led Experiment: Towards the Making of a New Somalia." Concept paper for the CEWARN II meeting. Kampala, Uganda, 11–12 September 2000.

Doyle, Michael. "Liberalism and the End of the Cold War." In *International Relations Theory and the End of the Cold War,* edited by Richard Ned Lebow and Thomas Risse-Kappen. New York: Columbia University Press, 1995.

Drimie, Scott. "Unravelling the Redistribution of Impendle State Land: Prospects and Process of Land Reform in Kwazulu-Natal, South Africa." Ph.D. thesis, Cambridge University, 2000.

Du Toit, Andries. "The End of Restitution: Getting Real About Land Claims." In *At the Crossroads: Land and Agrarian Reform in South Africa into the 21st Century,* edited by Ben Cousins. Bellville, South Africa: PLAAS; Johannesburg: NLC, 2000.

———. "Piloting Land Redistribution in the Western Cape." Report, PLAAS, University of the Western Cape, Bellville, South Africa, 1996.

ECDPM (European Centre for Development Policy Management). "The EC's Impact Studies on Regional Economic Partnership Agreements." Lomé Negotiating Brief no. 5, Maastricht, Netherlands, February 1999.

———. "Innovations in the Cotonou Agreement." Cotonou Information Kit 4, Maastricht, Netherlands, January 2001.

Eckert, J., J. Hamman, and J. Lombard. "Perceiving a New Future: Empowering Farmworkers Through Equity Sharing." *Development South Africa* 13, 5 (1996).

ECOWAS (Economic Community of West African States). Protocol Relating to the Mechanism for Conflict Prevention, Management, Resolution, Peacekeeping, and Security. Lomé, Togo, 10 December 1999.

Eismont, Maria. "Burundians Split on South Africa's Peace Force." *Business Day* (Johannesburg), 30 October 2001.

Ellis, Stephen. *The Mask of Anarchy: The Destruction of Liberia and the Religious Dimensions of an African Civil War.* London: Hurst and Company, 1999.

Elman, Miriam Fendius. "Testing the Democratic Peace Theory." In *Paths to Peace: Is Democracy the Answer?* Washington, D.C.: CSIA Studies in International Security, 1998.

Ero, Comfort. "The Future of ECOMOG in West Africa." In *From Peacekeeping to Complex Emergencies: Peace Support Missions in Africa,* edited by Jakkie

Cilliers and Greg Mills. Johannesburg: South African Institute of International Affairs; Pretoria: Institute for Security Studies, 1999.

Evans, David, Peter Holmes, and Ibbo Mandaza. *SADC: The Cost of Non-Integration*. Harare, Zimbabwe: SAPES Books, 1999.

Evans, Graham, and Jeffrey Newnham. *The Dictionary of World Politics*. New York and London: Harvester Wheatsheaf, 1990.

Fast, H. "An Examination of the Impact of Share Equity Schemes on Beneficiaries in the Western Cape and Mpumalanga." Report for the Surplus People's Project, Cape Town, and the Land and Agricultural Policy Center, Johannesburg, 1999.

Finnegan, William. *A Complicated War: The Harrowing of Mozambique*. Berkeley and Los Angeles: University of California Press, 1992.

Fisher-Thompson, J. "UN Important to US-Africa Peacekeeping Goals, US Official Says." *Washington File*, 11 January 2000.

Ford, K., and S. Katwala. *Reinventing the Commonwealth*. London: Foreign Policy Centre, 1999.

Fortna, Virgina Page. "United Nations Angola Verification Mission I." In *The Evolution of UN Peacekeeping*, edited by William Durch. New York: St. Martin's, 1993.

Francis, E. *Making a Living: Changing Livelihoods in Rural Africa*. London: Routledge, 2000.

Francis, E., and G. Williams. "The Land Question (in Kenya and South Africa)." *Canadian Journal of African Studies* 29, 3 (1993).

Frazer, J. E. "The African Crisis Response Initiative: Self-Interested Humanitarianism." *Brown Journal of World Affairs* 4, 2 (Summer/Fall 1997).

Friedman, Steven, Chris Landsberg, Zondi Masiza, and Maxine Reitzes. "State of Anxiety? Reconstructing the State, Democratisation and Economic Growth in Southern Africa." Centre for Policy Studies, April 1999.

Furley, Oliver, and Roy May, eds. *Peacekeeping in Africa*. Aldershot, UK: Ashgate, 1998.

Gambari, Ibrahim A. "Apartheid and Current Developments Inside South Africa: The Role of the United Nations." Lecture given to the African Studies Group, Fletcher School of Law and Diplomacy, Massachusetts, 30 April 1993.

———. "To Pretoria and Back." *West Africa* 3999 (23–29 May 1994).

Gaidzanwa, Rudo. "Women's Land Rights in Zimbabwe: An Overview." Occasional Chapter no. 13, Department of Rural and Urban Planning, University of Zimbabwe, Harare, 1988.

GAPWUZ (General Agricultural and Plantation Workers' Union of Zimbabwe). "Report on the Workshop on the Living Conditions of Farm Workers in Zimbabwe," Darwendale, Zimbabwe, 23–25 February 1997.

Geldenhuys, Deon. *The Diplomacy of Isolation: South Africa's Foreign Policy Making*. Johannesburg: Macmillan, 1994.

Geldenhuys, Deon, and Denis Venter. "Regional Cooperation in Southern Africa: A Constellation of States?" *International Affairs Bulletin*, December 1979.

Ginsberg, Anthony. *South Africa's Future: From Crisis to Prosperity*. Basingstoke, UK, and London: Pan Macmillan, 1998.

Goebel, Alison. "Process, Perception and Power: Notes from 'Participatory' Research in a Zimbabwean Resettlement Area." *Development and Change* 29, 2 (1998).

Goldstein, Joshua S. *International Relations*. New York: HarperCollins, 1994.

Goulding, Marrack. "The United Nations and Conflict in Africa Since the Cold War." *African Affairs* 98, 391 (April 1999).

Gramsci, Antonio. *The Modern Prince and Other Writings*. New York: International Publishers, 1959.

Greco, E. "New Trends in Peacekeeping: The Experience of Operation Alba." *Security Dialogue* 29, 2 (1998).

Grundy, Kenneth. *The Militarization of Southern African Politics*. London: I. B. Tauris, 1986.

Guest, Robert. "A Survey of Nigeria: Here's Hoping." *Economist*, 15 January 2000.

Gutteridge, W. "Military Ties." In *The Commonwealth in the 1980s,* edited by A.J.R. Groom and P. Taylor. London: Macmillan, 1984.

Hadland, Adrian, and Jovial Rantao. *The Life and Times of Thabo Mbeki*. Rivonia, South Africa: Zebra Press, 1999.

Hall, R. *The High Price of Principles*. New York: Africana, 1969.

Hall, R., K. Kleinbooi, and N. Mvambo. "What Land Reform Has Meant and Could Mean to Farm Workers in South Africa." Paper presented at the Human Sciences Research Council Conference, "Land Reform, and Poverty Alleviation in Southern Africa," Pretoria, 4–5 June 2001.

Hamman, J., and J. Ewert. "A Historical Irony in the Making? State, Private Sector and Land Reform in the South African Wine Industry." *Development South Africa* 16, 3 (1999).

Hanlon, Joseph. *Apartheid's Second Front: South Africa's War Against Its Neighbours*. London: Penguin, 1986.

Herbst, Jeffrey. *State Politics in Zimbabwe*. Harare: University of Zimbabwe Press, 1990.

Herz, John H. "Rise and Demise of the Territorial State." *World Politics* 9, 4 (July 1957).

Heyer, J. "Agricultural Development Policy in Kenya from the Colonial Period to 1975." In *Rural Development in Tropical Africa*, edited by J. Heyer, P. Roberts, and G. Williams. London: Macmillan, 1981.

Hill, C. "The Capability-Expectations Gap, or Conceptualising Europe's International Role." *Journal of Common Market Studies* 31, 3 (1993).

Hinga, S. N., and J. Heyer. "The Development of Large Farms." In *Agricultural Development in Kenya,* edited by J. Heyer, J. Maitha, and W. Senga. Nairobi: Oxford University Press, 1976.

Hirsch, John L., and Robert B. Oakley. *Somalia and Operation Restore Hope: Reflections on Peacekeeping and Peacemaking*. Washington, D.C.: U.S. Institute of Peace, 1995.

Holbrooke, R. C. "Conflict in Africa: The Search for Peace in the Congo." *Vital Speeches of the Day* 66, 6 (1 January 2000).

Holm, J., P. Molutsi, and G. Somolekae. "Development of Civil Society in Botswana." *Journal of African Affairs* 6 (1992).

Hoosen, S., and A. Collins. "Women, Culture and AIDS: How Discourses of Gender and Sexuality Affect Safe Sex Behaviour." Paper presented at the AIDS in Context Conference, University of the Witwatersrand, Johannesburg, 4–7 April 2001.

Hornby, Donna. "All We Need Is a Piece of Land." National Land Committee Investigation into Labour Tenancy, 1998.

———. "Tenure Rights and Practices on a State-Owned Farm: the Community of Ekuthuleni." In *At the Crossroads: Land and Agrarian Reform in South Africa into the 21st Century,* edited by Ben Cousins. South Africa: PLAAS; Johannesburg: NLC, 2000.

Hughes, David M. "Refugees and Squatters: Immigration and the Politics of

Territory on the Zimbabwe-Mozambique Border," *Journal of Southern African Studies* 25, 4 (1998).

———. "To Spread Opportunity Across Space: Smallholder-led Resettlement in Eastern Zimbabwe." Report to SAFIRE (Southern Alliance for Indigenous Resource), 2000.

Humphries, N. "Land Reform in the Western Cape, South Africa: Policy and Practice." B.A. thesis, St. Peter's College, Oxford, 2000.

Ibok, S. B. "The Effectiveness of African Regional and Sub-Regional Mechanisms to Prevent Ethnic and Racial Conflicts." Paper presented at the regional seminar of experts on the prevention of ethnic and racial conflicts, Addis Ababa, 4–6 October 2000.

ICG (International Crisis Group). "The Agreement on a Ceasefire in the Democratic Republic of Congo: An Analysis of the Agreement and Prospects for Peace." ICG Democratic Republic of Congo Report no. 5, 20 August 1999.

IGAD (Intergovernmental Authority on Development). "Declaration of the Seventh IGAD Summit of Heads of States and Governments." 26 November 1999.

———. "Report on the CEWARN II Workshop." Kampala, Uganda, 11–12 September 2000.

IGD (Institute for Global Dialogue). *The IGD Guide to the Southern African Development Community,* edited by Riaan de Villers and Kato Lambreechts. Johannesburg: Institute for Global Dialogue, 2001.

Ihonvbere, Julius. "Nigeria as Africa's Great Power: Constraints and Prospects for the 1990s." *International Journal* 46, 3 (Summer 1991).

IISS (International Institute for Strategic Studies). *The Military Balance 1996–1997*. Oxford: Oxford University Press, 1996.

Iloegbunan, Chuks. "King Solomon's Dilemma." *West Africa* 4319 (1–7 April 2002).

Ingram, D. *The Imperfect Commonwealth*. London: Rex Collings, 1976.

The Integrated Programme of Land Redistribution and Agricultural Development: A Response from Land NGOs. Prepared by the Centre for Rural Legal Studies (CRLS), Land Development Unit (LDU), Legal Resources Centre (LRC), Programme for Land and Agrarian Studies (PLAAS), Surplus People's Project (SPP), and Trust for Community Outreach and Education (TCOE) for the South African MALA Indaba on the IPLRAD, Johannesburg, 6–7 November 2000.

International Peace Academy. "Southern Africa's Evolving Security Architecture: Problems and Prospects." Report on Developing Regional and Subregional Security Mechanisms in Africa, Gaborone, Botswana, December 2000.

Isaacs, Dan. "Soldiers' Revenge." *BBC Focus on Africa* 13, 1 (January–March 2002).

Isaksen, Jan, and Elling N. Tjønneland. "Assessing the Restructuring of the SADC—Positions, Policies and Progress." Report commissioned by the Norwegian Agency for Development and Cooperation, Christian Michelsen Institute, Oslo, December 2001.

Jackson, Robert, and Carl Rosberg. *Personal Rule in Black Africa: Prince, Autocrat, Prophet, Tyrant*. Berkeley and London: University of California Press, 1982.

Jacobs, Susie. "Women and Land Resettlement in Zimbabwe." *Review of African Political Economy* 27 (1984).

James, D. "After 'Years in the Wilderness': Development and the Discourse of Land Claims in the New South Africa." *Journal of Peasant Studies* 27, 3 (2000).

———. "Hill of Thorns: Custom, Knowledge and the Reclaiming of a Lost Land in the New South Africa." *Development and Change* 31, 3 (2000).

Job, B. L. *Insecurity Dilemma: National Security of Third World States*. Boulder, Colo.: Lynne Rienner Publishers, 1992.

Johnson, P. *Eye of Fire: A Biography of Chief Emeka Anyaoku, Commonwealth Secretary-General*. Trenton, N.J.: Africa World Press, 2000.

Johnson, R. W., and L. Schlemmer. "Farmers and Farmworkers in Kwazulu-Natal: Employment Conditions, Labour Tenancy, Land Reform, Attitudes and Relationships." Helen Suzman Foundation for the Kwazulu-Natal Agricultural Union, Johannesburg, 1998.

Joseph, Richard. "The International Community and Armed Conflict in Africa—Post Cold War Dilemmas." In *Out of Conflict: From War to Peace*, edited by Gunner M. Sørbø and Peter Vale. Uppsala, Sweden: Nordiska Afrikainstitutet, 1997.

Kabemba, Claude. "Whither the DRC? Causes of the Conflict in the Democratic Republic of Congo, and the Way Forward." *Policy Issues and Actors* (Center for Policy Studies, Johannesburg) 11, 6 (March 1999).

Katjavivi, Peter. *A History of Resistance in Namibia*. London: James Currey; Paris: UNESCO; Addis Ababa: OAU, 1988.

Keegan, Timothy. *Rural Transformations in Industrializing South Africa: The Southern Highveld to 1914*. Basingstoke, UK: Macmillan, 1987.

Kennedy, Paul. *The Rise and Fall of the Great Powers*. New York: Vintage, 1987.

Keohane, Robert O. "International Liberalism Reconsidered." In *The Economic Limits of Modern Politics*, edited by John Dunn. Cambridge: Cambridge University Press, 1990.

———. "The Theory of Hegemonic Stability and Change in International Economic Regimes, 1967–1977." In *Change in the International System*, edited by O. R. Holsti, R. M. Siverson, and A. L. George. Boulder, Colo.: Westview Press, 1980.

Keohane, Robert, and Joseph Nye. *Power and Interdependence: World Politics in Transition*. Boston: Little, Brown, 1971.

Kindleberger, Charles. *America in the World Economy*. New York: Foreign Policy Association, 1977.

Kinsey, Bill H. "Determinants of Rural Household Incomes and Their Impact on Poverty and Food Security in Zimbabwe." Report for the Department of Urban Planning, University of Zimbabwe, and the Economic and Social Institute, Free University of Amsterdam, 1999.

———. "Emerging Issues in Zimbabwe's Land Resettlement Programme." *Development Policy Review* 1 (1983).

———. "Land Reform, Growth and Equity: Emerging Evidence from Zimbabwe's Resettlement Program." *Journal of Southern African Studies* 25, 2 (1999).

Kissinger, Henry. *Does America Need a Foreign Policy? Toward a Diplomacy for the Twenty-First Century*. New York: Simon and Schuster, 2001.

Kornegay, Francis. "Nigeria, Egypt and South Africa: A Stable Balance of Power in Africa." *South African Yearbook of International Affairs 1999/2000*. Johannesburg: South African Institute of International Affairs, 1999.

Kornegay, Francis, and Christopher Landsberg. "The HIV/AIDS Challenge to Southern Africa's Evolving Security Architecture." Unpublished paper, Johannesburg, December 2001.

Kozaryn, L. D. "US Will Offer Logistics Support to Congo Mission." U.S. Department of Defense News Release, American Forces Press Service, 18 February 2000.

Lahiff, E. "The Impact of Land Reform Policy on the Northern Province." In *At the Crossroads: Land and Agrarian Reform in South Africa into the 21st Century,* edited by Ben Cousins. Bellville, South Africa: PLAAS; Johannesburg: NLC, 2000.

Lamido, Sule. "I Will Surprise My Critics." Interview in *This Day,* 8 August 1999.

Lamont, James. "Mobile Phone Network Opens in Nigeria," *Financial Times,* 10 August 2001.

Landsberg, Christopher. "Directing from the Stalls? The International Community and South Africa's Multi-Party Negotiations Forum." In *The Small Miracle: South Africa's Negotiated Settlement,* edited by Stephen Friedman and Doreen Atkinson. Johannesburg: Raven Press, 1994.

———. "Exporting Peace? The UN and South Africa." *Policy Issues and Actors* (Centre for Policy Studies, Johannesburg) 7, 2 (April 1994).

———. "Pax Pretoriana vs. Pax Nigeriana." *L'Afrique Politique* 1 (2000).

———. "Promoting Democracy: The Mandela-Mbeki Doctrine." *Journal of Democracy* 11, 3 (July 2000).

———. "South Africa and Nigeria: Hegemons or Strategic Partners?" *Global Dialogue* 5, 2 (September 2000).

———. "South Africa and the Congo War." In *The African Stakes of the Congo War,* edited by John F. Clark. New York: Palgrave, 2002.

Landsberg, Chris, and Mark Suzman. "South Africa's Quest for Democracy." *The Oxford International Review* 11, 3 (1992).

LAPC (Land and Agriculture Policy Center). *Proceedings: Land Redistribution Options Conference.* Johannesburg: LAPC, 1994.

le Pere, Garth. "South Africa and Nigeria: A Strategic Partnership." *Global Dialogue* 4, 3 (December 1999).

le Pere, Garth, Anthoni van Nieuwkerk, and Kato Lambrechts. "South Africa and Africa: Reflections on the African Renaissance." Occasional Paper no. 17, Foundation for Global Dialogue, Bramfontein, South Africa, October 1998.

Leo, C. *Land and Class in Kenya.* Toronto: University of Toronto Press, 1984.

Leonhardt, Manuela. *Conflict Impact Assessment of EU Development Co-operation with ACP Countries: A Review of Literature and Practice.* London: International Alert and Safer World, 2000.

Levin, Richard. "Politics and Land Reform in the Northern Province: A Case Study of the Mojapelo Land Claim." In *Land, Labour and Livelihoods in Rural South Africa, Volume Two: Kwa-Zulu Natal and Northern Province,* edited by Michael Lipton, Frank Ellis, and Merle Lipton. Durban, South Africa: Indicator Press, 1996.

———. "Towards a National Implementation Strategy for Land Redistribution." In *At the Crossroads: Land and Agrarian Reform in South Africa into the 21st Century,* edited by Ben Cousins. Bellville, South Africa: PLAAS; Johannesburg: NLC, 2000.

Libby, Ronald T. *The Politics of Economic Power in Southern Africa.* Princeton, N.J.: Princeton University Press, 1987.

Lippman, W. *U.S. Foreign Policy: Shield of the Republic.* Boston: Little, Brown, 1943.

Lipton, Merle. "The Politics of Rural Reform in South Africa." In *Land, Labour, and Livelihoods in Rural South Africa: Volume One: Western Cape,* edited by Michael Lipton, Mike de Klerk, and Merle Lipton. Durban, South Africa: Indicator Press, 1996.

Lodge, Tom. *South African Politics Since 1994*. Cape Town and Johannesburg: David Philip Publishers, 1999.

LoveLife and ABT, Inc. "Impending Catastrophe Revisited: An Update on the HIV/AIDS Epidemic in South Africa." Kaiser Foundation, Parklands, South Africa, 2001.

Lynch, C. "Providing UN's Peacekeepers." *Washington Post,* 15 November 2000.

MacDonald, C. "The Construction of State and Development Subject in Rural KwaZulu-Natal: Implications of Dominant Discourses in the KwaZulu-Natal Land Reform Pilot Programme." *Transformation* 37 (1998).

MacIntosh, A., and A. Vaughn. "Experience of Agricultural Reform in South Africa: The Limits of Intervention." In *At the Crossroads: Land and Agrarian Reform in South Africa into the 21st Century,* edited by Ben Cousins. Bellville, South Africa: PLAAS; Johannesburg: NLC, 2000.

MacLean, G. "The Changing Perception of Human Security: Coordinating National and Multilateral Responses." United Nations Association Canada, 1999 [available at: http://www.unac.org/en/link_learn/canada/security/perception.asp], 2.

Mager, A. *Gender and the Making of a South African Bantustan: A Social History of the Ciskei, 1945–1959*. Oxford: James Currey, 1999.

Maier, Karl. *This House Has Fallen: Midnight in Nigeria*. New York: Public Affairs, 2000.

Malan, Mark. *SADC and Sub-Regional Security*. ISS Monograph Series no. 19. Pretoria: Institute of Security Studies, 1998.

Malan, Mark, and Jakkie Cilliers. "SADC Organ on Politics, Defence, and Security: Future Development." ISS Occasional Paper Series no. 19, March 1997.

Mamdani, Mahmood. *Citizen and Subject: Contemporary Africa and the Legacy of Late Colonialism*. Princeton, N.J.: Princeton University Press, 1996.

Mamila, K. "Mbeki MAP's Out Africa's Fresh Beginning." *Johannesburg Star,* 20 July 2001.

Mandaza, Ibbo, ed. *Peace and Security in Southern Africa*. Harare, Zimbabwe: SAPES Trust, 1996.

Mandaza, I., and A. Tostensen. *Southern Africa in Search of a Common Future: From the Conference to the Community*. Gaborone, Botswana: SADC, 1994.

Mankopi, S. "How to Provide Security of Tenure and Comparable Redress." In *At the Crossroads: Land and Agrarian Reform in South Africa into the 21st Century,* edited by Ben Cousins. Bellville, South Africa: PLAAS; Johannesburg: NLC, 2000.

Mansfield, Edward D. "The Concentration of Capabilities and the Onset of War." *Journal of Conflict Resolution* 36, 1 (1992).

Maphai, Vincent. "SA Should Not Rush in Where Angels Fear to Tread." *Business Day,* 14 March 2001.

Marcus, T., K. Eales, and A. Wildschut. *Land Demand in the New South Africa*. Johannesburg: LAPC, 1996.

Marcuse, Serbert. *Heroes and Civilisation*. London: Sphere, 1969.

Martin, Guy. "Francophone Africa in the Context of Franco-African Relations." In *Africa in World Politics: Post–Cold War Challenges,* edited by John W. Harbeson and Donald Rothchild. 2d ed. Boulder, Colo.: Westview Press, 1995.

Mather, C. "South African Agriculture and Rural Livelihoods in the Era of Liberalisation." In *At the Crossroads: Land and Agrarian Reform in South Africa into the 21st Century,* edited by Ben Cousins. Bellville, South Africa: PLAAS; Johannesburg: NLC, 2000.

———. "Wage Workers and Labour Tenants in Barberton, 1920–1950." In *White*

Farms, Black Labor: The State and Agrarian Change in Southern Africa, 1910–1950, edited by A. H. Jeeves and J. Crush. Oxford: James Currey, 1997.

Matlosa, Khabele. "The Electoral System and Election Management in Lesotho." Study for the Electoral Institute of Southern Africa, Johannesburg, July 2001.

———. "The Lesotho Conflict: Major Causes and Management." In *Crisis in Lesotho: The Challenge of Managing Conflict in Southern Africa,* edited by Kato Lambrechts. Foundation for Global Dialogue African Dialogue Series no. 2, Braamfontein, South Africa: Foundation for Global Dialogue, 1999.

———. "Lesotho's Political Turmoil and Prospects for the 1998 National Election." *Africa Insight* 27, 4 (1997).

———. "Military Rule and Withdrawal from Power: The Case of Lesotho." In *The Military and Militarism in Africa,* edited by Eboe Hutchful and Abdoulaye Bathily. Dakar, Senegal: CODESRIA Books, 1998.

———. "The 1993 Elections in Lesotho and the Challenge for the New Government, Southern African Perspectives." Working Paper Series no. 28, Center for Southern African Studies, University of the Western Cape, Bellville, South Africa, October 1993.

Matondi, Prosper. "Access to Land and Water Resources in Zimbabwe's Rural Environment." In *Environmental Security in Southern Africa,* edited by D. Tevera and S. Moyo. Harare, Zimbabwe: SAPES Books, 2000.

Mayende, G. "Didiza's Doing What She Should," *Johannesburg Mail and Guardian*, 25 August 2000.

———. "Myth and Reality in Land Reform." *East London Daily Dispatch,* 8 August 2000.

Mayer, M., and L. Kritzinger-van Niekerk. "Towards a South African Position on the Lomé Convention." Paper presented at the Development Bank of Southern Africa, Johannesburg, 1997.

Mazrui, Ali. "Hegemony: From Semites to Anglo-Saxons." In *Cultural Forces in World Politics*. Portsmouth, N.H.: Heinemann; London: James Currey, 1990.

Mbeki, Thabo. Interview. *Time,* 9 September 2000.

———. "Prologue." In *African Renaissance,* edited by Malegapuru William Makgoba. Cape Town: Mafube Publishing and Tafelberg Publishers, 1999.

———. "South Africa: A Workable Dream." Keynote address, Europe–South Africa 1995 Business and Finance Forum, Geneva, 27 June 1995.

———. "South Africa: A Year of Democracy." Speech delivered at the Bruno-Kreisky Forum, Vienna, 28 August 1995.

———. "South Africa: Two Nations." Statement at the opening of the debate on reconciliation and nation-building, National Assembly, Cape Town, 29 May 1998.

———. *The Time Has Come: Selected Speeches*. Cape Town: Tafelberg Publishers; Johannesburg: Mafube Publishing, 1998.

McClendon, T. *Genders and Generations Apart: Labour Tenants, Customary Law and Segregation in Natal*. New York: Heinemann, 2000.

McGeary, J. "Death Stalks a Continent." *Time,* 7 February 2001.

McIntosh, A., and A. Vaughn. "Enhancing Rural Livelihoods in Rural South Africa." In *Land, Labour, and Livelihoods in Rural South Africa, Volume Two: KwaZulu-Natal and Northern Province,* edited by Michael Lipton, Frank Ellis and Merle Lipton. Durban, South Africa: Indicator Press, 1996.

———. "Experiences of Agricultural Reform in South Africa: The Limits of Intervention." In *At the Crossroads: Land and Agrarian Reform in South*

Africa into the 21st Century, edited by Ben Cousins. Bellville, South Africa: PLAAS; Johannesburg: NLC, 2000.

———. "State and Capital in the Regeneration of a South African Peasantry." *Canadian Journal of African Studies* 29, 3 (1993).

McIntosh, G. "Don't Use Bantustan Solutions." *Johannesburg Mail and Guardian,* 31 March 1995.

McIntosh Xaba and Associates. "Review of the Land Reform Pilot Programme." Draft report for the South African DLA, European Union, the Department for International Development, and DANIDA, 1999.

"Military and Economic Pressure from South Africa Forces King's Yield South." *Scan,* 16 September 1994.

Mkandawire, Thandika. "Crisis Management in the Making of 'Choiceless' Democracies." In *State, Conflict, and Democracy in Africa,* edited by Richard Joseph. Boulder, Colo.: Lynne Rienner Publishers, 1999.

Mohamed-Siad, D. "The Djibouti Process. A People-Led Experience/ment: Towards the Making of a New Somalia." Concept paper for CEWARN II, Kampala, Uganda, 11–12 September 2000.

Moll, P. "The Structure of Commercial Agriculture in South Africa: A Quantitative Approach to Economies of Scale, Farm Size Change and Technical Change." Ph.D. thesis, Oxford University, 1988.

Moore, Donald. "Contesting Terrain in Zimbabwe's Eastern Highlands: Political Ecology, Ethnography, and Peasant Resource Struggles." *Economic Geography* 69, 4 (1993).

Morris, James. *Pax Britannica: The Climax of an Empire.* San Diego, Calif.: Harcourt-Brace, 1968.

Mortimer, Robert. "From ECOMOG I to ECOMOG II: Intervention in Sierra Leone." In *Africa in World Politics: The Africa State System in Flux,* edited by John W. Harbeson and Donald Rothchild. 3d ed. Boulder, Colo.: Westview Press, 2000.

Moyana, H. *The Political Economy of Land in Zimbabwe.* Aweru, Zimbabwe: Mambo Press, 1984.

Moyo, Sam. *Land and Democracy in Zimbabwe.* Harare, Zimbabwe: SAPES Books, 1999.

———. "The Land Question." In *Zimbabwe: The Political Economy of Transition, 1980–1986,* ed. I. Mandaza. Dakar, Senegal: CODESRIA, 1986.

———. "The Land Question and Land Reform in Southern Africa." In *Environmental Security in Southern Africa,* edited by Dan Tevera and Sam Moyo. Harare, Zimbabwe: SAPES Books, 2000.

———. *The Land Question in Zimbabwe.* Harare, Zimbabwe: SAPES Books, 1995.

———. *Land Reform Under Structural Adjustment in Zimbabwe.* Uppsala, Sweden: Nordiska Afrikainstitutet, 2000.

———. "Peasant Organisations and Rural Civil Society in Africa: An Introduction." In S. Moyo and B. Romdhane, eds., *Peasant Organisations and the Democratisation Process in Africa.* Dakar, Senegal: CODESRIA, 2000.

———. "The Political Economy of Land Acquisition and Redistribution in Zimbabwe, 1990–1999." *Journal of Southern African Studies* 26, 1 (2000).

Moyo, Sam, and John Makumbe. "The Socio-economic Environment and NGOs." In *NGOs, the State and Politics in Zimbabwe,* edited by Sam Moyo, John Makumbe, and Brian Raftopoulos. Harare, Zimbabwe: SAPES Books, 2000.

Moyo, Sam, Blair Rutherford, and Dede Amanor-Wilks. "Land Reform and Changing Social Relations for Farm Workers in Zimbabwe." *Review of African Political Economy* 84 (2000).

Moyo Sam, and Dan Tevera. "Regional Environmental Security in Southern Africa." In *Environmental Security in Southern Africa,* edited by Dan Tevera and Sam Moyo. Harare, Zimbabwe: SAPES Books, 2000.

Mukanda Mulemfo. *Thabo Mbeki and the African Renaissance*. Pretoria: Actua Press, 2000.

Muravchik, Joshua. "Promoting Peace Through Democracy." In *Managing Global Chaos: Sources of and Responses to International Conflict,* edited by Chester A. Crocker, Fen Osler Hampson, and Pamela Aall. Washington, D.C.: U.S. Institute for Peace, 1996.

Murray, C. "Land Reform in the Eastern Free State: Policy Dilemmas and Political Conflicts." *Journal of Peasant Studies* 23, 2/3 (1996).

———. "South African Land Reform: Case Studies in 'Demand' and 'Participation' in the Free State." *African Affairs* 96 (1997).

Muthaura, Francis. "Regional Blocs as the Only Viable Units in the Globalised Environment of the 21st Century—Experience from East Africa." Keynote address, Annual Conference of the Association of Third World Studies, Kenya Chapter, Eldoret, Kenya, 7 November 2000.

Mutua, Makau wa. "New Challenges in Southern Africa: From Regional Conflict to Internal Reconstruction." *Brown Journal of World Affairs* (Winter 1994).

Muyangwa, Monde, and Margaret A. Vogt. "An Assessment of the OAU Mechanism for Conflict Prevention, Management and Resolution, 1993–2000." International Peace Academy, New York, November 2000.

Mwagiru, Makumi. "IGAD Conflict Early Warning Mechanism: Legal and Institutional Aspects." Background paper for the CEWARN II meeting. Kampala, Uganda, 11–12 September 2000.

Mwanasali, Musifiky. "Peacebuilding in the Democratic Republic of Congo." Policy Briefing Series, International Peace Academy, New York, April 1998.

Myers, David. "Threat Perception and Strategic Response of the Regional Hegemons: A Conceptual Overview." In *Regional Hegemons: Threat Perception and Strategic Response,* edited by David Myers. Boulder, Colo.: Westview Press, 1991.

———, ed. *Regional Hegemons: Threat, Perception, and Strategic Response*. Boulder, Colo.: Westview Press, 1991.

Nathan, Laurie. "Towards a Conference on Security Stability, Development and Cooperation in Africa." Paper prepared for Asian Peace Research Conference, New Zealand, 1992.

Nattras, Nicoli, and Jeremy Seekings. "Two Nations? Race and Economic Inequality in South Africa Today." *Daedalus* 130, 1 (Winter 2001).

NEPAD (New Partnership for Africa's Development). Communiqué issued at the end of the meeting of the Implementation Committee of Heads of State and Government of NEPAD, Abuja, Nigeria, 23 October 2001.

Nhlapo, Welile. "South Africa and Peacekeeping: Looking to the Future." In *From Peacekeeping to Complex Emergencies: Peace Support Missions in Africa,* edited by Jakkie Cilliers and Greg Mills. Johannesburg: South African Institute of International Affairs; Pretoria: Institute for Security Studies, 1999.

"Nigeria and South Africa: Getting Down to Business." *Business in Africa,* June 2002.

Nkiwane, Tandeka C. "My Brother's Keeper: The Lesotho Crisis in Perspective." African Association of Political Science Occasional Paper Series 1, no. 1. Harare, Zimbabwe, 1997.

NLC (National Land Committee). "Land Reform Policy Proposals," Johannesburg, 1995.

Norton, A. R. "The Security Legacy of the 1980s in the Third World." In *Third World Security in the Post–Cold War Era,* edited by T. G. Weiss and M. A. Kessler. Boulder, Colo.: Lynne Rienner Publishers, 1995.

Ntsebeza, L. "Traditional Authorities, Local Government and Land Rights." In *At the Crossroads: Land and Agrarian Reform in South Africa into the 21st Century,* edited by Ben Cousins. Bellville, South Africa: PLAAS; Johannesburg: NLC, 2000.

Nye, Joseph, Jr. *Bound to Lead: The Changing Nature of American Power.* New York: Basic Books, 1990.

OAU (Organization of African Unity). "Declaration of the Assembly of the Heads of State and Government on the Establishment Within the OAU of a Mechanism for Conflict Prevention, Management and Resolution." Cairo, June 1993.

———. "Declaration on the Political and Socio-Economic Situation in Africa and the Fundamental Changes Taking Place in the World." Twenty-Sixth Ordinary Session of the OAU Summit, Addis Ababa, 9–11 July 1990.

———. "Interfacing the OAU Mechanism for Conflict Prevention, Management and Resolution with Africa's Sub-Regions and Arrangements: Elements of a Partnership Program." Addis Ababa, July 1999.

———. "Report of the Plenary." Twenty-Sixth Ordinary Session of the Council of Ministers. Addis Ababa, 23 February–1 March 1976.

———. "Report of the Secretary-General on the Situation in the Democratic Republic of the Congo." June 2000.

OAU and IPA (International Peace Academy). Report of the Second OAU/IPA Seminar on Peacekeeping and Peacemaking in Africa." Addis Ababa, 28 November–3 December 1998.

Obasanjo, Olusegun. "Africa's Rendevous with History." In *Africa: Rise to the Challenge,* edited by Olusegun Obasanjo and Felix Mosha. New York: Africa Leadership Forum, 1993.

———. *My Command.* London, Ibadan, and Nairobi: Heinemann, 1980.

———. "Nigeria, Africa, and the World in the Next Millennium." Address to the Fifty-Fourth Session of the UN General Assembly, 23 September 1999.

———. "Nigeria–South Africa: Bond Across the Continent." In *A New Dawn: A Collection of Speeches of President Olusegun Obasanjo,* edited by Ad'Obe Obe. Volume 2. Ibadan, Nigeria: Spectrum Books, 2001.

———. *Not My Will.* Ibadan, Nigeria: University Press, 1990.

———. *This Animal Called Man.* Abeokuta, Nigeria: Africa Leadership Forum Publications, 1999.

Obasanjo, Olusegun, and Felix Mosha, eds. *Africa: Rise to the Challenge.* New York: Africa Leadership Forum, 1993.

Odera, J. A. "Civil Society and Conflict Management in Africa: A Re-emerging Role." In *Out of Conflict: From War to Peace,* edited by Gunner M. Sørbø and Peter Vale. Uppsala, Sweden: Nordiska Afrikainstitutet, 1997.

Ohlson, T., S. Stedman, and R. Davies. *The New Is Not Yet Born: Conflict Resolution in Southern Africa.* Washington, D.C.: Brookings Institution, 1994.

Ojo, Olatunde. "Nigeria and the Formation of ECOWAS." *International Organisation* 34, 4 (Autumn 1980).

Ojo, Onukaba Adinoyi. *Olesegun Obasanjo: In the Eyes of Time.* New York and Lagos: African Legacy Press, 1997.

Olaniyan, Omotayo. "Nigeria and ECOWAS: A Role and Problem Analysis." In *Nigeria's External Relations: The First Twenty-Five Years,* edited by Gabriel Olusanya and R. A. Akindele. Ibadan, Nigeria: University Press Limited, 1986.

Olukoshi, Adebajo. "The State, Conflict, and Democracy in Africa." In *State, Conflict, and Democracy in Africa,* edited by Richard Joseph. Boulder, Colo.: Lynne Rienner Publishers, 1999.

Ott, Martin, Kings M. Phiri, and Nandini Patel, eds. *Malawi's Second Democratic Elections.* Blantyre, Malawi: Kachere Series, 2000.

Otunnu, Olara, and Michael Doyle, eds. *Peacemaking and Peacekeeping for the New Century.* Lanham, Md.: Rowman and Littlefield, 1998.

Parlevliet, Michelle. "The Role of Civil Society in Preventing Deadly Conflicts in Africa." Paper presented at the Fifth Meeting of the Independent International Commission on Kosovo, South Africa Institute of International Affairs, University of the Witwatersrand, Johannesburg, 25–26 August 2000.

Patel, Hasu P. "Zimbabwe's Mediation in Mozambique and Angola, 1989–91." In *Mediation in Southern Africa,* edited by Stephen Chan and Vivienne Jabri. London: Macmillan, 1993.

Patrick, Stewart. "Forging Hegemonic Consensus: America, France, and the making of the Postwar Order, 1945–1954." Ph.D. thesis, Oxford University, 1995.

Peters, Beverly. "HIV/AIDS: Uniting and Dividing South Africa and the United States." In *The Reality Behind the Rhetoric: The United States, South Africa, and Africa,* edited by Greg Mills and John Stremlau. Johannesburg: South African Institute of International Affairs and the Centre for Strategic and International Studies, 2000.

Peterson, J., and E. Bomberg. *Decision-Making in the European Union.* London: Macmillan, 1999.

Pinheiro, J. De Deus. "Can EU Development Assistance Contribute to Peace and Security?" Paper presented at a CESD/ISIS conference on "The Future of the EU's Common Foreign and Security Policy," Brussels, Belgium, 24 September 1998.

———. Commissioner's address. EU/SADC Ministerial Conference, Vienna, Austria, 3 November 1998.

Pisani, Andre du. "Security and Peace in Post Apartheid Southern Africa." *International Affairs Bulletin* 13, 3 (1992).

Platzky, L., and C. Walker. *The Surplus People: Forced Removals in South Africa.* Johannesburg: Ravan Press, 1985.

Powell, Colin. Remarks at the University of the Witwatersrand, Johannesburg, South Africa, 25 May 2001.

Prunier, Gérard. *The Rwanda Crisis: History of a Genocide.* New York: Columbia University Press, 1995.

Ramsamy, Prega. "SADC: The Way Forward." In *Regional Integration in Southern Africa, Comparative Perspectives,* edited by Christopher Clapham, Greg Mills, Anna Morner, and Elizabeth Sidiropolous. Johannesburg: South African Institute of International Affairs, 2001.

Ranger, Terence. "The Communal Areas of Zimbabwe." In *Land in African Agrarian Systems,* edited by T. J. Basset and D. G. Crummey. Madison: University of Wisconsin Press, 1993.

Rawls, J. *A Theory of Justice.* Oxford: Oxford University Press, 1971.

Renwick, Robin. "Rational Explanation for a Miracle." Book review. *The Financial Times,* 8 May 1997.

Rice, S. E. (Assistant Secretary for African Affairs). "US Policy Towards Sierra Leone." Testimony Before the Senate Foreign Relations Committee's Subcommittee on African Affairs, Washington, D.C., 11 October 2000.

Richards, Paul. *Fighting for the Rainforest: War, Youth, and Resources in Sierra Leone.* Oxford: James Currey; Portsmouth, N.H.: Heinemann, 1996.

Robertson, P. "A Common Purpose: The Commonwealth's Support for AAM." In *The Anti-Apartheid Movement: A 40-Year Perspective*. London: AAM Archives Committee, 2000.

Robbins, Steve. "Contesting the Social Geometry of State Power: A Case Study of Land-Use Planning in Matabeleland, Zimbabwe." *Social Dynamics* 20, 2 (1994).

Rotberg, Robert I. "Mandela and Mbeki." In *Ending Autocracy, Enabling Democracy*. Cambridge, Mass.: World Peace Foundation, 2002.

Roth, M., H. Dolny, and K. Wiebe. "Employment, Efficiency, and Land Markets in South Africa's Agricultural Sector: Opportunities for Land Reform." Draft report for the Land Tenure Center, Madison, Wis., and the World Bank, 1992.

Rutherford, Blair. "Another Side to Rural Zimbabwe: Social Constructs and the Administration of Farm Workers in Urungwe District, 1940s." *Journal of Southern African Studies* 23, 1 (1997).

———. "Traditions of Domesticity in 'Modern' Zimbabwean Politics: Race, Gender and Class in the Government of Commercial Farm Workers in Hurungwe District." Ph.D. thesis, McGill University, 1996.

———. *Working on the Margins: Black Workers, White Farmers in Postcolonial Zimbabwe*. London and Harare, Zimbabwe: Zed Books and Weaver Press, 2001.

Sachikonye, Lloyd, and Oliver Zishiri. "Tenure Security for Farmworkers in Zimbabwe." Working Chapter no. 27, Friedrich Ebert Stiftung, Harare, Zimbabwe, 1999.

SADC (Southern African Development Community). Annual Consultative Conference, Gallager Estate, Midrand, South Africa, Report 4.

———. Communiqué. Johannesburg, 28 August 1995.

———. Communiqué. Gaborone, Botswana, 28 June 1996.

———. Communiqué. Windhoek, Namibia, 16 March 2001.

———. Communiqué from the SADC Annual Consultative Conference, Royal Swazi Sun Convention Center, Mbabane, Swaziland, 20–22 February 2000.

———. Final communiqué of the SADC Summit of Heads of State or Government, Grand Baie, Mauritius, 13–14 September 1998.

———. "Protocol on Politics, Defense and Security in Southern Africa Development Community (SADC) Region." Maseru, Lesotho, 30 June 1996.

———. "Protocol on Trade." Gaborone, Botswana, 25 January 2000.

———. "Report of the Gender Division, 1999." Paper presented at International IDEA's Conference Towards Sustainable Democratic Institutions, Gaborone, Botswana, May 2000.

———. "Report on the Ministerial Meeting of the SADC Organ on Politics, Defense, and Security." Maputo, Mozambique, 8 May 1998.

———. *SADC Statistics: Facts and Figures 1999*. SADC Secretariat, Gaborone, Botswana, 1999.

———. *Southern Africa: A Framework and Strategy for Building the Community*. Gaborone, Botswana: SADC Secretariat, 1993.

———. "Subregional Report on Implementation of Agenda 21: Review of Progress Made Since the United Nations Conference on Environment and Development, 1992." UN Commission on Sustainable Development, New York, 7–25 April 1997 [available at: www.un.org/dpcsd/earthsummit].

———. "Towards a Southern African Development Community." Declaration by heads of state and government, Windhoek, Namibia, 17 August 1992.

———. "Treaty for the Southern African Development Community." Windhoek, Namibia, January 1992.

Sampson, Anthony. *Mandela: The Authorized Autobiography.* London: HarperCollins, 1999.

Sandbrook, Richard. *Closing the Circle: Democratisation and Development in Africa Between the Lines.* London: Zed Books, 2000.

SANDF (South African National Defence Force). "The SADC Intervention in Lesotho: A Military Perspective." Pretoria, May 2000.

———. "White Paper on Peace Missions." Pretoria, 24 February 1999.

Schirmer, S. "Land, Legislation and Tenants in Barberton, 1920–1950." In *White Farms, Black Labour: The State and Agrarian Change in Southern Africa, 1910–1950,* edited by A. H. Jeeves and J. Crush. Oxford: James Currey, 1997.

Schlessinger, S. "Transcending or Defending the World of States? The United Nations and Its Members." *Politik und Gesellschaft: International Politics and Society* 4 (1999).

Scoones, Ian. "Landscapes, Fields, and Soils: Understanding the History of Soil Fertility Management in Southern Zimbabwe." *Journal of Southern African Studies* 24, 4 (1997).

———. "Range Management Science and Policy: Politics, Polemics, and Pasture in Southern Africa." In *The Lie of the Land: Challenging Received Wisdom on the African Environment,* edited by M. Leach and R. Mearns. London: Heinemann, 1996.

Shackleton, S., C. Shackleton, and B. Cousins. "The Economic Value of Land and Natural Resources to Rural Livelihoods: Case Studies from South Africa." In *At the Crossroads: Land and Agrarian Reform in South Africa into the 21st Century,* edited by Ben Cousins. Bellville, South Africa: PLAAS; Johannesburg: NLC, 2000.

Shaw, Mark. "Crying Peace Where There is None? The Functioning and Future of Local Peace Committees of the National Peace Accord." Transition Series Research Report no. 31, Centre for Policy Studies, Johannesburg, August 1993.

———. "Organised Crime and State Responses in Southern Africa." In *Regional Integration in Southern Africa, Comparative International Perspectives,* edited by Christopher Clapham, Greg Mills, Anna Morner, and Elizabeth Sidiropoulos. Johannesburg: South African Institute of International Affairs, 2001.

Shevel, A. "AIDS Will Shrink Economy by 17% by 2010." *Business Report,* 29 November 2000.

Shivji, Issa, Sam Moyo, Welshman Ncube, and D. Gunby. "Draft National Land Policy for the Government of Zimbabwe." Discussion paper, Food and Agricultural Organisation and Ministry of Lands and Agriculture, Harare, Zimbabwe, 1998.

Sibanda, Philip. "Lessons from UN Peacekeeping in Africa: From UNAVEM to MONUA." In *From Peacekeeping to Complex Emergencies: Peace Support Missions in Africa,* edited by Jakkie Cilliers and Greg Mills. Johannesburg: South African Institute of International Affairs; Pretoria: Institute for Security Studies, 1999.

Sibanda, S. "Proposals for the Management of Land Rights in Rural South Africa." In *At the Crossroads: Land and Agrarian Reform in South Africa into the 21st Century,* edited by Ben Cousins. Bellville, South Africa: PLAAS; Johannesburg: NLC, 2000.

Sidaway, James, and Richard Gibb. "SADC, COMESA, SACU: Contradictory Formats for Regional Integration in Southern Africa?" In *South Africa in Southern Africa: Reconfiguring the Region,* edited by David Simon. Oxford: James Currey; Athens: Ohio University Press, 1998.

Simon, David, ed., *South Africa in Southern Africa*. Oxford: James Currey; Athens, Ohio: Ohio University Press, 1998.

Singini, R., and J. van Rooyen. "Serving Small Farmers: An Evaluation of the DBSA's Farmer Support Programmes." Report for the Development Bank of South Africa (DBSA), Midrand, South Africa, 1985.

Skalness, Tor. *Politics of Economic Reform in Zimbabwe: Continuity and Change in Development*. New York: St. Martin's, 1995.

Smith, A. *Stitches in Time*. London: Andre Deutch, 1977.

Smith, B. "The Role of Sub-Regional Organisations in Preventing African Conflicts." Paper presented at the Fifth Meeting of the Independent International Commission on Kosovo at the South Africa Institute of International Affairs, University of the Witwatersrand, Johannesburg, 25–26 August 2000.

Solomon, H. and J. Cilliers. "Southern Africa and the Quest for Collective Security." *Security Dialogue* 28, 2 (1997).

Sorrenson, M. J. K. *Land Reform in the Kikuyu Country*. Nairobi: Oxford University Press, 1997.

South African Commission on the Restitution of Land Rights. *Annual Report*. Pretoria, June 2000.

South African Department of Agriculture. "White Paper on Agriculture." Pretoria, 1995.

South African Department of Defence. "White Paper on Defence." Pretoria, 1977.

South African Department of Foreign Affairs. "The Millennium Partnership for Africa's Recovery Program" (MAP). Draft document 3a, Pretoria, July 2001.

———. Communiqué from the South Africa–Nigeria Bi-national Commission, Pretoria, 6 October 1999.

———. "South Africa as Chair of SADC and Review of the SADC Programme of Action." Pretoria, 20 November 1996.

———. "Statement on the SADC Summit and Accompanying Meetings in Blantyre, Malawi, 6–14 August 2001." Pretoria.

South African DLA (Department of Land Affairs). "Directorate: Redistribution Policy and Systems," *The Commonage Product*, 18 April 2000.

———. "Draft Land Policy Principles." From the National Conference on Land Policy, Kempton Park, South Africa, 31 August–1 September 1995.

———. "Farm Equity Scheme: Implementation Guide." Pretoria, 2000.

———. "The Food Safety-Net Programme: A Component of the Land Redistribution Programme." Draft discussion document, version 2.5, Pretoria, 2000.

———. Media briefing document for DLA Media Conference, Durban, South Africa, 22 June 2000.

———. "Mid-Term Review of the Pilot Land Programme." Report in association with the DANIDA, the European Commission and DFID, 24 September 1997.

———. *Proceedings of the National Conference on Land Policy, Kempton Park*. Pretoria, 1995.

———. "Report to the Minister on the Proceedings of the Commonage Workshop, 25 February 2000." Reprinted in *The Commonage Product*, 18 April 2000.

———. "White Paper on South African Land Policy." Pretoria, 1997.

———. "What the Extension of Security of Tenure Act (ESTA) Means for Owners and Occupiers: Know Your Land Rights," December 1997.

South African Government. "White Paper on Land Reform." Pretoria, 1991.

South African MALA (Ministry of Agriculture and Land Affairs). "The Commercial Farmer Programme: A Component of an Integrated Land Redistribution

Programme of the Ministry of Agriculture and Land Affairs," draft, 10 May 2000.

———. "An Integrated Programme of Land Redistribution and Agricultural Development in South Africa" (IPLRAD). Drafts, 8 May–23 October 2000.

———. "Land Redistribution for Agricultural Development: A Sub-Programme of the Land Redistribution Progamme."

Steppe, Masai. "The Windhoek Initiative: SADC Parliamentary Forum." Consultative meeting report, Windhoek, Namibia, 20–22 October 1993.

Stillwagon, Eileen. "HIV Transmission in Latin America: A Comparison with Africa and Policy Implications." *South Africa Journal of Economics* 68, 5 (December 2000).

Streek, B. "Land Reform Underspends Budget by R1.4 Billion." *Johannesburg Mail and Guardian,* 26 May 2000.

Stremlau, John. "African Renaissance and International Relations." In *African Renaissance,* edited by Malegapuru William Makgoba. Cape Town: Mafube Publishing and Tafelberg Publishers, 1999.

———. "Ending Africa's Wars." *Foreign Affairs* 79, 4 (July/August 2000).

Suberu, Rotimi T. "Can Nigeria's New Democracy Survive?" *Current History,* May 2001.

Summary of the Report of the Commission for the Socio-economic Development of the Bantu Areas Within the Union of South Africa. Pretoria, 1955.

Surplus People's Project, *Forced Removals in South Africa.* 5 vols. (Cape Town: SPP, 1983).

Swatuk, Larry, and Abillah H. Omari. *Regional Security: Southern Africa's Mobile "Front Line."* Southern African Perspectives no. 61. Cape Town: Centre for Southern African Studies, 1997.

Thomas, Caroline. *In Search for Security: The Third World and International Relations.* London: Harvester Wheatsheaf, 1987.

Throup, D. W. *The Economic and Social Origins of Mau Mau, 1945–1953.* London: J. Currey, 1988.

Tshuma, Lawrence. *A Matter of (In)Justice: Law, State and the Agrarian Question in Zimbabwe.* Harare, Zimbabwe: SAPES Books, 1997.

Tulya-Muhika, Sam. "Revival of the East African Co-operation and Its Institutional Framework." In *EAC, Perspectives on Regional Integration and Co-operation in East Africa.* Arusha: EAC, 2000.

Turner, S., and H. Ibsen. "Land and Agrarian Reform in South Africa: A Status Report." PLAAS Research Report no. 6, University of the Western Cape, Bellville, South Africa, November 2000.

UN (United Nations). "Report of the Panel on United Nations Peace Operations." New York, 21 August 2000.

UNAIDS. "AIDS and the Military." Geneva, May 1998.

———. "Report on the Global HIV/AIDS Epidemic." Geneva, June 2000.

———. "Report on the Global HIV/AIDS Epidemic." Geneva, December 2001.

UN Department for Public Information. "The UN and the Situation in Angola, May 1991–June 1994." Reference paper, New York, 1994.

UNDP (United Nations Development Programme). *Human Development Report 1999.* New York and Oxford: Oxford University Press, 1999.

———. *South Africa: Transformation for Human Development 2000.* Pretoria: UNDP, 2000.

UN Foundation. "Botswana to Lose One-Third of Economic Potential." *UN Wire,* 17 May 2000 [Available at: http://www.unfoundation.org.unwire/archives/UNWIRE000517.cfm].

———. "Disease May Cause Zero Population Growth in Zimbabwe." *UN Wire*, 5 June 2001 [available at: http://unfoundation.org/unwire/2001/06/05/index.asp].
UN General Assembly. "Declaration on Apartheid and its Destructive Consequences in Southern Africa." New York, December 1989.
———. "Report of the Panel on UN Peace Operations." Document A/55/305, New York, 21 August 2000.
UN Secretary General. "Report on the Question of South Africa." UN General Assembly and Security Council, New York, 10 January 1994.
———. "Report on Preliminary Deployment in the Democratic Republic of Congo," 15 July 1999, S/1999/790.
———. "Report Pursuant to Security Council Resolution 1216 (1998), Relative to the Situation in Guinea-Bissau," 17 March 1999, S/1999/294.
———. "Second Report Pursuant to Security Council Resolution 1270 (1999) on the UN Mission in Sierra Leone," 11 January 2000, S/2000/13.
"Update on the Land Rights Bill 1999." *Tenure Newsletter* 3, 1 (1999).
Urban Foundation. "Land Reform: An Analysis and a Challenge" and "Rural Development: Towards a New Future." *Policies for a New Urban Future* 4 (Johannesburg: 1990).
USEUCOM (U.S. European Command). "United States European Command Support to U.S. Policy in Africa." Theater engagement plan, Stuttgart, Germany, 2000 [available at: www.eucom.mil/Africa].
———. "USEUCOM Engagement Activities in Africa." European Command J-5 Strategic Plans and Policy Africa Division, Stuttgart, Germany [available at: www.eucom.mil/hq/ecj5_africa.htm].
U.S. Joint Chiefs of Staff. "National Military Strategy of the USA: Shape, Respond, Prepare Now: A Military Strategy for a New Era." U.S. Department of Defense, Washington, D.C., September 1997.
U.S. State Department. "Confidence and Security Building Measures: Communiqué, Second SADC-US Forum, Maputo, Mozambique, 11 May 2000." Bureau of Political-Military Affairs, U.S. State Department, Washington, D.C., May 2000.
———. "Foreign Military Training and DOD Engagement Activities of Interest, Volume 1." Joint report to Congress, Washington, D.C., 1 March 2000.
U.S. White House. *A National Security Strategy for a New Century.* Washington, D.C.: U.S. Government Printing Office, October 1998.
Vale, Peter. *The Case for Baskets: The Watershed Years.* Cape Town: Leadership Publication, 1991.
———. "The Case for a Conference for Security and Cooperation in Southern Africa." In *Southern Africa at the Cross Roads,* edited by Anthoni Van Nieuwkerk and A. G. Van Staden. Cape Town: South African Institute of International Affairs, 1991.
———. "Peace-Making in Southern Africa: Time for Questions." In *Out of Conflict: From War to Peace,* edited by Gunner M. Sørbø and Peter Vale. Uppsala, Sweden: Nordiska Afrikainstitutet, 1997.
Vale, Peter, and Ken Booth. "Security and Co-operation in Southern Africa: Post-Apartheid and Beyond Realism." *International Affairs* 71, 5 (1995).
———. "Security in Southern Africa After Apartheid: Beyond Realism." *International Affairs* 71, 2 (1995).
Vale, Peter, and Khabele Matlosa. "Beyond and Below: The Future of the Nation-State in Southern Africa." Working paper, Southern African Perspectives no.

53, Centre for Southern African Studies, University of the Western Cape, 1996.

Vance, Cyrus. *Hard Choices: Critical Years in American Foreign Policy.* New York: Simon and Schuster, 1983.

van den Brink, R., M. de Klerk, and H. Binswanger. "Rural Livelihoods, Fiscal Costs, and Financing Options: A First Attempt at Quantifying the Implications of Redistributive Land Reform." In *Agricultural Land Reform in South Africa: Policies, Markets and Mechanisms*, edited by J. van Zyl, J. Kirsten, and H. Binswanger. Cape Town: Oxford University Press, 1996.

Van Nieuwkerk, Anthoni. "Regionalism into Globalism? War and Peace? SADC and ECOWAS Compared." *African Security Review* 10, 2 (2001).

Vaughn, A., and A. McIntosh. "State and Capital in the Regeneration of a South African Peasantry." *Canadian Journal of African Studies* 29, 3 (1993).

Venâncio, Moisés. "Mediation by the Roman Catholic Church in Mozambique, 1988–91." In *Mediation in Southern Africa,* edited by Stephen Chan and Vivienne Jabri. London: Macmillan, 1993.

Venâncio, Moisés, and Carla Macmillan. "Portuguese Mediation in the Angolan Conflict in 1990–91," In *Mediation in Southern Africa,* edited by Stephen Chan and Vivienne Jabri. London and Basingstoke, UK: Macmillan, 1993.

"Vice President Gore and Governor Bush Participate in Second Presidential Debate." *CNN/AllPolitics*. Presidential debates transcript, 11 October 2000.

Vines, Alex. "Angola: 40 Years of War." Occasional Paper, Centre for Conflict Resolution, Cape Town. Published in *Track Two* 9, 2 (June 2000).

———. *RENAMO: Terrorism in Mozambique*. Bloomington and Indianapolis: Indiana University Press, 1991.

Vogt, Margaret A., ed. *The Liberian Crisis and ECOMOG: A Bold Attempt at Regional Peacekeeping*. Lagos: Gabumo Press, 1992.

Von der Ropp, K. "The Challenge of Change: Comparative Lessons from the Experiences of the EU and SADC." *ISS African Security Review* 2, 9 (2000).

Waever, O., et al. *Identity, Migration, and the New Security Agenda in Europe*. London: Pinter, 1993.

Waldmeir, P. *Anatomy of a Miracle*. London: Penguin, 1997.

Walker, C. "Relocating Restitution." *Transformation* 44 (2000).

Walker, Liz, and Leah Gilbert. "Women at Risk: HIV/AIDS—A South African Case Study." Paper presented at the AIDS in Context Conference, University of the Witwatersrand, Johannesburg, 4–7 April 2001.

Walt, Stephen M. "The Renaissance of Security Studies." *International Studies Quarterly* 3 (1991).

Warner, Jeroen. "Conflict on the Nile." In *Conflict Trends, Special Feature: Water Wars*. Umhlanga Rocks: Creda Communications, 2000.

Weiss, T. G., and M. A. Kessler. *Third World Security in the Post Cold War Era*. Boulder, Colo.: Lynne Rienner Publishers, 1995

Williams, Gavin. "Setting the Agenda: A Critique of the World Bank's 'Options for Land Reform and Rural Restructuring,'" *Journal of Southern African Studies* 23, 1 (1996).

———. "Transforming Labour Tenants." In *Land, Labour, and Livelihoods in Rural South Africa, Volume Two: KwaZulu-Natal and Northern Province,* edited by Michael Lipton, Frank Ellis, and Merle Lipton. Durban, South Africa: 1996.

Williams, G., J. Ewert, J. Hamman, and N. Vink. "Liberalising Markets and

Reforming Land in South Africa," *Journal of Contemporary African Studies*: 16, 1 (1998).

Williams, Rocklyn. "Beyond Old Borders: Challenges to Franco–South African Security Relations in the New Millennium." *African Security Review* 8, 4 (1999).

———. "Managing Regional Security," in *The IGD Guide to the Southern African Development Community,* edited by Riaan de Villers and Kato Lambreechts. Johannesburg: Institute for Global Dialogue, 2001.

Winter, G. *Inside BOSS: South Africa's Secret Police*. London: Passim, 1981.

Wixley, Sue. "Report from the Community Land Conference, 12–13 February 1994." NLC, Johannesburg, 1994.

World Bank. *Confronting AIDS: Public Priorities in a Global Epidemic*. New York: Oxford University Press, 1997.

———. *Governance: The World Bank's Experience*. Washington, D.C.: World Bank, 1996.

———. "Options for Land Reform and Rural Restructuring in South Africa." Land and Agricultural Policy Centre Conference, Johannesburg, October 1993.

———. "South African Rural Restructuring Program" (15 June 1993).

———. Zimbabwe. Agricultural Sector Memorandum. Vols. 1 and 2, no. 9429-Zim, World Bank, Washington, D.C., 1991.

———. "Zimbabwe: Country Economic Memorandum: Achieving Shared Growth," vol. 2. Economic report, Washington, D.C., 1995.

Wotshela, Luvuyo. "Homeland Consolidation, Resettlement and Local Politics in the Border and the Ciskei Region of the Eastern Cape, South Africa, 1960–1996." D.Phil thesis, Oxford University, 2001.

Wright, Stephen, and Julius Emeka Okolo. "Nigeria: Aspirations of Regional Power." In *African Foreign Policies,* edited by Stephen Wright. Boulder, Colo.: Westview Press, 1999.

Yates, Douglas. *The Rentier State in Africa: Oil Rent Dependency and Neocolonialism in the Republic of Gabon*. Trenton, N.J.: Africa World Press, 1995.

Yeros, Paris. "Peasant Struggles for Land and Security in Zimbabwe: A Global Moral Economy at the Close of the Twentieth Century." Working chapter, Harare, Zimbabwe: SAPES Books, 2000.

"Youth, Culture and Political Violence: The Sierra Leone Civil War" *African Development* 22, 2/3 (1997).

"Youth Still Ignorant on AIDS, Study Shows." *Johannesburg Star,* 18 July 2001.

Zacarias, Agostinho. *Security and the State in Southern Africa*. London: I. B. Tauris, 1999.

———. *The United Nations and International Peacekeeping*. London: I. B. Tauris, 1996.

Zartman, I. William. "African Regional Security and Changing Patterns of Relations." *Africa in the New International Order,* edited by Edmond J. Keller and Donald Rothchild. Boulder, Colo.: Lynne Rienner Publishers, 1996.

———, ed. *Collapsed States: The Disintegration and Restoration of Legitimate Authority*. Boulder, Colo.: Lynne Rienner Publishers, 1995.

Zimbabwe Land Tenure Commission. *Report of the Commission of Inquiry into Appropriate Land Tenure Systems*. 3 vols. Harare, Zimbabwe: Government Printers, 1994.

The Contributors

Adekeye Adebajo is director of the Africa Program at the International Peace Academy and adjunct professor at Columbia University's School of International and Public Affairs. He has served on UN missions in South Africa, Western Sahara, and Iraq. He is author of *Building Peace in West Africa: Liberia, Sierra Leone, and Guinea-Bissau* (Lynne Rienner, 2002) and *Liberia's Civil War: Nigeria, ECOMOG, and Regional Security in West Africa* (Lynne Rienner, 2002).

Jacqui Ala is senior tutor in the Department of International Relations at the University of Witwatersrand, Johannesburg. Her focus is on HIV/AIDS. She is also the coordinator of the International Relations Foundation course at the University of Witwatersrand, which received the Vice-Chancellor's Team Teaching Award for 2001.

Mwesiga Baregu is professor of political science and international relations at the University of Dar-es-Salaam. Until early 2002 he headed the Peace and Security Research Program at SAPES Trust in Harare, Zimbabwe. He is a member of the Executive Councils of the International Peace Research Association (IPRA) and the Africa Peace Research and Education Association (AfPREA). He has written and published numerous papers and edited a number of books on questions of political economy, peace and security, and democratization in Africa, focusing mainly on the Great Lakes region and southern Africa.

Talitha Bertelsmann-Scott, who hails from Pretoria, South Africa, was appointed as the EU/SADC research fellow at the South African Institute of International Affairs for 1997 and 1998. In 2000 she was appointed as research assistant and lecturer relief to the head of the Department of

Political Science at the University of Stellenbosch. In 2001 she moved to the UK, where she joined Christian Aid as their trade policy officer.

Jendayi E. Frazer is special assistant to the U.S. president and senior director for African affairs at the National Security Council. She is on leave from Harvard University, where she is assistant professor of public policy at the John F. Kennedy School of Government. As a Council on Foreign Relations international affairs fellow, she served as political-military planner with the Joint Chiefs of Staff in the Department of Defense and as director of African affairs at the National Security Council. She was a visiting fellow at the Center for International Security and Arms Control at Stanford University; a research associate at the Institute for Development Studies at University of Nairobi, Kenya; a member of the faculty of the Graduate School of International Studies, University of Denver; and editor of the journal *Africa Today*.

Ibrahim A. Gambari is Undersecretary-General/Special Adviser on Africa at the UN. He holds the record of being the longest serving ambassador/permanent representative of Nigeria to the United Nations (January 1990 to October 1999). From 1969 to 1974 he taught at the City University of New York and later at the State University of New York (Albany). He returned home to Nigeria to teach at Ahmadu Bello University in Zaria, first as senior lecturer (1977–1980), then as reader, and professor (1983). He was also chairman of the Department of Political Science at the University in Zaria (1982–1983), where he founded Nigeria's first undergraduate program in international studies. Professor Gambari was appointed director-general of the Nigeria Institute of International Affairs in October 1982, a position he held until his appointment as the minister of external affairs of Nigeria following the December 1983 military change of government.

Ruth Hall is a researcher in the Program for Land and Agrarian Studies at the University of the Western Cape, South Africa. At the time of writing, she was senior researcher at the Centre for Rural Legal Studies a non-governmental organization working on farmworkers' land and labor rights. During the past seven years, she has done research on land reform in South Africa and India, with a focus on gender equity issues in land redistribution and land rights.

Monica Kathina Juma has researched, taught, and carried out advocacy work in the areas of humanitarian assistance, disaster management, and refugee studies/forced migration for the past decade. Between 1995 and 2000 she carried out evaluations on the programs for the victims in Kenya

(1991–1998), commissioned by the UNDP and UK DFID. In 1997 she developed *Situational Analysis of Emergence in Kenya* for Action-Aid Kenya. In 2000 Dr. Juma served as a member of the International Academic Advisory Group to the UNHCR in the production of *The State of the World's Refugees* (2000). Her involvement in peacebuilding and conflict management work includes serving as a research associate at the International Peace Academy's Africa Program in 2001. She serves as a board member to the Refugee Advocacy Consortium of Kenya and the Eastern African Network for the Study of Forced Migration. She has written on human rights issues, regional security issues, and is currently coediting a book entitled *Doing Good: The Nature and Consequences of Humanitarian Assistance in Africa*.

Christopher Landsberg is the director of the Centre for Policy Studies in Johannesburg and the cofounder of the Centre for African International Relations at the University of the Witwatersrand, Johannesburg. He is a former deputy chair of the board of directors (2001–2002) as well as former deputy director of the CPS (1998–1999). During 1999–2000 he was a Hamburg fellow in the Center for International Security and Cooperation at Stanford University. He has published widely on South Africa's and Africa's international relations, particularly in the areas of governance, democracy promotion, development, peace, and security.

Prosper Matondi is an independent research fellow based in Harare, Zimbabwe. He has focused on land and natural resources management issues in Zimbabwe. He worked as a part-time coordinator of a project on the impact of the structural adjustment program on the rural landscape in Zimbabwe and was part-time coordinator of the Zimbabwe Land Research Network at the Southern Regional Institute for Policy Studies (SARIPS) in Harare.

Patrick Molutsi is director of the Political Participation and Methodology Programs at the International Institute for Democracy and Electoral Assistance (IDEA). He has taught at the University of Botswana, Gaborone, where he was appointed dean of the faculty of social sciences in 1996 and served in that position until 1999. He has researched widely on issues of elections, democracy, civil society, and political development in southern Africa. He is former member of the Governance Programme at SARIPS.

Sam Moyo is senior adviser and chair of numerous land networks, such as the South African Network on Land (SANL) and the Land Rights Network of Southern Africa (LRNSA), and a freelance land policy consultant based in Harare, Zimbabwe. Moyo has more than twenty-one years of research experience on rural development issues with a focus on land and natural resources management, civil society organizations, as well as capacity building and institutional development. He has worked as an associate professor at the Institute of Development Studies of the University of Zimbabwe and been associated with ZERO, a Harare-based regional environmental NGO. He has served as director of SARIPS in Harare and senior adviser on land policy matters to the various governments in the southern African region. He is currently vice president of CODESRIA located in Senegal.

Musifiky Mwanasali is an officer at the UN Sub-Regional Centre for Human Rights in Yaounde, Cameroon. He was a political analyst in the Center for Conflict Management, Department of Political Affairs of the Commission of the African Union. A native of the Democratic Republic of Congo, his area of policy research includes issues of peace, stability, democratic governance, and popular participation in central and southern Africa.

Tandeka C. Nkiwane is assistant professor of government at Smith College in Massachusetts. Formerly a lecturer in the Department of Political Studies at the University of Cape Town, she is the author of a number of journal articles and book chapters on southern African politics. Most recently, she is the recipient of the 2002–2003 HF Guggenheim Foundation award.

Kaye Whiteman is editor-in-chief/CEO of Business Media, a business publishing enterprise based in Lagos, Nigeria, publisher of the newsletter *Business Confidential*. From May 1999 to December 2000 he was director of information and public affairs in the Commonwealth secretariat. He was formerly editor-in-chief, general manager, and managing editor of the London-based weekly magazine *West Africa*. From 1973 to 1982 he was senior information official at the European Commission in Brussels, working on development issues. He has written extensively on West African affairs and European-African relations.

Gavin Williams is a fellow of St. Peter's College, Oxford. He has published a number of articles and edited several books on the politics of political economy and agricultural policies of African countries, particularly South Africa. He is currently writing a study of the history of the South African wine industry.

Agostinho Zacarias is principal officer in the office of the UN Undersecretary General Special Adviser on Africa. Prior to that he was senior government adviser at the UNDP Regional Bureau for Africa and served as the director of Mozambique's Institute for International Affairs (ISRI) in the Mozambique Ministry of Foreign Affairs. He was senior research associate at the International Institute for Strategic Studies in London. His publications include *The United Nations and International Peacekeeping* and *Security and State in Southern Africa*.

Index

Abacha, Sani, 33, 177, 196
Abubakar, Abdulsaalam, 177–178, 182
Abuja treaty, 207–208, 210
Academic community, democratic development and, 167
Adedeji, Adebayo, 1–2
Adeniji, Olu, 175
Africa Center for Strategic Studies (ACSS), 290
African Common Market, 215
African Crisis Response Initiative (ACRI), 280, 283–284, 290
African Economic Community (AEC): principles and mandate of, 207–208; SADC commitment to, 209
African National Congress (ANC), 327, 328, 330; land reform program of, 102–105; Reconstruction and Development Program, 98; United Nations and, 267
African Peace Council of Elder Statesmen (proposed), 180, 181
African renaissance, 171, 178, 183; goals and objectives of, 179–180; liberation legacy and, 186–187
African Renaissance and International Cooperation Fund, 188
African Union (AU), 205, 350, 351; Constitutive Act, 181, 184; military interventions and, 181; new regional organizations and, 210–211; Peace and Security Council of, 216
African-Caribbean-Pacific (ACP) grouping, 305; Lomé convention/Cotonou agreement and, 310–311; European Union trade agreements with, 311–313
Agricultural sector, impacts of HIV/AIDS pandemic on, 147. *See also* Land reform, in southern Africa
Ajello, Aldo, 266
Al-Turabi, Hassan, 233, 234
Allied Forces for the Liberation of Congo/Zaire (AFDL), 67–69
Amnesty International, 64
Anglo-American Corporation, 83
Anglo-German Treaty of 1890, 65
Angola: Armed Forces of, 264, 265; church-led resistance movement in, 165; conflict in, 257, 263; Congo military intervention and, 213; democracy in, 5, 40; memorandum of understanding on, 265; New York accord and, 262; opportunity for peace in, 352; South Africa and, 321; UN operations in, 261, 263–265
Annan, Kofi, 151, 189, 258, 261, 265, 269
Anyaoku, Chief Emeka, Commonwealth and, 317, 327, 330, 331–333, 337–338
Arab League, 236
Arab Maghreb Union (UMA), 207
Association of Southern African States (ASAS), proposal for, 37–38, 62, 211–212
Attlee, Clement, 320

Basotholand Congress Party (BCP), 185
Bicesse Peace Accords, 263, 264
Bin Laden, Osama, 232
Botha, P. W.: brutal regime of, 326–327; total strategy of, 59–60
Botswana, 256; average life expectancy in, 141; Commonwealth Ministerial Action Group and, 334; democracy in, 5; Democratic Republic of Congo and, 187; GDP growth rate in, 3; HIV/AIDS in, 132, 142, 150; Lesotho intervention of, 6, 185; U.S. engagement in, 281, 282
Bouteflika, Abdelazziz, 182, 183
Boutros-Ghali, Boutros, 267
Brahimi, Lakhdar, 267
Bureau of State Security (BOSS) of South Africa, 317
Burundi, peace agreement in, 188
Bush, George W., Africa policy of, 281, 286, 290
Buyoya, Pierre, 188

Callaghan, Jim, 324
Canada, decolonization and, 320, 323–324
Capri secessionist groups, 160
Carson, Johnnie, 229
Catholic Justice and Peace Organ, 165
Central African Federation, 320
Chiluba, Frederick, 41
Chissano, Joaquim, 8, 275, 276
Church-associated resistance movement, 165
Civil society, 161–170; authoritarian state and, 162; characteristics of, 163–164; church-related, 165; conceptions of, 161; conflict prevention role of, 167–168, 240, 245, 246; Cotonou agreement and, 312; democratic governance and, 169; environmental advocacy of, 166; human rights and, 165; human security process and, 167–169; liberation struggles and, 163; limitations and problems of, 162; minority groups and, 167; national security role of, 48–49, 347–348; research community and, 167; state control over funding of, 162; trade union movement in, 164–165; women's organizations and, 166
Civil wars, African; proliferation of, 260
Clinton administration: Africa policy of, 277, 281; "shaping engagements of," 288–292
Commercial Farmer Programme (South Africa), 100
Common Market of Eastern and Southern Africa (COMESA), 210, 245, 313–314; SADC and, 66–67
Commonwealth: Canada's role in, 320, 323–324; conflict resolution and, 335–336; Congo crisis and, 336; decolonization and, 319–328; democracy and, 331–335, 336; Goa Declaration on International Security and, 318; good governance and, 336; Harare declaration of, 332, 333; international security and, 319–328; Milbrook declaration of, 333; military operations and, 318–319; Mozambique and, 329–330; Namibian independence and, 329; Nigeria's membership in, 333, 338–339; post–Cold War policies, 329–331; and racism, 323; Rhodesian/Zimbabwean independence and, 321–323, 325–326; SADC and, 335–336; in Sierra Leone, 336; Singapore declaration of, 323; South African peacekeeping mission of, 330–331; and South Africa's Mbeki government, 336–337; South Africa's departure from, 319, 320; and UN peacekeeping operations, 319
Commonwealth Ministerial Action Group (CMAG), 333–335, 337
Confederation of South African Trade Unions (COSATU), 164
Conference for Security and Cooperation in Europe (CSCE), 37
Conference on Security, Stability, Development, and Cooperation in Africa (CSSDCA), 178, 179, 180
Conflict Early Warning and Response Mechanism (CEWARN), 239–241, 248
Conflict management and peacebuild-

ing: civil society's role in, 167–168, 246; democracy as means of, 4–5; development and, 271; diplomacy and, 189, 350; early warning mechanism for, 240, 270; European Union and, 308–309, 313; machinery, proposals for, 180; material conditions and, 257; Nigeria's efforts in, 179, 181–182; and peace prospects, 55; South Africa's approach to, 179, 181–182, 185–186; state commitment in, 246–247; UN-SADC cooperation in, 269–270. *See also specific country;* Intergovernmental Authority on Drought and Desertification (IGADD); Regional conflict; Southern African Development Community (SADC); United Nations peace operations

Congolese Rally for Democracy (RCD), 287

Constellation of Southern African States project, 34, 59

Contribution to the International Peacekeeping Account (CIPA), 288

Cook, Robin, 334

Côte d'Ivoire, restoration of constitutional rule in, 182

Coups d'état, African sanctions against, 181

Cuba: Angola and, 322, 329; Namibia and, 262–263; New York accord and, 262

Danjuma, Theophilus, 191

De Klerk, F. W., 178, 327, 328, 329, 330

Debt alleviation, 182, 183

Democracy: African adaptation of, 179, 181; and common values, 40–41; Commonwealth's commitment to, 331–335; and democratic peace theory, 54–55, 180; as development aid condition, 306; economic liberalization and, 53–54, 56–57; income distribution and, 54–55; security and, 4–5, 53, 55, 317, 346–347; and "zones of peace," 180. *See also specific country*

Democratic Republic of Congo (DRC): conflict in, 257; democracy of, 4; Inter-Congolese Dialogue (ICD) and, 269, 349; Lesotho and, 67–69; military intervention in, 6, 7, 41, 67–68; peace process and prospects in, 187, 189, 287–288, 349, 352; Rwanda's conflict with, 189; SADC military intervention in, 213–215; and South Africa, 189; UN missions in, 268–269, 286, 287–288, 349; U.S. engagement in, 281, 282, 287

Development aid, of European Union, 304, 305, 306, 308, 310

Development Bank of Southern Africa (DSBA), 115

Didiza, Thoko, 98, 99, 119

Dos Santos, José Eduardo, 186, 188, 264

East Africa, states of, 225

East African Community (EAC), 240; collapse of, 21; conflict preventive actions of, 244–245; reconstitution of, 207, 243–244; small arms monitoring of, 243. *See also* Greater Horn of Africa (GHA)

East African Customs Union, 244

Economic Commission for Africa (ECA), 180

Economic Community of Central African States (ECCAS), 207

Economic Community of West African States (ECOWAS), 178, 190, 207; failures of, 175–176; peacekeeping mission of, 167, 350

Economic Community of West African States Cease-Fire Monitoring Group (ECOMOG), 25, 190–191, 270, 285

Economy, southern African, 259; causes of poor performance of, 3–4, 35; HIV/AIDS pandemic and, 142, 258; and liberal market reforms, 56–57. *See also specific country*

Educational sector, and HIV/AIDS pandemic, 135, 143, 145–147

Environmental security: advocacy groups for, 166; early warning mechanism for, 240

Ethnic groups, and democratic reforms, 167

European Development Fund, 310

European Economic Community (EEC), SADCC and, 307
European Political Cooperation (EPC), 303, 307
Regional economic preference agreements, 312–313
European Union (EU): as peacekeeper, 308–309; security defined by, 301; South Africa's relations with, 20–21, 311–312
EU-Africa relations: African-Caribbean-Pacific (ACP) grouping and, 311–313; Common Foreign and Security Policy (CFSP), 303–306, 309–309; development aid in, 304, 305, 306, 308, 310; direct engagement in, 304–305; Lomé convention/Cotonou agreement and, 305–306, 310–313; Zimbabwean crisis and, 305–306
EU-SADC relations, 302, 306–309; ministerial conferences and, 309; promotion of peace and stability in, 308–309, 313; regional economic preference agreements and, 312–313, 314; Regional Indicative Program funding and, 304; regional integration and, 313–314; trade agreements and, 311–313
Extension of Security of Tenure Act (ESTA) of South Africa, 108, 111

Food Safety-net Programme (South Africa), 100, 117
Forum for Early Warning and Early Response (FEWER), 239–240
France: African policy of, 196, 321; Nigeria and, 175–176
Fraser, Malcolm, 327
Front for the Liberation of Mozambique (FRELIMO), 265–266, 329
Frontline States (FLS), 62, 322; and apartheid South Africa, 57, 58, 176, 327, 328; disbanding of, 37; formation of, 2, 60; SADCC/SADC and, 20, 61, 211

G-8 powers, Africa's partnership with, 351
Gambari, Ibrahim, 177
Garang, John, 234
George VI, 320
Global AIDS Fund, 151
Globalization, 183, 338; African renaissance and, 179; organized crime and, 259; poverty and, 134; regional integration and, 21–22; security and social justice implications of, 346; United Nations and, 349
Goa Declaration on International Security, 318
Good governance, 244, 271; as development aid condition, 306; liberal democracy and, 53–54; World Bank's political conditionality and, 53
Gore, Al, 286
Great Lakes region, 225
Greater Horn of Africa (GHA), 225–248; economies of, 228–229; forced displacement in, 229; history and nature of insecurity in, 225, 226–229; human rights abuses in, 229; illicit ownership of arms in, 227–228; institutional development needs in, 247–248; insurgencies in, 228; peace initiatives in, 229–231; types of states in, 227
Guelleh, Ismail Omr, 235–236, 237
Guinea-Bissau, ECOMOG military mission to, 190, 191

Hain, Peter, 334
Hanekom, Derek, 98, 105
Harare declaration of 1991, 67
Health care sector, impacts of HIV/AIDS pandemic on, 144–145, 148
Heath, Edward, 322–323
Hegemony: in Africa, 174–175; conceptualizations of, 173–174; and hegemonic stability concept, 174
HIV/AIDS, 3; business and economic impact of, 142–145; and child- and female-headed households, 147–148, 149; economic impact of, 258; education sector impacted by, 135, 143, 145–147; farming sector and, 147; health care sector and, 144–145, 148; as human security threat, 132, 150–151; malnutrition and, 134–135; military and peacekeeping

forces infected with, 153–154; misinformation and lack of knowledge about, 140–141; orphaned children's vulnerability to, 146, 149–150; population and demographic impacts of, 141–142; and prevention/education programs, 140, 141, 151; prostitution and, 139–140; regional cooperation and, 151–152; risk factors for, 132–141; sexual abuse and, 137, 140; social norms/sexual practices and, 136–138; stigmatization and, 135–136; and traditional security concerns, 152–154; urban migration and, 137–138; women's status and, 138–140
Holbrooke, Richard, 132, 286–287
Horn of Africa: conflict systems in, 246; states of, 225. *See also* Greater Horn of Africa (GHA)
Human rights: abuses, 186, 229, 333; as development aid condition, 306; movement, 165; South Africa and, 186–187, 188
Human security: arms proliferation and, 242; civil society and, 167–169; concept of, 131–132; democratic governance and, 169; HIV/AIDS and, 132; nature of regional conflicts and, 160–161; SADC and, 160; and social justice paradigm, 346–347

Ibok, Sam, 217
Income distribution gap, 54–55
Indian Ocean Commission grouping, 210
Integrated Programme of Land Redistribution for Agricultural Development in South Africa (IPLRAD), 99, 119
Intelligence institutions, and early warning systems, 49
Intergovernmental Authority on Drought and Desertification (IGADD), 245; early warning mechanism of, 239–243; mandate of, 229–231; Partners Forum proposal, 233; and People to People peace initiative, 238–239; and small/intermediate arms proliferation, 241–243; and Somali peace process, 235–238; and Sudan peace process, 231–235, 238; treaty, 240
International Law Enforcement Academy for Africa (ILEA), 294
International Monetary Fund (IMF), 312; structural adjustment programs of, 56
International Peace Academy, conflict management approach of, 167–168
Inter-State Defence and Security Committee (ISDSC), 9, 38, 39, 63, 348; DRC intervention of, 67–68
Inter-State Politics and Diplomacy Committee (ISPDC), 8–9
Islam, Sudan peace process and, 231–232, 233

Jiang Zemin, 182
Joint Combined Exchange Training (JCET), 290, 294–295

Kabila, Joseph, 189, 268, 269
Kabila, Laurent, 67, 68, 267–268
Kagame, Paul, 189, 269
Kapwepwe, Simon, 322
Kenya: land reform in, 103, 120; regional cooperation strategy of, 244, 245; and Sudan peace process, 232–233; women's land ownership in, 139
Kiplagat, Bethuell, 227
Kissinger, Henry, 175, 324, 325–326
KwaZulu-Natal Province: HIV/AIDS prevalence in, 132; land reforms in, 107, 110

Lamido, Sule, 191
Land and Agricultural Policy Centre (LAPC) of South Africa, 104
Land Redistribution for Agricultural Development (LRAD) of South Africa, 99–102, 117, 119
Land reform, in southern Africa: community-driven, 91; and land restitution, 90–91; sources of conflict in, 90, 91; and structural adjustment programs, 91; variable approaches to, 90–91. *See also* South African land reform; Zimbabwean land reform

Land Reform (Labour Tenants) Act, 106, 108
Langa commission, 185
Legal aid centers, 165
Lesotho: COMESA and, 67; constitutional crisis in, 185–186; democracy in, 4, 40–41; Democratic Republic of Congo and, 67–69; economy of, 310; military intervention in, 185–186; royal coup in, 67; South Africa's intervention in, 6, 40, 41
Letsie III of Lesotho, 67
Liberalization, African economy and, 56–57
Liberia, Nigeria's interventions in, 190
Lomé convention, 285, 307, 309, 324, 336; Cotonou agreement and, 305–306, 310–313; development aid and, 310
Luanda Mutual Defense Pact, 349
Lusaka agreement, 61, 264, 265, 268, 325; and Frontline States (FLS) formation, 2; implementation of, 287; OAU and, 214; Political Committee of, 214–215

Maastricht Treaty, 303
Machakos declaration, 234–235
Machel, Samora, 329
Macmillan, Harold, 320
Malawi: challenges to democracy in, 5; economy of, 310; resistance movement in, 165; SADC summit in, 23, 189, 275–276
Mandela, Nelson, 171, 177, 181, 185, 186, 188, 196, 267, 327, 328, 330; Commonwealth membership and, 331, 333, 336; and OPDS institutionalization, 64; as SADC chair, 38–39
Manley, Michael, 329, 331
Margai, Albert, 322
Masire, Ketumile, 59, 189
Mauritius, democracy in, 5
Mbeki, Thabo, 178–197, 269; African renaissance and, 171, 178, 179–180; conflict mediation of, 181; consultative strategy of, 186; on democracy, 179, 180; foreign and security policy of, 178–182; and North-South relations, 182–184; and Olusegun Obasanjo, 178–179, 194; peacemaking role of, 187–189, 196; value-driven approach of, 178
Mboya, Daniel, 232
McKinnon, Don, 334
Menzies, Robert, 320
Merafe, Mompati, 334
Migration: and regional tensions, 35; urban, HIV/AIDS pandemic and, 137–138
Military interventions: African Union Constitutive Act and, 181; of South Africa and Nigeria, 182, 185–186, 187, 213; as traditional security approach, 32, 33
Military personnel, HIV/AIDS risks for, 153–154
Military spending, 245
Millennium Africa Recovery Plan (MAP), 183
Mkapa, Benjamin, 8, 276
Mobutu Sese Seko, 58, 67–68, 267–268
Mokhehle, Ntsu, 67, 185
Moshoeshoe II, 185
Movement for Democratic Change (MDC) in Zimbabwe, 4; land reform and, 77, 86, 87–89
Mozambique, 262; civil war in, 265; COMESA and, 67; Commonwealth diplomacy in, 329–330; Lesotho intervention and, 185; liberation movement in, 329; National Resistance Movement (RENAMO), 5, 265–266, 329; peace agreement in, 265–266; UN peacekeeping in, 257, 261, 266
Mswati III, King of Swaziland, 19
Mudenge, Stan, 66
Mugabe, Robert, 4, 8, 37, 59, 186, 324, 329; ascension to power, 326; Commonwealth and, 334–335; European Union and, 305; land issue and, 89, 352; Mbeki government and, 187; OPDS and, 64, 213
Muluzi, Bakili, 5
Museveni, Yoweri, 136
Muzorewa, Abel, 324–325

Nairobi Initiative on Small Arms and Light Weapons, 242
Namibia/South West Africa, 326; COMESA and, 67; conflict in, 257;

Congo military intervention and, 187, 213, 287; democracy in, 4–5, 41; independence of, 329; South Africa's mandate in, 262–263; UN peace operations (UNTAG), in, 261, 262
Nassau Declaration on World Order, 318
National African Farmers Union (NAFU), 120
National Department of Agriculture (NDA) of South Africa, 111; black commercial farming class and, 99; Broadening Access to Agriculture Thrust of, 116; land transfers and, 118; liberalization policies of, 98
National Land Committee (NLC), 109, 120
National Union for the Total Independence of Angola (UNITA), 4, 50, 263, 264–265
Native Trust and Land Act, 114, 115
Nehru, Pandit, 320
New African Initiative (NAI), 183–184
New Partnership for Africa's Development (NEPAD), 178, 184, 350–351
New Sudan Council of Churches (NSCC), People to People peace initiative of, 238–239
New York accord, 262
Ngong, Namanga, 268
Nigeria: Abacha regime's human rights abuses in, 333; anti-apartheid and liberation movements and, 176; common market goal of, 175–176; Commonwealth membership of, 333, 338–339; democracy of, 177, 195; economy of, 177, 192; and France's subregional presence, 175–176; and giantism, 174; military interventions of, 182; as peacekeeper, 179, 181, 189–191; as regional hegemon, 171–172; religious/ethnic divisions in, 78; repression and human rights abuses in, 176–177, 186; Sierra Leone involvement of, 285; South Africa's partnership with, 174–175, 192–197. *See also* Obasanjo, Olusegun
Nigeria–South Africa Binational Commission (BNC), 192–193
Nonaligned Movement, 183
Nongovernmental organizations (NGOs): land reform and, 98, 102, 112; regional security role of, 247–248. *See also* Civil society
North American Free Trade Agreement (NAFTA), 22
North Atlantic Treaty Organization (NATO), 37; regional interventions of, 24, 25
Nujoma, Sam, 5, 186
Nyerere, Julius, 320

Obasanjo, Olusegun, 171, 178–197, 285, 327; African renaissance and, 171; conflict mediation of, 181; democracy and, 180; economic diplomacy policy of, 192; foreign and security policy of, 178–182; institutional approach of, 178; and North-South relations, 182–184; peacemaking role of, 187–189, 196; and Thabo Mbeki, 178–179, 194
OMEGA Plan, 183
Operation Blue Crane, 309–310
Organ on Politics, Defense, and Security (OPDS), 211, 212–213, 275–276; establishment of, 63–64; functions and goals of, 5–6, 38; inconclusive status of, 68; institutional framework of, 22–23; operationalization of, 64, 286; politics of, 38–39; security performance of, 31; weaknesses and ineffectiveness of, 6, 160. *See also* Southern African Development Community (SADC)
Organ on Politics, Defense, and Security Cooperation (OPDSC): influential position of, 353; operationalization of, 26–27, 49, 346, 348–349; regional structures and mechanisms in, 8; review of, 7, 26–27; SADC relationship with, 348; security conceptualization of, 47–48; and state transformations, 48
Organization for Economic Cooperation and Development (OECD), 338
Organization of African Unity (OAU), 2, 176, 178, 180, 181, 236; Abuja

treaty and, 207–208, 210; peacebuilding and conflict management approach of, 167–168; and regional economic communities, 207–209, 215–218; regional interventions of, 209; regional security mechanisms and, 215–220; regions of, 207; Rhodesia/Zimbabwe liberation and, 322; SADC and, 215; and sanctions against putschists, 181; and state interference, 205. *See also* African Union (AU)
Organized crime, transnational proliferation of, 258–259

Peace movements, and national security planning, 48. *See also* Conflict management and peacebuilding
Peacekeeping: of African Crisis Response Initiative (ACRI), 283–284; of ECOWAS states, 350; forces, and HIV/AIDS, 153–154. *See also* United Nations peace operations
People to People peace initiative, 238–239, 245
People's Democratic Party of Nigeria, 195
Phosa, Mathews, 195
Political instability, democratization and, 35
Popular Liberation Movement of Angola (MPLA), 263, 264
Portugal, African empire of, 321
Poverty: and development aid, 310; Millennium Africa Recovery Plan (MAP) and, 183; small arms proliferation and, 242; trade liberalization and, 311–312, 313
Powell, Colin, 279–280
Preferential Trade Area, 66

Ramaphosa, Cyril, 195
Ramphal, Shridath, 324–325, 326, 332, 333
Reconstruction and Development Program (RDP), 98, 109
Regional conflict: endemic and multifaceted nature of, 159–161; military solutions to, 257; territorial, 64–65; trade and, 65–66; water resources and, 65. *See also* Conflict management and peacebuilding
Regional integration and development: Abuja treaty and, 207–208, 210; affection model of, 21; gain model of, 21; globalization and, 21–22; New African Initiative (NAI) and, 183–184; power model of, 22; and regional economic communities (RECs), 207–209, 215–218; regional models of, 21–22; security linked to, 244, 248, 271; threat model of, 21–22
Regional security: challenges, 346–353; civil society's role in, 48–49, 347–348, 349; collective arrangements/models for, 5, 25–26; common values/vision in, 40–41, 47; defense industry and, 49; democracy and, 4–5, 53, 55, 317, 346–347; evolving architecture of, 2–7; extraregional actors in, 347, 348, 350, 351; hegemonic states and, 25–26, 350; HIV/AIDS crisis and, 348; insecurity sources and, 47; institutional bridge-building and, 349–350; interdependence and, 46; interregional cooperation in, 350; land reform and, 347, 348; leadership changes and, 59; legal framework for, 49; militaristic point of view in, 34–35, 39; nonmilitary agents of, 48–49, 59, 60; operational issues in, 49; partnership building in, 347, 350–351; people-driven process in, 246; political commitment and, 326–247; poverty and social justice challenges in, 347–348; power management in, 46; process-based, 245–246; UN Charter and, 23–24; variables of fear and fragmentation in, 45–46. *See also* Human security; Southern African Development Community (SADC)
Regional security community: definition of, 206; organizations in, 210–211; Sirte declaration and, 210. *See also* Organization of African Unity (OAU)
Regionalization, of southern Africa, 57–60, 207

Renwick, Robin, 327
Rice, Susan, 285
Rwanda: Democratic Republic of Congo's conflict with, 189; genocide, 189, 261; U.S. engagement in, 282, 283

Salat Hassan, Abdul Kassim, 237
Sankoh, Foday, 285
Saro-Wiwa, Ken, 333
Savimbi, Jonas, 4, 40, 264
Security: concept, 226, 301–302; concept of order in, 43; concepts of peace and justice in, 42–43; developmental perspective on, 244, 248, 271; economic aspects of, 43; idea of "the good life" in, 42–44; in international system, 32–33, 317; legitimacy and policy capacity issues in, 33–34; liberal democratic model of, 53–54; militarism in, 32, 33; nonmilitary phenomena and, 33–34; people- versus state-centered approach to, 31–32; and political process, 44; in third world, 32–35. *See also* Human security; Regional security
Sexwale, Tokyo, 195
Sierra Leone: Nigeria's interventions in, 190, 191, 285; peace operations in, 260, 284, 285
Small- and medium-arms proliferation, 259; in Greater Horn region, 241–243; Nairobi declaration on, 242
Smith, Arnold, 323
Smith, Ian, 321, 325
Smuts, Jan, 262
Social justice, as security paradigm, 346
Social movements, and national security planning, 48–40. *See also* Civil society
Somalia: peace process in, 235–238, 246; peacekeeping debacle in, 283; state collapse of, 235; U.S. engagement in, 282, 283
South Africa: Angola and, 263; Commonwealth agenda and, 320–328; Commonwealth membership of, 319, 320, 331; Commonwealth Observer Mission in, 330–331; Congo military intervention and, 187, 213; Delhi and Nassau CHOGMs and, 318, 326; democracy and, 5, 177, 186–187, 188, 192, 195; destabilization policy of, 34, 176; economy/gross domestic product (GDP) of, 63, 177, 259; embargoes against, 266–267; European Economic Community (EEC) and, 307; European Union and, 20–21, 306, 307; Frontline States and, 60; giantism and, 174; HIV/AIDS prevalence in, 132, 141, 142; Human Development Report of 2000, 55; human rights promotion of, 186–187, 188; interregional relations of, 20–22; justification for apartheid crimes in, 317–318; Lesotho intervention of, 185–186; Lomé convention accession of, 311; macroeconomic liberalization impacts in, 55; migration impacts on, 35; military of, 63; military interventions of, 182; New York accord and, 262; Nigerian partnership with, 174–175, 192–197; peacemaking/peacekeeping approach of, 179, 181, 185–186, 188; postapartheid foreign policy, 57–58, 59, 62–63; race and class divisions in, 178; as regional hegemon, 20, 25, 45–46, 58, 171–172, 186, 350; SADC's relations with, 20–21, 308, 311; social divisions in, 192; South West Africa/Namibia and, 262; subregional distrust of, 172; trade disputes of, 65–66; trade policy of, 176, 187, 194; transitional phase of, 330–331; U.S. engagement in, 281, 282; "White Paper on Peace Missions," 185; Zimbabwe's relations with, 7, 41, 68. *See also* Mbeki, Thabo
South African Department of Land Affairs (DLA): land reform program of, 99–102, 105–112; responsibilities and objectives of, 98–99, 100; "Review of the Land Reform Pilot Programme," 107, 113–114; Settlement/Land Acquisition Grants (SLAGs) of, 98, 108–109, 111–112

South African Development Trust (SADT), 102, 115
South African land reform, 97–121; activist movements and, 97; and agricultural development, 99–102; ANC policy in, 102–105; beneficiaries of, 98, 112, 117, 118; betterment schemes in, 115–116; and black commercial farmers, 99; contradictions of, 111–112; emergent farmers as focus of, 99, 116, 117–121; equity-share schemes in, 110–111, 117; farmer support programs (FSPs) in, 115–116; in former bantustans, 112, 115–116, 119; in historical/comparative perspective, 114–117; land invasions in, 121; land reform pilot projects in, 109–111; land/tenure rights in, 107–108, 119; land redistribution in, 108–111; land restitution in, 106–107, 113, 114; land transfers in, 118–120; and native reserves, 114–115; nongovernmental organizations and, 98, 102, 106, 109, 120; outgrower schemes in, 111, 116–117; race and, 99, 100; radical market liberalization policies of, 98; settlement/land allocation grants (SLAGs) and, 98, 100, 108–109, 111–112; supply-side approach to, 113–114; and violence against white farmers, 112, 121; and women's land rights, 102, 112, 119–120; World Bank redistribution model and proposals for, 98, 99, 102–105, 120
South African National Defense Force (SANDF), 185
South West African People's Organization (SWAPO), 262. *See also* Namibia/South West Africa
Southern African Customs Union (SACU), 176, 312–313
Southern African Development Community (SADC), 176, 178, 245, 328; African Economic Community (AEC) functioning and, 209; Cairo declaration, 216; Common Defence Pact, 349, 353; common market goal of, 66–67; Commonwealth and, 335–336; conflict prevention and mediation in, 36–37, 167, 309–310; Council of Ministers, 22, 26–27; creation of, 20, 46; Declaration of Heads of State, 36; DRC invasion and, 268; economic development in, 3–4, 37; Electoral Commissions Forum, 4; expanded mandate and geographic base of, 210; external donor funding of, 1; Gaborone summit, 22–23, 61, 63, 212–213; government structure in, 22; hegemonic institutional bridge-building doctrine of, 350; history of conflict in, 19–20; HIV/AIDS pandemic and, 3, 151–152; human security and, 160; implementation capacity of, 4; ineffectiveness of, 59, 160; integrated economic–security management system proposal of, 211–212; interregional cooperation doctrine of, 350; leadership of, 189; Lesotho intervention and, 185–186; Malawi summit of, 23, 63, 189, 275–276; Mechanism for Conflict Prevention, Management, and Resolution, 215–217; member states, 61; militaristic view of security in, 39–40; New Partnership for Africa's Development (NEPAD) and, 350–351; OAU and, 215; Parliamentary Forum, 4; peacebuilding and conflict management, 167; regional economic communities and, 215–220; regional integration mandate of, 2–3, 21, 51–62, 209–210, 308; regional interventions of, 25, 59–60; sector on Political Cooperation, Democracy, Peace, and Security, 61–62; security issues in, 35–41, 256–259; South Africa's relations with, 20–21, 307–309; standby force proposed for, 40; state linkages in, 57; state-centric paradigm in, 352; trade protocol, 65–66; Treaty on Defense and Security, 22, 58, 211, 212; and U.S. bilateral security assistance, 292–294; and water resources, 65. *See also* EU-SADC relationship; Organ on Politics, Defense, and Security (OPDS)
SADC Protocol on Politics, Defense, and Security Cooperation, 8–10, 40,

346; operationalization of, 348–349

Southern African Development Coordination Conference (SADCC): formation and purpose of, 2, 20, 61, 207; infrastructure development and, 307; Inter-State Defence and Security Committee (ISDSC), 275; SADC Allied Forces' DRC operations and, 20, 23, 24–25, 213–215, 217; South Africa's exclusion from, 58; South Africa's racist regimes and, 322

Southern African Regional Police Chiefs Cooperation Organization (SARPCCO), 294

States, southern African: centrality of, in security agenda, 205; democracy in, 40–41; foreign policy agenda of, 67; of Greater Horn of Africa, types of, 227; HIV/AIDS pandemic and, 150, 151–152, 154; leadership changes in, 59, 68; militarization and, 34–35; regional security role of, 47–48. *See also specific state*

Structural adjustment programs, 312; educational impacts of, 139; and land reform strategies, 91

Sudan: Dinka/Nuer Wunlit accord and, 238; peace process, 231–235; People to People program in, 238–239; and UN sanctions, 234

Swaziland, 336; democracy in, 3, 40–41, 352; economy of, 310; HIV/AIDS prevalence in, 132; and overhaul of OPDS, 7

Talbott, Strobe, 279, 280

Tanzania, 60; Democratic Republic of Congo and, 187; democracy prospects in, 5; regional cooperation strategy of, 244, 245; Rhodesia and, 322

Territorial border disputes, 64–65

Thatcher, Margaret, 325, 326, 327, 328

Trade: EU–South Africa, 311–313; as major foreign-policy concern, 65–67

Trade, Development, and Cooperation Agreement (TDCA), 311–312

Trade liberalization: Cotonou agreement and, 311–313; negative impacts of, 311–312; and poverty alleviation, 313

Trade unions: and democratic governance, 169; reformist agenda of, 164–165

Trudeau, Pierre, 323

Uganda: HIV/AIDS initiative in, 136, 144, 150, 154; regional cooperation strategy of, 244, 245

UNITA. *See* National Union for the Total Independence of Angola

United Democratic Front of South Africa, 328

United Kingdom: and colonial reparations, 76–77, 84; and Mozambique, 329. *See also* Commonwealth

United Kingdom Department for International Development, 83

United Nations, 255–271; Charter, as framework of regional security arrangements, 23–24; Development Programme (UNDP), 83; Economic Commission for Africa (ECA), 180; goals and ideals of, 255; HIV/AIDS pandemic and, 132, 135, 151, 152, 258; human security concept of, 131–132, 150; regional organizations' cooperation with, 269–271; South African apartheid and, 266–267

United Nations peace operations, 260–269, 283–288; Angola Verification Mission (UNAVEM I), 263–264; Brahimi report on, 261, 347; Commonwealth countries' contribution to, 319; current, characteristics of, 260; in intrastate conflicts, 260; Mission in the Democratic Republic of Congo (MONUC), 197, 260–261, 268–269, 286, 287–288; Mission in Sierra Leone (UNAMSIL), 197, 284, 285–286; Observer Mission in South Africa (UNOMSA), 267; and regional initiatives, 349; resource constraints on, 288; SADC and, 269–271, 275, 276–282, 286, 349; small arms proliferation and, 242; Somalia and, 235; Sudan conflict and, 234; and southern Africa's security capacity, 350, 351

United States: African Crisis Response Initiative (ACRI) and, 283–284, 290, 291–292; African policy of, 275–297, 302; Agency for International Development (USAID), 83; and bilateral security assistance, 290–294; bureaucratic divisions on Africa, 283–288; communist expansion in Africa and, 321; embassy bombings and, 232, 278; as hegemonic power, 173–174; humanitarian assistance of, 289, 296–297; military-to-military engagement programs of, 290–292; Namibian crisis and, 329; National Security Strategy of, 277; noncombatant operations of, 289; peacekeeping and, 280, 283–288; post-Somalia posture of, 283; regional capacity-building and, 286; SADC and, 275–278, 279–282, 291–294; selective engagement policy of, 282–282; Sierra Leone conflict and, 285; trade and, 278
U.S. European Command (USEUCOM), 281, 289, 292, 294–296
U.S. National Security Council (NSC), African Affairs/Global Affairs bureaus in, 283–288

Verwoerd, Hendrik, 319
Vorster, B. J., 59, 325

Wade, Abdoulaye, 183
Water resources, as foreign-policy issue, 65
Wilson, Harold, 321, 322
Windhoek treaty of 1992, 2–3, 35–36, 64
Women: education of, 139; and gender-biased development policies, 138, 139; HIV infection rates for, 138; land ownership of, 138–139, 147; marginal economic position of, 138–139; political and decisionmaking roles of, 166; prostitution of, 139–140; and social norms regarding sex, 136–137, 139
Women's organizations, 166
World Bank: good governance concept of, 53; and South Africa's land reform, 98, 99, 102–105, 120; structural adjustment programs, 56, 312; and Zimbabwe land reform, 82, 83
World Trade Organization (WTO), 313

Youth/student movement, reemergence of, 167

Zaire, civil war in, 267–268. *See also* Democratic Republic of Congo
Zambia, 60; civil society and progressive NGO actions in, 350; democracy and, 4, 41; and liberation of Rhodesia, 322
Zimbabwe, 332; crisis of 2000–2001, 305–306, 334–335; Democratic Republic of Congo military intervention and, 187, 213, 287; economy/gross domestic product of, 66; election of March 2002 in, 352; European Union and, 305–306; HIV/AIDS in, 141, 153; independence struggles of, 322; land issues in, 187; Lesotho intervention and, 185; OPDS proposal of, 212; security situation in, 187; South Africa's relations with, 7, 41, 68, 189; task force on, 351–352
Zimbabwe African National Union (ZANU), 322, 324
Zimbabwe African National Union (Patriotic Front) (ZANU[PF]), land reform and, 76, 77, 82, 84, 86, 88–89
Zimbabwe African Peoples' Union, 322
Zimbabwe Congress of Trade Unions (ZCTU), 164
Zimbabwean land reform, 73–93, 334, 352; agrarian context of, 79–80; beneficiaries selection in, 78–79; and brutality against farm workers, 81; Commercial Farmers' Union (CFU) and, 81, 82, 89; conflict mediation in, 91–92; constitutional reform process and, 87; Economic and Social Adjustment Program (ESAP) in, 79–80, 82–83; and fast-track resettlement program in, 86, 89–90; historical conflicts in, 74; Inception Phase Framework Plan in, 81, 85–86, 92; interest groups in, 76; international capital and donors and,

82–84, 85, 86; institutional processes and actors in, 81–82; and Land Acquisition Act of 1992, 87; land acquisition conflict factors in, 77–78; land acquisition means in, 76–77; land occupations and evictions and, 74, 77, 86–88; Land Redistribution and Resettlement Program (LRRP) in, 79, 80, 84–85, 92; land rights and tenure in, 80–81; land use practice alterations in, 79–80, 83; market-oriented conception of land use in, 79; nongovernmental organizations and, 77, 81, 83, 85; politics and, 77, 88–90; regional dimension of, 90–91; ruling party's role in, 82; tourism and outcropping focus in, 79–80; and United Kingdom compensation, 76–77, 84; violence in, 82, 87–88; and women's land ownership, 139

Zuma, Jacob, 181, 188, 189, 192

About the Book

From the ongoing war in Angola to sporadic instability in Zimbabwe and Lesotho, to the conflict in Congo, to issues of land reform and the ravages of AIDS, southern Africa faces varied and complex threats to its peace and security. The authors of *From Cape to Congo* assess the region's major security challenges, as well as the roles of local, regional, and external actors in managing them. Their theoretically informed—but practical—approach encompasses political, economic, and military arenas.

Mwesiga Baregu is professor of political science and international relations at the University of Dar-es-Salaam (Tanzania) and also former head of the Peace and Security Research Programme at SAPES Trust in Zimbabwe. **Christopher Landsberg** is director of the Centre for Policy Studies in Johannesburg and cofounder of the Centre for Africa's International Relations at the University of Witwatersrand (South Africa).